DYNAMICS OF INDUSTRIAL REVOLUTION 4.0: DIGITAL TECHNOLOGY TRANSFORMATION AND CULTURAL EVOLUTION

PROCEEDINGS OF THE 7TH BANDUNG CREATIVE MOVEMENT INTERNATIONAL CONFERENCE ON CREATIVE INDUSTRIES (BCM 2020), BANDUNG, INDONESIA, 12 NOVEMBER 2020

Dynamics of Industrial Revolution 4.0: Digital Technology Transformation and Cultural Evolution

Editors

Ratri Wulandari, Idhar Resmadi, Vika Haristianti, Rahmiati Aulia, Riky Taufik Afif, Gema Ari Prahara & Aulia Ibrahim Yeru
Telkom University, Bandung, Indonesia

CRC Press
Taylor & Francis Group
Boca Raton   London   New York   Leiden

CRC Press is an imprint of the
Taylor & Francis Group, an **informa** business

A BALKEMA BOOK

CRC Press/Balkema is an imprint of the Taylor & Francis Group, an informa business

© 2021 The Author(s)
Typeset by MPS Limited, Chennai, India

The right of the 7th Bandung Creative Movement International Conference on Creative Industries (BCM 2020) to be identified as author[/s] of this work has been asserted by him/her/them in accordance with sections 77 and 78 of the Copyright, Designs and Patents Act 1988.

Although all care is taken to ensure integrity and the quality of this publication and the information herein, no responsibility is assumed by the publishers nor the author for any damage to the property or persons as a result of operation or use of this publication and/or the information contained herein.

Library of Congress Cataloging-in-Publication Data

A catalog record has been requested for this book

Published by: CRC Press/Balkema
           Schipholweg 107C, 2316 XC Leiden, The Netherlands
           e-mail: enquiries@taylorandfrancis.com
           www.routledge.com – www.taylorandfrancis.com

ISBN: 978-1-032-04451-4 (Hbk)
ISBN: 978-1-003-19324-1 (eBook)
ISBN: 978-1-032-04452-1 (Pbk)
DOI: 10.1201/9781003193241

Table of contents

Digital technology transformation and cultural evolution in time of pandemic

Innovation of products, creative industries management and marketing

Aesthetic evolution in digital era

Digital education for creative industries

Digital technology and cultural evolution

Preface

The 7th Bandung Creative Movement (BCM) held on 12 November 2020, live from Telkom University in Bandung, gathered people from creative sectors dealing with creative industries and digital technology.

Under the theme *Dynamics of Industrial Revolution 4.0: Digital Technology Transformation and cultural evolution*, 7th BCM discussed how the digital world and connectivity transformed in accordance with human needs and social culture. It also underlined how technology and community influence each other to continuous innovation by integrating aesthetic, emotional aspects, and culture with the latest technology.

The conference examined issues on:

- Aesthetic evolution in digital era.
- How and to what extent does the digital technology influence environmental transformation?
- What is the relation between Digital Technology and cultural evolution? How digital technology changes people behaviour and culture, and vice versa?
- What is the importance of Creative Technology and data in the creative industry?
- Discussion on innovation of Products, Creative industries management and marketing
- Digital education for creative industries

In response to the pandemic, issues related to covid-19 and digital technology were also discussed. How the creative world & digital technology respond and answer to the pandemic.

The keynote speakers, that came from various backgrounds and from different countries, are:

1. Vichaya Mukdamanee, BFA, MFA, PhD, Silpakorn Thailand
2. Mumtaz Mokhtar (Assoc. Prof. Dr.) PhD, UiTM Malaysia
3. Florian Heinzelmann, PhD, Dipl.-Ing. (FH), M. Arch., SBA, SHAU Architecture and Urbanism, The Netherlands
4. Dr. Ira Wirasari, Telkom University, Indonesia

The parallel session presented 64 papers coming from collaborative and individual works. All papers are divided into 7 sub themes as offered in this open access proceeding. We believe and hope that readers will find 7th BCM an enriching overview on digital creative world worth sharing.

The Editors

Dynamics of Industrial Revolution 4.0: Digital Technology Transformation and Cultural Evolution –
Wulandari et al (eds)
© 2021 The Author(s), ISBN 978-1-032-04451-4

The 7th Bandung Creative Movement International Conference

Chairman
Mahendra Nur Hadiansyah, S.T., M.Ds.

Reviewers:
Kunto Adi WIBOWO, Ph.D *(Padjadjaran University)*
Dr. Jasni DOLAH *(Universiti Sains Malaysia)*
Prof. Dr.Hj. Aan KOMARIAH, M.Pd *(University Indonesia of Education)*
Dr. Mumtaz MOKHTAR *(Universiti Teknologi MARA)*
Dr. Astrid KUSUMOWIDAGDO, S.T., M.M. *(Ciputra University)*
Dr. Muhizam MUSTAFA *(Universiti Sains Malaysia)*
Maulana IBRAHIM, Ph.D *(Khairun University)*
Prananda Luffiansyah MALASAN, M.Ds., M.Phil., Ph.D *(Bandung Institute of Technology)*
Dr. Roro Retno WOELAN, S.Sos., M.Pd. *(Telkom University)*
Dr. Didit Widiatmoko SOEWARDIKOEN, M.Sn. *(Telkom University)*
Dr. Riksa BELASUNDA, Drs., S.ST., M.Ds. *(Telkom University)*
Dr. Ira WIRASARI. S.Sos., M.Ds. *(Telkom University)*
Dr. Moh. Isa Pramana KOESOEMADINATA, M.Sn. *(Telkom University)*
Dr. Arini ARUMSARI, S.Ds., M.Ds. *(Telkom University)*
Dr. Fajar CIPTANDI *(Telkom University)*
Dr. Djoko MURDOWO, MBA *(Telkom University)*
Punto WIJAYANTO, S.T., M.T. *(Trisakti University)*
Ersy ERVINA, S.Sos, M.Par. *(Telkom University)*
Nur Arief HAPSORO, S.T., M.T. *(Telkom University)*
Dandi YUNIDAR, S.Sn., M.Ds. *(Telkom University)*
Irwan SUDARISMAN, S.T., M.T. *(Telkom University)*
Grisna ANGGADWITA, S.T., MSM. *(Telkom University)*
Ahmad Nur Sheha GUNAWAN, S.T., M.T, *(Telkom University)*
Wirania SWASTY, S.Ds., M.AB. *(Telkom University)*

Editors:
Ratri WULANDARI, S.T., M.Sc.
Idhar RESMADI, S.Ikom., M.T.
Vika HARISTIANTI, S.Ds., M.T.
Rahmiati AULIA, S.Sn., M.M.
Riky Taufik AFIF, S.Pd., M.Pd.
Gema Ari PRAHARA, S.Sn., M.Ds.
Aulia Ibrahim YERU, S.Ds., M.Sn.

Telkom University

School of Creative Industries

Keynote and Featured speakers

Dynamics of Industrial Revolution 4.0: Digital Technology Transformation and Cultural Evolution –
Wulandari et al (eds)
© 2021 The Author(s), ISBN 978-1-032-04451-4

Mixed media art in Thailand: The case study of Vichoke Mukdamanee

V. Mukdamanee
Silpakorn University, Bangkok, Thailand

ABSTRACT: In Thailand, although many artists had already explored the possibility of mixed media art, the history of term *mixed media art* officially originated in the 37th National Art Exhibition in 1981. Vichoke Mukdamanee is among the Thai pioneer artists who had been deeply interested in mixed media. For over 40 years of his art career, Vichoke Mukdamanee has created many mixed media works, originating from his interest in the bonds between the environment, technology, and life. By various materials, including wood, metal, brass, bronze, aluminum, clothes, earthenware, scraps, and ready-made objects, Mukdamanee's mixed media art reflects the artist's perspectives toward the change in external factors. His artwork expanded into more profound concepts related to life, referring to rural life, Buddhist philosophy, and a family's love and bond. The artist attempted to establish a link between his concepts and internal overflowing emotions (love, happiness, suffering, and sadness) and express it through painting, collage-assemblage, and installation.

1 INTRODUCTION

1.1 *What is mixed media art?*

The terms "mixed media art" or "mixed media" are complicated and confusing. Not only do those outside the art sphere usually wonder "What are artists mixing?" when hearing the terms, experienced individuals in the art circle are sometimes uncertain of the extent of mixed media art. The extent of mixed media sometimes seems to cover various types of creative work. However, at the same time it demonstrates specific characteristics, making mixed media art distinctive and unique.

According to Collins English-language dictionary, the definition of mixed media is "the integrated use of different forms of media, especially within the arts." In Thai, the term mixed media means a combination of different forms of media under the meaning of art. The British Tate Art Museum defines mixed media as art derived from a combination of various types of media and materials, starting in 1912 based on the Cubist collage art by Pablo Picasso and Georges Braque (Tate, 2020). Cubist collage art influenced other artists in their period and has continued to impact others, opening up new horizons for art practitioners to recognize that essentially art can be made of anything or any combination of things. Moreover, another commonly heard term is "multi-media". Although multi-media is also a combination of various types of media, it is often referred to with regard to electronic media, such as videos, movies, sounds, and computers.

"Mixed media" refers to artwork in a modern sense as it was only coined around a century ago. Formerly, artwork was generally created with only one technique, such as with oil on canvas, color on paper, and rock-carved, wood-carved, or bronze-molded sculptures. Although artists in the past mixed various techniques, no one defined or distinguished the technique. Cubist and Dada artists utilized materials to represent vital contents in artwork. The artists in this era discovered a new way of expressing everyday human life accounts; they put or installed utility objects, including newspaper sheets, magazine pages, furniture, or a television, as parts of artwork. Mixed media art does not necessarily recount stories through painting; it can also reveal objective qualities and functions of multiple media and materials.

1.2 *Mixed media art in Thailand*

A clear example of the use of the term "mixed media" in Thailand's art realm is the National Art Exhibition in which a contest in the mixed media art category began in 1981 (the 27th National Art Exhibition). In the contest, Arkom Duangchaona was the first to be awarded a silver medal for the mixed media category (no one was presented with the gold medal). Mixed media art continued to exist in the 28th National Art Exhibition but ceased to be part of the contest for the following eight years until a piece was presented with a silver medal for the mixed media category at the 34th National Art Exhibition in 1991. The name of the awarded work was "New Symbolic from Environment No. 2" by Vichoke Mukdamanee. From then on, mixed media fine arts in Thailand have been organized in alignment with the National Art Exhibition. (In certain years, mixed media art was absent, or no one was received an award; yet, it was not long until mixed media re-emerged in subsequent years.)

The definition of mixed media in the National Art Exhibition is constantly developing. For instance, in an application for the participation of the 61st Fine Arts Exhibition (2016), mixed media was categorized as the fourth type apart from painting, sculpture, and printmaking. Mixed media was defined as "Fine artwork utilizes different art approaches, such as painting mixed with sculpture and/or more than two types of materials like ready-made materials, natural materials, synthetic materials, technological materials and mixed media installation."

The confusion lies in how to distinguish mixed media from painting and sculpture as mixed media is defined by technical conditions (a mixture of two or more types of media and/ or materials) while painting and sculpture are distinguished by dimensions of work (two and three dimensions). With different conditions, the types of work become overlapped. Some can be classified as both "painting" and "mixed media" at the same time while others may be classified as "sculpture" or "mixed media".

Therefore, using the term "mixed media" to describe the features of each piece of work depends on the intention of the person classifying the work. To focus on the dimensional aspect of the work, artists, critics, and curators often call their work paintings or sculptures. However, if they want to present the aspect of technical mixtures, whether two-dimensional or three-dimensional, all the work can be classified as mixed media art. In addition, there are such words as mixed media painting, mixed media sculpture, mixed material painting, mixed technique painting, and mixed technique sculpture. These represent important evidence of the flexibility and complexity of mixed media art created and disseminated throughout today's art world.

2 METHODOLOGY

In this paper, the author tries to observe and analyze the art pieces made by Vichoke Mukdamanee. The progression between artworks, and how it influences art in Thailand. Art criticism methods were used to analyze the artwork. In general, art criticism could be used to responding to, interpreting meaning, and making critical judgments about specific works of art. In this case, the artwork mentioned is related to the case study of mixed media artist, Vichoke Mukdamanee.

3 THE CASE STUDY OF A THAI MIXED MEDIA ARTIST: VICHOKE MUKDAMANEE

3.1 *About the Artist*

Professor Vichoke Mukdamanee is an artist who created contemporary artwork. He began creating his early fine artwork in 1973 from human figurative shapes and accounts. He developed mixed media art based on the stories, nature, and environment found the Thai society under the influence of modern technology, and thereafter installation art using various materials, including wood, metal, brass, bronze, aluminum, clothes, earthenware, scraps, and finished materials. In that period, mixed media work creation was done with painting processes, of which the contents dealt with life, society, and environment along with traditional philosophy, scientific progress, and current beliefs influenced by Buddhist ones as well as the future world (Department of Cultural Promotion, Ministry of Culture, 2002).

After his solo exhibition "Modern Existence 1992" at the National Gallery in February 1992, Vichoke's image as a "mixed media artist" became known in the spheres of artists, art theories, critics, collectors, and the public interested in art in Thai society. The artwork in the exhibition was created with many forms of materials, such as twigs, metal sheets, clothes and nylon ropes, ceramics, newspaper sheets, plastic sheets and tubes, gold leaf, spray colors, oil colors, watercolors, acrylic colors, and so on. Art materials were mixed with natural, industrial, and ready-made ones to show colors and shapes that yielded "symbols" reflecting the artist's perspectives toward the changing circumstances of the era which impacted people's lives. The artist stated in the exhibition catalog that "Life, mankind, nature, environment and all other things are influenced by modern technology and material prosperity. The modern existence consists of both conflicts and relationships in the forms of hidden beauty, completeness, and power. The said circumstance and atmosphere has given me concepts and driven me to express them through fine art creation, which focuses on contents of shapes with structures and symbols that convey and reflect the current modern existence" (Mukdamanee, 1992).

3.2   The Artworks

For over 40 years in his art career, Vichoke Mukdamanee has created many mixed media works, originating from his interest in the bonds between the environment, technology, and life. The used materials reflect the artist's perspectives toward the change in external factors. The artwork expanded into more profound concepts related to life, referring to rural life, Buddhist philosophy, and a family's love and bond. The artist attempted to establish a link between his concepts and internal overflowing emotions (love, happiness, suffering, and sadness) and express it through painting and collage—assembly and installation. The artist was able to manage the materials to present the contents without losing the materials' original objective value and at the same time express his identity. Whether a particular piece of work was made of paper, wood, metal, or plastic, its certain identities explicitly conveyed the artist's signature. Vichoke stated "I usually started many pieces of work by drawing to generate shapes, movements and compositions. Afterwards, I gradually added techniques onto the work again and again till I was satisfied: patching, coloring, painting, perforating, and adding textures. Some criticized me that my additions were too much, but I think individual moderation is different, depending on individual tastes. As an artist, I added details till I was satisfied and felt that the materials in front were well managed and belonged to me. The big picture should be able to represent myself…" (Mukdamanee, 2007).

Looking back at Vichoke's work between 1974 and 1984, when the artist graduated from the Department of Painting, the Faculty of Painting Sculpture and Graphic Arts, Silpakorn University, until he received a scholarship to continue his study at the Faculty of Art and Design, Tokyo Gakugei University in Tokyo, Vichoke showed his interest in the study of a human's structural shape through the creation of oil paints on canvas. The influence of the art of Cubism led by Pablo Picasso and Georges Barque, which was spreading to the contemporary art sphere in Thailand, inspired Vichoke to analyze and curtail the shapes and movements of human bodies to become an overlapping area, yielding a semi-abstract monochrome work in a solemn atmosphere. The flat plate shapes appearing in Vichoke's painting were adjusted to show weight, depth, and complexity, yielding a seemingly living, moving structure, aligned with his explanation in the catalog of the exhibition "Modern Existence." The artist himself talked about his work in the period "…I used shapes derived from architectural structures and human bodies to create paintings. The shapes were to move in accordance with the movement of human bodies under an architectural structure of a

Figure 1.   Structure with internal planes (oil on canvas, 116 x 100 cm, 1974).

definite volume. I also used light and shade to control zooming in and out of the deep, shallow, and lateral aspects of my work. My work is of definite structures, showing stillness and firmness" (Mukdamanee, 1992).

4   CONCLUSIONS

When observing Vichoke's work over a ten-year period, we can see the development of his techniques in many ways, which were still present in his later work. Almost every piece of his work relies on line drawing techniques to create the main structure of the work. Some are geometrical shapes—squares and circles put together—while others are distorted to become independently moving shapes. Afterward, the artist added details, using painting and material management techniques linked to and developed from the said structure. He resorted to pounding and perforation to make holes in linear directions, scratching to make deep and shallow incisions, and patching and tying materials to make shapes and textures, all teasing with the styles and movements of his painting strokes and paintbrush traces. He utilized a line drawing process and composition to fix directions, shapes, and movements to create the relative rhythms of lines and spaces.

The materials Vichoke used to create artwork were transformed—twisted, pulled, burned, and pierced to make new shapes. Some were painted or sprayed to have different colors and textures. It is noticeable that the artist's techniques aligned with the objective nature of each type of material. For instance, paper was folded, or hand pressed to create texture or sealed with glue. Wooden materials were burned, sawed, and pounded. Metal materials were twisted. Cloths were tied. The artist inserted his ideas into the processes and materials, expressing his identity by transforming the meanings of the materials which became part of the artwork. In addition, he managed to make his various materials coexist. The natures of oil color, acrylic color, and spray color blended with gaudy colors and shiny, slippery, and reflective textures of scientific materials. Some were mixed with wood, cloths, and baked clay, yielding natural gentleness, warmth, new aesthetic harmony, and unity.

From the beginning of painting aiming to curtail the shapes of living things, Vichoke's paint strokes became so acute and solid that he could simply present essential structures. We can even understand the origins of his strokes and linear perforations, coming from the shapes of humans, animals, trees, flowers, the surroundings, or certain objects. The artist intended to use lighter paint strokes and abandon his preliminary concrete inspirations, keeping only abstract contents. The curtailed structures were left with just visible lines and dots connected to one another like symbols or signs invented to convey certain messages. When Vichoke used plastic, laminate plates, and aluminum plates, the symbols and signs derived from his strokes were deeply engraved on the surfaces of the materials. We can compare these characteristics with pieces of wood or rocks used by ancient tribes to communicate their accounts or record happenings. Sometimes the letters were conveyed in the forms of incomprehensible pictures or illegible symbols. We can study the origins of the materials, colors, and shapes by comparing the attitudes of the people and the events in the era. If the letters symbolized spoken voices, the traces in Vichoke's mixed media work resembled symbols that conveyed his perspectives and thoughts. They were from his imagination and the artist used them to represent nature, living things, the environment, and the existence and awareness of his identity amid the volatile circumstances of prosperity and the decay of - era-.

Vichoke Mukdamanee is an important case study of mixed media artists in Thailand who pioneered work by using various types of materials in his paintings, sculptures, and installations. The artist has been developing his concepts and work processes continuously for over 40 years, focusing on mixing natural materials, scraps, industrial materials, and creative ideas from his awareness of the impacts of the new social matters on the environment, local cultures and traditions, ways of life, and beliefs.

REFERENCES

Art Gallery, Silpakorn University. 2015. An Application Form for the 62nd Fine Arts Exhibition (2016). Bangkok: Art Gallery, Silpakorn University.

Art Gallery, Silpakorn University. 2015. Roster of Award Winners in the National Fine Art Exhibitions (the 1st to the 60th from 2010 to 2014), in the 61st National Fine Art Exhibition. Bangkok: Silpakorn University, pp. 143–164.

Dictionary.com. *Collins English Dictionary - Complete & Unabridged 10th Edition*, HarperCollins Publishers. http://www.dictionary.com/browse/mixed-media. Retrieved July 6, 2020.

Vichoke Mukdamanee. 2002. *Collage Art in Thailand*. Bangkok: Art Gallery, Silpakorn University.

Vichoke Mukdamanee. 2002. *Mixed Media and Collage Art in Thailand*. Bangkok: Art Gallery, Silpakorn University.

Vichoke Mukdamanee. 2007. Post-modern Art (published art catalog for an art exhibition) by Vichoke Mukdamanee. Bangkok: Art Gallery, Silpakorn University, p. 134.

Vichoke Mukdamanee. 1992. *Work Creation Concepts*. From Art Catalogs to…the Modern Existence, Bangkok: Amarin Printing Company Limited, p. 11.

Tate Online Resource. Mixed Media. *Tate*. http://www.tate.org.uk/learn/online-resources/glossary/m/ mixed-media. Retrieved July 6, 2020.

The Royal Society of Thailand Society of Thailand. 1987. An art vocabulary Dictionary in Thai-English. Bangkok: The Royal Society of Thailand Society of Thailand, p. 116.

Dynamics of Industrial Revolution 4.0: Digital Technology Transformation and Cultural Evolution –
Wulandari et al (eds)
© 2021 The Author(s), ISBN 978-1-032-04451-4

Art framework for the industrial revolution 4.0

M. Mokhtar
Universiti Teknologi MARA, UiTM, Selangor, Malaysia

ABSTRACT: The Industrial Revolution 4.0 (IR 4.0) had an impact on the form of art production and the art industry itself, eventually having huge implications for all of society and all aspects of life, including economy, education, and politics. The arts community needs to be aware and view the very broad framework of inter-art relationships and how IR 4.0 took place so that the production of the work is more relevant, up-to-date, and progressive. Several documents were reviewed to identify the dynamic framework of art within the IR 4.0. Art framework related to the IR 4.0 is detailed with components of the artist as co-creator, hybrid types of production, and attributes of a super smart society. Several key points should be referenced by humans so that they can be further prepared, better equipped, and more realistic for society 5.0.

Keywords: art framework, Industrial Revolution 4.0, society 5.0

1 INTRODUCTION

Among the factors of art development are international technology, the dynamics of artforms, and the art community itself. I-Suke (2020) reported that more than 15,000 visitors visited the Leonardo da Vinci exhibit at the National Art Gallery, Kuala Lumpur even though the work exhibited was just a reprint. Regardless, the advanced digital technology managed to captivate the audience and satisfy Malaysians who have only been able to see such artwork in books and movies. However, there are still some constraints in the art development.

In conjunction with the da Vinci exhibit, the display of Young Contemporary artwork caused surprises where there were works that were touched and damaged as a result of the behavior of the visitors, especially with regard to selfies. However, the gallery gave a clear justification regarding the adequate management of the exhibition operations. In a February 10, 2020 article from the Malaysiakini online newspaper, 10 Feb 2020 revealed the news was revealed that there was a release of four works by Ahmad Fuad Osman in the exhibit titled *At the End of The Day Even Art Is Not Important* even though the exhibition session is in progress. The realease was done by the gallery. The gallery took the action to control the confusion of the general public which the gallery said was not yet able to interpret the work at a higher level. In this case, the development of art needs to be driven wisely to cover all aspects that are in line with current developments.

2 THE DYNAMIC OF MALAYSIAN ART IN THE INDUSTRIAL REVOLUTION 4.0 (IR4.0)

The existence of IR 4.0 can be traced back to the 2000s. During that time, Malaysia experienced many deviations in social, political, and economic conditions. There are many kinds of art forms created in Malaysian art such as site-specific installation, web art, interactive CD, sound art, light art, performance, digital photography, alternative prints, fax, and mobile phone. In Table 1, Hasnul (2008) listed 35 paradigm shifts of modern to postmodern art styles that occurred in Malaysia. The table shows the variation in the processes, existence, output, performances, values, interpretation, and appreciations. At present, art forms have also become blurred with so-called painting, print, and

DOI 10.1201/9781003193241-2

Table 1.   Paradigm Shifts by Hasnul (2008).

FROM	TO	FROM	TO	FROM	TO
Master narrative	Discourse	Centralize	Multicentered	Hierarchy	Network
Safe	Provocative	Single discipline	Multidiscipline	Sequence	Simultaneous
Aesthetic	Socio-politic	Linear	Nonlinear	Hand skill	Brain skill
Formalism	Parody, hybrid	Form	Information	Goods	Services
Modern	Post-modern	Fix	Change	Global competition	Global collaboration
Homogeneity	Multiculturality	Content	Context	Dominance	Synergy
National	Global	Singular meaning	Multiple meaning	A passive audience	Interactive
Exclusive	Participate	Product	Time	Physical attributes	Intellectual attributes
Mass media	New media	Mass	Customisation	Specialization	Convergence
Status quo	Deconstruction	Artist-centered	Audience-centered	Single direction	Cyclical
Prescriptive	Choice	Review of end product	Review of process	Isolated specialist	Multi-skill generalist
Nation state	Transnational	Independence	Interdependence		

sculpture, thus a new media art term transpired in contemporary art. Suhana Nordin and Mokhtar (2015) stated that new media art required different understanding thus, the diversity of art, language and its principles needed to be highlighted. Besides hypertextual and virtual attribute in new media art, they added that the art medium itself represented as a message while data is the form.

A word dynamic can be understood as constant change with a positive value. The IR 4.0 launched at the World Economic Forum in 2016, showing that the boundary between the physical, digital, and biological will be more blurred. The situation is embodied through the elements of Artificial Intelligent (AI), Autonomous Vehicles, and the Internet of Things (IoT). The Malaysian Young Contemporary Art 2016 winner, Fuad Arif, created installation art, combining classical music synchronized with Quranic text translation animated on the screen and presented in a dark, closed gallery space. Visual and audio elements were combined with the spatial environment, requiring the audience to focus on whether to hear the sound or read the visual, to be in a real situational site or to meditate into the inner soul, or be able to adapt to everything at one time. Piliang (2018) stated that art development was really affected by the social-cultural environment. He added that the dynamic of its development is exaggerated by a dynamic community, network society, and the IR 4.0. For him, co-creator is the name of a "new" artist, who is no longer working alone. The form is also no longer the final production created by an artist but is art resulting from the ideas and an assortment of contributions. An established Malaysian sculptor, Ramlan Abdullah (2018), viewed other people to be part of his creative process. His public sculptures involved those who walked safely though his artwork in the city and those who participated along the creation. He added, art and technology are intertwined in the context of media application, human interaction, and the process itself. In 2017, Malaysia introduced Dasar Industri Kreatif Negara (DIKN) National Creative Industry Policy which catered to the enhancement of three major areas which are Creative Multimedia (film, advertising, design & animation), Creative Art and Culture (crafts, visual art, music, performing, creative writing and fashion textile), and Creative Art and Heritage (museum, archive, restoration, and conservation). Since then, various initiatives were launched by several agencies in order to promote art locally and globally. Mazlan Othman (2019) in Senikini#26 mentioned that the creative industry is the industry of the future in Malaysia.

Alvin Toffler (1990) mentioned that world technology control will be managed by those who have power in economics and politics. Since the IR 3.0 Malaysian art scene was supported by educational institutions, political power, and social dynamics, facing forward to the IR 4.0 there needs to be a high quality of a nation who engineered the success of the Industrial Revolution. Japan established society 5.0 attributes that are technology-based and human-centered. According to Yuko Harayama (2017), humans must remain the central actors and digitalization the means. There need to be initiatives to converge the physical space and cyberspace by fully utilizing ICT (Information and Communication Technology). Mayumi Fukuyama (2017) stated that all citizens are dynamically engaged through IoT, big data, robots, and AI, including culture and art. The uncertainty aroused among Thai artists and craftsmen as to whether or not change their art, craft, and design or to

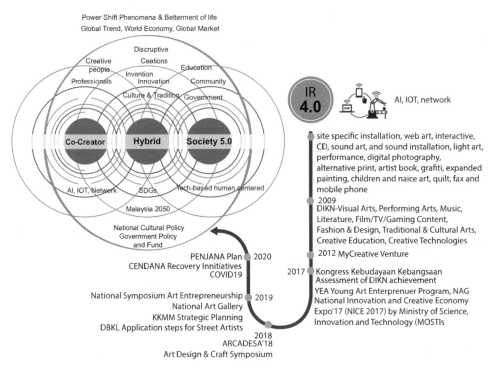

Figure 1. Malaysian art tagline and art framework in the Industrial Revolution 4.0.

preserve it. Consequently, Veerawat Sirivesmas (2018) stated that the main justification is based on an understanding of the history and culture before a paradigm shifts happen. Masterpieces, authenticity, and intellectual property have become new considerations in art production today. Since the Giclee print was introduced for high-quality digital art as original artwork, Intellectual Property (IP) and ownership certificates ideas for selling artwork instead of the tangible product itself. Javier Pes (2019) referenced Maurizio Cattelan's $120,000 banana with duck-tape entitled "Comedian" which was eaten up as performance art. According to Cattelan, the banana work that was eaten is only a banana and is no longer a piece of real work. Ownership of the work is subject to the ownership of the original certificate.

3 ART FRAMEWORK IN IR 4.0

In Figure 1, an art framework for IR 4.0 shows how art functions and its current significance. The framework consists of components, linkages, and boundaries. The components of the art framework consist of co-creator, hybrid art form, and society 5.0. Every component is linked to each other and local cultural policies and other relevant government policies as well as financial allocation being an internal factor that controls the development of art in addition to external factors that are global in nature.

Co-creators consisted of multidisciplinary skills of an artist or professional team. They were creative people that endeavored with AI, IoT, and network system. With IR 4.0, creation of an art form converted to the hybrid mode either exists in actual things, simulated or virtual form, or a combination thereof. The creation of hybrid artwork occurred through the innovation, creation and even disruptive processes. When a work was produced by the process of collaboration it required an equivalent understanding or a clear agreement that ultimately produced the value of commonality.

Local identity and cultural values are needed to overcome the challenges of global acceptance and the value of authenticity. Art for art's sake or art for society turned into to art that accomplishes the betterment of human life. Thus, the consideration of sustainable life is crucial nowadays. The sustainable development goals, or also known as SDGs ,involved every community. The individuals should be technology-based and human centered. They will be supported by various support systems, including the political power, economic stability and funding, education, and social interactions.

4 CONCLUSION

In conclusion, every component in the framework is interrelated and consists of local and global factors. The art form evolved according to the development of the technology introduced. Revolution is closely related to the keywords *change, replacement, movement, flow,* and *improvement* due to force, pressure, or coercion. The latest technology will take over the previous methods from various aspects of art production, including, materials, tools, systems, functions, processes, and how to appreciate them. Super smart artists as part of a super smart society today need critical and creative thinking skills. Not only that, but they also need to merge with other entities to produce a piece of work. Amalgamation of co-creators involving artists, AI, and robotic technology will be more interesting. Hybrid art and design generate a new language of art that opens up new understanding and appreciation. The definition of "beauty" and aesthetic will be transformed. It seems that art will be more subjective for most communities, but the fact is more intellectual as well as contextual for the super smart audience to "read" and communicate about art. For example, alternative prints maintain the concept of matrix in the understanding of print, but how the effect of the print is produced is so broad that the human brain itself is needed to print the shading effect of a material. The data will replace images that are typically treated as symbols or metaphors and need to be described, transcribed, and cryptographed as informative signs. As a creative human artist cannot not rely much on technology, they challenge themselves on how to manipulate it in order to express and execute creative solutions, ideas, and the betterment of the whole ecosystem. Living in a borderless world today has the potential to create social ills. To compete with technology, it is important that humans realize that they are still human created by the Great Creator and should know what the purpose of their life in the world is. It is up to the government, private agencies, institutions, and all communities to lead society in the right direction. However, true knowledge will guide us all to the perfect life.

REFERENCES

Ramlan Abdullah. 2018. The Transformation of Art Towards Industrial Revolution: A Case Study. The Construction of Langkawi Sundial From Idea, Fabrication and Installation. *Proceedings of the Second International Symposium Art, Craft and Design in Southeast Asia 2018 ARCADESA#2* (Facing the Challenges of 4th Industrial Revolution). Malaysia: National Art Gallery & faculty of Art & Design, UiTM. pp. 32–33.

Bernama. 2020. February 11, 2020. Balai Seni Negara Sahkan Penurunan Karya Ahmad Fuad Osman, Available: https://www.astroawani.com/berita-malaysia/balai-seni-negara-sahkan-penurunan-karya-ahmad-fuad-osman-230377. Retrieved September 22, 2020.

Mayumi Fukuyama. 2018. Society 5.0 Aiming for A New Human-Centered Society, Japan, SPORTLIGHT. July/August, pp. 47–50.

Wartawan Sinar Harian. July 15, 2020, Peluang Lihat Karya Agung Leonardo Da Vinci di Balai Seni Lukis. Available: https://www.sinarharian.com.my/article/37885/BERITA/Nasional/Peluang-lihat-karya-agung-Leonardo-Da-Vinci-di-Balai-Seni-Lukis. Retrieved September 22, 2020. © 2018 Hakcipta Terpelihara Kumpulan Karangkraf.

Yuko Harayama. 2017. Society 5.0: Aiming for A New Human-centered Society; Japan's Science and Technology Policies for Addressing Global Social Challenges. *The Economist* Limited 2017.

Hasnul. 2008. Under-Deconstruction; Contemporary Art in Malaysia After 1990 in Timelines, Malaysia National Art Gallery, pp. 228–279.

i-Suke. 2020. Karya Agung Leonardo da Vinci Dipamer Dalam Bentuk Digital, Balai Seni Negara Catat Sejarah Terima Kunjungan Luar Biasa! *The Star*. Available: https://www.mstar.com.my/xpose/isuke/2019/08/01/pameran-mona-lisa. Retrieved September 22, 2020 Hakcipta Terpelihara © 2020. Star Media Group Berhad (10894D).

Jabatan Kebudayaan dan Kesenian Negara. 2019. Dasar Kebudayaan Kebangsaan. Retrived September 15, 2020. Available: http://www.jkkn.gov.my/ms/dasar-kebudayaan-kebangsaan

Malaysia Ministry of Communication and Multimedia.2019. Strategic Planning of Malaysia Ministry of Communication and Multimedia (2019–2023), pp. 55–66.

Mazlan Othman. 2019. Trusting Malaysian Creatives into the Future in SENIKINI#26 Edisi Khas 10 Tahun Arthopea, Kuala Lumpur: National Art Gallery.

Mumtaz Mokhtar. 2019. Facing the Challenges in the 4th Revolution Industry, in SENIKINI #26 Edisi Khas 10 Tahun Arthopea, Kuala Lumpur: National Art Gallery.

Pes, J, (2019). *Maurizio Cattelan's $120,000 Banana Was Ejected From Art Basel Miami Beach After Drawing Unsafe Crowds (and Getting Eaten)*. Artnet News. https://news.artnet.com/market/cattelan-banana-art-art-basel-1725678

Suhana Nordin and Mumtaz Mokhtar. 2015. Discussion: Diversity in Malaysia, New Media Art. International *Journal of Business and Administrative Studies* I(3), 94–98. DOI: https://dx.doi.org/ 10.20469/ijbas.10003-3

Yasraf Amir Piliang. 2018. Co-Creation as A Basis of Creative Industry in The Era of Industrial Revolution 4.0. *Proceedings Second International Symposium Art, Craft and Design in Southeast Asia 2018 ARCADESA#2* (Facing the Challenges of 4th Industrial Revolution). Malaysia: National Art Gallery & faculty of Art & Design, UiTM. pp. 11–19.

Veerawat Sirivesmas. 2018. The Shifting Paradigm, Beyond the Disruption of Design Crafts in Thailand, From the Perspective of Jewelry Design Instructor. *Proceedings of the Second International Symposium Art, Craft and Design in Southeast Asia 2018 ARCADESA#2* (Facing the Challenges of 4th Industrial Revolution) Malaysia: National Art Gallery & faculty of Art & Design, UiTM. p. 20–25.

A. Toffler. 1991. *Power Shift*. United States of America: Bantam books Group, Inc.

A. Toffler. 1970. *Future Shock; A Study of Mass Bewilderment in the Face of Accelerating Change*. London: The Bodley Head.

–. 2020. *Karya Ahmad Fuad diturunkan agar 'tak disalah erti'*. Malaysiakini. https://m.malaysiakini.com/hiburan/510342

Dynamics of Industrial Revolution 4.0: Digital Technology Transformation and Cultural Evolution –
Wulandari et al (eds)
© 2021 The Author(s), ISBN 978-1-032-04451-4

Digital knowledge improvement for Indonesian small and medium enterprises: Cultural change in digital mental

I. Wirasari
Telkom University, Bandung, Indonesia

ABSTRACT: Cultural changes in society affect many areas of life, including the business sector as well as small and medium enterprises. During a pandemic, there are changes in the way people think, act, and socialize. The COVID-19 pandemic has altered the world's economic order to such a large degree that the International Monetary Fund predicted negative global economic growth in 2020. In Indonesia, economic activities have decreased drastically, especially with the government-mandated, large-scale social restrictions and health protocols such as the use of masks and social distancing. The first strategy for Indonesian small- and medium-scale enterprises in the new normal is to conduct marketing research on consumers to meet their needs. Marketing research is part of the STP (segmentation, targeting, and positioning) marketing strategy, and is more suitable and appropriate to meet consumer needs. Although qualitative research methods and analyzing branding strategies were used, the current study analyzed how community, especially small business actors, adapts to this pandemic. Mental changes in society were analyzed as well as cultural changes in society's digital mental state. The results of the study showed mental changes along with the development of digitalization in all sectors.

Keywords: Cultural changes, digitalization, small and medium enterprises

1 INTRODUCTION

Reviewing the data from the Ministry of Cooperatives and small- and medium-scale enterprises (SMEs) of the Republic of Indonesia, micro, small, and medium enterprises (MSMEs) have experienced good development and growth over the years. In 2010, the total number of MSME units was 52,769,426. In the latest news in early 2020, that number has reached 63 million. In a pandemic such as the COVID-19 we are experiencing now, SMEs are competing to be able to maintain their business.

The first strategy for new normal SMEs is to conduct marketing research to all consumers to meet their needs. Marketing research is part of the STP (segmentation, targeting, and positioning) marketing strategy. By conducting marketing research, this type of strategy is more suitable and appropriate to meet consumer needs.

The development of SMEs in Indonesia demonstrates a good pattern. The existence of support from the government in certain ways affects the growth rate of the number of micro, small, and medium enterprises. The use of technology and communication facilities, the allocation of business credits, and the reduction in the Final Income Tax rate, are several factors that encourage the development of SMEs in Indonesia. Even so, this growth is still considered slow because several supporting factors are considered not very effective.

These factors include the media for promotion and branding. SMEs' actors, who originally carried out promotions and branding with conventional media, are now starting to switch to digital media. The transition to digital media is a mental change that business owners must accept. However, this is not easy because the mental changes involved in going from conventional to digital means, including behavior changes that relate to cultural changes, must be adapted by SMEs. Subsequent social changes exist in changes that are fundamental or only complete previous changes. As an example, a change in the promotion media in Indonesia is the nature of completing previous deficiencies.

Based on the information above, the research problems were identified as follows.

(1) SMEs are still adapting conventional branding and promotion patterns.
(2) Changes from conventional media promotion and branding require an overall change in the mentality of business actors.
(3) A branding strategy is needed to support mental change in the way of thinking from conventional media to digital. Thus, the problems are the appropriate digital branding strategy for SMEs in Indonesia and how it affects the mental change of business actors.

2 RESEARCH METHODOLOGY

Bogdan & Taylor (1975) in Moleong (2007) stated that qualitative methodology is a research procedure that produces descriptive data in the form of written or oral words from people as well as their observable behavior. Qualitative research aims at obtaining the complete picture of a matter according to the human point of view studied. Qualitative research is related to the ideas, perceptions, opinions, or beliefs of the people being studied.

3 LITERATURE REVIEW

Brand values/core ideas communicated to an audience have different weights and pressures depending on the characteristics of the product. Luxury and signature products place emphasis on the products themselves. Retail/culinary emphasize the ambience/atmosphere of an interior retail space. Service in general emphasizes behavior/attitude/hospitality of the business actors. Consumer goods emphasizes frequent communication through various media (Ollins, 2008).

Based on Ollins (2008), there are the four vectors through which a brand emerges. They are product, behavior, environment, and communication. The four vectors are interrelated in changing the knowledge of businesspeople from conventional thinking to digital, both for branding and promotion purposes. Brand management should be treated as a resource in every way equal to financial management or IT management, as a corporate resource which will work effectively when it embraces every part of the organization (Ollins, 2008).

4 DISCUSSION AND RESULT

4.1 *Small and medium business branding strategy in the new normal*

Before creating a branding strategy for SMEs, a mapping is needed. Things that must be mapped and analyzed are as follows.

(1) **Marketing Research.** The first strategy for the new normal SMEs is to conduct marketing research or research to all consumers in order to meet consumers' needs. Marketing research is part of the STP marketing strategy. By conducting marketing research, you can discover which strategy is more suitable and appropriate to meet consumer needs.
(2) **Product Portfolio Evaluation.** The strategy for the next new normal SME is to evaluate the products that will appear when entering the new normal era, where consumers will be more careful about using new products even at very economical prices. There is even a possibility that consumers will instead use cheaper products with standard quality because consumers tend to be cautious and aware that the crisis will recur.
(3) **Evaluate Prices and Pay Attention to Competitors.** Evaluate the problem of price because consumers tend to reduce their purchasing power to be more careful about buying and

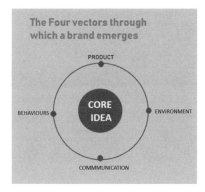

Figure 1. The four vectors through which a brand emerges. Source: Ollins (2008).

consuming. To neutralize the decline in the purchasing power of consumers, MSMEs must have more creativity in determining economical packages or promotional packages that are attractive to consumers, e.g., product packaging. SMEs can do promotional packages by providing 3-in-1 packages or cheaper price selling products with smaller packages. Another sales strategy is to offer wholesale prices to consumers given the trend of group buying or panic buying. Such strategies make consumers choose SME products over competing products.

(4) **Focus sales on the online channel.** The last new normal SME strategy is to focus on online business, considering that this new normal era has forced the switch to online channels due to changes in consumer behavior. Moreover, with the condition of the COVID-19 virus outbreak, mobilization is limited and social distancing is encourged, so that consumers look for products through the marketplace. To take advantage of this change in consumer behavior by shifting sales focus to online channels, one must be aggressive in launching selling on websites, social media, and e-commerce.

Based on the results of the mapping above, it can be concluded that there are three important components in a branding strategy, namely, content and database advertisement. In terms of content, SMEs must be able to create content that is attractive and in accordance with the target market. Taking advantage of what is currently popular can also increase audience engagement with the content. SMEs must also collect and analyze databases because it serves to maximize promos to the right audience. Furthermore, ads for promotion must also be done because they are useful for expanding the achievement of content created digitally to new users outside the database that are still in accordance with the target market. Various types of digital marketing tactics and strategies basically have the same goal: to promote a product or service to increase brand awareness which in turn increases the number of purchases.

4.2 *Collaboration*

In addition, it is important for MSME actors to collaborate with various parties to be able to move more quickly and effectively. In increasing the SME business, Jalur Nugraha Ekakurir is now launching COD (Cash On Delivery) Retail feature, a service product to facilitate online buying and selling activities through cash transaction on product delivery time. This is designed to make it easier for people to buy necessities online and to encourage SMEs to continue to grow in the midst of the COVID-19 pandemic in the face of the new normal.

4.3 *Soft selling*

Soft selling is when you adverstise a new product by releasing a product teaser that contains product knowledge, prices, and launch dates. A timeline is then created to address pre-orders and such.

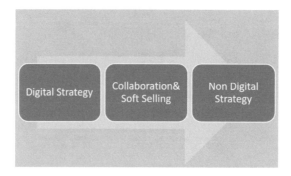

Figure 2.   Branding strategy flow.

Scheme of Cultural Change from Conventional to Digital

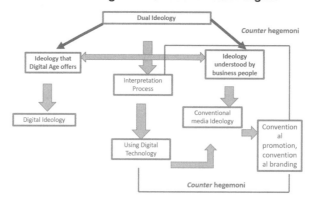

Figure 3.   Scheme of cultural change.

4.4 *Non digital strategy*

Expand Sales Territory. SMEs depend on customers and employees from one region. Today, this is very risky as the COVID-19 crisis in the red zone could stop a company's sales and operations. It is important, then, that SMEs diversify their location to minimize disruption and maintain income.

   Increase knowledge about business. For SMEs, new technology has made it easier to expand their local footprint and even go global. For example, to handle customers and fulfill orders, an add-on for an e-commerce platform can translate a retail website into multiple languages and help ship products around the world.

4.5 *Mental change to the digital age*

Associated with the theory of cultural politics, branding and promotion have actually become desirable for business actors, both large, medium, and small. It can be said that this desire is a reference for the expectations of the business actor. Within that desire are elements of digital branding and promotion. These elements form a culture in society, and within the elements there are certain goals of the ruling class regarding carrying out their ideas to society.

   Based on the description above, those in the ruling class must compete with one another so that the culture offered by them is accepted by the community. It can be concluded that the battle for the power of media branding and promotion is not just a power struggle between conventional and digital media, but is broader than that, namely a battle of ideology.

16

In truth, there are many businesses disappearing of which we are not aware. These businesses are reluctant to adapt to the changing era because they are too comfortable with the glory they have achieved in the past. Apart from being too comfortable, there are also some businesses that don't know how to deal with this digital transformation. They were stunned to see new start-ups popping up and grabbing their customers, one after another.

There are some businesses that have adapted successfully and others that keep trying but still fail. The successful transformation of a business, organization, or company is not determined by one person. In fact, digital transformation requires all parties in an organization to adapt. Skills such as the ability to take advantage of technology to simplify and speed up work are essential for helping a business adapt to the digital era.

REFERENCES

Bogdan dan Taylor. 1975. *Metodologi Penelitian Kualitatif*. Remadja Karya, Bandung.

Moleong, Lexy J. 2007. *Metodologi Penelitian Kualitatif. Edisi Revisi*. PT Remaja Rosdakarya, Bandung.

Shimp, Terence, A. 2003. *Periklanan Promosi dan Aspek Tambahan Komunikasi Pemasaran Terpadu*, Jilid 1 (edisi 5), Jakarta: Erlangga.

Lee, Monle & Carla Johnson. 2013. *Principles of Advertising, A Global Perspective, Second Edition*, Routledge, England.

Morissan, M.A. 2010. *Periklanan Komunikasi Pemasaran Terpadu*, Kencana, Jakarta.

Olins, Wally, 2008. *The Brand Handbook*, Thames & Hudson, England.

Olins, Wally, 2014. *Brand New, The Shape of Brands to Come*, Thames & Hudson, England.

Sugiyono. 2018. *Metode Penelitian Kualitatif*, Bandung: Alfabeta.

Creative technology, data, and creative industry

Dynamics of Industrial Revolution 4.0: Digital Technology Transformation and Cultural Evolution –
Wulandari et al (eds)
© 2021 The Author(s), ISBN 978-1-032-04451-4

Board games as tools for developing character independence in Malang Regency

C.U.C. Nursyifani, L.T. Atmaji & G. Febriani
Bina Nusantara University, Malang, Indonesia

ABSTRACT: Ages 0–5 are the ages during which a child's brain develops very rapidly. During this time, children learn by imitating so that the characters formed at the beginning of a child's development are similar to the characters of the people closest to them. At those ages, children learn to develop cognitive, psychomotor, discipline, independence, social, and emotional character through activities at home and at school (preschool). Children learn these things by using games and their daily habits. Currently, there are a lot of educational games, one of those being a board game. The research method used is qualitative with a child psychology approach (4–6 years), teacher opinion, and visual communication design theory. This psychological approach is used to determine a child's character so that it has an impact on the preparation of the concept of the game which includes the rules.

Keywords: board game, characters, preschool

1 INTRODUCTION

Children begin to learn things by imitating older people. According to Bandura, social learning theory can form an individual personality in response to social stimuli, which will have an impact on the good formation of character of a nation's generation. The process of observing and imitating the behavior and attitudes of others is an act of learning. The Bandura theory explains human behavior in the context of continuous reciprocal interaction between cognitive, behavioral, and environmental influences. Environmental conditions around children are also very influential in social learning patterns (Bandura 1974).

One characteristic of psychological development in kindergarten children aged 4–6 years is the emergence of children's desire to take care of themselves or be independent. Independence is a positive habit and this attitude of independence is also a component of the formation of social life skills, namely the ability of children to be able to adjust to their social environment (Sidharto & Izzati 2007).

Therefore, alternative media is needed to help children develop character from an early age that is fun so that children of preschool age can socialize and act according to existing rules. Schools have a variety of instructional media for preschool children in terms of character development using a play approach method. There are so many types of learning media that can stimulate children's development through games.

Learning activities for preschoolers are dominated by doing daily activities and playing, therefore educational games are often found in school playgroups and kindergartens. Games provided by schools aim to help children grow and develop. Games that are suitable for the preschool-aged children include interactive books, block games, board games, etc.

In the current digital era, game-based teaching media easily can be found on practical digital/smartphone tools and certainly is very interesting for preschool-aged children. However, digital learning doesn't adequately stimulate a child's motor skill, so children become lazy to move their bodies because they are too focused on the smartphones. One tool that has the potential to stimulate

Table 1. Development stages of children aged 48–72 months.

Stage Development*	Child Development
48–60 Months	Stand on one foot 6 seconds, Looping 1 foot, Dance, Drawing (a cross, a circle), Drawing people with 3 body parts, Buttoning up doll clothes or clothes, Call the full name without assistance, Nice to mention new words, Nice to ask about anything, Answering questions with correct words, The talk is easy to understand, Can compare/distinguish something from its size and shape, Call the numbers, count fingers, Call the names of the day, Self-dressing without help, Brushing teeth without assistance, React calm and not fussy when left by the mother.
61–72 Months	Walking straight, Stand with one foot for 11 seconds, Draw with 6 parts, draw complete people, Catch a small ball with both hands, Draw a quadrilateral, Understand the meaning of the opposite word, Understand conversations that use 7 or more words, Answering questions about what objects are made of and their uses, Known numbers, can count numbers 5-10, know colors, Expressing Sympathy, Follow the rules of the game, self Dressing without help.

* *Pedoman Pelaksanaan: Stimulasi, deteksi dan intervensi dini tumbuh kembang anak ditingkat pelayanan kesehatan dasar.* Kementrian Kesehatan Republik Indonesia 2013.

children is board games because this game can stimulate a child's thinking, language development, psychomotor abilities, and emotions.

According to the Pedoman Pelaksanaan: Stimulasi deteksi dan intervensi dini tumbuh kembang anak ditingkat pelayanan kesehatan dasar Kementrian Kesehatan Republik Indonesia 2013, children have characteristics that grow from the time of conception until the end of adolensnce. Development is the increase in the structure and function of the body which is more complex in the development of psychomotor, speech, and language abilitites, as well as socialization and independence. In terms of character development, preschoolers need to be given stimulation, especially related to the exercise of independence and socialization. Another stimulation that also needs to be grown are the cognitive and psychomotor abilities of children. Table 1 shows the stages of development of children aged 48–60 months and 60–72 months.

The definition of a tabletop game is a game that is played on the surface of a table. One type of tabletop game is a board game. The definition of a board game is a game in which there are rules on how to play which are equipped with several game components such as tokens, pawns, or pieces that can be moved on a special board. As time has evolved, the types of board games today are more varied (Tan et al. 2015):

1. *Classic Board Games/Family Games.* Players race around the board game or follow specific paths to reach goals. Sometimes a point collection system is also used. The essence of this game lies not in the game but from the experience of togetherness players. An example of this type of game is Snake and Ladder.
2. *Euro-Style Games.* This game requires players to collect points. The winner of this game is the player who collect the most points. Examples of this type of game are Catan, Power Grid, Carcassonne, and Lancaster.
3. *Deck-Building Games.*This game is similar to trading card games—each player has several sets of cards that will be used to play. Examples of this type of game are Dominoes and Thunderstorms.
4. *Abstract Strategy Games.* The essence of this game is the players collide strategy to defeat or trick each other. Examples of this type of game are Chess, Checkers, and Push Fight.
5. *Strategy Games.* This game has a story that is very important to direct the player. This game involves cooperation and competition and requires a high level of thinking. Examples of this type of game are Risk, Empire, Arkham Horror, and so forth.
6. *Card-based Strategy Games.* A strategy game where cards are a very important element. An example of this type of game is 7 Wonders.

The variations of the games aim to make players more challenged with the flow of the game. Therefore, in making games, a game development process is needed which is divided into several stages. The game development process is broadly divided into the following stages (Nugroho 2013):

1. Research Phase and Concept Development. At this stage, basic ideas, objectives, themes, target audiences, technology, media (platforms), and various other limitations are formulated. This research stage becomes a crucial stage, various basic elements of a game are arranged here.
2. Formulation of Gameplay. At this stage, the game designers formulate gameplay/game mechanics that will be used in a game. This gameplay also regulates how a player can meet the objectives of the game and get a pleasant playing experience.
3. Arrangement of Asset and Level Design. This stage focuses on the conceptualization of all the characters and assets (including sound/music) needed. At the same time, the team also began to do the level design or grouping of levels of difficulty and various appropriate assets at each level (if there are more than one level) so that the game can present an optimal playing experience.
4. Test Play (Prototyping). At this stage, a prototype/dummy is presented to test the gameplay and various concepts that have been arranged, both at each level and as a whole, as well as making various improvements needed. This stage also serves to provide a complete picture for the whole team so that it can facilitate the process of further development.
5. Development. At this stage, all concepts (characters and assets) that had previously been arranged began to be fully developed. The game engine began to be developed, and all elements began to be integrated.
6. Alpha/Close Beta Test (UX-Initial Balancing). The main focus at this stage is to find out if all the main components of the game have been able to provide user experience as expected as well as to detect technical problems that have not been detected in the previous stages.
7. Release. At this stage, the game is ready to be released and introduced to the target players. When a game has been released to the public, it does not mean the development process is complete. Games in general continue to be optimized (updated). This is to ensure that the game that is presented is really able to provide the maximum playing experience.

The literature study above states that the development of children aged 4–6 years includes cognitive, motoric, and character development. At this age, the child begins to develop an independent character. Games that are suitable for the age of preschoolers include interactive books, block games, board games, etc. These games can stimulate a child's thinking, language development, psychomotor ability, and emotions.

The targeted findings in this study are able to compile content related to developing the character of independent preschool children (4–6 years) in Malang Regency. The purpose of this research is to help teachers and parents in adding variety to the game they play in terms of developing children's character through non-digital learning tools.

2 METHOD

The research method used is qualitative with a child psychology approach (4–6 years), teacher opinion, and visual communication design theory. The qualitative approach is a study aimed at describing and analyzing the phenomena, events, social activities, attitudes, beliefs, perceptions, and thoughts of people individually or in groups (Sukmadinata 2005), while the psychology approach is used to determine a child's character so that it has an impact on the preparation of the concept of the game which includes the rules of the game.

This research took place in two kindergarten locations in Malang. The primary research object is preschool children, both male and female, aged 4–6 years, as well as parents and teachers as secondary research objects. Data sources used in this study include written data in the form of field notes, research results, observations, scientific articles from previous research artists, and in-depth interviews. Data collection methods include the following.

Figure 1.   Top That! game, Fold It! game, and Mash Up Monsters game.

Figure 2.   Saya Bisa! board game prototype test to preschool childrens.

1. Observation and identification are carried out to observe the condition of the object of research and to identify the problem under study. Observation locations were carried out in kindergartens, board game cafes, and board game developers.
2. Documentation and observation are carried out together before the interview process is carried out until the interview process takes place. On the next visit, the researcher began to compile an interview protocol that would be submitted to the principal, teachers (four people), board game developers (three people), board game café staff (two people), and pre-school children (five children aged 5 years).
3. Interview (in-depth interview) using semi-structured techniques with instruments in the form of interview guides. The selection of speakers is based on experts in their fields.

3   RESULTS AND DISCUSSION

Based on the results of interviews with psychologists, independence is the ability to solve problems on your own. The independence of pre-schoolers can be seen when they are able to complete tasks, tidy up things, and help others. Preschoolers are happy if they get a reward or praise for completing a given task.

The results of an interview with the principal stated that the media owned by the school in supporting the development of independence characters were in the form of picture books and daily habituation. Children aged 4–6 years tend to be curious and really like to be given a gift when they are able to complete the task. Gifts do not have to be expensive objects or items, but enough with the provision of star stickers or the words "smart kids".

The results of an interview with the board game designer found that children like playing games by playing mix and match. That is, children like games with the aim of matching the same picture. Based on previous literature studies, the game to be used is Euro-style games, where the player who collect the most points is the winner.

Examples of card games recommended by experts include "Top That!" and "Mash Up Monsters". These games use cards as clues to the mission to do. The rules of the game are almost the same, only different themes and materials. The flow of an easy game becomes important because children aged 4–6 years have limitations in reading and understanding instructions.

The author created a prototype board game called Saya Bisa! Using previous games as a role models, the theme of this game is the daily activities in preschool children. Children are trained to be brave and actively answer or carry out a mission provided. The components contained in this game are image boards containing surrounding objects, meeple/pawns, question cards and mission cards, gold and silver coins, and medals.

4 CONCLUSIONS

The board game prototype Saya Bisa! made based on the results of observations and interviews that have been conducted. Board game prototype Saya Bisa! is the theme of daily activities using the help of illustrations of surrounding objects. The use of illustrations is because preschool children are not fluent in reading. This game teaches children with a happy atmosphere. Children easily absorb new things with the method of play.

The advantage of the concept given is that this game can develop a character of independence with several kinds of challenge. Children dare to answer, dare to tell stories, and can complete a challenge. The disadvantage of this game is that if there is no adult assistance, so children will have difficulty in running the game. The next research recommendation is to simplify the flow of the game so that children can play without too much assistance from adults.

ACKNOWLEDGMENTS

The authors want to thank Wikan Prabowo, Kummara/Manikmaya game designer, the H'Dr Comic Café staff, and Tabletops Boardgames Library staff, who participated as experts for the interviewing this research. The authors also want to thank to PAUD Al-Furqan Malang and RA Miftahul Jannah-DAU for contributing as an object of research.

REFERENCES

Bandura, A. 1974. Behavior theory and the models of man. *American Psychologist* 29(12):859– 869.
Kementrian Kesehatan Republik Indonesia. 2013. *Pedoman Pelaksanaan: Stimulasi,deteksi dan intervensi dini tumbuh kembang anak ditingkat pelayanan kesehatan dasar,* Jakarta 13–14.
Nugroho, Eko. 2018. Soal game, jangan sampai kita blunder. Retrieved from https://kumparan.com/eko-nugroho/soal-game-jangan-sampai-kita-blunder-ngobrolgame/full.
Nugroho, Eko. 2013). 7 tahap pengembangan game. Retrieved from https://tekno.kompas.com/read/2013/08/21/1226508/7.Tahap.Pengembangan.Game?page=all.
Sidharto, S. and Izzaty, R. E. 2007. Pengembangan kebiasaan positif: 16–19. Yogyakarta: Tiara Wacana.
Sukmadinata, N.S. 2005. Metode penelitian pendidikan:60 Bandung:Remaja Rosdakarya.
Sukmasari, R.N. 2016. Manfaat main board game bagi anak: latih strategi hingga kontrol energi. Retrieved from http://m.detik.com/health/read/2016/03/16/143225/316 6187/ 1301/manfaat-main-board-game-bagi-anak-latih-strategi-hingga-kontrol-emosi?l992203755.
Tan, S., Suwasono, A.A., and Yuwono, A. 2015. Perancangan Board Game Pengenalan Dinosaurus Untuk Anak Usia 8–12 Tahun. *Jurnal DKV Adiwarna*, 1(6):10.

Branding of muslim scuba dress: The case study of Rizka Haristi in Bandung

S.B. Haswati & S.M. Ridjana
Telkom University, Bandung, Indonesia

ABSTRACT: The growing of the fashion industry in Indonesia has driven competitiveness within the creative market, marked by numerous prestigious fashion events held every year. As a Muslim fashion brand established since 2015 in Bandung, Rizka Haristi has had to compete with similar brands to create the market opportunity, especially in West Java. Despite Rizka Haristi success in several fashion shows and its sales even reaching a peak in 2018, fluctuating profit is undeniable. It is assumed that the lack of emotional relationship with its consumer, also the use of single promotion media, has become the primary factor of this fluctuation. Hence, the company requires an advertising solution to increase their brand awareness. By conducting qualitative research using various methods, this paper generated a creative strategy toward a particular target audience: bridesmaid. By offering a special package, the program could help the brand to build a more emotional connection and stabilize the profit in the long run.

Keywords: branding, Muslim dress, scuba material, fashion, bridesmaid

1 INTRODUCTION

The fashion industry significantly contributes to Indonesia's economic growth, especially from the creative sector. The national exports ranked first at 56% and Gross Domestic Product (GDP), with the second rank of 18.15% after culinary (Rusiawan et al. 2017). As an impact, it captures the interest of both fashion workers and fashion enthusiasts in Indonesia. Now the public could attend regular prestigious Muslim fashion events in some big cities: the Muslim Fashion Festival (MUFFEST), Jakarta Modest Fashion Week (JMFW), etc. The industry also consists of fashion shows, fairs, talk shows, and design competitions such as contests for products of Muslim fashion and the business environment. It strongly indicates the massive potential of the Muslim fashion industry, especially in Bandung and DKI Jakarta, to transform Indonesia to be the center of the Muslim fashion world.

The journey of Rizka Haristi (RH) began since September 2015. The purpose of the brand is to accommodate women who encounter the difficulty of getting an elegant but comfortable fit-body Muslim dress with an affordable price. With competition among fellow Muslim fashion brands, RH introduces the benefits of customized Muslim dresses made from scuba with a minimalist and elegant design to look beautiful at all events. Scuba or rubber (stretch) that is an elastic fabric made from the core of a rubber thread at a time in the process of making yarn (Astiti 2016). Generally, scuba material is widely used for sportswear. This material has the nature of thick material but is elastic, not easily tangled and neat pieces of fiber material (Septiana & Siagian 2019) so it is used as an innovation in the use of Muslim RH dresses.

This innovation has brought RH to various national Muslim fashion events such as the Indonesia Hijab Festival in Bandung (2018), Jakarta Modest Fashion Week (2018), and Muslim Fashion

DOI 10.1201/9781003193241-5

Festival (2018–2019) in Jakarta. At the same time, RH was achieving the highest sales in November 2018 and sold 392 Muslim dresses through offline sales at the fashion bazaar and online events conducted on social media on Instagram. However, the data starting from July 2018–June 2019 shows the sales fluctuate, since RH sales rise only when they take part in fashion shows or bazaars at certain events. Unfortunately, sales may decline again right after shows and fairs, or in short, sales tend to be unstable.

It is expected that RH can attract more attention from women, especially bridesmaids as the target audience, which consisted of female students, career women, even the young housewives aged 22–30 years. A bridesmaid is anyone who is supposed to be the closest person, family member, or best friend of the bride who supports them at the wedding. To look remarkable by standing alongside the bride, the dress used by the bridesmaid makes an essential point in the togetherness and remains in harmony with the beauty of the wedding dress (sam Kim & Lee 2014). The color selection of a bridesmaid dress can create its impression on a wedding with various models and bridesmaid dresses be made according to their respective characteristics. Due to 400,311 couples who got married in West Java recently (Indonesia 2018), this trend can be seen as a huge market opportunity. Thus, it could support momentum for RH to increase its brand awareness in Bandung.

Brand awareness is one of the stages in knowing the ability of how the target audience recognizes, is interested, remembers, and feels familiar with a brand, while awareness, perceived quality, and loyalty to the brand can influence the target audience's purchasing power for a particular product (Rahman & Triadi 2019). Promotion is also one of the efforts of the brand to build brand awareness and attachment to the consumer experience of a brand (Moriarty et al. 2008). By using promotional mix (including advertising) to deliver product messages, a brand may reach a broader target audience (Wariki et al. 2015). Advertising itself is a form of communication that contains messages sent through particular media, where advertising becomes effective when consumers react according to the wishes of the ad maker (Moriarty et al. 2008).

In the previous promotion, RH only used social media content on social media on Instagram as the only media to deliver communication messages, whereas in advertising the media or the means to convey product messages usually use coordination in a mix of media with diverse types such as conventional, digital, or combination of both. The lack of resonance with consumers' belief in product messages also impacted on the lack of personal bonding between the brand and consumers (Moriarty et al. 2008). Therefore, RH must consider how to implement the right strategy to increase its brand awareness: not only persuasive and creative but most important, it effectively works.

2 RESEARCH METHODS

This research utilizes a qualitative approach as the data collection and facts are based on the observations of the authors, through questionnaires, interviews, and literature studies on phenomena that occur in the community (Sugiyono 2007). Thus, the data are collected through observations, interviews, questionnaires, and literature review to enrich the impression or insight from human behaviors (Kothari 2004). The method of analysis focuses on three characteristics, one of which is demographic (social character), which is fundamental in choosing and identifying the target audience to design messages and select the media according to the target. It is supported by SWOT (Strengths, Weakness, Opportunities, and Threats) analysis studies to explore knowledge about products promoted to consumers since SWOT is an instrument to find out and identify product problems from the internal factor, namely strengths and weaknesses. In contrast, opportunities and threats will describe the marketing influence of external elements (Moriarty et al. 2008).

Moriarty also stated that the AOI method (Activity, Opinion, and Interest) determines the target audience from personal (psychographic) driving factors, namely lifestyle aspects such as activities, interests, and opinions on a product or phenomenon. At the same time, the design process used AISAS as one of the marketing communications models to analyze consumer behavior and designing appropriate media strategy (Sugiyama & Andree 2010).

3 RESULT AND DISCUSSION

3.1 *Communication message*

The benefits of RH products are providing color selection consultations, from models to customized sizes so that consumers can look beautiful according to their personalities, while the consumer insight from the bridesmaid phenomenon becomes a very important moment in beautifying the appearance. They want Muslim dresses that show character and self-privilege. So, RH wants to portrait the brand as "Muslim dress that is customized so that it can look beautiful according to the character and personality of yourself on a special day".

With the tagline "Stunningly Beauty, Be You Be True", RH believes women can look beautiful and confident according to their character. By using scuba dress, the ladies would be fascinated as if the dress is made to exude their own persona. The communication strategy is used in providing information on product excellence. To provide the best service, appreciation and surprise to convince the target audience to make a purchase, this design utilized FACET Model of Effects Communication approach in the form of affective responses to the stage of resonance of belief (Moriarty et al. 2008). If the viewer could be triggered and feel the energy from the brand message seen through advertisements, they will continue to look forward and share their experiences so that others can feel the same way (Petrescu 2014).

3.2 *Visualization*

The visual pays attention to details on product quality and cohesiveness along with the bridesmaid themes. It also requires the use of informative and persuasive copywriting with advertising approach models such as Compliment Ads (praise) and Question Ads in the form of the use of questions in the headline so that it attracts the target to be more deeply attached to a message to the visual of the ads (Collins 2014).

In the design of logo making, the primary colors used are purple, gold, and ash by using color mixing which results in a series of colors that are: bright colors (tints), tone colors (tones), and dark colors (shades). These colors may trigger specific responses and harmony with the message (Meilani 2013). The supporting logo reads "Be You, Be True" by serif typefaces to give the impression that emphasizes the character of an elegant woman.

3.3 *Media strategy*

The media mix conveys the messages according to the analysis of the target audience and is designed with the AISAS communication model. Attention (A) is a step to shape the first impression of the

Figure 1.   Promotion media of special bridesmaid package RH. (Source: Ridjana 2020)

Figure 2. The TVC of bridesmaid special package on YouTube and Instagram. (Source: Ridjana 2020)

RH brand. Thus, the several advertisings are placed on Instagram, flyers are put in beauty salons (MUA or Brides), Muslim salons, and Muslim fashion bazaars based on the target audience's interest in fashion. Also, the poster is set on digital signage in the mall lobby based on the results of an analysis of activities that are often carried out by the target audience.

Interest (I) is the stage to persuade the target audience to know more about the RH brand and to interact and follow information about the brand. By using media that can provide detailed information in the form of visual products with quality graphics, the placement is still similar as in the attention stage. Next, the Search (S) directs the target audience to explore the brand through digital media, which consumers can access by clicking links and scanning barcodes.

When it comes to Action (A) step, the brand will communicate a personal emotional impact on the target audience to tie consumer awareness in recognizing brands, by broadcasting a TVC video placed on YouTube and Instagram TV (IGTV). Finally, Share (S) disseminates RH brand information in the form of word-of-mouth, buzzer, or influencer who were exposed to information by publishing their experiences with brands using social media.

3.4 *Design result*

This design prioritizes "Bridesmaid Special Package" packaging as an innovation to increase the awareness of the target audience in recognizing brands. Packaging can communicate products consistently, effectively in conveying messages and being brand reminders (Moriarty et al. 2008). Not only does this protect the product, but the packaging also provides differentiation between competitors and convincing the target audience to purchase the product (Rahman & Triadi 2019). The design gift is a membership card as a "surprise" after purchasing a product with special packaging as a strong brand element in creating consumer appeal, where this membership will later provide privileges such as getting discounts, following the activities carried out by the brand in the next promotion, and priority queues in purchases (Kurnia & Stanley 2013). In this case, the member card is also a benchmark media that has an impact on increasing the number of consumers.

The end of the TVC offers this membership card as a form of reward for purchasing products. The essence of the message is a cohesiveness to "friendship does not mean having to stay together, but it can also be with the nature of mutual understanding with each other". It is similar to the RH brand where one of its advantages is that it provides consultations on the selection of models, colors, and sizes according to the character of the self-visualized. A storytelling video uses the reality of life as a story that can arouse the emotions of the target audience to cause affection for the brand (Collins 2014).

Since meaningful advertising tends to be more effective in the long term (Haswati 2018), the target audience will get certain prizes after purchasing a "Bridesmaid Special Package" product and sharing experiences with the RH brand. The purpose of using merchandise in visual design is as a reminder of Rizka Haristi, giving affection and personal confidence to the target audience, and disseminating information about the brand.

4 CONCLUSION

The tight competitiveness among market players—especially in Muslim fashion, provoke RH Muslim dress to raise its brand awareness that contains information on excellence and product quality. RH perceives itself as a Muslim fashion brand providing customized Muslim dresses with consultation on the selection of colors and models to look beautiful following one's personality at special moments. In communicating the message, this paper analyzed the target audience's behavior in-depth then design creative strategies and sustainable media strategies in order to increase brand awareness. Altogether, the branding activity such as creative strategies and media would impact growing consumers, especially bridesmaids as the primary target audience.

In designing the creative strategy, it is highly recommended for RH to present "Bridesmaid Special Package" as special offers in the form of membership cards that provide an emotional impact in the form of a target audience's confidence in the brand. The communication model of affection and resonance, media strategies based on AOI, and SWOT strategies are expected to have an impact on increasing the number of RH consumers to maintain sales stability in the long run.

REFERENCES

Astiti, N. D. 2016. *Penerapan Material Scuba Terhadap Material Rib Sebagai Aplikasi Eksplorasi Teknik Tekstil Pada Busana Ready to Wear*. Skripsi. Telkom University.

Collins, T. 2014. *100 Ways to Create a Great Ad*, Laurence King Publishing.

Haswati, S. 2018. Sell and Tell: A Story of Dairy & Cocoa Print Advertising During Indonesian Colonial Period. *5th Bandung Creative Movement International Conference on Creative Industries 2018* (5th BCM 2018), 2019. Atlantis Press.

Indonesia, B.-S. 2018. Statistical Yearbook of Indonesia 2018. BPS Central Jakarta, Indonesia.

Kothari, C. R. 2004. *Research Methodology: Methods and Techniques*, New Age International.

Kurnia, P. R. and Stanley, J. R. 2013. Pengaruh Customer Satisfaction Dan Membership Card Loyalty Terhadap Store Loyalty Pada Industri Ritel Kategori Minimarket Di Jakarta. *Journal Of Management and Business Review*, 10(1):16–28.

Meilani, M. 2013. *Teori Warna: Penerapan Lingkaran Warna Dalam Berbusana*. Humaniora, 4:326–338.

Moriarty, S., Mitchell, N., and Wells, W. 2008. *Advertising Ed.8*, Kencana.

Petrescu, M. 2014. *Viral Marketing and Social Networks*, Business Expert Press.

Rahman, Y. and Triadi, A. 2019. *Perancangan Cerita Webtoon Mengenai Budaya Palang Pintu. Desain Komunikasi Visual, Manajemen Desain dan Periklanan (Demandia)*, 4:15–15.

Rusiawan et al., W. 2017. *Data Statistik Dan Hasil Survey*. Jakarta: Badan Ekonomi Kreatif. Badan Pusat Statistik.

sam Kim, Y. and Lee, J.-a. 2014. *Fashion Styles and Aesthetic Values Represented in Bridesmaid Dresses.* 한국의류산업학회지 *pISSN*, 16, 2014.

Septiana, M. G. and Siagian, M. C. A. 2019. Penerapan Motif Kain Ulos Tumtuman Pada Busana Ready to Wear Deluxe. *eProceedings of Art & Design*, 6.

Sugiyama, K. and Andree, T. 2010. *The Dentsu Way: Secrets of Cross Switch Marketing from the World's Most Innovative Advertising Agency*, McGraw Hill Professional.

Sugiyono, S. 2007. *Metode Penelitian Kualitatif Kuantitatif Dan R & D. Bandung Alf.*

Wariki, G. M., Mananeke, L., and Tawas, H. 2015. Pengaruh Bauran Promosi, Persepsi Harga Dan Lokasi Terhadap Keputusan Pembelian Dan Kepuasan Konsumen Pada Perumahan Tamansari Metropolitan Manado. *Jurnal EMBA: Jurnal Riset Ekonomi, Manajemen, Bisnis dan Akuntansi*, 3.

Dynamics of Industrial Revolution 4.0: Digital Technology Transformation and Cultural Evolution –
Wulandari et al (eds)
© 2021 The Author(s), ISBN 978-1-032-04451-4

Digital comic design of food waste for teens

S. Hidayat & D.E. Heryadi
Telkom University, Bandung, Indonesia

ABSTRACT: Indonesia is the second biggest contributor to food waste in the world. This unstable issue is a severe problem facing Indonesia, and the younger generation must acknowledge the impact of food wastage to attain a better future. This study is based on data acquired from questionnaires, interviews, and literature reviews. The research method is qualitative, supported by theories relating to the design. The media that matches the results of the data is digital comics for teens who need to know about food waste. This digital comic media was published via the internet and received positive responses from the readers. The media-designed results are considered able to increase awareness and knowledge of adolescents about food waste in Indonesia.

Keywords: Digital Comic, Food Waste, Teenager

1   INTRODUCTION

The lack of awareness of the Indonesian people toward food wastage earns Indonesia second place in the world as the country with the most food waste, as reported in 2016 by The Economist Intelligent Unit (EIU) with the Barilla Center for Food and Nutrition Foundation (BCFN). Therefore, knowledge about food waste needs to be given to the people of Indonesia, especially teenagers so as to have a better impact in the long term. Adolescents tend to be influenced by the environment outside the supervision of parents and school, so it would be better if insights about food waste are also presented practically in daily activities.

Indonesia has a fan of comics since the 1930s. It started with comic strips published in newspapers and magazines. Comics in Indonesia then evolved into a Japanese style influenced by popular Indonesian publisher *Elex Media Komputindo* when they produced translated Japanese comics (*manga*) around the 2000s (Aditya & Apsari 2019). The community's interest in comics grew in both readership and artistry, creating a large hobby and profession all over the country. As a big entertainment category in Indonesia, comics have the potential to share messages about food waste.

Currently, comic reading activities have been upgraded to digital media, including scanned comic book sites and webcomics. The website Webtoon.com is one of the most popular webcomic sites in Indonesia, with 60 million users worldwide. Through digital comics on the Webtoon website, information can be easily reached by teenagers.

2   RESEARCH METHODS

Comics contain the alignment of images that are deliberately arranged to convey messages and create aesthetic products to the reader (McCloud 1993). In starting the comic concepts and writing storylines, comic creators must pay attention to the limits that media has, from how far comics can visually narrate the story to how deep the message can be reached (Einser 2000). Comics also have a good communication effect, as can be seen from the combination of images and text, so messages from comics can be conveyed and presented more optimally (Lesmana et al. 2015). Comics have

Table 1. Comparison Result between 2 Comics

Comic Design	Title	Positive	Negative
	Digital comic about eating manner[*]	Good response from the audience, effective learning value, and is considered suitable for publication by media experts	Using blogs for publication
	Tanggap: waspada gempa bumi[†]	Comprehensive disaster mitigation theory and published on Webtoon	Using posters and advertisements on one social media only and the narratives are very theoretical

[*] by Muti'atul Mawaddah in 2016
[†] by Putra Arif Prasetyo in 2019

changed different mediums from time to time, with portable gadgets such as smartphones, tablets, and laptops becoming daily necessities over the last ten years. In this matter, comics have evolved into digital formats for better use. Digital comics were published online and have been accepted worldwide, especially in Asia (Aditya &Apsari 2019). To make comics a campaign media, it is obligatory to be able to influence public behavior over a broad scope in a limited time by communication activities and media to have non-commercial benefits for society (Atkin 1989).

A comparison of similar media and themes is used in the analysis. In this case, two comics have been chosen to obtain accurate data, and the results of the analysis are shown in Table 1.

Table 1 shows how to design a better comic referring to the latest trends and community target. To deliver messages about food waste, the digital comic has to be accessed on the internet so it is easier to share on various social platforms. The comic with a lot of theory might bore the teenagers, and the comic is expected to be entertaining but still informative.

To collect data, the author distributed questionnaires to adolescents aged 12–18 and received 101 responses, and interviewed the food waste campaign *Piring Bersih* founder. In the questionnaire results, 66% of teen respondents said they often left their food, and the rest stated that they are not used to leaving food unfinished. The majority of the reasons expressed were because they were too full, followed by reasons such as the taste of the food, not liking a particular part of the food, they got spoiled food, or they lost the mood to eat. Furthermore, in an interview with Faulina Diani Safira as (Clean Plate) campaign founder, she explained what adolescents can do to help Indonesia avoid food waste: (1) know their food portion, (2) encourage a proper eating schedule, and (3) share what to do when they eat outside.

3 RESULT AND DISCUSSION

The important role of the community in improving food sustainability in Indonesia became the main message of the comic. The form of the message is not designed too explicitly because the messages apply to entertainment media.

The title of the comic is *Sepiring Liburan* (A Plate of the Holiday). Each episode shows the efforts of food making, food waste side effects, and steps to reduce food waste for teenagers. The digital comic is published on an Webtoon to reach a larger audience and increase engagement (Figure 1).

The Webtoon comic *Sepiring Liburan* has been read by 10,800 people, followed by 698 people, and scored 9.73/10 by viewers. Audiences responded through comments that they are new to the major side effects of wasting food; it showed that their sympathy toward food waste was stronger than before (Figures 2, 3).

4 CONCLUSION

Sepiring Liburan shares advanced knowledge about food waste so that readers can understand the dangers and be able to apply that awareness in their daily activities. The results from the comics show a very good response. Readers conveyed that they have learned lessons about food waste properly from comics and the design of this digital comic has the potential to increase awareness to reduce food waste in Indonesia.

ACKNOWLEDGMENTS

Our deepest appreciation goes to *Piring Bersih* as project contributor, Faulina Diani Safira as an interviewee, all the questionnaire respondents, and Webtoon readers. This article would not have been possible without their help and encouragement.

Figure 1.   Webcomic digital banner and S*epiring Liburan* Webtoon home page.

Figure 2. *Sepiring Liburan* comic thumbnail.

m.th 27 Mei 2020 | Laporkan

baru tau ngga ngehabisin makanan dampaknya bisa
sampai sejauh ini:(ide komiknya bagus banget,
menambah wawasan. Semangat lanjutin ceritanya ayaa!

MEMBALAS   👍 2   👎 0

"I never knew we can get that much of a bad impact just by wasting food, this comic idea is great, really
informative. Keep it up!"

E

"This is great! especially that scene where the brother said 'it takes a long time to grow a plate of rice', it
caught the feeling about not wasting food and I'm moved. I think the next episode will be good too! I'm
curious, keep it up!"

Figure 3. *Sepiring Liburan* comment section.

REFERENCES

Aditya, D. K., and Apsari, D. 2019. The influence of the advancement of social media in the visual alnguage
of Indonesian comics strips. *Bandung Creative Movement International Conference on Creative Industries
2018*, p. 156.

Atkin, C. K. 1989. *Public Communication Campaigns*. Sage Publications.

Einser, W. 2000. *Comics & Sequel Arts*. Poorhouse Press.

Lesmana, M. E., Siswanto, R., and Hidayat, S. 2015. Perancangan Komunikasi Visual Komik Berbasis Cerita
Rakyat Timun Mas. *EProceedings of Art & Design,* 2(1), 112.

McCloud, S. 1993. *Understanding Comics: The Invisible Art*. Harper Collins.

Dynamics of Industrial Revolution 4.0: Digital Technology Transformation and Cultural Evolution –
Wulandari et al (eds)
© 2021 The Author(s), ISBN 978-1-032-04451-4

Designing verbal messages and visual media for the tourism destination of *Curug Putri*

S. Nurbani, J. Haiba, Y.A. Barlian & A.R. Ramadhan
Telkom University, Bandung, Indonesia

ABSTRACT: Curug Putri Campground is a natural tourist destination in Palutungan, West Java that has a uniquely shaped waterfall resembling a princess and a mythical story believed by the surrounding community. That makes this location full of potential for tourism yet due to a lack of promotion and the emergence of competitors in the area, the number of visitors coming to this place has been decreasing. The purpose of this research is to design a main message and visual media to promote Curug Putri Campground. The research method used is qualitative. The main verbal message is designed through the analysis of creative strategies of word meaning and visual media strategies using creative strategy theory and visual media. By designing a verbal message and visual media appropriately, it is the hope that this promotion can be delivered effectively, leading to an increase in visitors to Curug Putri which would help to improve the local economy.

Keywords: verbal message, visual media, word meaning, Promotion, Curug Putri, creative strategy

1   INTRODUCTION

Indonesia has many tourist destinations. If the government is able to take advantage of the existing potential and is able to work with local communities, they could work together on development that would help improve the country's economy. Tourism has the potential to overcome welfare problems if developed professionally.

Palutungan Curug Putri Campground has made various efforts such as completing and maintaining the beauty of the area in an effort to compete with other tourism destinations. Curug Putri has many advantages over other locations such as having a large piece of land, complete facilities, easy access, and a unique waterfall which is believed to be a miracle. However, due to the lack of promotion, Palutungan Curug Putri Campground has experienced a decline and fluctuation in the number of visitors since 2014.

Based on the results of interviews with the director of CV. Putri Mustika Tourism, promotions have been carried out in the form of word of mouth and direct marketing promotions by visiting public and private agencies as well as schools. Direct marketing can build relationships between buyers and sellers more effectively (Kotler &Armstrong 2008). Promotions are felt to be less effective, so creative strategies are needed to achieve the desired results. Therefore, based on these phenomena and problems, Palutungan Curug Putri Campground needs to be promoted by designing appropriate message strategies and visual media so as to have the desired effect on the target audience.

1.1   *Word meaning*

Words take on different meaning depending on how they are used in everyday life. According to Abdul Chaer (1994), a lexical meaning can also be called a true meaning. For example, "water" means a type of liquid that is used every day. A grammatical meaning is the result of grammar or grammatical processes. Contextual meaning is the meaning of a word or lexicon that appears based on a particular context. Referential is a meaning that has a reference to it in the real world. Non-referential meaning is the opposite of referential meaning. Denotative meaning is the original meaning, the original, or even the actual meaning that a word has that does not have any other hidden meaning. Connotative meaning is another meaning that uses the word. Conceptual meaning is the meaning possessed by a word that is independent of any context or association. Associative meaning is the meaning of words that arise because of the relationship of these words with other things outside the language. Word meaning describes several words as words that have a common or similar meaning. Term meaning is the opposite of the meaning of the word. Idiom meaning is the meaning of a word contained in a certain group of words, where the meaning formed is different from the original meaning of the word. Proverb meaning is similar to an idiom meaning in that it arises due to the formation of certain phrases or collections of words.

1.2 *Advertising*

Advertising is a complex form of communication that sets goals and uses strategies to influence the thoughts, feelings, and actions of consumers (Moriarty et al. 2011). Advertising or an "ad" is the overall broad communication about a product, service, or goods paid by a particular sponsor (Morissan 2010).

1.3 *Creative strategy*

According to Lee and Johnson (2011), the attractiveness of advertising is the approach taken in advertising to attract the attention of the target audience to influence their feelings toward the product/service. The attractiveness of advertising is Informational/Rational (Aggressive Sales); this attraction focuses on the practical and functional needs of consumers for products or services. Emotional Attractiveness (Persuasive Sales) is attraction that uses emotional messages and is designed around images expected to touch the heart. Combination Attraction combines informational/rational and emotional appeal.

AISAS is an advertising design model of *The Dentsu Way* that is effective for the target audience with behavior changes happening now due to the development of the internet. AISAS stands for Attention, Interest, Search, Action, and Share (Sugiyama &Andre 2011).

1.4 *Media*

The word "media" has the mediator of the message from the sender to the recipient, or the intermediary introducing the message or in Arabic known as *waasai* (Arsyad 2002). According to Belch (in Morissan 2010), the media is an intermediary who sends messages including television, newspapers, radio, and other supporting media. From the above definition, the media is an intermediary or messenger including broadcast media, print media, digital media, outdoor media, and other supporting media.

1.5 *Visual communication design*

Visual Communication Design can be defined as an amalgamation of applications and skills from design elements such as layout, color, typography, visuals, and communication for business and industrial needs. Visual communication design is an art to convey a message of information using the form as the language that is conveyed through media in the form of design (Anggraini and Nathalia 2018).

2 RESEARCH METHODS

In conducting this research, the authors used qualitative research methods because most of it refers to the phenomena that occur in society. Strengthened by the explanation from Moleong, qualitative research is research that is intended for the phenomenon of the behavior, perception, motivation, and action holistically by means of description (Moleong 2005). Data collection uses triangulation of data, namely observation, interviews, and literature study. Observation is a method of looking directly into the field (Sugiyono 2013). The data was obtained based on direct observation of the tourist destinations of Bumi Perkut and Palutungan Curug Putri on July 10, 2019 and August 18, 2019.

3 RESULT AND DISCUSSION

3.1 *Concept of verbal message*

Verbal messages, commonly referred to as copywriting, or in this case *the tagline,* are obtained from a creative strategy by combining Unique Selling Proposition (USP), Benefit, and Insight from the target audience. From these three elements, the proposition can be taken as the main message that Curug Putri has complete facilities and unique waterfall shapes, reflecting the shape of a mythical princess who was the daughter of heaven and water. This waterfall is believed to be efficacious and able to provide new and unique experiences for visitors. From this angle, a tagline is taken from the key phrase *Beyond the Magical Curug.*

The types of meanings used in the design of verbal messages in the form of taglines and headlines are contextual and associative. In this case, the word "*beyond*" contains contextual meaning that will depend on what is discussed, in this case referring to the facilities in Curug Putri as the selling power of this tourist area which is generated from the USP of this Putri waterfall tour. The word "*The magical*" is included in the associative meaning—in this case, the myth of a heavenly princess and water believed to be efficacious. The word "*Curug*" is included in the conceptual meaning because the concept of Curug is a waterfall.

Therefore, with the formation of the contextual, association, and conceptual meanings, verbal messages, in this case, a *tagline*, can be conveyed clearly to the target audience and can be received clearly without dual or multiple meanings. Henceforth, this verbal language will be strengthened or the visual language will be strengthened so that it the minds of consumers become clearer over the meaning or message conveyed by advertisers (Nurbani and Nanda 2019).

3.2 *Visual media*

3.2.1 *Target audience*
To obtain strategies and the right media in accordance with the target audience, the activities of the target audience will be deepened to discover how effective the media is in promoting the Curug Putri. The results from the mood board above show that the target audience likes things related to nature and hanging out with friends, traveling, culinary, trying new and unique things, following trends, and liking tranquility.

3.2.2 *Typography*
In the design of the promotion of Curug Putri Campground, the Sans Serif typeface is used to make it more friendly and modern. It uses Balbeer fonts for headlines and letter affirmations and use Gotham fonts for body copy.

3.2.3 *Color*
The color used is an earth tone. A grayish white color is from the small rocks of the mountains, dark green is the color of the leaves, the maroon color is the brownish color of the earth, and the

Table: AISAS

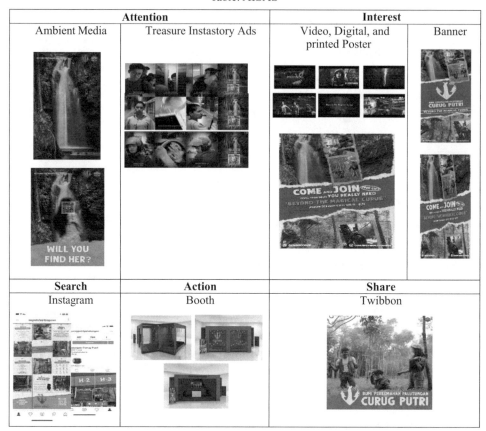

Source: Authors' Documentation

orange-yellow color matches the sun. So, it is expected that the colors bring the impression of comfort and strength.

3.2.4 *Design results*

Attention

Ambient media is able to give a deep massage to the target audience by providing a direct experience so that the target audience can immediately feel the truth. The choice of location of the elevator at the shopping center is the result of a survey of places often passed on by the target audience.

Interest

At the stage of interest, it uses information communication and persuasion strategies that are packaged with a video. Videos will be placed in the media using YouTube and Instagram. For YouTube videos containing Instagram address information the target audience can be directed to Instagram. Through the Instagram swipe up features, digital posters on Instagram ads that containing booth information can directing the information to Instagram feed. The banner that will be installed at the mall is also installed on the side of the road which contains information about the booth.

Search

The search stage uses information communication and persuasion strategies. Instagram content introduces the background, myths, facilities, and figures of workers who are tired of their activities and become a guide and complete information about the existence of brand activation. By using information communication strategies and brand activation persuasion in the form of booth experience, where visitors can feel and get information about Curug Putri, visitors have the opportunity to get free merchandise. The booth experience is made with three sides like a pop-up.

Share
The entry requirement to the booth is that visitors share their experiences on social media with the #BuperBuangBaper hashtag. Twibbon will be used when the target audience shares their activities at the booth and when visiting the Palutungan Curug Putri Campground.

4 CONCLUSION

The main advertising message is very important in determining what will be communicated to the target audience, so that the target audience can understand and accept the message well and the decision to purchase or use the product can be highly considered. Aside from a good message, visual media strategies also determine the message to be communicated effectively. Both of these are obtained from determining the right creative strategy so that promotion can be done effectively. This will affect the main goal of increasing the number of visitors to come to the Curug Putri Campground so that the region's economy can be lifted up and indirectly help solve the nation's problems related to poverty.

ACKNOWLEDGMENT

Thank you to all parties who provided the data and thank you to the previous researchers. Thank you to PPM Telkom University for providing internal funding for this research.

REFERENCES

Arsyad, Azhar. 2002. *Media Pembelajaran*, edisi 1. Jakarta: PT. Raja Grafindo Persada.
Belch, George E. and Michal, A. 2009. *Advertising and Promotion: An Integrated Marketing Communication Perspective, 8th edition*. New York: Pearson Education.
Chaer. 1994. *Linguistik Umum*. Jakarta: Rineka Cipta
Kotler, Philip and Armstrong, Garry. 2008. *Prinsip-prinsip Pemasaran*, Jilid 1, Erlangga, Jakarta
Lia Anggraini, S. and Nathalia, Kirana. 2018. *Desain Komunikasi Visual; Dasar- dasar Panduan Untuk Pemula*. Bandung: Penerbit Nuasa.
Moleong, Lexy J. 2005. *Metodologi penelitian kualitatif*, Bandung: Remaja Rosdakarya
Monle lee dan Carla Johnson. 2011. *Prinsip-prinsip Pokok Periklanan dalam Persfektif Global*. Kencana Prenada Media Group.
Moriarty, Sandra, Nancy Mitchell, Wells, William D. 2011. *Advertising Edisi 8*. Jakarta: Kencana Prenada Media Group.
Morissan. 2010. *Periklanan komunikasi pemasaran terpadu*, Jakarta: Penerbit Kencana
Nurbani, S. and Nanda Ayu R. Dewi. 2019. Designing Verbal Message And Visual Media Of Quick Chicken. *6th Bandung Creative Movement 2019*, Bandung, Indonesia, October 2019. Telkom University, pp. 446–450.
Sugiyama, Kotaro and Andre, Tim. 2011. *The Dentsu Way*. New York: McGraw-Hill.
Sugiyono. 2013. *Metode Penelitian Pendidikan Pendekatan Kuantitatif, Kualitatif, dan R&D*. Bandung: Alfabeta.

Dynamics of Industrial Revolution 4.0: Digital Technology Transformation and Cultural Evolution –
Wulandari et al (eds)
© 2021 The Author(s), ISBN 978-1-032-04451-4

Measurement method to test the strength of peg and tie joints against tensile strength and press on simple bamboo structure

A.N.S. Gunawan & S. Mohamad
Universiti Sains Malaysia, Penang, Malaysia

ABSTRACT: The search for an effective connection tool for assembling bamboo is mostly done by researchers and architects. Either conventional or trying to change the bamboo into the form of other materials. The search for a new connection tool wasn't followed by test regarding the strength of the bamboo strings against compressive and tensile forces. The goal of testing the strength of the tool connected and bamboo aims to see the pattern of damage to the bamboo that will occur due to the use of the tool connected. Testing is done by creating a model of the test object circuit structure simply with the use of the tool Universal Testing Manual (UTM) Ibertest type of Eurotest. The results of the test show a lot more damage caused by power urges the bamboo on the hollow part of the bamboo as the space/layout of the connection pegs.

Keywords: connection tool, bamboo, tensile force, compressive force, the strength of the urges

1 INTRODUCTION

Many researchers, practitioners, and architects try to renew stitch bamboo as a building structure. The update is an effort of invention and a creation tool to connect new use in stringing the bamboo for the structure of the building. Morisco (1998) and Pathurrahman (1998) conducted a study increase in the strength of the connection on the bamboo to make the connection fill the bamboo with the aim of making the bamboo that will be spliced into a composite, similar to research done by Hogan and Archer 2010) by filling in the mortar and gave the steel reinforcement on the part of the bamboo that will be spliced. Nugraha (2012) conducted a similar study but using resin as a material filler and did variation testing with a wide variety of corner styles (0°, 45°, 60°).

Analysis of the resistance of the lateral joints of wood and mortar fillers, known as Morisco Mardjono joints, was carried out by applying EYM (European Yield Theory). This analysis aims to formulate the strength of the Morisco Mardjono lateral joint system which is influenced by the geometry data connection, the bending moments of the bolts and bamboo fulcrums, and the material fulcrum points (Awaludin 2012). However, testing the re-facing tool to connect the new and the old did not do much. The physical condition of the bamboo, which is hollow, is composed of parallel fiber; the nature of the expansion and shrinkage create a problem for the construction of bamboo as a structural element of the building.

There are three common means of connecting: tie, stake, and substitution. It is necessary to test the effectiveness of the power of each system based on materials used. In the coupling structure of the building, the structural elements have to meet the requirements of the strength against a tensile force and compressive force, or both because part of the structure is subjected to traction, pressure, or both (Salvadori 1990). It turns out it is influenced also by how to compose the elements of the structure of bamboo which will have an impact on the stability of the building reduction because of the connection factors between bamboo stem by resistance elements (Sassu et al. 2012). A common problem is to equate how to connect with the use of a connection system which isn't an appropriate function of the mechanic is received on a connection of the bamboo.

DOI 10.1201/9781003193241-8

To recognize further related to the behavior of the connection due to the use of the tools connect a special method for testing is needed. Scientific writing describes one of the techniques of measurements of the strength of bamboo and provides a means of connecting that is used as well as the impact of damage to the mechanical well on the bamboo and on the tools used.

2 RESEARCH METHODS

2.1 *Stimuli*

This research used the quantitative method, utilizing a comparative study and an experimental study. Before doing the testing, exploration studies were carried out in the literature related to the principles of work and distribution of the load and the force on a series of bamboo construction and experiment in the circuit of the simple construction of bamboo, such as the use of test equipment compressive and tensile strength.

The results of the observation and search of a comparative study found how there are two kinds of connection base. The first is the connection with the belt (rope) and pegs.

2.2 *Subject*

This research was done in an effort to discover how to make a simple circuit according to the principles of the compressive force, The tensile force received and borned, will be distributed on each rod element in the series of truss system/truss system (Salvadori 1981 in Gunawan et al. 2013) trunks interconnected with joints on the ends of the rod and distributes the load on the dots connect the gusset on the truss system/truss system by using a means of connecting a rope or a means of connecting pegs.

2.3 *Research procedures*

First, make a model of the test object with a variety of connection devices of different types. The model in the form of an equilateral triangle with length l2 is 2 x l1. Then the value of h can be calculated by calculating the Pythagorean formula, as follows:

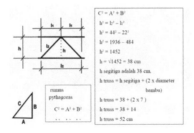

Figure 1. The formula of calculation of the dimensions of the model will be made. (Source: Ahmad Nur Sheha Gunawan, 2013)

The second stage is the manufacture of the test object.

Figure 2. The test specimen to a compressive force and drag created in the form of simple construction. (Source: Ahmad Nur Sheha Gunawan, 2013)

The third stage is to test the strength of the test specimen laboratory test by using the tool Univeral Testing Manual (UTM) Ibertest type Eurotest. Universal Testing Manually is a machine used to test the tensile stress and compressive strength at material or materials with a variety of standards and compression on materials, components, and structures. In the case of this test, the bamboo material strung together in a series of structurally simple with a means of varying connection. Machine Universal Testing Machine can do tensile testing with many standards and compression tests on materials, components, and structures.

Figure 3.   Manual testing images laying objects on measuring University (UTM)Eurotest type. (Source: Ahmad Nur Sheha Gunawan 2013)

The fourth stage is the laying of the test object on the testing tool.

Figure 4.   Manual testing images laying objects on measuring University (UTM) Eurotest type. (Source: Ahmad Nur Sheha Gunawan 2013)

After the model test objects are created and ready to test, the model test object is brought into the laboratory for testing the test tap and drag using the tool Universal Testing Manual (UTM) Ibertest type Eurotest with a capacity of the capacity test load up to 20 tons. The purpose of this test is to see the performance of the connection at the point of connection with the given treatment of compressive load and tensile load. The test object is laid on the tool UTM Ibertest type Eurotest which then gives the load to fit the performance you want to see, e.g., compressive or tensile strength. A large burden of work is set by the load control and the data recorded digitally in the computer instruments testing tool. The control of the load on the tool is set digitally, so that when the test object is damaged, then shifted, and the shape of the tool is deformed, the test will stop and generate measurement data in the form of data maximum load, maximum strength, and displacement/shift of position.

3 RESULTS AND DISCUSSION

Testing is done by creating a model of the test object 1:1. The specimen was tested with the machine tool UTM Ibertest type Eurotest.

The model was made for testing the press. The experimental data of test force laboratory structure and material civil engineering Institute of Technology Bandung (ITB) in the form of numeric data/numbers and the image data in the form of recording the process and results of testing.

By using Microsoft Excel, the measurement results data are displayed in the form of numerical data and graphics which are then interpreted as a description of the results of the measurement model testing. Data measurement results in the form: maximum load, maximum power, and a shift/position of a series of the truss. After the trial was carried out, the following data were obtained.

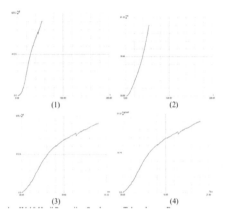

Figure 5. The results of testing the connection press: (1) compressive weight force (kgf) vs. time (s); (2) displacement distance (mm) against time (s); (3) compressive weight force (kgf) against sliding (mm); and (4) the compressive weight of the style/field press against the percentage of strong heavy press style %Lo.

Press testing on the test object by using a means of connecting bolts shows that the load maximum pressure capable of being held by 750.2 kg, while the maximum power capable of being held by of 46.9 kg/cm^2, the displacement distance due to the drag maximum is 55,745 mm.

Figure 6. The damage on the model test press with machine UTM. (Source Ahamd Nur Sheha Gunawan 2013)

From the test, it is known that the damage to bamboo is caused more by the force of the bamboo against the hollow part of the bamboo as a place for connection pegs. The stiffness of the post (related to the type of material) also plays a role in the breakage. Damage to bamboo with wooden pegs is different from damage caused by the stiffness of metal pegs. The amount of tensile strength and compressive strength acting on a series of simple specimens is not the main cause of damage to the joined bamboo stems. Holes that are too big or too small also have a role in the damage to the bamboo strung. Weakening due to improper perforation causes the friction force of the pegs against the bamboo (in the holes) because it is loose so that the force acting on the pegs to bamboo causes the bamboo to break, especially in joints with hard-made pegs such as metal. Whereas on soft pegs such as wood and bamboo, more damage occurs to the pegs.

So, it can be said that the weakening of the joint is also influenced by the size and position of the hole, the type of peg material. In structural elements that are dominant, the tensile force tends to damage because the bamboo which functions as a tensile rod will result in a reduction in the area of the tensile rod which affects the tensile strength where the distribution of the tensile load is not evenly distributed but there is a right stress concentration on the edge of the hole of the one-way connection tool. tensile force. This can be explained through the theory of elasticity (Suryoatmojo, 1997 in Gunawan 2013). An element that has a hole in the middle is loaded with a centric dance load will cause an uneven load distribution (stress concentration occurs), right on the edge of the large hole in the direction of tensile stress. An element that experiences a compressive force will experience a bending force up to the maximum yield stress and buckling occurs because of the instability of the compressive element.

In the model with a tie object, bamboo does not suffer significant damage, but the structural structure of bamboo changes shape. This is due to the elastic-plastic binding material of bamboo.

4 CONCLUSION

The test results and exposure above concluded that the damage to the structure of bamboo is not only determined by the size of the style, but also the related issue of the type of bamboo (the physical properties of bamboo are arranged by the parallel fiber), layout connection, large hole connection, the connection type, and the material of the tool connect.

It can be an input related to the creation of a means of connecting the new to further consider physical form, the nature of the character of bamboo, and the laying of the tool connected. In particular, a means of connecting based stake.

The idea that appears related to new connection tool is how to create a means of connecting bamboo that is strong without damaging it, related to the bamboo physical form with fibers shaped in parallel direction.

REFERENCES

Barry, R. 1984. *The Construction of Buildings. 3rd edition Vol. 3: Single Storey Frames, Shells and Lightweight Coverings*. London: Granada

Frick, Heinz. 2004. *Ilmu Konstruksi Bangunan Bambu Pengantar Konstruksi Bambu*. Yogyakarta: Penerbit Kanisius.

Frick, Heinz. 1997. *Pola Struktural dan Teknik Bangunan di Indonesia*. Yogyakarta: Penerbit Kanisius.

Frick, Heinz. and Purwanto, L.M.F. 1998. *Sistem Bentuk Struktur Bangunan, Dasar-Dasar Konstruksi Dalam Arsitektur*. Yogyakarta: Penerbit Kanisius.

Frick, Heinz., L and Setiawan, Pujo. 2001. *Ilmu Konstruksi Struktur Bangunan, Cara membangun Kerangka Gedung Ilmu Konstruksi Bangunan 1*. Yogyakarta: Penerbit Kanisius.

Hadjib, N. and Karnasudirdja, S. 1986. *Sifat fisik dan mekanis bambu andong (Gigantochloa verticillata Mur.), betung (Dendrocalamus asper Back) dan ater (Gigantochloa ater Kurz)*. Laporan Intern Pusat Penelitian dan Pengembangan Hasil Hutan dan Sosial Ekonomi Kehutanan Bogor.

Jassen, J. 2011. Draft ISO: N315. Laboratory Manual on Testing Methods for Determination of Physical and Mechanical Properties of Bamboo. *Draft ISO/TC 165/WG9, Determination of Physical and Mechanical Properties of Bamboo* .

Morisco. 1999. *Rekayasa Bambu*. Yogyakarta: Nafiri Offset.

Schodek, D. L. 1998. Dalam D. L. Schodek, *Struktur*. Bandung: PT. Refika Aditama.

Dynamics of Industrial Revolution 4.0: Digital Technology Transformation and Cultural Evolution –
Wulandari et al (eds)
© 2021 The Author(s), ISBN 978-1-032-04451-4

Periodization of the development of local fashion brand in Bandung in 1994–2018

W.N.U. Bastaman, A.S. Hardy Shafii
Universiti Sains Malaysia, Penang, Malaysia

R. Febriani
Telkom University, Bandung, Indonesia

ABSTRACT: Bandung, known as the city of education, has attracted many people from various regions, helping to build an open and diverse atmosphere. Its proximity to Jakarta (Place), the capital of Indonesia and the largest business center in the country, allowed Bandung to receive information on the latest trends and business. These two aspects were then able to give birth to many new ideas, one of which was the phenomenon of the emergence of local fashion brands in Bandung in the late 1990s which continue to grow today. This research maps out Bandung's local fashion brand from 1994–2018, based on their periodization and genre. This mapping is expected to be a reference for designers, crafters, entrepreneurs, and industry stakeholders to develop Bandung's local fashion brand in the future. This research uses qualitative methods through literature study and secondary data, further reinforced by interviewing influential designers and people in the industry. As a result, it can be concluded that Bandung has experienced three periodizations of development of local fashion brands.

Keywords: local brand, Bandung, creative industry

1 INTRODUCTION

Bandung is the capital of the West Java Province and the 5th largest city in Indonesia. It has long been known for its beautiful, natural potential. Because of its good air quality, the city of Bandung was also planned as the Dutch East Indies' capital replacing Batavia (Kunto 2014). Its geographical location (Place) naturally attracts many people to stay in Bandung. Besides that, the location, with its proximity to Jakarta, makes Bandung able to easily receive information on the latest trends. Bandung is also known as a city of education, another important aspect as it attracts many young people to live there. The number of young people in Bandung has reached 60% of the total population (People) (Resmadi 2017). The existence of young people with various backgrounds creates an atmosphere of openness in Bandung, and this conversation then produced ideas for their environment thereby increasingly making the city of Bandung a more livable place (Bandung Dossier Team 2013).

Places, people, and ideas are three strengths of Bandung (Ekomadyo et al. 2016). These three strengths had a significant impact on the city of Bandung in the 1990s. The phenomenon resulted in the birth of a fashion brand in Bandung, which was then widely adopted in various other cities in Indonesia. This phenomenon was also reinforced by the emergence of Western popular culture in Bandung in the 1970s through music (Yujin 2017). According to data from the Ministry of Cooperatives and Small and Medium Enterprises and the Office of Trade and Industry, the number of local fashion brands in Bandung in 2012 reached 551. However, in fact, the number may be more than that because there are still many local fashion brands that only operate online and do not have a brick and mortar store. Therefore, they are not considered official business entities and so not listed (Soei et al. 2015). The KICKFEST event was the first clothing festival in Indonesia originating from the city of Bandung. It took place in September 2019 in Malang, with the number of local brands participating reaching 100. In addition, the Brightspot Market event was held in October 2019 in Jakarta, where 150 local brands participated. Because of this potential, Bandung was initiated as a creative city in 2015 (Aritenang 2012; Irawati & Nasional 2011; Unesco 2015). Through this research, researchers will map the development of a local fashion brand based on each period's periodization and distinct features. This mapping is expected to be a reference for designers, crafters, entrepreneurs, and stakeholders to develop Bandung's local fashion brand in the future.

2 METHODOLOGY AND DISCUSSION

The research was conducted using qualitative methods through document studies and in-depth interviews from 2018–2019. Researchers interviewed the owner and Creative Director of some of the leading fashion brands in Bandung who had been in business 5–10 years. Interviews were conducted in semi-structured interviews and direct observation. Researchers visited the actual store and observed the social media of local brands. The data obtained through these documents, such as data from journals, books, and popular articles, were compared with interviews. Based on these data, the mapping of periodization, actors, local brands that developed at that time is known, and other important events impact further developments.

2.1 *Pioneer Era (1994–1996)*

Table 1. The Pioneer Era (1994–1996)

1906–1983	1970	1983	1990	1993	1994	1996
Bandung History Dutch Colonial (1906–1945) until New Order Era (1983): Westernized	Birth of Aktuil music magazine (1970), rock and British music invasion	• Press restriction • Foreign media enter Indonesia • Mainstream music start to raise	• MTV • ESPN: skateboarding • Punk, hardcore, metal music communities thrived underground	Pas Band (underground band) recording 1st album	• DIY spirit • Reverse Studio Music established (Dxxxt, Helvi, Richard Mutter) and develop become to Reverse Clothing Company • The rise of punk, metal, hardcore local band • The first skateboarding shop established	347 established. This becomes the pioneer of Bandung's local brands. Its design and inspired by the style of skateboarding style, music, and design.

The first period was The Pioneer Era, which became an important point early at the start of the local fashion brand born in Bandung. Since Bandung was established until the New Order government beginning in 1983, Western lifestyles strongly influence Bandung. In the 1970s, an up-to-date and critical music magazine Aktuil was established which focused on rock music news. During the New Order government, the media were finally restricted. Then the presence of foreign press makes the news circulating tend to be neutral. The era of mainstream music eventually flourished. But punk, hardcore, and metal music continued to grow underground (Resmadi 2018). The presence of TV also brought on a new wave of MTV and ESPN. A new wave of loud music and extreme sports such as skateboarding and BMX further developed into one solid community. In 1993, Pas Band, one of Bandung's underground bands, managed to record an album and distributed it independently. This spirit finally gave birth to the Reverse Music Studio. Here, all underground music, skateboarding, and BMX Bandung communities gather (Resmadi 2017). Reverse Music Studio is also slowly turning into a Reverse Clothing Company. We can find various kinds of band merchandise, tapes, artwork, and fashion items related to music, recording, and BMX. In 1996, Bandung's pioneer local fashion brand, 347, was born, which offered fashion items inspired by skateboarding and surfing.

2.2 *Distro and clothing company Era (1997–now)*

Table 2.   The Distro and Clothing Company Era (1997–now).

1996	1997	1998	2002	2006	2007	2008	2012
The rise of various music scene & created a new fashion trend then became a local fashion brand, Distro (distribution store) & Clothing Company	• Asian Financial Crisis • Rupiah collapsed • Reverse Clothing company closed • No more imported music merchandise	• Distro and clothing company began to design and produce their own product • Also, their collaboration with a local band to produce their merchandise such as t-shirt.	• Many Indonesian youngsters imitated the style of the pioneer distros and clothing company in Bandung itself and other cities until now • Besides music, art, and design, street style trends greatly influence their product designs	• Kreative Independent Creative Kommunity (KICK) established • In collaboration with the Indonesian Ministry of Industry, KICK held Bandung Indie Clothing Expo • Internet is easier to access. Social media such as Friendster is used widely.	First KICKFEST held in Bandung and still held annually until now in various cities in Indonesia	Facebook is widely used.	• The offline store starting to shift to an online store • Several distros and clothing companies began to collapse

After the Reverse Clothing Company and 347 were established, many of the local fashion brands were developed. Some local fashion brands will eventually be able to have independent distribution or offline stores. Otherwise, it will usually join a particular Distro (distribution store) and use the sales consignment system. The term "Distro" has come to represent a local brand that stands for this era, whether it has independent offline stores or not (Kim 2017). Unfortunately, in 1997, the Asian financial crisis occurred, and the Rupiah collapsed. Reverse Clothing Company that were focusing on the sale of imported merchandise products collapsed. In 1998, to overcome difficulties after the economic crisis, the system focused on designing and locally producing its products (Irawati & Nasional 2012), and began actively collaborating with a variety of local musicians at the time and bringing the community to become the main consumer. In 2006, a community was finally created to accommodate a local fashion brand called the Kreative Independent Creative Community (KICK). It began with a showcase and bazaar and performances from local musicians. The event continues to be held every year since, not only in Bandung but in other major Indonesian cities as well. In 2008, when Facebook began to be widely used, the product sales process began to change becoming online. At its peak in 2012, the distro slowly began to collapse. Local fashion brands that have survived until now can adapt to challenge and have a strong community behind them.

2.3 *Local brand Era (2008–now)*

The last period is the local brand era. After the Distro and Clothing Company era, local fashion brands are varied and known by the term "Local Brand". In 2008, Happy Go Lucky was born, the first curated store in Bandung. Saadiah Adzani (2019), former Creative Director of Happy Go Lucky, said the concept is similar to Distro, which collects several local fashion brand products in one place but with the thematic theme. If Distros are very thick about local musicians, a curated store comes with current fashion trends. This was followed by the first curated local fashion brand event in Jakarta, Brightspot Market. Similar to Brightspot Market, Bandung also held the Trademark Market and the Lookats Market. The online shopping phenomenon started spreading in 2010. Iqra Tanzil (2018), Creative Director from Imagery Bags, said besides Facebook, there are also new

Table 3. The Local Brand Era (2008–now)

2008	2009	2010	2011	2013	2014	2017
Happy Go Lucky or well known as HGL, the first curated local brand store, established in Bandung	• First Brightspot Market held in Jakarta. • Brightspot Market become a barometer for similar events in other cities, especially in Bandung.	• Facebook, Kaskus, and Blackberry are widely used as a marketing channel and the "online shopping" phenomenon began to spread • Brodo, a footwear brand, established • Trademark Market held in Bandung	Kaskus thread: Indonesian Brands -One Stop Fashion News-established	Instagram began to be widely used as a marketing channel and made people easier to online shopping	Local brand starting with social media and building web stores	• People familiar with the marketplace (Tokopedia, Shopee, Zalora, etc.) • Some local brands also launched physical stores

information platforms, such as Kaskus and BlackBerry Message Group. With more open access to information from the Internet, a new concept of local fashion brands emerged. Agit Bambang from Amble Footwear and Fahmi from Hijack Sandals (2019) said that the Local Brand has its specialty, such as footwear, bags, or jewelry. This is different from the Distro that provides the entire product from head to toe. Anya Kardin from Kar Jewelry (2019) said that Instagram's birth opened up online shopping opportunities. Although the Local Brand already has a website, major sales channels are still through WhatsApp, Line, email, or marketplace. However, in the last three years, people are more familiar with using the site and the advent of markets that generally use the website base.

3 CONCLUSION

The local fashion brand in Bandung experienced three periods of development. Distro, Clothing Company, or Local Brand are local fashion brands. The name Distros is already attached to several local fashion brands born in the late 1990s or 2000s. In the era of Distro and Clothing Company, more focus is on developing apparel products that complement one another from head to toe, making the products offered more specialized in the period of Local Brands. Distro or Clothing Company, generally very attached to a particular music genre or music community. But in Local Brands usually, they complement each other to define specific communities. This research is expected to provide a map of local brand development periodization in Bandung's city. It could guide young entrepreneurs to understand business development in Bandung and allow them to make business forecasts.

REFERENCES

Aritenang, Adiwan. 2012. *The City of Bandung: Unfolding the Process of a Creative City.* SSRN Electronic Journal. 10.2139/ssrn.2295227.
Ekomadyo, Agus Suharjono & Pradita Candrawati. 2016. *Kriteria Placemaking untuk Fashion Hub. Prosiding Temu Ilmiah IPLBI 2016.*
Bandung Dossier Team. 2013. *UNESCO City of Design Bandung.* Application.Bdg.
Data Statistik dan Hasil Survei EKONOMI KREATIF Kerjasama Badan Ekonomi Kreatif dan Badan Pusat Statistik. 2016.
Ekonomi Kreatif Bandung. 2018. http://creativeconomy.bandung.go.id/. Https://en.unesco.org/creative-cities/bandung (2015)

Irawati, I. and Nasional, I. T. 2011. *City as Idea Generator for Creative Industries: Case Study: Bandung's Creative Industry (Clothing and Indie Music Industries)*. In *3rd World Planning Schools Congress, Perth*.

Kim, Y. 2017. *Making "Creative" Movement: Transformation of Urban Culture and Politics in Bandung, Indonesia. Geographical Review of Japan Series B*, 90(1):17–25.

Kunto, H. 2014. *Wajah Bandoeng tempo doeloe*. Granesia, Bandung.

Resmadi, I. 2018. *Jurnalisme musik dan selingkar wilayahnya*. Kepustakaan Populer Grame dia.

Resmadi, Idhar. 2017. *Pentingnya Pemikir Desain di Kota Desain*. https://idhar- resmadi.net/2017/12/14/pentingnya-pemikir-desain-di-kota-desain/

Resmadi, Idhar. 2017. *Tongkrongan Penting Anak Musik di Bandung Pada 1990-an*. https://www.djarumcoklat.com/article/tongkrongan-penting-anak-musik-di-bandung-pada- 1990an

Soei, C. T. L., Satyarini, R., and Prasetya, I. 2015. *Identifikasi Key Success Factor pada Indus tri Clothing di Kota Bandung. Research Report-Humanities and Social Science*, 2.

Digital transformation of environment

Dynamics of Industrial Revolution 4.0: Digital Technology Transformation and Cultural Evolution –
Wulandari et al (eds)
© 2021 The Author(s), ISBN 978-1-032-04451-4

Planning private spaces for design students to support the optimization of online learning

A. Farida, W. Liritantri & M.S. Hanafi
Telkom University, Bandung, Indonesia

ABSTRACT: As an effort to prevent the spread of the COVID-19 outbreak, the government stipulated that all tertiary institutions eliminate lecture activities on campus and pivot to online lecturing. However, this change resulted in several problems for students, one of which regarding space in which to learn from home. Because of that, space design is needed to support students to perform online learning more sufficiently both in terms of space layout and adequate facilities. This design was made based on the results of a questionnaire from 100 varied design students majoring in interior design, architecture, products, visual communication, and craft. The design students as a subjects (as subjects) were chosen because the nature of their assignments were more dynamic so that their facilities needed to become more diverse. This design was carried out using qualitative methods, namely analyzing questionnaire data as well as quantitative data with descriptive analysis from literature studies. By designing this online learning space, it is hoped that students can optimize the online learning process.

Keywords: space, optimization, online learning, layout, facilities

1   INTRODUCTION

This article is in response to the West Java provincial government policy which stipulated that face-to-face teaching and learning activities were to be postponed until January 2021. In addition, the Minister of Education and Culture, Nadiem Makarim, revealed that distance learning can be applied permanently after the COVID-19 pandemic is over. Teaching and learning activities using technology will be fundamental. The use of technology provides an opportunity for schools to do various models of learning activities. Based on this decision, careful planning for adequate an online learning space to support online learning is necessary. For design students, online learning has higher challenges because of the more dynamic and diverse nature of lectures. Lectures are not restricted only to theory classes, but also have to be taken into consideration with regard to practice studies and variations of assignments make the online learning process of design students more complicated.

   The main problem such as lack of concentration in learning can be overcome by arranging the layout of the space to be more private. A clear domain separation will ensure proper control of privacy in the private space. An operational definition of privacy, namely avoidance of unwanted interactions with others, involves information flowing from person to person. Unwanted interactions can be controlled by rules (attitude, avoidance, hierarchy, etc.), through the meaning of psychology (withdrawal, daydreaming, intoxication, lack of appetite, etc.), through behavioral cues, by structuring activities in time (being a particular individual or group certain not met), through spatial separation, and through physical equipment (walls, fields, doors, curtains, locks—architectural mechanisms that selectively control or filter information) (Rapoport 1977).

   In addition to setting the space as a private domain, the study room also needed adequate facilities. Referring to the theoretical basis, online learning spaces can be categorized as independent learning spaces. The minimum area ratio for independent study is 4 m^2/student, and facilities in the room

DOI 10.1201/9781003193241-10

must include: furniture, information equipment, and storage furniture (Badan Standar Nasional Pendidikan 2011)

2 METHODS

The research method was conducted using qualitative methods in the form of analyzing question-naire and quantitative data with descriptive analysis from literature studies. Questionnaire data was synchronized with literature studies obtained from books, research journals, and the internet. The data was then be processed (then processed) and analyzed. The conclusions obtained from these results were the basis for creating models of online learning spaces

The data collection includes primary and secondary data. The primary data collection was carried out through a questionnaire and interview with the research subjects. Subjects were design student that already have experience with online learning activities from the previous semester. The primary data was supplemented by secondary data from print and electronic media.

3 ANALYSIS

3.1 *Questionnaire data*

Design Major	Total
Interior	55
Textile and Craft	4
Visual Communication	13
Architecture	14
Product	14
Total	100

Figure 1. Respondent major.

Being in Semester	Total
1–2	17
3–4	22
5–6	25
7–8	36
Total	100

Figure 2. Questionnaire. Source: Personal Source

Details of the questionnaire's responses can be seen in Figure 1, with a total number of 100 respondents with different design majors, specifically: interior design, textile and craft, visual communication, architecture, and products. Design student respondents were currently in various semesters ranging from semesters 1–8 (Figure 2).

3.2 *Identification of problems*

The results of the questionnaire found that when students do online learning activities at home, the majority of them do so in their bedrooms (Figure 3). Therefore, the appropriate planning of student

Online Learning Place at Home	Total
Separate study room	3
Bedroom	75
Guest room	1
Living room	19
Terrace	2
Total	100

Figure 3.   Online learning place at home. Source: Personal Source

The Biggest Obstacle When Doing Online Learning	Total
Lack of concentration	48
Unavailability of adequate facility	21
Lack of privacy	15
External interference	6
Communication limitation	10
Total	100

Figure 4.   Online earning constraints. Source: Personal Source

private rooms, specifically bedrooms, as a means of online learning spaces needs to be done to support the requirements for appropriate learning activities.

From the data obtained it can be concluded (Figure 4) that the biggest obstacles felt by students when learning online are: lack of concentration, lack of facilities, and lack of privacy when learning online.

3.3   *Determination of technical needs*

The student bedroom, originally a room for rest, has become an online study room as well. Therefore, we must calculate the dimensions and facilities that can fulfill both of these space functions properly and appropriately in one room.

Standard dimensions of the space occupied by one person as a bedroom are seen in Figure 5. Figure 6 shows the standard dimension of a space occupied by one person as a study room.

Minimal Dimension	Capacity	Furniture
3.15 x 2.25=7.09 m^2	1 person	1 set of study tables and chair, 1 single bed, and 1 wardrobe

Figure 5.   Bedroom imension tandar. Source: Ernst & Peter Neufert 2000

Minimal Dimension	Capacity	Furniture
2.38 x 1.52= 3.61 m^2	1 person	1 set of study table+chair, 1 piece of storage furniture

Figure 6.   Study room imension tandar. Source: Julius Panero 2003

To get more detailed dimensions, Figure 7 calculates in more detail what facilities are needed based on space and activity.

No	Space	Activity	Facility	Measurement (PxL) cm	Circulation	Total m²
1	Bedroom	Sleeping, Resting, Changing clothes, Getting ready	1 Single bed, 1 Wardrobe, 1 Storage furniture	100 x 200 100 x 60 60 x 60	30%	5.1
2	Study Room	Online learning , Doing assignment, Reading books	1 Table for computer/laptop , 1 Table for assignments, 1 Chair, 1 Storage furniture	110x50 120x70 50x50 120x45	30%	3.3
	Total					8.4

Figure 7.   Bedroom and study room imension. Source: Personal Source

Although the bedroom and study room have different needs for facilities and activities, with the right layout it all can be arranged in one room. Students prefer to do the online learning process in their bedrooms because the bedroom is the most private room in the residence so that being in there can reduce distractions from external factors. Thus, good acquiescence with the student's private bedroom is very important to support the two different room functions.

The minimum dimensions for a bedroom are 5.1 m², while for a study room it is 3.3 m². Therefore, from the table above (Figure 7) we can conclude that the ideal room for resting and online learning has a minimum area of 8.4 m², with the main facilities needed being one single bed, one wardrobe, one desk for working on college assignments, one laptop table for online lectures, study chairs, and two pieces of furniture for storage.

The spaces must also arrange to meet the different activities that must be facilitated inside it. For the bedroom, the activities are sleep, rest, changing of clothes, and getting ready. As for the learning space, the activities therein are online learning, doing assignments, and reading books. For these activity (activities), human space must be available in the form of a comfortable circulation space, and then a circulation space of at least 30% of the estimated space is needed.

In addition, there are also other factors that are needed and desired by students to support online learning such as facilities and tools that can accommodate learning activities, e.g., laptops, lamps, stationery, and bookshelves. Placement of sockets and a stable internet network are also things to consider. The comfort factor in the study room must also be considered because students will conduct online learning on average 2–4 hours each day. From the Figure 9 diagram below, it can be concluded that the things that must be considered to construct student comfort when doing online learning are room acoustics, space atmosphere, stable network, lighting, and pleasant air circulation.

3.4   Design concept

To ensure the privacy of each space in the bedroom, a clear separation of sleep or rest zones and study zones must be carried out. It is also useful for increasing student concentration while studying. Furniture layout is arranged so that when conducting lectures online these zones will not intersect one another. Adjusting the visibility of the laptop camera with the surrounding room, as well as setting a domain or apparent room divider between the bedroom zone and the study room zone must also be applied to the design of the online study room.

Layout of the facility settings are adjusted to each domain so that the effectiveness of the activity flow in each space is created. The size of the furniture is also adjusted to the effectiveness and comfort for the capacity of one student. The window placement is beside the study room to maximize the light and natural air to create pleasant space for study.

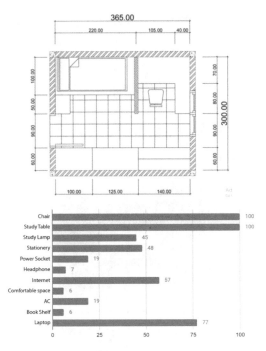

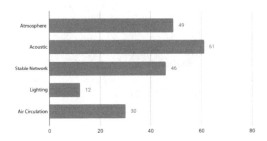

Figure 8.   Other facilities. Source: Personal Source

Figure 9.   Comfort factor during online learning. Source: Personal Source

The colors used in the study room were bright colors that are soft. Bright colors are believed to increase concentration in the learning process such (as) egg yolk, sky blue, or salmon(,) (and) green (Trihanondo et al. 2017). In addition, bright colors can make the room feel more spacious. Bright colors can be combined with neutral colors so that the stimulus presented is not too excessive. However, for a study room that is located in the bedroom, students are advised to use bright colors that remain soft so that the main function as a resting room is not interrupted.

4   CONCLUSIONS

The shift from face-to-face lecture activities to online lecture activities resulted in several problems for students. The main problems arising from this shift are: lack of concentration, unavailability of adequate facilities, and lack of privacy in the online learning process. From research it is known that the place where the majority of students undertake online learning is in their private bedrooms. Therefore, planning a private bedroom as an adequate online learning space to support the learning process of students needs to be prepared.

Figure 10. Bedroom layout. Source: Personal Source

Figure 11. Perspective testing domain. Source: Personal Source

Figure 12. Perspective study domain. Source: Personal Source

Figure 13. Perspective 1. Source: Personal Source

The minimum dimensions for a bedroom are 5.1 m², while for a study room they are 3.3 m². Then we can conclude that the ideal room for a place to rest and do online learning must be at least 8.4 m² in size. The main facilities that must be included are: one single bed, one wardrobe, one desk for working on college assignments, one laptop table for online lectures, study chairs, and two pieces of furniture for storage. To ensure the privacy of each room, a clear separation of sleep or rest zones and study zones must be carried out. In addition, the atmosphere and comfort of online study rooms also needs to be considered because students will conduct online learning

Figure 14.   Perspective 2. Source: Personal Source

Rated Factors	Excellent	Very good	Good	Poor	Very poor
Design to improve concentration	6	4	0	0	0
Adequate facilities	8	2	0	0	0
Design to improve privacy	3	7	0	0	0
Total	17	13	0	0	0

Figure 15.   Student opinion. Source: Personal Source

on average 2–4 hours each day. Another questionnaire was also conducted to review the student bedroom design for 10% of the previous respondents, as seen in Figure 15.

This research is preliminary research for online study space planning. For more accurate results it is necessary to study this topic in more detail and depth.

ACKNOWLEDGMENTS

This paper was (a) research search conducted by the first author, and also became joint research with a student at Telkom University for her practical work and the third author. This research wouldn't have occurred without the data provided from all respondents from different design majors.

REFERENCES

Badan Standar Nasional Pendidikan. 2011. Rancangan Standar Saran dan Prasarana Pendidikan Tinggi Program Pascasarjana dan Profesi, Pemerintah Indonesia.
Ching, Francis D.K. 1994. Terjemahan oleh Paulus H. Adjie. Arsitektur, Bentuk Ruang dan Susunannya. Jakarta: Erlangga
Donny Trihanondo SDs., MDs, Tri Haryotedjo SDs., MDs., Iqbal Prabawa Wiguna SSn.,MSn. 2017, Pisikologi Ruangan pada Program Studi Intermedia dalam Mendukung Atmosfer Akademik, 490
Neufert, Ernst. 1996. Terjemahan oleh Dr. Ing Sunarto Tjahjadi, jilid 1, Data Arsitek. Jakarta: Erlangga
Panero, Julius and Martin Zelnik. 2003. Dimensi Manusia & Ruang Interior. Jakarta: Erlangga.
Rapoport, Amos. 1977. Human Aspects of Urban Form: Towards A Man-Environmental Approach to Urban Form And Design, New York: Pergamon Press.
https://jabar.suara.com/read/2020/06/03/090839/sekolah-di-jawa-barat-masih-tutup-sampai-januari-2021-belajar-di-rumah accessed May 2020
https://www.kompas.com/tren/read/2020/07/03/155830065/menteri-nadiem-wacanakan-belajar-jarak-jauh-permanen-setelah-pandemi-covid accessed May 2020

Dynamics of Industrial Revolution 4.0: Digital Technology Transformation and Cultural Evolution –
Wulandari et al (eds)
© 2021 The Author(s), ISBN 978-1-032-04451-4

Digital data storage to reduce workplace density.
Case study: Indonesian bureau of logistic, Jakarta

W. Liritantri, A.D. Handoyo & G.I. Mahodim
Telkom University, Bandung, Indonesia

ABSTRACT: In line with business development of an office, the need to hire additional employees increases. However, some office spaces cannot accommodate an increase in staff which therefore results in an increase in workplace density. Digital data storage in and off of premises can be used to change the physical storage of a business. The research method used is the qualitative method. Observation, data collections gained through field notes, and calculation of the physical data storage were carried out to obtain data. The aim of this research is to provide the data on the space saving calculation of workplace when using digital data storage by replacing the physical data storage. The result showed that the use of digital data storage can reduce high workplace density but no significant space was saved when using digital data storage off the premises versus on the premises.

Keywords: workplace density, digital data storage, space saving, reduced density

1 INTRODUCTION

Density is an object measure that is subdivided into a measure of social density and a measure of spatial density (Hayduk 1983). In the office, density means the calculation of space between the number of employees in the working area. Workplace density is also determined in the number of square meters needed by employees and the surrounding facilities to support the work. High workplace density faced by offices, which happens when the number of employees is greater than the expansion of the office area, leads to a reduction in workspace area per person.

Office density is divided into three points (Simmons 2018): high density that is around $7–14 \text{ m}^2$ per employee; average density is around $14–23 \text{ m}^2$ per employee; and spacious is $23–46 \text{ m}^2$ per employee. The Indonesian Bureau of Logistics states that in order to have an average density, 500 employees must have an approximate area of $11,500 \text{ m}^2$, and to have a spacious work place, those same 500 employees must have an area of approximately $23,000 \text{ m}^2$. Therefore, the Indonesian Bureau of Logistics, with its 17 floors and building area of $16,800 \text{ m}^3$, has an average density.

Along with the growing development of the Indonesian Bureau of Logistics, the head office itself needs more space to accommodate its employees as it currently has inadequate working spaces, unergonomic spaces, lack of circulation, and lack of document storage. From the surveys conducted, paper documents are one of the main problems that the office is facing. Almost every room has its working area filled with documents that cannot be stored in the filing cabinets due to lack of space. Figures 1 and 2 show the office's inadequate working space.

In this digital era when digital products are a necessity, digital data storage for archiving and document storage is also essential. In addition, digital data storage makes an office more environmentally friendly. Electronic documents are more efficient than paper documents which require physical, and often bulky, filing cabinets in which to store them (Rotenstreich).

Saving documents in a digital archive such as a cloud server or an on-premises server is considered more efficient and effective as the files can be accessed in anywhere, at any time. They're also faster to access than paper documents (Raymond & Okoro 2013)

Digital data storage in an office is mostly divided into two methods: (1) cloud storage and (2) on-premises server (Seal 2019). If the office considers using a cloud server, the office doesn't even

DOI 10.1201/9781003193241-11

Figure 1. Bulog office working area. Source : Personal Documentation

Figure 2. The density in the working space. Source : Personal Documentation

have to provide a place for data storage. For on-premise servers, the general size for the server room is a minimum of 2 m in length and 2 m in width (Darmansyah 2020). The common element that all on-premises server rooms need are racks for the hardware. The most common size for these racks is only 213 cm in height, 68 cm in width and 78 cm in depth. Knowing the size of the storage for an on-premises or even a cloud server that doesn't need space, one can imagine the wasted space that could be reallocated after the bulky filing cabinets are removed.

A good office layout aims to have its office administration as close as possible (Eyre 1989). To make an efficient and ideal working layout, the following things have to be considered: workflow, supervision, floor space, working space, hallways, proximity of workers ad-equipment, noisy machines, natural lights, privacy, and appearance. Modern office space optimization is heading toward a more connected, collaborative, and flexible work environment, which helps increase employee efficiency and productivity (Accruent 2018). By using digital storage in the office, it is expected that we will discover how much space can be saved if using digital storage on and off the premises.

2 RESEARCH METHODS

The research method used for this research is the qualitative approach. Data collections were also conducted in observation and field surveys in the main research location, which is the Indonesian Bureau of Logistics in Jakarta. The calculations considered are the circulation, office density, human mobilization, document storage, and other factors related to documents and filing.

The collection method that was used includes primary and secondary data. The primary data were obtained through field surveys and observations, while the secondary data was obtained from literature, books, and journals that give data researching information about digital data storage. Data collection through observation is carried out to obtain primary data while the secondary data is gained through the written sources. From the field survey, the data used is only data from the 6th, 9th, and 10th, floors because the activities on these floors are main focus of the office, its where the administration works, and they're the floors the the highest density.

3 RESULT AND DISCUSSION

3.1 *Physical data storage and digital data storage*

Paper documents, which are not considered green and efficient nowadays, are still common in the Indonesian Bureau of Logistics office. Document storage or archive storage can be found in every floor of the office. Figure 3 is a picture of the over capacity and how documents are stored.

Figure 3.   The document storage in the Indonesian Bureau of Logistics. Source: personal documentation

When using cloud data, physical data is completely unnecessary. If indeed the physical documents are still needed, they will only be kept for one year. Data that is older than one year will only be available in electronic form. Thus, overcapacity archive storage can be avoided. Figure 4 shows an example of on-premises data storage.

The benefit of using digital data storage is that workers have unlimited access to files, and files can be accessed at any time, and from anywhere. In addition, the minimum space required for using on-premises data storage is around 2 m².

3.2 *Space saving using digital data storage*

As mentioned from the field survey, the data used is only data from the 6th, 9th, and 10th floors. The required spaces in the office are shown in Table 1.

Table 1 shows that the archive room is mostly available on every floor. If the archive room was taken away and changed into cloud data, then the archive room and circulation space could be converted into employee work space. The calculations are shown in Table 2.

Figure 4. Server room, on-premises data storage. Source: pinterest

Table 1. Indonesian Bureau of Logistics office space for working area only and document/archive storage.

Floor	Working area (m²)	Circulation (m²)	Archives Room and Circulation (m²)	Total Area (m²)
6	692.32	175,696	34.67	902.686
9	721.76	161.678	129.883	1013.321
10	707.63	118.6	52.962	879.192

Table 2. Space saved calculation.

Floor	Space Saved (m²)
6	34.67
9	129.883
10	52.962
Total	217.515

Table 3. The working space with storage room added as a working space.

Floor	Working area (m²)	Archive room (m²)	Total (m²)
6	692.32	34.67	726.99
9	721.76	129.883	851.643
10	707.63	52.962	760.592

3.3 Space density calculation after using digital data storage

The office is utilizing 15 out of the building's 17 floors and each floor has around 33 persons or workers occupying it. The area needed for average density of 33 workers is around 735.79 m² on every floor. But for the spacious area, they would need 1103.68 m² for every floor. If the 6th, 9th, and 10th floors can save space around 217.515 m², then the space saved from the other floors would be around 1087.575 m².

Tables 3 and 4 show that by changing the archive room into a working space it could upgrade the density from dense to average. From the result it can add around 0.2–0.5% area of space.

Table 4. The working space ratio after using digital storage in space density.

Space Density	Space needed Per person	Space needed for 33 persons	Existing working area 6th, 9th, 10th floors	Working area after using digital storage calculation
High Density ratio	7–14m^2	231–462 m^2		
Average ratio	14–23 m^2	462–735.79 m^2	692.32 m^2 6th floor 721.76 m^2 9th floor 707.63 m^2 10th floor	726.99 m^2 6th floor
Spacious ratio	23–46 m^2	759–1103,68 m^2		851.643 m^2 9th floor 760.592 m^2 10th floor

4 CONCLUSION

The purpose of using digital data storage instead of physical data storage is that it would increase the work space in the Indonesian Bureau of Logistics' head office. In fact, based on the calculation this step will save around 217 m^2 on the 6th, 9th, 10th floors in total. Having on-premises data storage will save approximately 213 m^2, adding around 0.1–0.5 % of workable office space. As an alternative, using both physical and digital data storage in the office still saves space but it is not optimal. The result of using digital data storage off-premises is an option for offices that need more space for its employees. As a result, having more space for the office means that space density will decrease. In this case, the average density ratio turns into spacious density.

ACKNOWLEDGMENTS

This paper was a research continuation from the Telkom University Student Final Project: The Redesign of Indonesian Bureau of Logistics Head Office, which was made as a graduate require-ment from The Telkom University. This research wouldn't have achieved its results without the data provided by the Indonesian Bureau of Logistics Head Office.

REFERENCES

Bulog. 2018. *Sekilas Perum BULOG*. Accessed June 15, 2020, <http://www.bulog.co.id>
Darmansyah, Y. 2020. *Rangkuman Standarisasi Ruang IT Server*. Accessed 15 June 2020, <http://academia.edu>.
Eyre, E. C. 1989. *Office Administration*. London: Macmillan Education LTD.
Hayduk, L. A. 1983. Personal Space: Where We Now Stand. *Psychological Bulletin*, 293–335.
Rotenstreich, S. n.d. *The Difference Between Electronic and Paper Documents*. Accessed June 20, 2020, <www.seas.gwu.edu>
Simmons, K. S. 2018. *How Much Office Space Do I Need (Calculator & Per Person Standards)*. Accessed 2020, <https://aquilacommercial.com/learning-center/how-much-office-space-need-calculator-per-person>
U. Raymond, Okoro. 2013. Office of the Future-Digitizing Record Keeping. *International Journal of Computing Academic Research*. 2(2):75–87.

Redesign of an interior HVAC system in order to limit the spread of the COVID-19 virus in co-working spaces

A.D. Handoyo
Telkom University, Bandung, Indonesia

E. Wicaksono
Universitas Pelita Harapan, Tangerang, Indonesia

ABSTRACT: The existence of the COVID-19 pandemic has affected the world of design. The current habit and design process are pushed to be able to adapt new habits in the post-pandemic era. Public areas such as shared workspace have become one of the prioritized places for implementing health protocols as they work collectively. This study aims to identify the most optimal solution so that the existing building design can meet the health protocol standards in the new era of normality. Through precedent study, this research analyzes the ventilation system of co-working space in Bandung. The observation focused on public areas that have the longest duration of use. It was found based on the study that the design of open workspaces is relatively safe with cross ventilation to dilute the air. However, enclosed space design requires additional attributes such as UVC lamps to kill germs to clean the air.

Keywords: UVC, COVID, co-working space, air conditioning, interior design

1   BACKGROUND

The condition of the SARS-CoV-2 pandemic (hereafter referred to as COVID virus) demands the manager of buildings to adapt the old design to new normal requirements through a process of a redesign (Yatmo 2020; Hatmoko 2020; Tabinas 2020). In general, people spend most of their time at home (Gilrandy et.al. 2020) or the office/co-working space (Turner 1971; Heidegger 1971; Pramadesty 2018). Strong airflow from an air conditioner may spread a droplet that carries the virus (Lu et al. 2020). The COVID virus also tends to be stable and has longer life outside of its host body in a low temperature and humid environment such as in a space with an air conditioner (Hillside 2020). The risk of spreading a disease will expand if there is less air exchange inside the room, just like SARS cases at Hotel Metropole Hongkong in 2003 and the emergence of new contagion clusters in offices.

For the sake of energy efficiency, some building managers only recycle air that has been cooled down in the room. If not designated adequately, the air conditioning system may become a primary incubator as well as a source of disease.

This case is different with an air conditioning system in an airplane or hospital that is specifically designed with HEPA (High-Efficiency Particulate Air) system that can block particles with a diameter of 0.3 microns or higher, with 99% or even higher efficiency (Schoen 2014). However, this HEPA filter has a limitation, which is its expensive price. An alternative system for artificial airing is required and proposed to prevent the spread of the virus at an affordable price.

This research aims to analyze the airing system inside an existing design in adapting new habitual activities, by taking a study to the design of co-working space in the city of Bandung. Co-working space is chosen not only because this place serves as an office, but also as a home office concept that is supported by various facilities.

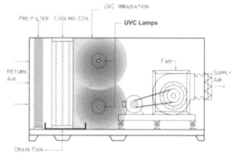

Conventional AHU System

Schematic Drawing UVC for AHU Application

Figure 1. The placement of UV ray inside AHU system.

Table 1. Comparison between the adaptation of new habit in controlling the risk.

Effort	Avoid	Shift	Improve
Elimination (remove the virus) Engineering controls	1. Room with high density (crowded space) 2. Rooms with closes air conditioning system without new airflow. 3. Use of sharing application.	1. Physical distancing. 2. Pressure control inside a room. 3. Vertical separation between clean and dirty. 4. Optimizing natural ventilation to dilute the air. 5. Routine cleaning.	1. Technology to kill virus: UV, plasma, ozone. 2. Technology adaptation to filter virus: HEPA.

Morawska et al. (2020) argues that health protocols in adapting new habits can be divided into four categories according to their level of effectivity: virus elimination as a source of disease, engineering control, administrative control, and personal protection. This study focuses on the first and second level because is more relevant to the design and effectivity in limiting the spread of the virus. Many researchers suggest that this protocol be implemented in the home (Heath 2020; Gilrandy et al. 2020) and office (Serres 2020; Libanori 2020). Both categories can be divided further into three groups in its application, some need to be avoided, shifted, and improved from existing condition (TUMI 2020).

ASHRAE (American Society of Heating, Refrigerating and Air-Conditioning Engineers) recommends the counter measure of COVID spread by using HVAC (Schoen 2014). First, to implement air dilution with optimizing natural airing with opening doors and windows, and second, to control the direction of air from the supply point back to the return point, regulate the air inside the room, design personal ventilation openings, personal airing inside the room, air filtering, and UVGI (). Considering the dangers of direct UVGI exposure to humans, UVGI is installed as an additional filter from the centralized air conditioning which is placed on the AHU system.

This proposition uses ultraviolet (UV) ray that is proven to deactivate the virus. A correct application is needed so this UV ray can be effective in dealing with COVID-19 pandemic inside a building system (Hibaru 2020).

2 METHOD

This research is conducted through observation and surveys simultaneously with descriptive analytics about HVAC system in Bandung Digital Valley (BDV). BDV was designed as a coworking space especially for startups in the technology industry. In the initial stage, observations are made to analyze the ventilation system in the room that has the most users and the longest duration of use. The analysis is focused on the direction of air movement by comparing where the position of the air supply and the return point. Therefore, the movement of air in the room can be designed in such a way that it doesn't mix clean air with dirty air. This research is exploring solutions on how existing conditions can be improved so that they can minimize the spread of COVID by engineering the spatial planning, ventilation system, and minimizing user capacity. This research compares the before and after condition from the redesign proposal in the shared workspace and communal space.

3 RESULT AND DISCUSSION

Based on the observation, it was found that shared working space has the most frequent use and the longest duration of use. Almost all rooms in BDV are enclosed spaces using air conditioning as a ventilation system. Shared workspace and communal space are not exceptions. Coworking space in BDV is integrated inside a single building utilizing centralized air conditioning as the primary airing system and is supported by a split system in several parts. Air conditioning works by sucking air from the room then mixes with clean air from outside. The mixture from Cooling Tower enters through the Air Handling Unit (AHU), is filtered, and then distributed through air evenly from each AHU to every room. The situation of working space in BDV is shown in Figure 2.

Figure 2.   Existing environment inside a coworking area in BDV.

The working desk is arranged in a group with a capacity of six people. Two people in the middle are facing each other and there are two others on each side, as shown in Figure 3. In the existing design, clean air is coming out of the supply outlet on the ceiling (blue color). Clean air mixes with the air in the room and is used (orange color) to become dirty air (light green color). Then, the dirty air is sucked in by a return inlet on the ceiling. Air movement has the potential to spread droplets that have already fallen and may contain the virus to mix with clean air on the ceiling. Also, with this close proximity of layout (less than 1 meter), each person has a greater exposure from infected individual to droplets (see dark green color) (Nicas & Jones 2009; Li 2011).

Figure 4 illustrates two situations that can be implemented to adapt new habits in BDV. The first and the best scenario is to open the window to dilute the inside air with the outside (see light blue color) (Sun et al. 2011). The amount of air can be controlled so that the flow of cross ventilation that enters the room is exactly what the occupants need to feel comfortable.

The second scenario, if the first scenario is not possible because of using the fixed window and air conditioner, an AHU system must be equipped with UVGI irradiation as a filter to clean air contaminated by the COVID virus (Schoen 2014). This system must also be modified in order

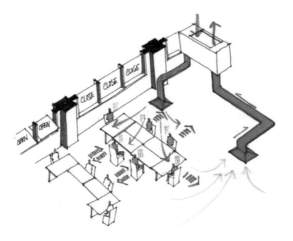

Figure 3.   An illustration of existing layout of working space and HVAC system in BDV.

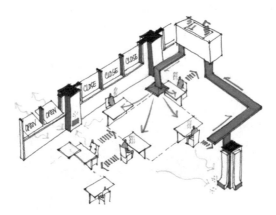

Figure 4.   An illustrated simulation of adapting the new habit in BDV.

to optimize fresh air. Learning from the air conditioning system in the hospital, the supply outlet remains to be placed on the ceiling while the return inlet must be modified as close as possible to the floor. By following the law of gravity, zoning of air in space is divided into two parts, namely clean air at the top, and dirty air (containing droplets/microdroplets) is at the bottom. The dirty air collected below is not expected to disperse and can be sucked in directly at the return point (Fennelly et al. 2004; Wainwright et al. 2009). Of course, changes in the position of the inlet return must adjust the conditions and placement of walls, columns, and other interior elements.

Regarding the arrangement of the furniture layout, the suggestions are: the working area is to be placed radially below the suppy outlet ot the clean air (dark blue color) to create a positive pressure room that can be used by the occupants. The radial arrangement of the working table results in maintaining a safe distance between users, as mentioned by Nicas and Jones (2009) and Li (2011). Using a zigzag sitting pattern can minimize the air flow that may contain the virus to the person behind. This experiment and solution will be more successful if it is implemented together with new normal habits and other health protocols such as wearing masks, washing hands frequently, and/or using face shield.

4 CONCLUSION

Based on this study, it is found that utilization of an air conditioning system in a close room increases the risk of spreading the virus. First, the impact can be reduced by putting in more clean air to dilute the air in the interior. This effort can be done by optimizing natural ventilation through window openings and artificial airing system if it is not possible to open the window. On the other hand, introducing more fresh air will have an impact on the performance of a heavier AC engine. Second, if the building is using a central air conditioner, the UVG system can be integrated into the AHU. In addition, the placement of lamps in AHU ensures the UV rays do not disturb the occupants. In the interior, the supply and return point are designed in such way so the air can be circulated, UV-ed, filtered, as quick as possible. The return inlets are positioned as low as the floor level to clean up the fallen droplet. Therefore, the rooms are designed to separate the clean air and dirty (or may contaminated) air. Third, redesigning the layout of workspace. Creating zig-zag seating arrangement not only reduces rooms capacity but also increases a safe distance between occupants (more than 1–3 meters). This study recommends that other studies be conducted related to how to create an air conditioning system that still optimizes fresh air but has high energy efficiency.

REFERENCES

Fennelly, K.P., J.W. Martyny, K.E. Fulton, I.M. Orme, D.M. Cave, and L.B. Heifets. 2004. *Coughgenerated aerosols of Mycobacterium Tuberculosis: A new method to study infectiousness.* American Journal of Respiratory and Critical Care Medicine 169:604–609.

Gilrandy S. and Apriliyanthi, S. Atidesa. A. 2020. *Dream House that Respond to Pandemic Situation. Webinar.* Indonesia, May 16, 2020

Hatmoko, A. 2020. *Isu Utama Pasca Covid. Berubahkah Tatanan Arsitektur Pasca Covid-19?* Webinar. IAI Sumatera Barat.

Heath, O. Biophillic Design. *How to create interior spaces that enhance our physical and mental wellbeing.* Webinar. Singapore, May 18, 2020

Heidegger, M. 1971. *Poetry, Language, Thought. Building, Dwelling, Thinking.* New York: Harper & Row

Ibold, S., Medimorec, N., Wagner A. Peruzzo, J. 2020. *The Covid 19 Outbreak and Implications to Sustainable Urban Mobility. TUMI Transformative Urban Mobility Initiative.* Retrieved 16:23, July 23, 2020 from https://www.transformative-mobility.org/news/the-covid-19-outbreak-and-implications-to-public-transport-some-observations

Infrastructure Guidance for COVID-19/Alternate Care Sites. June 9, 2020. *The HILLSIDE.* Retrieved 07:51, August 1, 2020 from https://thehillside.info/index.php?title=Infrastructure_Guidance_for_COVID-19/Alternate_Care_Sites&oldid=2128.

Li, Y. 2011. *The secret behind the mask.* (Editorial.) *Indoor Air* 21(2):89–91.

Libanori, M. 2020. *The Power of Colors. Smarter Impact*: Webinar Series. Webinar. Singapore, May 7, 2020

Lu, J., Gu, J., Li, K., Xu, C., Su, W., Lai, Z....Yang, Z. 2020. *COVID-19 Outbreak Associated with Air Conditioning in Restaurant, Guangzhou, China, 2020.* Emerging Infectious Diseases, 26(7):1628–1631. https://dx.doi.org/10.3201/eid2607.200764.

Memarzadeh, Farhad. 2011. *Literature review of the effect of temperature and humidity on viruses.* ASHRAE Transactions 117(2).

Morawska, J.W. Tang, et al. 2020. *How can airborne transmission of COVID-19 indoors be minimised?, Environment International (2020),* doi: https://doi.org/10.1016/j.envint.2020.105832.

Nicas, M. and R.M. Jones. 2009. *Relative contributions of four exposure pathways to influenza infection risk. Risk Analysis* 29:1292–303.

Pramedesty, R., et al. 2018. *Co-Working Space Sebagai Solusi Kebutuhan Ruang Kerja Berdasarkan Karakteristik Startup Kreatif.* Idealog: Ide dan Dialog Desain Indonesia, [S.l.], 3(1):50–60.

Schoen, L. 2014. *ASHRAE Position Document on Airborne Infectious Diseases.* Atlanta: ASHRAE

Hibaru. *UV LAMP & UVC- Membunuh Bakteri, Virus, Jamur, Lumut DLL (2020, June 9). PT Hibaru.* Retrieved 21:51, August 1, 2020 from http://www.hibaru-online.com/uv-lamp-uvc-membunuh-bakteri-virus-jamur-lumut-dll

Serres, A. 2020. *Human Centric Design.* Smarter Impact: Webinar Series. Webinar. Singapore, May 5, 2020

Sun Y., Z. Wang, Y. Zhang, and J. Sundell. 2011. *In China, students in crowded dormitories with a low ventilation rate have more common colds: Evidence for airborne transmission.* PLOS ONE 6(11):e27140.

Tabinas, J. 2020. *The Response of Architecture to Pandemic: How COVID Impact the Design?* The Architecture of/in/on/from the new normal. Webinar. Malaysia, May 9, 2020

Turner, J. 1971. *Housing by People: Towards the autonomy in Building Environments.* New York: Pantheon Books

Wainwright, C.E., M.W. Frances, P. O'Rourke, S. Anuj, T.J. Kidd, M.D. Nissen, T.P. Sloots, C. Coulter, Z. Ristovski, M. Hargreaves, B.R. Rose, C. Harbour, S.C, Bell, and K.P. Fennelly. 2009. *Cough-generated aerosols of Pseudomonas aeruginosa and other Gram-negative bacteria from patients with cystic fibrosis.* Thorax 64:926–31.

Yatmo, Y. 2020. *Evidence Based Design:Arsitektur Setelah Covid-19. Berubahkah Tatanan Arsitektur Pasca Covid-19?* Webinar. IAI Sumatera Barat, April 29, 2020.

Dynamics of Industrial Revolution 4.0: Digital Technology Transformation and Cultural Evolution –
Wulandari et al (eds)
© 2021 The Author(s), ISBN 978-1-032-04451-4

Finding lighting balance within the ecosystem of Taman Teras Cikapundung

R.H.W. Abdulhadi & M.T.M. Raja
Telkom University, Bandung, Jawa Barat, Indonesia

M. Akkaya
Kadir Has University, Istanbul, Turkey

ABSTRACT: Taman Teras Cikapundung park restoration has succeeded in creating an open space for public use. This park has various functions, as a gathering place, improving aspects of economics and as nature conservation. From an economic point of view, this park is considered to be able to create new values for the community, however from the preservation point of view, deeper observation is needed, especially in terms of lighting design. The research was conducted with comparative observations through field studies and literature, by making comparisons between existing conditions and how lighting should emphasize nature conservation. From this study it was found that the lighting in this park still prioritizes recreational and economic functions without paying attention to conservation. This can be seen from the selection of lighting, through the direction of the light, spectral distribution, and shielding that is not in accordance with the provisions of nature conservation.

Keywords: lighting pollution, lighting Taman Teras Cikapundung, nature conservation, lighting and nature conservation,

1   INTRODUCTION

The restoration of the Teras Cikapundung Park is an effort initiated by Balai Besar Wilayah Sungai Citarum with the Bandung's regional government to organize, restore its infrastructure in the form of open spaces with several functions such as educational facilities, recreational facilities, commercial space, and as a means of nature conservation (Direktoran Jenderal Penataan Ruang Departemen Pekerjaan Umum 2008). The park is open to the public and can be accessed late into the night. The atmosphere at night is added with the lighting design that is presented. One lighting design which catches the attention is the dancing fountain equipped with colored lighting which adds value to recreational functions. Other existing lighting features serve as a safety and security factor for visitors. As a park that has a fairly complex function, the balance between education, recreation, commerce, and conservation functions is important.

Based on location, this park is located on the banks of the Cikapundung River and very close to the river area and the green area of Babakan Siliwangi, in which there are many flora and fauna ecosystems along the river banks which should also be part of conservation. One way that this has been done in the context of nature conservation is preservation of urban forests, maintaining the cleanliness of the forests and river streams from waste, and fish breeding in existing ponds. In terms of function, this has been able to provide benefits to the community, but for the preservation of nature and ecosystems that live in urban forests and river streams and riparian area, there are other problems that need to be addressed.

The problems that arise in this park are caused by activities that function until the night, where lighting is a must for the safety and comfort of visitors. On the other hand, lighting is a problem for the riverbank ecosystem for both floral and fauna (Bennie et al. 2016). Riverbank ecosystems are important to humans; the loss of ecosystems in riverbank areas will cause the loss of aesthetic, economic, recreational, and other characteristics that have human value (National Research Council 2002). Another disadvantage for the ecosystem is changes in the food chain that occur in riverbank areas, so that the balance of the ecosystem is disturbed (Manfrin et al. 2017). With the destruction of the food chain, it will directly affect humans. In fact, research from several places in the river area shows that the breakdown of the food chain will cause the growth of algae, and in worst conditions the river oxygen levels decrease and damage fish habitats, causing an unpleasant odor (Longcore & Rich 2016). This, of course, will have an impact on humans by losing the economic and recreational aspect. In terms of area coverage, this park is not too large, so that artificial lighting that occurs at night will have a significant impact on the riverbank ecosystem (Longcore & Rich 2016).

The purpose of this study is to provide an evaluation and solution to the lighting design at Teras Cikapundung in relation to its function as a conservation area. Evaluation and solution are to be met in terms of armature selection, and color spectrum of the light used in relation to the balance of the garden's functions as nature conservation.

2 RESEARCH METHODOLGY

The research method used is comparative observation. Observations were made by paying attention to the type of luminaire, light color temperature in each luminaire, lighting control device, and its light distribution. The results from these observations are then compared with lighting standards for environmental conservation. This research method is used to provide an evaluation of lighting and the impact that occurs in this park in the field of conservation so that it is expected to provide improvements in the future.

Data collecting was carried out through direct observation at the park. List of luminaires with its specification such as types of luminaires, color temperature, light control system, and light distribution is then processed through table list as data set.

Through data set table, a lighting condition at the park can be seen. Furthermore, a comparison through accordance of luminaires, color temperature, lighting control device, and its lighting distribution as ecosystem friendly lighting can be compared. Comparison was using a standard from the Australian Government Department of Environment and Energy 2019. The National Light Pollution Guidelines for Wildlife has a broad and clear statement about how good lighting should be applied to preserve ecosystem.

Table 1. Data set luminaires.

No.	Types of Luminaires	Color temperature	Lighting control device	Lighting distribution
1	Pole luminaires for general illumination	5000 K	none	downward wide (symetric 45 degree)
2	Floor mounted uplight for trees	3600 K	None	upward-Wide (symmetric 45 degree)
3	Bollard at bridge	3600 K	Shielded with opaque glass	difused
4	Perimeter lighting with LED strip	Blue light	None	diffused
5	Orientation lighting	3600 K	Indirect light	downward
6	Flood lighting	3000 K	Flood light	upward and downward > 45 degree

3 RESULT AND DISCUSSION

Lighting mitigation which are used on different habitat should be considering five aspects. Aspects which considered to be important are the how much light for human to perceive its surrounding in terms of safety and consideration to nature, spectrum of lamp, intensity of light, direction of light, and duration (Longcore& Rich 2016). Based on the survey at the park, lighting at Teras Cikapundung has several functions. The main lighting is in the form of pole lighting which is used to provide general lighting and provide a safety factor in the garden. The type of lamp used are pole luminaires and provides lighting in a wide direction, with a light spread of more than 45° downward. This lamp functions as the lighting for the parking lot bordering the river area, lighting the sitting area, and the amphitheater. The type of lamp used is an LED with the color spectrum used is cold white or around 4000K.

The use of this pole lighting is considered to meet the standard of illumination at conservatory area in terms of need, light direction, light intensity of light, and duration, but in terms of spectrum which related to the types of lamp which is used is not correct, the use of LED light in cold color temperature ca. 4000 K contain much blue spectrum in it is considered not appropriate for conservation. The use of LED lighting could be altered with high pressure sodium lamp, or warm white LED lamp which has long wavelength (Pawson & Bader 2014.)

The second lighting is accentuation lighting. The type of luminaire which is used are floor mounted luminaires and provides lighting in a wide direction, with a light spread of more than 45° upward. This lamp functions as the lighting for accentuating trees. The type of lamp used is an LED with the color spectrum used is warm white or around 3600 K.

The light used is an LED type but with a lower color temperature, around 3600 K, thus not too harmful for the environment. The incorrect application comes from the type of luminaire which is used; there should be a proper shielding to minimize light spill from the luminaire which causes a lot of light to be wasted. Apart from having a harmful impact on pollution for nature, also in a certain direction of view it will cause glare for visitors (Australian Government Department of Environment and Energy 2019)

Figure 1.   General illumination at Teras Cikapundung in the form of pole lighting.

Figure 2.   Accent illumination at trees at Teras Cikapundung in the form of floor-mounted up-lighting.

Figure 3.   Perimeter illumination at the amphitheater and bridge at Teras Cikapundung in the form blue LED strip light, and bollard.

Figure 4.   Orientation illumination at stairs at Teras Cikapundung in form of recessed lighting.

Figure 5.   Flood lighting directed to river stream.

The third lighting used is a lighting parameter that functions to limit the pedestrian area to the river area, including those used under bridges. Perimeter lighting is uses two methods: by forming area boundaries through the use of LED strips and the use of light bulbs that are arranged to limit pedestrian areas and river areas.

The incompatibility of this perimeter illumination using LED strip lamps concerning environmental issues is the application which is not hidden or integrated to features at parks and the use of blue colored light. The use of blue as the color of choice has a very bad impact, especially on the perimeter and under the bridge area (Pawson & Bader, 2014). The use of bollard lamps in the perimeter area is still considered adequate and can be used because the wrapping material used around the lamp is opaque glass so that it can still be tolerated, and the color of the lamp used is warm white or around 3600 K.

The other lighting in this area that is felt to be quite good is the orientation light on several steps so that the distribution of light is specifically directed toward the stairs. The use of directional light minimizes light spill and helps with visitor orientation.

The use of special lighting for recreational such as dancing fountain is not considered to be harmful, since it is not always turned on unlike other lighting which is always turned on. Another lighting application that is considered to be harmful is the use of floodlighting directed at the river and trees in the nature area. The lamp that is used is high pressure sodium, which has yellow light spectrum, but the direct illumination is considered to be harmful for the ecosystem.

4 CONCLUSION

In this research it was found that the lighting design at Teras Cikapundung Park as a whole cannot be said to be appropriate for nature conservation. Lighting is only intended for the safety and comfort of visitors by prioritizing aspects of recreation and economic value, but in the long run these aspects can be disrupted by disruption of the ecosystem in this park. The need for humans to perceive and have activities should be balanced with the conservation of nature, especially at a park that has a close relation to nature and has a conservatory function. Inappropriate use of lighting distribution, spectrum, or choice of lamp, and lack of shielding will become harmful for the park's ecosystem.

The form of research by prioritizing the balance between ecosystems and humans is a form of research that is flared discussed in developed countries. The development of technology and applications in lighting is then questioned in relation to the environment. The strength of this research is that it can provide practical solutions for lighting at Teras Cikapundung Park, but it still has shortcomings due to the need for complete quantitative data in terms of lamp spectrum, and more in-depth lighting simulations, as well as relationships with other researchers, especially from the environmental field to provide more optimal result. Recommendations for further research can be in the form of solution to provide smart lighting system or lighting distribution control system which can be adjusted to the occupant of Taman Teras Cikapundung and its environment, thus creating a balance between recreation, finance, and the environment.

ACKNOWLEDGMENT

We would like to thank those who helped carry out this research. Our gratitude is addressed to Telkom University lecturers who helped develop and become a source of inspiration in this research. We also express our gratitude to the Bandung's City Government and Dinas Pekerjaan Umum who have worked hard to realize, develop, and manage the Taman Teras Cikapundung. We would also like to thank the community and parties who have managed to create a Cikapundung terrace garden; without good management this park would not have become our source of inspiration.

REFERENCES

Australian Government Department of Environment and Energy. 2019. National Light Pollution Guidelines for Wildlife.

Bennie, J., Davies, T.W., Cruse, D., and Gaston, J. 2016. Ecological effects of artificial light at night on wild plants. *Journal of Ecology* 104(3):611–620.

Direktoran Jenderal Penataan Ruang Departemen Pekerjaan Umum. 2008. *Pedoman Penyediaan Dan Pemanfaatan Ruang Terbuka Hijau (RTH) Di Kawasan Perkotaan Permen PU No. 5/PRT/M/2008.* Indonesia.

Longcore, T. and Rich, C. 2016. Artificial Night Lighting and Protected Lands: *Ecological Effects and Management Approach.*

Manfrin et al. 2017. Artificial Light at Night Affects Organism Flux Across Ecosystem Boundaries and Drives Community Structure In The Recipient Ecosystem.

National Research Council. 2002. Riparian Areas: Functions and Strategies for Management. Washington, D.C: The National Academies Press.

Pawson, S.M. and Bader, M.K. 2014. Led lighting increases the ecological impact of light pollution irrespective of color temperature. *Ecological Applications.*

Dynamics of Industrial Revolution 4.0: Digital Technology Transformation and Cultural Evolution –
Wulandari et al (eds)
© 2021 The Author(s), ISBN 978-1-032-04451-4

Effects of early adolescent characteristics in circulation design for a junior high school building

K.P. Amelia, I. Hanom, W. Lukito & S.N. Siregar
Telkom University, Bandung, Indonesia

ABSTRACT: Good architecture is when data fulfills the function of a building and provides psychological comfort to its users. The function can be fulfilled by design guidelines applicable dimension standards, in this case issue raised is circulation in the building. Unique characteristics of these early adolescent can be anticipated in designs based on these characteristics, one of which was the role of circulation. This research is a qualitative descriptive study with a comparison of three selected Junior High School. The point being compared is the design decision in designing circulations for the three Junior High Schools. The early adolescent's characteristics approach in circulating design being considered good to facilitate users of the building. The design process makes psychological factors an approach in hope of achieving a match between the user's subject. This is sn an indicator of success in a design that has been successfully accommodated according to the needs of its users.

Keywords: early adolescent, characteristic, circulation design, Junior High School

1 INTRODUCTION

School is a place where teenagers spend their daily time to getting a formal education or socializing with friends informally. Time spent by the teenager can be said all day because it spends time generally, 6 hours every day. Good architecture is architecture that can facilitate / accommodate user activities and main function of architecture itself (Salura 2001:3) From the range of intensity of activity and use of buildings, it can be concluded the importance of the role of an architecture in accommodating the activities in the school. Another factor that influences a design decision is to consider the user of the architecture. In addition to the spatial dimensions of standards, design decisions are needed in the study of design psychology from its users.

In the context of the analysis raised, this study focuses on building users, namely students with the definition of adolescents aged 13–15 years with the category of early adolescents. Early adolescents have unique psychological character and development. According to the State Administration Agency Team, in Syfa, 2019 that the development of psychology is the changes experienced by individuals or organisms toward the level of maturity or maturity that takes place in a systematic, progressive and continuous way both concerning physical or psychological.

A design of the school is expected. In addition to being a place for student activities, there are the activities of teaching and learning, informal socialization, and many more activities student do at school. Design can help develop psychological characteristics of adolescents. A building, the elements forming its space can form/create psychological impression on its users (Caudil 1978), for example a narrow corridor and a low ceiling will create a different impression with a wide corridor and has a high ceiling. The unique characteristics of early adolescent are expected to be accommodated in the design of the junior high school building so users can feel comfortable and the spatial need can be completed.

DOI 10.1201/9781003193241-14

2 METHOD

This study uses a qualitative descriptive method, making comparisons based on the results of a survey conducted on three designs of Junior High School building. Analysis was conducted by referring to the type of space organization in architecture, circulation, and psychological/ psychological characteristics of early adolescents. The case study of this study was conducted sampled at 3 junior high schools in West Java and Jakarta assuming the following number of students.

Table 1. Number off peers in every study case.

Junior High School	Theory Class	Peers/Classes
A	12 classes	10-15 peers
B	18 classes	10-15 peers
C	12 classes	10-15 peers
2	upper class	18 peers

* Curriculum used: Cambridge curriculum

The survey was conducted by documenting the atmosphere of the space in the building and mapping the layout of the Junior High School Building. The analysis is done by discussing two elements in architecture in a building, which is the application of spatial organization patterns (spatial layouts) and the application of circulation patterns used in buildings design. These two points are explained in each case study to explain each of the conditions in the object. The results of the processed analysis of the survey data are then compared so that conclusions can be drawn.

3 ANALYSIS

Important characteristics of concept development in early adolescents, according to Santrock (2013), consist of seven concepts: abstract and idealistic; differentiated; contradiction with them self; the functioning self, real, and ideal true and false selves; and self-conscious and self-protective. In general, the characteristics of adolescents can be explained as individuals who are looking for an identity, expressive and crowd-like or hanging out with friends, even though early adolescents who are still looking for identity are sometimes unstable and often feel insecure with themselves. A good architectural design is a design that can provide psychological comfort to its users (Caudil 1978). In addition to providing an activity container with its functions, architecture can provide psychological comfort to its users, one of which is a psychological approach in design. These concepts and characters can be implemented in the design, to accommodate the characteristics of its users in school building case studies, are early teens.

According to Syfa (2019), the application of user characteristics into the space to be used as the main reference in the design as a problem-solver in the designing process are:

1. Consider the hierarchy of space based on the level of privacy/orientation-based needs.
2. Minimize the bulkhead in space, prioritizing the open-plan concept.
3. Application of open space area.
4. Categorize the room into different zone areas, thus psychologically humans will interact naturally.

These points can be implemented in building designs. There are six ordering principles according to D.K. Ching in the design process: axis, symmetry, hierarchy, datum, rhythm, and transformation. The order is a reference from the design as a whole guideline, which is then derived in spatial elements. Among other things, the organization of space and circulation in a building.

Circulation and organization in buildings are considered sufficient to represent the design of the space in Junior High School case studies. Assume that the circulation and organization of buildings is a part of the building where flow circulation of students and teachers in large numbers under certain conditions, and also illustrate the concept of flow circulation design of the building as a whole.

Space organization is the basic layout of a building in compiling patterns of relationships between rooms. Building design can regulate the flow of building user activity in addition to the spatial function distribution is by the basic arrangement of spatial organization. Horizontal circulation is a space that is used as a means of circulation or an intermediary space from one room to another, types of positions, materials, etc. Horizontal circulation can provide different visual sequence.

3.1 *Spatial organizations*

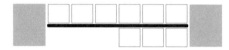

Figure 1. Radial in Case A.   Figure 2. Linear in Case B and Case C.

Two of the three schools use radial space organizations where users are asked to be at one point first and then spread out according to the space they want to go to, but the use of linear organizations can also be used in one case study with the application of a long hallway as a reference for spatial planning. The application of spatial organization, in addition to being influenced by the concept of drafting design, is influenced by the form of the site conditions. According to building main function, it will be easier for Junior High School buildings with radial space organization, given the need for sufficient space and there is a large enough area for students to gather compared to buildings with linear space organizations.

3.2 *Horizontal circulations*

Horizontal circulation room serves as a link between the space in the school and the place of social interaction activities outside of class hours. This room is a corridor that connects space with a minimum area of 30% of the total area of the entire building and the minimum width of the corridor is 1.75 m (Adler 1979). Corridors that do not have walls on one side must use handlers with a height of 90 cm (Neufert 2000).

3.2.1 *Case A (double-loaded and linear)*
Even though the space organization was arranged radial with a fairly large lobby on the first floor of the building, Case A's classrooms were arranged linear on the first and second floors. In addition to a wide corridor aproximately 3 m, there are voids on the 2nd floor which also gives a broad impression. The design of the floor pattern helps to show the elevation of the floor and the difference in classrooms. Along the corridor there is a shoe storage area for students. With a wide circulation design, it provides enough space for students to move and gather and can provide additional space for students to sit along the circulation.

3.2.2 *Case B (double-loaded and radial)*
Case B classrooms are on the 2nd and 3rd floors with the application of the double-loaded corridor design. Space requirements for standing people with both of hands open width is according to the standard 1.75 m (Adler 1979) with linear space organization. Therefore, students can gather or carry out activities with their friends in circulation. At the ending circulation there is quite large on one side. Utilized as a public area/library, so students will prefer to gather in a larger public area/library than in the middle of the corridor.

3.2.3 *Case C (double-, single-loaded, and radial)*

In Case C according to Figure 7, there is a circulation with single-loaded and double- loaded. Users are accepted in a fairly large lobby area in front of the building, so that it is then directed by the circulation that focuses on the intended space. Although there are no long corridors, two types of corridors are formed in Case C: double-loaded and single-loaded. Circulation of the double-loaded corridor is formed inside the building, after entering the user's lobby, is directed into a double-loaded corridor. On the other side of the class there is a corridor which is directly facing the outside building, so that sunlight enters the corridor.

The use of this circulation design makes it easier to compare with the previous case, the organization of radial and double-loaded spaces that are formed giving enough space for students to have activities and users to gather. Single-loaded corridors provide a different atmosphere of the corridor that can provide comfort for building users, especially students. The use of different materials on the side that is directly related to the outer space as a treatment solution of the building from the direct sun can simultaneously provide an aesthetic element in the building.

Table 2 is a summary analysis in \three case studies were carried out.

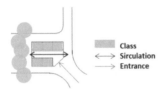

Figure 3. Layout sketch of Case A.

Figure 4. Corridor situation of Case A.

Figure 5. Sketch layout in Case.

Figure 6. Circulation situation in Case.

Figure 7. Sketch layout in Case.

Figure 8. Circulation layout in Case.

Table 2. Circulation application design in every case.

Junior High School	Spatial Organization	Horizontal Circulations
A	Linear	Double-Loaded
B	Radial	Double-Loaded
C	Radial	Single-Loaded
		Double-Loaded

4 CONCLUSIONS

Psychology and human behavior are two of the approaches in the design process of interior architecture that can be raised to achieve an agreement between human space, product design, and the user's subject. In a junior high school case study with users predominantly early adolescents, the characteristics of the early adolescents are a reference from the expected designation process. Broadly speaking, these three case studies have no problem in the extent of circulation in the lobby and corridor areas with an average area of 6 m. Here is the conclusion of the analysis obtained.

Radial space organization can be the main choice in the design of junior high schools, considering the characteristics of early adolescents who need space and gathering areas for students in an area that can be wider and more spread out. Linear organization with a corridor area according to the standard can lead the building users to not move in the corridor, so users will prefer other open spaces or in class double-loaded circulation is a type of circulation that is commonly used and based on space efficiency factors and site design limitations, these conditions can be optimized with a good design, supported by other space-forming elements, and also a single-loaded circulation. Good planning is planning that has a basic approach that is appropriate for the main user, taking into account the psychological and physical comfort of the user of the building.

ACKNOWLEDGMENTS

This paper was a research continuation from Telkom University Student Final Project: Redesign of Interior Space Edu Global School Junior High School Building in Bandung, a graduate requirement from Telkom University. This research wouldn't been possible without data provided from each Junior High School.

REFERENCES

Adler, D. 1979. *New Metric Handbook*. Grate Britain: Hartnolls Ltd.
Caudil, W.W. 1978. *Architecture and You: How to Experience and Enjoy Building*.
Ching, Francis, D.K. 2007 *Architecture: Form, Space, and Order Volume 3*. Jakarta. Erlangga.
Neufert, P. 2000. *Architects Data Third Edition*. Oxford: Blackwell Science.
Nurafni, Syfa. 2019. *Proses Perancangan Ulang Interior SMP International Edu Global School Bandung*. Telkom University.
Salura. P. 2001. *Berarsitektur, Membuat, Menggunakan, Mengalami dan Memahami Arsitektur*. Architecture Communication: Bandung.
Santrock, J. 2013. *Childhood Development*. 14th Edition, New York: McGraw-Hill Education. http://bekasi. binus.sch.id/facilities/ accessed May 2020 http://www.sekolahmutiarabunda.com/smp-mutiara-bunda-1 accessed May 2020.

Dynamics of Industrial Revolution 4.0: Digital Technology Transformation and Cultural Evolution –
Wulandari et al (eds)

Temporary spatial transformations in residential area corridors due to the impact of tourism. Case study: Jalan Jaksa, Jakarta

V. Haristianti
Telkom University, Bandung, Indonesia

W.D. Pratiwi
Institut Teknologi Bandung, Bandung, Indonesia

ABSTRACT: This study aims to determine the extent to which the impact of the event affects the creation of a temporary territorial transformation of the corridor structure. This research is qualitative research. The research variables are changes in soft space found in residential corridors, including the width of the road area on the sidewalk, and the garden of the residence. Sampling was carried out by means of before and after studies which emphasized the observation of literature study results and direct observation. The results showed that the significance of sidewalk changes can be seen during the day and at night where there is a change in function, as well as the crowd. Changes in the function of the sidewalk area and road buildings when there are activities are not merely spatial changes, but also affect the territorial structure, namely the occurrence of changes in depth sequences in the spatial strata.

Keywords: temporary spatial transformation, tourism area, digital mapping, depth sequence changing

1 INTRODUCTION

Tourism as an integral part of global business is highly dependent on seasonality, economic activities and human behavior and society in general (Corluka 2019). In its implementation, the built environment as a place to carry out an activity has a very close relationship with tourism. Habraken (1998) likens the built environment as an organism. He said that every change that occurs is a representation of the values adopted from the time of the ancestors to the future generations and changes in the built environment itself based on changes in the cultural value system adopted by the community (agent) who has power (controls). The result of the movement of people carrying out activities in the built environment at one time is called an event. The nature of the space used by humans to carry out events can be permanent or temporary. In permanent space, the function of space will remain the same under any circumstances. Whereas in temporary space, the function of the space will be different at a certain time.

The process of transformation contains the dimensions of time and the socio-cultural changes of the people who occupy a place, emerge through a long process and are always related to activities that occur at that time. (Alexander 1987, Pakilaran 2006 in Pratiwi 2009). In the process of transformation, there is a term called territory which means space under regulation or supervision (Habraken 1998). Territorial depth can be measured by the number of crossings required to move from the outermost region to the deepest region. This is shown in the Depth Sequence Diagram, namely the principle relationship for entering the transition between private and public spaces which is described in different ways to be able to access territorial areas (Susanti et al. 2018).

This paper is intended to highlight the relationship between the built environment and tourism. Specifically, it will discuss how spatial transformation occurs in temporary spaces in the corridor

DOI 10.1201/9781003193241-15

of a settlement area due to events. The residential area that will be the object of study is Jalan Jaksa, Central Jakarta. This road is known to have a long history. The development of a residential area into a tourism area has occurred since the end of 1968 until now. Since 2011, Jalan Jaksa has been designated as a Night Tourism Area. The contents of the DKI Jakarta Provincial Governor Regulation Number 53 of 2011 concerning Guidelines for City Design for Special Areas of the Jaksa Street Corridor states that the emphasis on the arrangement of the Jalan Jaksa corridor is on the arrangement of mass of buildings, facades, pedestrian tourist routes and public space planning. In more detail, Jalan Jaksa is projected to be built into a central corridor for tourist accommodation, entertainment and snacks that are attractive and nuanced to local Jakarta culture and are active for 24 hours, but still comfortable to live in and friendly to pedestrians. Jalan Jaksa is expected to become a special corridor for left-to-time traffic through traffic restrictions and setting maximum parking standards.

The ebb and flow of objects and tourist attractions in Jalan Jaksa is greatly influenced by the Indonesian economic situation (Haristianti & Pratiwi 2020). The changes that occurred on Jalan Jaksa were very dynamic. In this case, the transformation process occurs due to supply-demand in the form of visitor needs, as well as tourists and the response of local communities. Therefore, the discussion regarding temporary spatial changes in the corridor of Jalan Jaksa is considered worthy of discussion because it has many relationships with other aspects of society, including economic and social aspects. The purpose of this paper is to determine the extent to which the impact of the event which causes temporary spaces in the corridor to appear at certain times has an effect on the creation of territorial transformation in the corridor structure. The research, which was carried out as an academic exercise, is expected to produce new knowledge related to spatial transformation of the Corridor on Jalan Jaksa. The collected information is also expected to be a recommendation for related parties (for example local governments) to monitor the course of changes that have occurred in this area so that it becomes more focused and sustainable.

2 RESEARCH METHOD

The research method used in this paper is a qualitative method (Creswell 2002) with a time setting of before and after studies (also known as the pretest / post-test design (Kumar 2005) with a number of contacts twice. The sample is carried out by comparisons of two time periods, namely past conditions from Google Earth Satellite digital data, as well as direct observations. The aim is to obtain a clear picture of the changing situation in the corridor of the case study area to assess the direction of its temporary spatial transformation. Soft space attribute that can be used as a benchmark for assessing spatial transformation, including the width of the road area on the sidewalk, public open space for residents, the garden of the occupancy and road attributes.

2.1 *Data collection method*

The primary data collection method uses field observation methods compared with the results of documentation in the form of past photos obtained from satellite photos and also digital documentation from various sources. At this stage, the writer acts as a non-participant (Kumar 2005). In the first observation, the authors compared the results of satellite photos from 2004 - 2014 and examined the spatial parts of the residential corridors that are likely to change when viewed from satellite capture by means of montage. After that, the results of these observations are used as a reference for conducting direct surveys. As for the second survey stage (direct survey), the sample was selected by non-random or probability sampling by selecting the parts of the corridor that were seen to have changed from the data obtained in the first survey. To enrich the information, the authors also conducted unstructured interviews with business owners and visitors who were in the case study location in the sampling area.

2.2 Data analysis method

Data analysis was carried out in a qualitative way (Creswell 2002). After the field observation process is complete, the results of the literature and field documentation are directly compared and analyzed by means of data coding and text data analysis (Kumar 2005) for further descriptive interpretations based on predetermined variables. To enrich the results of the analysis, the authors also collect secondary data in the form of theory and earlier research as well as the results of personal documentation from residents of Jalan Jaksa as well as documents from internet reviews related to special events (for example: Jalan Jaksa festival, Republic of Indonesia anniversary) which occurs at the case study location and is considered the peak season time to enrich the description of the interpretation results.

3 RESULT AND DISCUSSION

3.1 Result

The results of satellite mapping observations in the years 2004–2014 show that there are many points that have undergone spatial changes. The results of these changes can be seen in the image below:

Figure 1.   Map of distribution of spatial change in settlements on Jalan Jaksa. (source: author documentation)

The mapping of the satellite photo observation results above is then used as a reference when making direct observations. The results of direct observations show that, apart from the main zone (zone 1) there are also several other zones that have changed. From the results of direct observations, it is found that the changes that occur in roads and corridors (sidewalks) cannot be separated from the role of street vendors (PKL) who are on Jalan Jaksa and its surroundings. After doing the mapping, the results show that the street vendors already have a place / zoning that is devoted to their trading. Then, the PKL category was divided into three sample zones. The sampling itself was carried out at three different PKL special points in zone 1, 2 and zone 3.

From the distribution map below (Figure 2), three different zones of corridors and public spaces are usually used by street vendors for selling. Interestingly, from the observations it was found that the thing that distinguishes zones 1, 2 and 3 is the time to sell street vendors. For street vendors selling in zones 1 and 2, their presence is at night. During the day, this area is not used for selling and functions only as a sidewalk as well as an ordinary road shoulder. However, in the evening

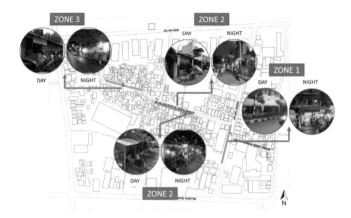

Figure 2.   Map of the distribution of case study sampling. (source: author documentation)

before sunset, this area will begin to be crowded with sellers who make preparations to sell at night until it approaches midnight. Zone 1 and zone 2, will be crowded at night. Zone 1 is more crowded with migrants from outside Jalan Jaksa, while zone 2 will be crowded with local residents because near area 2 there is a gazebo which residents use as a shared outdoor space. Whereas in zone 3, crowds occur during the day. Street vendors in this area trade from morning to evening and this area will be quieter at night.

The purpose of street vendors selling every day in this area is as a place for office employees located around Jalan Kebon Sirih to eat during lunchtime breaks. In addition to changes in function and the busyness of the sidewalk area during the daytime and at night, the sidewalks also often undergo renovations and also changes from street vendors where at some point, street vendors change their building structure from temporal to more permanent. sidewalks change frequently. These changes include in terms of maintenance (excavation, material replacement) carried out by the government. In addition, it can also be seen how some street vendors often change their selling areas to become more permanent on occupied sidewalks. In zone 2, some also show that the sidewalks in the corridor of Jalan Jaksa and its surroundings undergo a temporal spatial transformation due to changes in usage during the day and at night. In addition to the changes in the sidewalk, there are other public space points which are also allegedly changing frequently in this area, including the karang taruna gazebo and the gazebo where residents gather also the sidewalks

3.2   *Discussion*

The change in the function of sidewalks and road shoulders when there is an activity compared to the absence of this activity is not merely a spatial change, but also affects the territorial structure of the open space. The existence of activities allows space to form new territories where the levels can be seen in the illustration image below which is adapted from the theory of Habraken, 1998 regarding depth sequence diagrams:

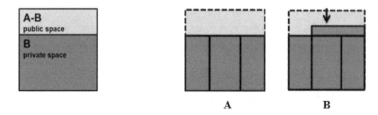

Figure 3.   Illustration of the rise of the sidewalk territorial structure to become more private during the activity.

84

When viewed from the perspective of the existence and function of sidewalks and road shoulders, the increased activity of residents leads to an increase in the territorial structure of the sidewalks and road shoulders where the initial function determines that the area is a free area (public space) but when the activity occurs, the area experiences layers of imaginary levels. Where some of the areas are semi-public areas, namely areas where street vendors, or residents sit, indicating that pedestrians cannot enter the area as freely as they can if there are no street vendors or residents doing activities. Meanwhile, when viewed from the point of view of B to A (private area to public area), this situation causes a decrease in the level of territory or level as described in the illustration below:

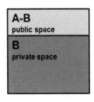 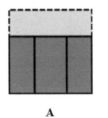 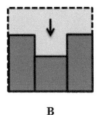

A   B

Figure 4.   The illustration of the decline in the territorial structure becomes more public on the residents' yard when there is activity on the sidewalk.

From the illustration above, it can be explained that when viewed from private (B) to public (A-B), the time when the activity takes place is the time when the territorial structure decreases. This can be proven by changing the use of private facilities such as the main gate and garage, where when there is no activity it is the private area of the owner of the residence, while when there is an activity it turns into a public area that can be used by residents as a place to wait for food, a place to chat, etc. So it can be concluded that the spatial transformation of the corridor can cause changes in the territorial strata of the public space.

4   CONCLUSION

The existence of digital media is very helpful in the process of mapping the direction of the corridor's spatial transformation that occurs. The spatial transformation of the corridor on Jalan Jaksa and its surroundings can cause changes in the territorial strata of the public space. The direction of the changes that have occurred has not yet fully led to the Regulation of the Governor of DKI Jakarta Province Number 53 Year 2011 concerning Guidelines for City Design for Special Areas of Jalan Jaksa Corridors. Currently, the condition of Jalan Jaksa corridor continues to decline. For this reason, the role of the government is needed especially to monitor the direction of transformation and improve the quality of events that are on the agenda of the Jaksa Street corridor, including the Jaksa Street Festival and the Celebration of Indonesian Independence. This research was conducted based on the experiences obtained from the findings, and observations of researchers when conducting field studies in research locations (empirical). It is possible for further research to develop this topic towards phenomenological research.

REFERENCES

Corluka, G, 2019. Tourism seasonality–an overview.
Creswell, J. W,2002. *Research design: qualitative, quantitative, and mixed methods approaches. Second edition*, Sage Publications, International Education and Professional Pubisher.
DKI Jakarta Provincial Governor Regulation No. 53 of 2011 concerning City Design Guidelines for the Special District Corridor for the District Attorney.

Habraken, N.J, 1998. *The structure of the ordinary: form and control in the built environment.* The MIT Press, Massachusetts.

Haristianti, V. and Pratiwi, W.D, 2020. Transformasi spasial hunian pada eks-backpacker enclaves studi kasus: jalan jaksa, jakarta pusat. *RUAS (Review of Urbanism and Architectural Studies)*, *18*(1), pp.52–63.

Kumar, R, 2005. *Research methodology: a step by step guide for beginner.* London, Sage Publication.

Pratiwi, W.D, 2009. *Tourism in traditional Bali settlement: Institutional Analysis of Built Environment Planning,* Verlag Dr Muller.

Susanti, I.S., Dewi, N.I.K. and Permana, A.Y., 2018. Tatanan teritorial dalam proses transformasi hunian. *Jurnal Arsitektur ZONASI*, *1*(1), pp.27–37.

Dynamics of Industrial Revolution 4.0: Digital Technology Transformation and Cultural Evolution –
Wulandari et al (eds)
© 2021 The Author(s), ISBN 978-1-032-04451-4

Data digging: Evaluation of Indonesia's built heritage information

R. Wulandari
Telkom University, Bandung, Indonesia

W.A. Rahmy
University of Florida, Florida, USA

ABSTRACT: A monument, a built heritage, needs information and narration to be shared with the public as part of their story that enrich their value as a cultural heritage. Digital technology has given us data and repositories on almost everything. It has made online research easier. This study is an empirical study on how to use and develop data digging for architectural history research on a monument or an object of a built environment using cases studies. From the case studies, it was understood that the information of an object being spread out are mostly incorrect thus need correction. Data digging with keyword research can confirm information of a built heritage, correct the mistaken information, and add other relevant information. Online repositories for Indonesian built heritage are available not only in The Netherlands, but also in other countries, in other languages, which need to be selected and listed.

Keywords: information technology, digital repository, built heritage,

1 INTRODUCTION

The world of the built environment has a record of its development, particularly a record of a building or a monument, even perhaps a record of the building's landscape and environment, or even a city. This record might be the note on its construction history, its design and planning, its social history that involved events, the research done on it afterwards, trading record, guest book, or even design drawing. All of these records can be found scattered in the building itself, in the contractor office, at the architect's studio, photograph at the owners' property, painting or story by an artist or a traveler, a magazine, a newspaper, even postcard and stamps. The information contained in the records could be very helpful for an architecture historian in understanding a historic monument.

A monument or site, historic monument/site in this case, needs evaluation on its origin, authenticity, integrity, and history to be valued as heritage. The information needed including the time of construction or inauguration, changes happened, original function. The information gained from archives and records can help historian and architectural historian in determining a monument's age, architectural style, changes from its original design, layer of history, layer of physical changes in the building, its landscape, even its surrounding.

Archive and historical data have been used regularly by historians. In the last decade, architecture historians in the Netherlands used archives and historical data to do research on built environment at their former state colony, one of it is Indonesia. Since the rise of digital technology, with its many facets, archives and data have been digitized and put online for public information and research use. This big data of historical archives and records can be accessed freely by anyone around the world.

The Dutch government service, the Cultural Agency, in cooperation with National Archives, university, library, and Dutch architectural historian have been making workshops on *digging 4 data* to introduce and popularize the rich online repository of the built environment in their former state of colony. From the cooperation, a guideline on how to do research on archive base was published (Akihary et al. 2017).

However, is this Dutch archive repository the only one that Indonesian researchers can count on in determining a value of a building, a monument, or even a region? Is there any other repository that can be consulted for research needs? And how to do it? This study is an empirical research with a study case that practiced and searched further use of archive and records repository online as well as trying to seek if there is another repository available to be consulted.

2 DIGGING 4 DATA

It is without doubt that the digital world, the digital information and communication technology, the computerized technology have changed our world in general. It has changed the way we seek and process information. It has provided people with big data and endless repository on everything in life, not to mention the heritage world. The digital information and communications technologies (ICT) have produced a wide range of applications for collecting and processing historical data, documenting and monitoring the physical conservation of objects and monuments, visualizing historic structures and environments, and creating interactive information (Brizard & Derde 2007).

Digging for Data was popularized in Indonesia by a Dutch architectural historian as *Digging4Data* is a method in researching the built environment in their former state of colony, particularly Indonesia. The data digging has been recently introduced in Indonesia through a workshop in 2014. The workshop was held together by National Archive of Indonesia and the Netherlands, University of Delft, and Cultural Heritage Agency of the Netherlands (RCE) (Akihary et al. 2014). The workshop was followed by several Indonesian universities and heritage communities. However, the method is still less understood and only few were starting using it.

The digging for data method uses repositories online and offline from books, archives, records, photographs, maps (Pauline & van Roosmalen 2014). The offline repositories are available in the library of government services, universities, books. In the meanwhile, the online repositories are available the internet. However, not all the information from the internet can be taken for granted as a valid source.

Akihary (2014) listed several valid and selected repositories from Indonesia and the Netherlands, containing text documents, photographs, films, maps, archives, magazines, and newspapers. These repositories are to be consulted for research on Indonesia's built environment (colonial architecture and town planning) from 1620–1950. The selected repositories are Arsip Nasional Republik Indonesia (ANRI); Atlas of Mutual Heritage VOC and WIC documents; Koninklijke Bibliotheek (KB, National Library); Delpher; Koninklijk Instituut voor de Tropen; Leiden University Libraries; Koninklijk Instituut voor Taal-, Land- en Volkenkunde (KILTV, Royal Netherlands Institute of Southeast Asian and Caribbean Studies); Nationaal Archief (National Archive); Het Nieuwe Instituut Nederlands (former Architectuur Instituut, NAi); Stichting Bibliografieën en Oeuvrelijsten van Nederlandse Architecten en Stedenbouwkundigen (BONAS); Perpustakaan Nasional Republik Indonesia (PNRI); Pusat Dokumentasi Arsitektur; Nationaal Museum van Wereldculturen (NMVW); Rijksmuseum Volkenkunde (Collection & Library); Rijksmuseum Tropenmuseum; Universitaire Bibliotheken Leiden; KITLV Collection; University of Technology, Delft Repository on European colonial architecture c.1850–1970; Towards A New Asian Partnership (TANAP) or portal for Dutch East India Company Archives and Research. Most of the information in the archives, offline or online, are available in Dutch and Indonesian. This gives limitation to user or researcher needing information since Indonesia researcher do not speak Dutch unless they are historian who studied Dutch.

3 METHOD

This study was an empiric study using data digging with study cases as method. Data digging was used as a method in testing and researching for correct information of a building from the colonial era in Indonesia. Public buildings and plantation site have been chosen as object of study. Public buildings were chosen because they are visible and recognizable by public, located in the city center, is listed, and acknowledged by public as a heritage property. Meanwhile, plantation site was also chosen as non-building study case because this site was created by the Dutch during colonial era.

The empiric study was done through keyword search of the chosen buildings and site in several languages. Languages used for keyword searching were Dutch, Indonesian, English, French, and Spanish. Several languages were used to find out if there is other information or repositories available online in other language than Indonesian and Dutch. Asian languages were not used due to author's incapacity in Asian languages other than Malay. As for keywords used, name of buildings or site were primary keyword, followed by buildings' function, name of region, name of the buildings' architect where available.

Information found in the online repositories were then compared to existing information already provided by local government or local communities. Different information was crosschecked to ensure validity of the data as well as the source of the information whether the source is reliable.

4 RESULT AND DISCUSSION

4.1 *Result*

The first chosen public building for the study was Gedung Gas Negara (PGN) Bandung located at Braga Street in Bandung. It was chosen because of its location in the city center, its visibility to public, and the visibility of its information to public. The building was designated as the city cultural heritage protected by local law and classified as "A" class heritage which means no physical changes can be made to the building. For the need of public information and socialization of the law as well as the building statutes, a placate was put by the government on the building façade. The marble placate gives information on the building's name, time of construction or inauguration, name of the architect, the building's function and other added information, and the name of the law protecting the building.

On the marble placate on Gedung Gas Negara's façade, it was said that the building was built in 1930 by an architect named R.L.A. Schoemaker and that it was functioned as gas factory. A question was raised on the information about the building's former function as a gas factory. The question was raised because the typology of the building is an office typology with divided rooms and a meeting hall. There is no storage or production facility present in the building. Thus, information saying that it functioned as a factory needed to be crosschecked and confirmed.

A data digging was done to confirm the mentioned question. First data digging was through book repository. A book written by C.V. van Dulleman and a book written by Huib Akihary became the two first repositories. From van Dulleman's book, it was understood that the building was built in 1919, and not 1930. It was also found in the first book that it was designed by the architect C.P. Wolff Schoemaker. In the meanwhile, no information of the building was found from the second book.

Next, data digging was done through the internet using keywords that would match the building. Keywords used were former name of the building, former name of the gas company, the street address. The keyword came out from following website https://www.indischeliterairewandelingen. nl/. On the website, little information in Dutch was saying that the building was built in 1919 by architect C.P. Wolff Schoemaker. The web also mentioned that the building was used as a central office for the gas company. Information from this website confirmed the one from van Dulleman's book and counter every information written in the placate installed on the building's façade. Thus, most of the information written on the marble placate on the façade are incorrect. Other information using keywords from other languages were not found for this building.

The data digging method was also used to test the availability of information on another public building and site. The second chosen study case for building was religious buildings, in this case the Indonesian mosques. For the Indonesian mosques, keywords used were name of the mosques, words "Indonesian mosques", region name. For the second study case, information searched were

Figure 1. Information about Gedung Gas Negara provided by the city, Paguyuban Pelestarian Budaya Bandung.

Figure 2. Gedung Gas Negara (PGN) Bandung, (Source: https://www.indischeliterairewandelingen.nl/)

those related to construction date, the builder (not architect), physical form, and shape. Surprisingly, information on Indonesian mosques can also be found in French repositories, mostly as research publication results. Several repositories that provided information on Indonesian mosques are: https://www.persee.fr/; https://www.gutenberg.org/; https://revue-archipel.fr/index_en.html; and https://brill.com/view/journals/bki/2/1/article-p384_20.xml

The data digging was also tested to get information about site (landscape) with plantation site as the case. Keywords used for plantation case was name of the plantation, former name of the plantation, name of the plant, region name, company name, name of former owner. Beside the previously mentioned repositories, information concerning plantation company was also found in Google books repository, and in legal document available in the google books library.

Data digging used for Indonesian mosques and plantation site provided information related to their history, form, year of construction, and people involved in the construction or development of the object. Every gathered information from data digging helped confirm the validity and accuracy of existing information known by local citizen, government, public in general, also researcher and academician.

4.2 *Discussion*

In Bandung, there are 100 buildings that are recognized as heritage by the local heritage law. Each of the building is marked with a marble placate containing information of each building. However, the information contained might not be valid or not 100% correct.

From the case of Gedung Gas Negara, it was confirmed that information written locally, been red by citizens, is not a valid information. Material written loud and clear on the building's façade turned out to be almost completely wrong. Only information about the law protecting it is correct. In the meanwhile, this information is being read by every passerby, every citizen, and every visitors of the building. Unless the information is corrected, the missing information is spread out and would be considered as fact by those who read it.

There are factors that could cause the misinformation of a monument. Several possibilities that could occur are the government has no valid source when making the information, the source used was considered credible but was not crosschecked or confirmed, the information searched was using limited available source, or taking for granted the already known information without further research. For whatever the condition, confirming information on a monument is necessary, especially when the monument is designated as heritage property. Valid historical information must be provided to support the designation and to support the value of the monument.

Digging for data in this case must be done prior to a monument's designation as a heritage property to evaluate its value. It should also be done to confirm every information already known by public. Validity of every information concerning a building, or a site must be ensured prior to public awareness publicity. Valid and accurate historical information of a heritage property is a capital for the object's narration to public.

From the case of Indonesian mosques and plantation site data digging, it was found that creativity in creating keywords related to the object is a fundamental skill. Foreign language skill of a researcher would be beneficial in digging for data activity. A researcher who wishes to do digging for data of Indonesia's built heritage needs to understand Dutch and several other European and perhaps Asian languages. However, with the aid of technology and online tools, the online translation services could do a little help on such research especially in creating keywords. Researching keywords in another language helps researchers in finding out if there are other repositories from other countries outside Indonesia and the Netherlands having some information on the built heritage researched. This is true for the case of mosque where French repositories were found to have some resources on it.

Some information concerning landscape and social situation can also be found on Project Gutenberg as information written in books related to the keyword researched. Other online repositories that could be useful as well are universities dissertation repositories. Some universities provided their students' dissertation online. Along with other repositories, Google books was also found to contain some information on the searched object or at the least, something related to searched object. By all means, in accordance with Akihary et al.(2014), selected Dutch repositories are primary source for the Indonesian colonial heritage data.

5 CONCLUSION

Historical data research is needed to confirm information of every historical object. Not every present existing data is valid and accurate. It is necessary to find out detailed information from offline and online repositories to confirm historical information of a built heritage to avoid informational mistakes.

Repositories are available not only in The Netherlands, but also in other countries in other languages. Consulting repositories in other countries using other languages will help enrich historical information of a colonial heritage property. Thus, it is important for a researcher to train their ability in keyword researching of an object of their study. The keyword research would be beneficial for the researcher to find more information not only from the listed sources, but also from other possible sources. Online repositories itself need to be selected, the information inside needs to be checked and rechecked to get a valid accurate historical data on an object of built heritage.

Capability in using online repositories, if offline is difficult to access, is important in research of historical built heritage. When the built heritage is related to history of colonialism, then there are more repositories to be consulted from both countries—ex-colonizer and ex-colony. All these repositories can be used to find information on landscape, city history, urban planning. Online repositories are free and open access, but one must be cautious in choosing a valid repository. A list of trusted sources should be made and updated to make digging for data more efficient and effective.

REFERENCES

Huib Akihary et al., 2014. Collecting and Connecting Historical Data for Inner City Development in Indonesia. Workshop Report Jakarta, Indonesia, October 27–28.

Huib Akihary, Nadia Purwestri, and Pauline K.M. van Roosmalen. 2017. Digging4Data How to do research on the built environment in Indonesia, 1620–1950. Jakarta, The Hague, Amersfoort.

Brizard, Tamara and Willem Derde. 2007. Basic Guidelines for Cultural Heritage Professionals in the Use of Information Technologies. *How Can ICT Support Cultural Heritage*. http://media. digitalher-itage.se/2010/07/Basic_Guidelines_TII.pdf.

Pauline K.M. van Roosmalen. 2014. A repository for sources about European colonial architecture and town planning (c.1850–1970): Creating a digital (research) tool. Workshop Historical Data for Inner City Development Jakarta. October 27–28.

Pauline K.M. van Roosmalen. 2014. Patience & Perseverance: How to go about historical research Workshop Historical Data for Inner City Development Jakarta October 27–28.

Dynamics of Industrial Revolution 4.0: Digital Technology Transformation and Cultural Evolution –
Wulandari et al (eds)

Study of controlling the layout and construction on pedestrian foot-bridge based on regulation

N.A Hapsoro & H.F.S Rusyda
Telkom University, Bandung, Indonesia

C.N. Bramiana
University of Malaya, Kuala Lumpur, Malaysia

ABSTRACT: Pedestrian facilities in Indonesia are still very inadequate. One of the most riskiesty pedestrian facilities that is underestimated is the pedestrian foot-bridge. The research objective of controlling the arrangement of the pedestrian foot-bridge construction is to control the design and location of the pedestrian foot-bridge construction, and to make the control criteria and determine the appropriate control components. This research is done with qualitative methods, namely with literature review. With this following study, the result is expected to be able to optimize the location of crossing bridges, increasinge the level of security, safety, and comfort of pedestrians to cross the street.

Keywords: pedestrian foot bridge, pedestrian, regulation, control, digital

1 INTRODUCTION

Indonesian people do not have a habit of walking. In a 2017 study conducted by researchers from Stanford published in the *Nature Journal*, Indonesia was listed as the laziest country for walk in the world (Muhammad 2019). Weather factors, minimal safety, security, and comfort factors all greatly influence the people's reluctance to walk. Meanwhile, based on the number of death records in 2016, 5,005 people died due to road accidents—that's at least 14 pedestrians every day (Rahapit 2020). Generally, pedestrians are injured or die when hit by a speeding vehicle (Ihsan 2019).

Infrastructure and facilities for pedestrians in Indonesian cities are still inadequate (Wardiningsih & Hendarto 2019). One of the most underestimated pedestrian facilities is the pedestrian foot-bridge. Good pedestrian crossings must be made with regard for proper visibility and accessibility, traffic patterns, traffic stages, prohibitions to turn right, duration/time that can be used by pedestrians, and safe measures of traffic that will allow pedestrians to traverse. For more complete regulations of crossing facilities, refer to the Technical Guidelines for the Engineering of Pedestrian Facilities in the City Area SK.43/AJ 007/DRJD/97, issued by the Department of Transportation, Directorate General of Land Transportation. Some legal bases that can be referred to as the basis for controlling the construction of pedestrian crossing bridges are as follows:

- Law No. 14 of 1992 concerning Traffic and Road Transportation (UU No. 14 1992, 1992): Pedestrians are required to walk on the facilities that have been provided and road users, especially, must prioritize pedestrian safety.
- Law No. 4 of 1997 concerning Disabled Persons (UU No. 4 1997, 1997): Persons with disabilities receive facilities that support their independence to use roads and public facilities.
- Law No. 28 of 2002 concerning Buildings (UU No. 28 2002, 2002).
- Law No. 38 of 2004 concerning Roads (UU No. 38 2004, 2004).
- Law No. 26 of 2007 concerning Spatial Planning (UU No. 26 2007, 2007).

DOI 10.1201/9781003193241-17

- Government Regulation No. 43 of 1993 concerning Infrastructure and Traffic (PP No. 44 1993, 1993).
- Government Regulation No. 34 of 2006 concerning roads (PP No. 34 2006, 2006).
- Minister of Public Works Regulation No. 29/PRT/M/2006 concerning Guidelines on Technical Requirements for Buildings (PERMEN PUPR 29/PRT/M/2006, 2006).
- Minister of Public Works Regulation No. 30/PRT/M/2006 concerning Technical Guidelines for Facilities and Accessibility in Buildings and Environments (PERMEN PUPR 30/PRT/M/2006, 2006).
- Minister of Public Works Regulation No. 06/PRT/M/2007 concerning General Guidelines for Building and Environmental Planning (PERMEN PUPR 06/PRT/M/2007, 2007).
- Decree of the Minister of Transportation No. KM 65 of 1993 concerning Support Facilities for Traffic and Road Transportation Activities (Mentri Perhubungan 1993).

If in an area of planning this element is ignored, then the possibility that occurs is the emergence of conflict between pedestrians with traffic flow that can cause obstacles, congestion, and endanger drivers themselves (Nawir & Rusmiyati 2019). This is a conclusion obtained from previous studies in the form of literature studies, as well as case studies that occurred in cities such as Surabaya (Jusmartinah 2011), Jakarta (Kautsar & Hamima 2013), Bandung (Koswara et al. 2014), Yogyakarta (Priastama 2015), and Tarakan (Nawir & Rusmiyati 2019). Therefore, regulating the construction of pedestrian footbridges is very important. With the following studies, it is expected to optimize the location of crossing bridges, increasing the level of safety, security, and comfort of pedestrians who will cross the road.

2 METHODS

This research is done with qualitative methods (Creswell & Poth 2018), namely literature review (Snyder 2019). The data obtained are taken from journals, articles, and regulations. At the data analysis stage, using a prescriptive qualitative analysis method. The scope of this study contains the layout, control criteria, components of pedestrian foot-bridge in urban environments that cross over highways, and or railroads, which include upper buildings, basements, connecting stairs, and the surrounding environment.

3 RESULTS AND DISCUSSION

By looking at the problems, and the impact caused if the arrangement is not regulated, it is necessary to have a control measure on the construction of pedestrian foot bridges. This is related to the increasingly dense traffic flow and the many problems in it, especially in big cities. It also relates to service to the community by improving the quality of infrastructure and facilities of a city. The issues considered in controlling the pedestrian footbridge construction are accessibility, safety, security, convenience, and aesthetic.

3.1 *Accessible*

Accessibility is concerned with the ease at which pedistrians move through pedestrian so that circulation is smooth and does not complicate the users. The target is the location of the pedestrian footbridge that is easily reached. The indicator is that the location of the pedestrian footbridge must be easily accessible and easily visible, and must be accessible to all groups, including the disabled. The following are the control components of the accessibility control criteria

Location: Elevated/bridges are provided at different locations This type of crossing cannot use zebra cross; pelican crossings have disrupted the vehicle traffic; roads with high-frequency pedestrian accidents; and are easily visible and accessible (Departemen Pekerjaan Umum 1995a). The maximum distance from the activity centers, the crowd, and bus stops is 50 m; the minimum distance from the intersection is 50m (UU No. 4 1997, 1997).

Dimensions of Space: Availability of stairs and ramp. The width of the footbridge, stairs, and ramp is at least 2 m so that the disabled can use it (UU No. 28 2002, 2002).

3.2 *Safety*

Safety refers to the safety within the pedestrian crossing bridge for the people using it. The goal is to provide safety guarantees for pedestrian footbridge users. The indicator is the bridge structure must be able to support the load inside the bridge, and users on the footbridge must be visible from the outside. The following are the control components of the safety control criteria

1. Stairs: There are no holes that can endanger the stairs; must be equipped with a handrail.
2. Structures: Structural planning must be carried out on a combination of fixed and uniform loads; Active soil pressure must be calculated based on standard pressure theory.
3. Visibility: There is nothing blocking the view from the outside towards the pedestrian foot bridge; There is good lighting during the day and at night.
4. Backrest of the footbridge. The minimum height of the backrest is 1.35 m from the surface of the floor to the top edge of the backrest (Departemen Pekerjaan Umum 1995b); each rod must be taken into account and be able to bear the vertical and horizontal forces that work simultaneously at 0.75 kN/m. For the pedestrian crossing over the road with high-speed traffic, the back structure must act as a safety wall covered with 12×12 mm wire and a minimum height of 3 m.

3.3 *Security*

Security refers to the sense of security against various disturbances that result from inside a pedestrian footbridge. The goal is to provide security guarantees for pedestrian footbridge users. The indicator is the user inside the footbridge must be visible from the outside. Visibility refers to the fact that there is nothing blocking the view from the outside toward the pedestrian footbridge. There is also good lighting during the day and at night.

3.4 *Convenience*

Convenience concerns the state of the pedestrian footbridge that provides a sense of comfort. The goal is to provide a guarantee of comfort for pedestrian footbridge users. The indicator is the location of the pedestrian footbridge should be easily accessible and visible, must be accessible to everyone, including the difable, and the bridge should be able to see clearly in the bridge. The following are the control components of the comfort control criteria

1. Location: Visible and easily accessible; The maximum distance from the activity centers and the crowd and bus stops is 50 m. The minimum distance from a crossroads is 50 m.
2. Dimensions: Availability of stairs and ramp; The crossing bridge width is at least 2 m (UU No. 38 2004, 2004).
3. Visibility: There is good lighting during the day and at night.
4. Ramp: The ramp slope in the building must not exceed 7° (the angle between the slope of the ramp and the horizontal plane). The slope calculation does not include the start or suffix (curb ramps landing). The prefix and suffix of the ramp is even more gentle. While the slope of a ramp outside the building is a maximum of 6°, the horizontal length of one ramp (with a slope of 7°) must not exceed 900 cm. The length of the ramp with lower slope can be longer. If the length of the ramp exceeds the provisions, then every 9 m there is a borders as a temporary resting place; borders at the beginning or end of a ramp must be free and flat so that it is possible to rotate a wheelchair with a minimum size of 160 cm. The ramp's minimum width is 95 cm without a railing and 136 cm with a railing. The flat surface prefix or suffix of a ramp must have a texture so it is not slippery either when it rains. The width of the ramp edge is 10 cm designed to prevent the wheelchair's wheel from falling in or out of the ramp. The ramp should be equipped with a

handrail which is guaranteed to be of sufficient strength as the handle when the difable is not with the driver.
5. Stairs: Must have an optrade and antrade dimension of uniform size. Must have a slope of the stairs less than 60°. There are no holes that can endanger the stairs users. Must be equipped with a handrail minimum on one side of the stairs. The length of the handrail must be increased by the edges (the top and bottom of the stairs) with a length of 30 cm. The handrail should be easy grip hold with a height of 65–80 cm from the floor, free from intrusive construction elements and the edges should be rounded or deflected either toward the floor, wall, or pillar.
6. Railing: The minimum height of the railing is 1.35 m from the surface of the floor to the top edge of the railing (Departemen Pekerjaan Umum 1995b). If the length of the bridge is more than 40 m, protection must be installed against the sun and rain (Departemen Pekerjaan Umum 1995b).

3.5 Aesthetic

Aesthetic is concerned with the state of the pedestrian crossing bridge that provides visual enjoyment. The goal is to guarantee the beauty of the city. The indicator is the location of the pedestrian footbridge placement must also pay attention to the composition of the city facade, and the shape of the bridge must adjust to the characteristics of the surrounding environment. The following are the control components of the comfort control criteria

1. Location: Placement should not be blocking the view towards the landscape or landmarks.
2. The Bridge's Shape: Keep attention to the design of pedestrian foot-bridges to keep them in harmony with the atmosphere and characteristics of the surrounding environment. At the bottom of the outside side of the railing can be installed elements that function to plant ornamental plants whose shape and dimensions must be in accordance with applicable regulations (UU No. 38 2004, 2004).

Planning the pedestrian bridge should be done not only by the government but should also involve the community. The government can use the correspondence method to get a point of view from the general public as well as from experts. JMP and SPSS are the most commonly used software to analyze data text. To analyze the performance of this pedestrian bridge, simulation methods can be used. Commonly used software are VISSWAL and SIMWALK. This software is able to predict the movement of pedestrians by taking into account the points of destination and the interactions between pedestrians.

4 CONCLUSION

The ineffective function of the pedestrian footbridge can be due to several aspects, namely, accessibility, safety, security, convenience, and aesthetic. The purpose of managing the construction of the pedestrian footbridge is to control the location and design of the pedestrian footbridge construction, and to establish control criteria and determine the appropriate control components. The expected target of managing construction of the pedestrian crossing bridge is as a guideline for the local government in determining the laying and type of pedestrian crossing bridge that considers the accessibility, safety, security, convenience, and aesthetic factors.

The continuation of the decision-making process from the pedestrian bridge design stage, in determining the location and design of the bridge, would be better if it involved the community and experts. To find out the performance of a pedestrian bridge that accommodates human movement, simulation is needed. This is influenced by human behavior that tends to be random and also because of the interaction between humans in the movement area.

REFERENCES

Creswell, J. W. and Poth, C. N. 2018. *Research Design: Qualitative, Quantitative, and Mixed Methods Approaches*. Los Angeles: Sage Publications, Inc.

Departemen Pekerjaan Umum. 1995a. *Tata Cara Perencanaan Fasilitas Pejalan Kaki Di Kawasan Perkotaan. No. 011/T/Bt/1995.*

Departemen Pekerjaan Umum. 1995b. *Tata Cara Perencanaan Jembatan Penyeberangan untuk Pejalan Kaki Di Kawasan Perkotaan. No. 027/T/Bt/1995.*

Ihsan, D. N. 2019. *Maut Mengintai Pejalan Kaki di Jalan Raya, Jeda.id*, October 11. Available at: https://jeda.id/stories/maut-mengintai-pejalan-kaki-di-jalan-raya-2148.

Jusmartinah. 2011. *Pendekatan Konsep Desain yang Manusiawi Guna Meningkatkan Minat Penggunaan Jembatan Penyeberangan Orang di Kota Surabaya. Jurnal Teknik WAKTU*, 09.

Kautsar, L. H. R. and Hamima, S. 2013. *Analisis Jembatan Penyeberangan Orang (JPO) Transjakarta sebagai Alternatif Perpaduan Infrastruktur dengan Ruang Terbuka Hijau Melalui Pemanfaatan Sistem Informasi Geografis (SIG) dan Penerapannya di DKI Jakarta. Geo-Environment Scholars Championship.*

Koswara, E. S., Roestaman, and Walujodjati, E. 2014. *Efektifitas Penggunaan Fasilitas Jembatan Penyeberangan Orang (JPO) (Studi Kasus pada Fasilitas Jembatan Penyeberangan Orang di Jl. Soekarno Hatta Bandung). Jurnal Kalibrasi Sekolah Tinggi Teknologi Garut*, 13.

Mentri Perhubungan. 1993. *Fasilitas Pendukung Kegiatan Lalu Lintas Dan Angkutan Jalan, Keputusan Menteri Perhubungan, KM 65.*

Muhammad, F. 2019. *Jakarta Kota Orang Malas Jalan Kaki, Benarkah. CNBC Indonesia*, April 19. Available at: https://www.cnbcindonesia.com/lifestyle/20190407105522-33-65061/jakarta-kota-orang-malas-jalan-kaki-benarkah.

Nawir, D. and Rusmiyati. 2019. *Studi Analisis Fasilitas Jembatan Penyeberangan Orang di Kota Tarakan. Borneo Engineering: Jurnal Teknik Sipil*, 3(1).

PERMEN PUPR 06/PRT/M/2007. 2007. *Pedoman Umum Rencana Tata Bangunan Dan Lingkungan.* in *Peraturan Menteri Pekerjaan Umum.*

PERMEN PUPr 29/PRT/M/2006. 2006. *Pedoman Persyaratan Teknis Bangunan Gedung.* in *Peraturan Menteri Pekerjaan Umum.*

PERMEN PUPR 30/PRT/M/2006. 2006. *Pedoman Teknis Fasilitas Dan Aksesibilitas Pada Bangunan Gedung Dan Lingkungan.* In *Peraturan Menteri Pekerjaan Umum.*

PP No. 34 2006. 2006. *Jalan.* in *Peraturan Pemerintah Republik Indonesia.*

PP No. 44 1993 1993. *Kendaraan Dan Pengemudi.* in *Peraturan Pemerintah Republik Indonesia.*

Priastama, P. 2015. *Analisis Dan Perancangan Kebutuhan Jembatan Penyeberangan Orang (Studi Kasus Jalan Diponegoro dan Jalan Laksda. Adisutjipto Yogyakarta. Universitas Atma Jaya Yogyakarta.*

Rahapit, A. 2020. *Data Kecelakaan Pejalan Kaki di Indonesia Nomor Dua Terburuk. ASKARA*, January 24. Available at: https://askara.co/read/2020/01/24/460/data-kecelakaan-pejalan-kaki-di-indonesia-nomor-dua-terburuk.

Snyder, H. 2019. *Literature Review As a Research Methodology: An Overview And Guidelines.* Journal of Business Research, 104:333–339.

UU No. 14 1992. 1992. *Lalu Lintas dan Angkutan Jalan.* in *Undang-Undang Republik Indonesia.* Republik Indonesia.

UU No. 26 2007. 2007. *Penataan Ruang.* in *Undang-Undang Republik Indonesia.* Republik Indonesia.

UU No. 28 2002. 2002. *Bangunan Gedung.* in *Undang-Undang Republik Indonesia.* Republik Indonesia.

UU No. 38 2004. 2004. *Jalan.* in *Undang-Undang Republik Indonesia.* Republik Indonesia.

UU No. 4 1997. 1997.*Penyandang Cacat.* in *Undang-Undang Republik Indonesia.* Republik Indonesia.

Wardiningsih, S. and Hendarto, D. 2019. *Kajian Jembatan Penyeberangan Orang (JPO) Sebagai Elemen Perkotaan (Studi Kasus: JPO Stasiun Lenteng Agung, Jakarta Selatan). IKRA-ITH Teknologi*, 3(2).

Digital technology transformation and cultural evolution in time of pandemic

Dynamics of Industrial Revolution 4.0: Digital Technology Transformation and Cultural Evolution –
Wulandari et al (eds)
© 2021 The Author(s), ISBN 978-1-032-04451-4

Featured animation design for cultural respect and understanding in Tjap Go Meh's narration

I. Wirasari
Telkom University, Bandung, Indonesia

F.B. Mohamed
Universiti Teknologi Malaysia, Malaysia

D.K. Aditya, N.D. Nugraha, A. Erdhina & S. Fathiani
Telkom University, Bandung, Indonesia

ABSTRACT: *Lontong Tjap Go Meh* is one of the most popular *Chinese Peranakan* dishes in Indonesia. Initially, this dish was served at the *Tjap Go Meh* celebration. Uniquely, this dish is actually not found in China. The similarity with *Ketupat Lebaran* has a connection with the spread of Islam in Java and the acculturation with the local culture. Unfortunately, not many people know about the origin and philosophy of this dish. In the *Chinese Peranakan* community in Indonesia itself, especially the younger generation, they mostly do not know about the history behind the *Lontong Tjap Go Meh*, other than it is a dish passed down by previous generations. *Tjap Go Meh*'s celebration in Indonesia can be said as something new for them, especially since this celebration was banned during the New Order regime. This cultural-based research intends to reintroduce the origins and philosophy of *Lontong Tjap Go Meh* through media that can be enjoyed by the younger generation, namely short animation.;his media form is easily accessed easily and is more effective, especially in this COVID-19 pandemic era. With qualitative research supported by observational data collection, literature study, and interviews with the qualitative method, it is hoped that the messages tconveyed through character and setting designs can be effectively received.

Keywords: Lontong Tjap Go Meh, Chinese Peranakan, acculturation, featured animation

1 INTRODUCTION

Indonesia is a country that has a variety of cultural wealth, starting from the original cultural heritage of the archipelago as well as the culture of migrants overseas. Historical records prove that many civilizations of other nations entered Nusantara through international trade, learning, exploration, the spread of religion, and colonial conquest. One of the overseas cultures that most influences the culture of the Nusantara is the Chinese overseas culture. The Chinese overseas culture manifests itself in a number of cultural artifacts in the archipelago, ranging from architecture, fashion, absorption language, culinary, to some Islamic culture in several places. The Chinese overseas that live in Nusantara for generations are called the *Chinese Peranakan*. The most sublime influence of the *Chinese Peranakan* culture in our daily life is the culinary culture. Without us knowing, several culinary dishes that we enjoy every day come from the process of acculturation, assimilation, and amalgamation, which originated from the results of Chinese initiatives spreading across the country. Most of the Chinese Peranakan were born from inter-marriage and do not speak in their father's language anymore. Most of the Chinese Peranakan live in Java and they often view themselves as Javanese people, but on other hand, the patrilineal system among the Chinese makes them consider themselves Chinese.

DOI 10.1201/9781003193241-18

The reason why this research connects with the COVID-19 pandemic is because of the philosophy within the *Lontong Tjap Go Meh* itself. The origin of the rice cakes originally came from rice balls, meaning of the family reunion. COVID-19 greatly changed social interactions, therefore many families could not gather because of need to social distance in order to reduce and stop the spread of the virus. That is why this animation project discusses the value of celebrating family gatherings for the younger generations.

The philosophy in *Lontong Tjap Go Meh* sounds simple, but it is also complicated to describe as the narration needs some deep cultural understanding because of the acculturations and lengthy and complicated historical trivia. ;t is said that, for the Chinese, dishes are not only something that is served for eating, but also play a role in diplomacy, friendship, as a cure for diseases, respect for one's ancestors, and also to avoid negative energy. It is a pity due to Soeharto's New Order Regime, which lasted over 30 years, that the *Chinese Peranakan* lost their relationship with their ancestors' cultural artifacts and values. Back then, not many *Chinese Peranakan* celebrated *Tjap Go Meh* until 1999, when former president, Abdulrahman Wahid, changed Soeharto's regulations in the Indonesian–Chinese society. Because of that, the celebration of the *Tjap Go Meh* was merely new for all children and teenagers who live after 1998.

Lontong Tjap Go Meh is one of the most famous *Chinese Peranakan* culinary dishes in Indonesia. Everybody in Indonesia, especially the *Chinese Peranakan* community, knows the taste of this unique dish well. Contrary to the dish, not everyone in Indonesia knows about the history and origins behind the dish. In fact, even in China, there are no dishes similar to *Lontong Tjap Go Meh* itself. *Lontong Tjap Go Meh* has similar components as *Ketupat Lebaran*, the famous dish served in Idul Fitri celebrations. The dish contains solid steamed rice cakes mixed with chicken curry, which is served with marrow slice, bean sprouts, fried shallots, and crackers. In Malaysia and Singapore, the dish is very similar with their *Laksa*. The similar components and the philosophy with the *Ketupat Lebaran* (which also did not exist in the Arab and other Middle Eastern countries, except the curry) made the two dishes become parts of Indonesian people's traditional culinary assets that came from two different custom and religion's assimilation. Some of stories of its origin state that the two dishes were introduced by either Sunan Kalijagaone of the Muslim's Nine apostles, or *Wali Sanga,* who spread Islam in the Java Island. Sunan Kalijaga used the cultural and acculturation approach during his missionary to spread Islam, such as *Wayang Kulit*/Shadow Puppet. The term *Tjap Go Meh* itself refers to the Hokkian people's celebration on the 15th day of the Lunar New Year [In Chinese, *Tjap Go Meh* is known as *Yuan Xiao Jie* (元宵节)]. In the traditional Chinese custom, on the 15th day, the Chinese should serve rice balls or rice cakes. *Lontong*, or the rice cakes themselves, are believed to be adapted from the traditional rice cakes that was served with pork soup. But, to honor the native Muslims community, the Chinese serve this rice cake with chicken curry called *Opor Ayam*. From this narration, we have learned that the Chinese overseas in the past had a relationship with the Islamic culture in Indonesia, especially in Java. It is also believed that Admiral Zhang He, from Ming's dynasty, has brought and spread Islam in North Java's coast during his diplomatic journey.

2 RESEARCH METHODS

Since the research wants to create animation assets such as character and background designs, the research will use the visual methodology approach. Visual terms here are referred to everything that is seen and made by human beings, such as paintings, drawings, posters, advertisements, and also statues, monuments, and constructions. Those things were created by human beings with messages that could be interpreted. Meanwhile, the data collecting for this research will use three models namely observation, interviews, and literacy studies.

(1) Observation: The research will observe some objects related to *Tjap Go Meh* festivals in Indonesia, especially in some places in Java. Any details on Chinese cultural artifacts that are related to the *Tjap Go Meh* festival will be observed as data, and then will be used as visual references;

(2) Interviews: The research will interview some Chinese cultural expertise and some Chinese descendants to obtain primary data on their origin and knowledge about the history of the *Tjap Go Meh* celebration in Indonesia, as well as its relationship with the *Lontong Tjap Go Meh*. But due to the pandemic, this step is still pending.

(3) Literacy Studies: They are conducted to obtain secondary data. Literacy studies are also carried out with a view to getting visual references, and to get references about everything related to the origin, including documentation about *Tjap Go Meh* in Indonesia and also in Southeast Asia, especially Malaysia, which has similarities to Indonesia. Visual references in this study are not only in the form of photographic recording data, but also the work of several character designs and settings from a number of comics and animations with the visual communication approach.

3 RESULT AND DISCUSSION

The research wants to explore some media that could inform and communicate the message about the philosophy. The medium that this research would take is a short feature animation. The short feature animation should use the suitable media because it will be broadcasted through social media such as a YouTube, Instagram, or even in another online or broadcasting channel. This research has considered to use these online media because it is significant due to the increasing numbers of internet users during the work from home and, of course, study from home in this COVID-19 pandemic era.

This is not the first time for us to find other animation projects that share the history and philosophy about *Tjap Go Meh*. The previous research and project created by the students of the multimedia concentration in Telkom University's Visual Communication Design Department had brought a dynamic and good quality of the animation for this topic. However, it lacks the historical facts due to the limitation of the final project timeline. This condition is understandable for this research because the previous project teams did not have any more details of the Chinese Peranakan references. Furthermore, this research wants to flesh out what the previous project had done before, especially with more historical accuracy.

The new narrations of the animation will consist of the reunion of a small Indonesian–Chinese *Peranakan* family for the celebration of the 15th day of the Lunar New Year during a pandemic era. The small family will have a chat at the dining table, discussing the history of the dishes that are served on the table. Then, the story rewinds back to how the Chinese overseas came to Nusantara and established a good relationship with their fellow Muslim natives, and how the dishes were introduced.

There will be two types of animation styles used in the project: first, the usual 2D animations that are commonly used in children's animations to illustrate the situations today; and second, 2D animations based on the Chinese puppet and Javanese Shadow puppet to illustrate the past scenes. The collaboration between the two styles is considered to deliver the message that we should remember and respect the past, learn how our ancestors paid respect to others, how they have established the values of tolerance, and how the diversity builds our customs.

4 CONCLUSION

Even though the COVID-19 pandemic has changed every aspect of our lives, including this research and the project within, the research is still ongoing. The researche only changes the media, which is easy to access during the study from home policy. In order to adopt the messages and the spirit to communicate to make a relationship with the audience to get the cultural respect like the *Lontong Tjap Go Meh* philosophy, this research will continue the project. With this short animation project, the researchers hope that the messages about respecting the diversity in values and the philosophy of gatherings and reunions delivered to young audiences, either to local natives or the *Chinese*

Figure 1. Sample of animation asset design. (Source: Priska Agari, Asy SyifaRahma, Firda Ayu Nopianty, 2019).

Peranakan, will show that this nation will strengthen in numbers when it searches for similarities in others as well as learns to value generations of the past while still embracing the future.

ACKNOWLEDGMENTS

The researcher wants to thank and show appreciation for Priska Agari, Asy SyifaRahma, Firda Ayu Nopianty, and Mr. Arief Budiman., S.sn., M.Sn. from the Visual Communication Design, Telkom University, Department in the Multimedia Program for helping with the visualization concept.

REFERENCES

Agari, P. and Budiman, A. 2019. Perancangan Storyboard Untuk Film Animasi 2D Lontong Cap Gomeh. *e-Proceeding Art Des.*, 6(3):4050

Arikunto, Suharsimi. 2013. *Prosedur Penelitian Suatu Pendekatan Praktik*. Jakarta: Penerbit Rineka Cipta

Bromokusumo, A. 2013. *Peranakan Tionghoa dalan Kuliner Nusantara*. Jakarta: Kompas Media Nusantara.

Ghifari, A. S. R. *Perancangan Background Untuk Film Animasi Pendek 2d Lontong Cap Gomeh*. Universitas Telkom, 2019.

Gondomono. 2002. "Pengantar Untuk Pelangi Cina Indonesia." PT. Intisari Mediatama, Jakarta

KOMINFO, 2020. "Penggunaan Internet Naik 40% Saat Bekerja dan Belajar dari Rumah." Kementerian Komunikasi dan Informatika RI, Jakarta

Nopianty, et al. 2019. Perancangan Karakter Untuk Film Animasi Pendek 2d Lontong Cap Go Meh, *e-Proceeding Art Des.*, 6(3):3835

Setiono, B.G. 2003. *Tionghoa dalam pusaran politik*. Jakarta: Trans Media.

Sidharta, M. 2006. Jejak-jejak Koki Diplomat. In Wibisono (ed.), *Etnik Tionghoa di Indonesia*, 52–61, Jakarta: PT. Intisari Mediatama

Soewardikoen, D.W. 2019. *Metodologi Penelitian Desain Komunikasi Visual*. Jakarta: PT Kanisius.

Dynamics of Industrial Revolution 4.0: Digital Technology Transformation and Cultural Evolution –
Wulandari et al (eds)
© 2021 The Author(s), ISBN 978-1-032-04451-4

Breaking logo's rule: Promoting social distancing to prevent COVID-19 spread by changing brand's logo

R.A. Siswanto & J. Dolah
Universiti Sains Malaysia, Penang, Malaysia

I. Resmadi
Telkom University, Bandung, Indonesia

ABSTRACT: In the current COVID-19 pandemic situation, a logo can convey social campaigns about social distancing. By delivering this social campaign, some brands have changed their logo shape without shifting their identity and recognizability. On the other hand, turning or twisting a logo could be seen as destroying it. However, this logo modification phenomenon shows that brands must be adaptive and flexible in responding to social situations to show their empathy and build positive perceptions and images in society. The method used in this study is the qualitative research method with a case study approach. The results of this paper aim at providing a picture of the creative process of making a logo that can respond to social phenomena. Logos can react to social phenomena, and go through a deconstruction of form, without having to lose its character and identity. This research shows that in the digital age the rigidity of a logo can be reduced by media, which allows a logo to be more flexible and fluid.

Keywords: logo design, branding, dynamic identity, campaign, COVID-19

1   INTRODUCTION

According to the World Health Organization (WHO), maintaining a distance of 2 meters between people could minimize the spreading of COVID-19 (Centers for Disease Control and Prevention 2020). This protocol, which later was known as "social distancing", became commonly discussed due to the global pandemic of COVID-19 that began in 2020. Social distancing itself is referred to as an action or measure taken to minimize the disease spread by reducing contact between large crowds. However, it's not only people who practice social distancing; several brands are also keeping the distance by tweaking their logos amid the coronavirus pandemic. Coca-Cola, McDonald's, Audi, and Volkswagen are some of the companies that have promoted "social distancing" into their logos by adding extra spaces in between in their logo elements.

These brands suggest people be aware of the current situation to keep the distance between people. This phenomenon escalates to become paradoxical and contradictory because logos should never be tweaked and must remain consistent in certain forms (Wheeler 2017). However, what is currently happening is that logos can then change shapes and become more fluid, flexible, and adaptive. Logos can respond to social phenomena, although it must break the rules. The rise of the number of brand logos that can react to the COVID-19 social phenomenon shows that in the current digital era, logos must be able to compromise and so be dynamic in responding to various issues, especially in social media. Brands must create empathy that is humane and show its alignment with the community while still paying attention to the part of visual identity while maintaining its distinctive and robust characteristics (Kotler et al. 2016).

Some previous literature shows that the logo must be dynamic in this digital era because one of them is the demand for digital media. In the sense of "Dynamic Identities," a company brand should not be static, but continue to grow in response to technological developments. Dynamic identity also emphasizes that changes in color, patterns, and shapes can change from external factors or factors outside the designer (Van Nes 2012). In addition to technological change factors and external factors, some changes in a brand's identity are also due to several things, including criticism, aesthetics, and communication ethics (Guida 2014). Brand identity also must be easy to adapt and flexible with certain content, situations, and contexts to respond to various things, and brand identity or visual identity must have the ability to respond and react to the surrounding environment (Felsing 2010). From some of the literature, it can be said that during the COVID-19 pandemic, a brand can respond to social phenomena through a campaign method related to changes in its visual identity (color and shape).

The novelty that would like to be displayed in this paper is how a social campaign's case study is distancing by deconstructing the logo. The logo has a distinctive and potent visual identity and can also be an exciting medium in conveying social campaigns without losing its distinctive and identical visual identity.

2 METHODS

This research is aimed at answering the question of how brands change and keep their identity when they change their logo in order to promote the social distancing recommendation while the identity of the brand still has to be recognizable. This is very important because according to Wheeler (2017), a consistent logo and recognizability is key for a successful branding. Therefore, it is expected that we could understand how far the logo distortion can be done. To answer the question, the qualitative research method is used in this paper with a case study approach. The case was chosen based on the validity of the campaign released by the brands, not fan-made or unofficial versions. The sample is determined based on the date of the release between April 1, 2020 to May 31, 2020 as the WHO recommendation to prevent the COVID-19 spread was released.

The analysis that will be used is to do a matrix analysis by discussing each visual element. Then, each visual element will be examined along with the social context that influences the creative process of changing the logo. Several stages of analysis used in this paper are analyzing the visual form of each logo, and the related social context of the logo change. Atlas.Ti software is used as the tool at the analysis stage to minimize the human error factor.

3 RESULTS AND DISCUSSION

According to the results of the McDonald's, Volkswagen, Audi, and Coca Cola logo analysis, it can be said that the shape changes designed by these big companies are still part of a dynamic visual identity. These patterns are part of an interesting and unique campaign, because in creating positive perceptions and building empathy about COVID-19, companies can deconstruct logos, even though these changes clearly do not change their unique identities and characteristics (colors and shapes). So, the conclusions obtained from the visual analysis results above are that the logo can change more dynamically because it is influenced by external factors, and in this context, the COVID-19 pandemic. However, the change in a logo must also ultimately see changes or shifts in harmony without changing the distinctive essence of the visual identity. Dynamic logo changes are only possible if there is still a boundary line between the social context achieved and the change that still maintains its visual identity. From the analysis results obtained, a dynamic logo in response to a social phenomenon is very possible without having to radically change the entire logo, but what shape and color are the strongest visual identities by adding or reducing parts of the shape of a logo. Even so, the community must be able to perceive the logo's identity.

 Source: McDonald's official Facebook account	(Specimen 1) McDonald's social distancing campaign on McDonald's official Facebook page. Posted in April 2020. What has changed: The M logo split into two parts. What has remained: The red and yellow colors. How the logo is still recognizable: McDonald's logo is considered as an iconic logo. It is used globally and is very easy to associate the red and yellow colors with the specific curvy shape of the M logo. Therefore, even though the M logo is split, the red and yellow color still maintains, so the split M logo will always be recognized as the McDonald's logo.
 Source: Volkswagen's official Instagram account	(Specimen 2) An Instagram post on Volkswagen's official account (verified) on April 3rd. What has changed: The V part moved upward creates a distance with the W part. What has remained: The circle, the W, and the blue color remains consistent. How the logo is still recognizable: Overall, the V shape is still read as the letter V and the W also did not shift. The original logo's addition is attached to the left-hand corner as an identity that the VW logo has not really changed.
 Source: Audi official Twitter account	(Specimen 3) A Tweet on Audi's official Twitter account (verified) in April 2020. What has changed: The four rings now have space in between the movement shown on the 30-second video, with a "Keep Distance" tagline underneath. What has remained: On 0.20', the rings close back together, forming Audi's regular logo. How the logo is still recognizable: The shape of this logo is a link between the four circles that make up the Audi logo. However, from the new logo in response to social distancing, the characteristics of the circles then have their respective distances. The strength of the Audi logo is in the shape of a circle which amounts to four. The harmonization of the four circles can still be recognized as part of Audi's identity, although in this campaign, there is a distance between the circles.
 Source: CNN	(Specimen 4) LED advertising board in New York City showing modified Coca-Cola's logo. What has changed: The spaces between the letters and beside the dashes in letters have changed. What has remained: Coca Cola font. How the logo is still recognizable: There are not too many changes in this logo except the spacing between letters and the hyphen in letters. If you note the continuity of the Coca Cola letters, it can still be recognized.

Figure 1.

4 CONCLUSIONS

This research shows that the paradigm of a logo must be rigid and making it inflexible is increasingly irrelevant because, based on the case studies analyzed, indicating that the role of the logo is more than just a marker of a brand, but it can also be a media in showing empathy and concern for social situations and problems. As Kotler said, brands in the digital age must be more humane and behave, so that people will appreciate the brand, which will undoubtedly add to the brand's positive assumptions (Kotler et al. 2016). This research is still in the initial stages, where it is necessary to conduct studies that are more of studying the phenomenon or the deeper technical context. However, this research can show that in the digital age, the rigidity of a logo can be reduced by media, which allows a logo to be more flexible and fluid.

REFERENCES

Centers for Disease Control and Prevention (CDC). 2020. *Social Distancing, Quarantine, and Isolation*; CDC: Atlanta, GA.

Felsing, U. 2010. *Dynamic identities in cultural and public contexts*. Müller.

Guida, F.E. 2014. *Dynamic identities for the Cultural Heritage*. In *Le vie dei Mercanti-XII Forum Internazionale di Studi* (pp. 1113–1120). La Scuola di Pitagora Editrice.

Kotler, P., Kartajaya, H., and Setiawan, I. 2016. *Marketing 4.0: Moving from traditional to digital*. John Wiley & Sons.

Van Nes, I. 2012. *Dynamic Identities: How to create a living brand*. BIS Publishers.

Wheeler, A. 2017. *Designing brand identity: an essential guide for the whole branding team*. John Wiley & Sons.

Dynamics of Industrial Revolution 4.0: Digital Technology Transformation and Cultural Evolution –
Wulandari et al (eds)
© 2021 The Author(s), ISBN 978-1-032-04451-4

Home interior wall treatment to support sensory games for toddlers in Indonesia during the pandemic situation

R. Rachmawati, I. Hanom & A. Sidarta
Telkom University, Bandung, Indonesia

ABSTRACT: The COVID-19 pandemic situation forced people to do activities from home, including parents of toddlers in Indonesia that faced new challenges of accompanying their children to play and learn at home. Toddlers learn from their surrounding environments through their five senses. Therefore, a game method that stimulates the senses is needed to be played at home, and one suitable medium for this is the wall surface. This study aims to determine what types of simple sensory games can be used as interior wall treatments for toddlers to play at home. The qualitative method is used in this research through the collection of literature and a questionnaire from respondents who are parents of toddlers. The results of this study are the division of wall treatments that can be a guide for parents, designers, or architects to process the walls as an exploration game medium to stimulate the senses of homebound toddlers.

Keywords: interior, wall treatment, sensory games, toddler

1 INTRODUCTION

The COVID-19 pandemic situation, especially in Indonesia, is still ongoing and there are no signs of abatement. Therefore, all activities such as work, study, play, and so on are carried out at home (Choerotunnisa 2018). Some parents are aware of the inconvenience of this, where in addition to having to work from home to meet their daily needs, they must also spend extra time to accompany their children to learn at home. This is certainly a double pressure for employees who are also mothers who have toddlers. Moreover, they have a new role to assist their toddlers who are still in school that now went under a distance learning policy (learning from home) (Vibriyanti 2020). For this reason, effective play media for toddlers are needed to help ease the activities of mothers at home. Basic games that are usually applied at home are still restricting the toddlers, therefore it is necessary to create play facilities for toddlers at home that can provide a comfortable atmosphere without making them feel confined (Oktaria and Putra 2020).

Toddlers will experience sensorimotor maturation that affects concentration, posture, balance, and daily behavior. Thus, treatment is needed as early as possible in the form of a brain gym which uses a lot of sensory skills. The sensory game does not have to always use sophisticated equipment; it can also be done with simple methods. The most important goal is to activate the child-friendly space that supports their activities at home (Kaiser 2020).

Sensory games, in the current pandemic situation, are safe to play at home and will greatly help children participate in activities that are beneficial for their development. There are games that can support the quality of toddler education with their five senses. Most sensory activities are part of the development of a child since birth (Galeti et al. 2020). This game is very useful to improve the brain development of children. However, this type of game often causes the room to become messy and troublesome for parents (Winahyu 2020). Therefore, an efficient form of play is needed that can stimulate the senses and support the quality of children when playing at home while not bothering parents when accompanying them. One part of the space that is considered efficient for

DOI 10.1201/9781003193241-20

sensory game application is the wall element. The following will discuss the results further and discussion of this research.

2 RESEARCH METHODS

The research method used is a qualitative method, in which an analysis of the latest literature reviews the development of children's play activites during a pandemic situation. It is then associated with user experience in the field, obtained through a questionnaire. The first step is capturing the phenomenon experienced by toddler (0–5 years old) in Indonesia during this pandemic when they are playing games at their own home. After that, further analysis is carried out on the needs of the game that has been done so far, especially the sensory games. There were 50 respondents who are parents as well as workers, where they participate in awork from home (WFH) system as well as accompanying their toddler to play at home during this pandemic. The result from the questionnaire will be a foundation to design a sensory game as a room treatment during the pandemic situation.

3 RESULT AND DISCUSSION

3.1 *Result*

The questionnaire was given to 50 respondents with the following criteria: the occupation of parents, age of the children, and their experience of playing sensory games (Figure 1). Based on respondents' experience, as many as 92% of them had played sensory games at home.

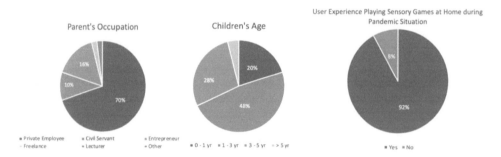

Figure 1.   Diagram of respondents' background.

Based on the data obtained, the average young working mothers during the COVID-19 pandemic from March–July (4 months) did their work from home while also caring for their children. As many as 68% of them have children in the age range of 0–3 years old, where these children are categorized as toddlers, and in that age range their role is dominated as sensorial explorer. Naturally, they will learn from their environment through what is felt by their five senses. For this reason, the first important educational stage for children at this age is sensory play (Sanders 2016). Of all working mothers' respondents, 92% were proven to have had sensory play activities with their children while at home during this pandemic situation (Figure 2). As many as 75% of working mothers choose the living room as the best area to do their office work, supervise their children, as well as play with their children (Figure 2).

As many as 50% of those who choose the living room said that the reason for this because this room is easily accessed from other rooms so it is easier to supervise the children. The other 46% mentioned the reason was because the living room is the widest area, and 4% of the rest said that this area is the most popular with children.

Of the various elements in the living room interior, the wall is the most effective and efficient element that can function as a sensory game wall treatment. As many as 97.8% of respondents

Figure 2.   User experience in sensory activities at home during the pandemic.

Table 1.   Interior element selection for sensory games.

No	Interior Element	Percentage
1.	Wall Treatment	49%
2.	Floor Treatment	17%
3.	Furniture	34%

Table 2.   Sensory games for interior wall treatment.

No.	Type of Activity	Type of Game	Percentage
1	Identifying shape/ color (visual)	Introducing 3D shapes, getting to know colors, playing snakes and ladders	30%
2	Drawing (visual, action)	Coloring with paint/crayon	8%
3	Moving things (visual, action)	Moving water and ice cream stick, color sorting	26%
4	Training hearing sense (sound)	Distinguishing the sound of animals, playing piano, identifying notes	6%
5	Playing Lego (visual, action, touch)	Playing puzzle, mega block, Lego, blocks, scrabble, wooden pairs of numbers, and uno stacko	20%
6	Recognizing texture (touch, feel)	Playing using pattern box, sensory beads/ hydrogel, rice, kidney beans, sponge, oobleck, and dough	44%

agreed that in addition to stimulating the five senses, the application of sensory boards to the wall can also help the child's growth stages from sitting, crawling, standing, to walking. This is also in accordance with the literature which states that the selection of interior elements of the wall as a medium for sensory game application is based on respondents' experience data where as many as 49% agree to choose wall treatment as the place for sensory game applications for toddlers (Table 1).

Based on Table 1, the wall area gets the most votes from respondents. This phenomenon is related to the study that the wall area is an alternative interior element that can be maximized so that it does not take up too many spaces and it can take advantage of the child's narrow room (Hindiarto et al. 2015). As for the toddler (0–3 years old) anthropometry data, it was taken based on median data on Indonesian children's height. Indonesian children aged 0–3 years old have a height of about 58–86 cm (Muljati et al. 2016). This data is used as a reference to determine the dimensions of length and height in the wall area where the sensory games for toddlers can be applied. For a sensory board attached to a wall, the maximum height dimension is 90 cm with a length that can vary. To be applicable in the design of sensory game wall treatments, there are various types of activities and games that were chosen by the respondents as explained in Table 2.

111

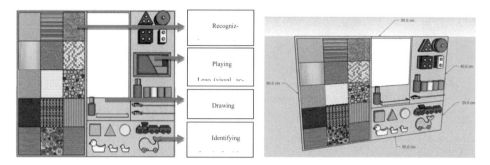

Figure 3.　Sensory games as interior wall treatment at home.

The application of a wall treatment in the form of sensory games is dominated by the activity of recognizing texture (44%). Toddlers are quite happy to play this game. In fact, they play it repeatedly for a duration of 0–60 minutes. Another activity chosen is identifying shapes/colors (30%) as well as moving things according to its shape and color (26%). Thus, the following are the sensory game distribution chart that can be applied as an interior wall treatment at home during the pandemic (Figure 3).

The results of the interior wall treatment application in the form of sensory board games in the living room were tested again and received a good response from respondents. In the application, 83.3% of parents were satisfied and agree that if this sensory wall was applied in their home they would use it. The respondents who chose to agree (84.4%) and 75.6% of them also feel that toddlers are not easily bored of it, so they can play longer on the side of the wall. Another positive impact is there are 48.9% of parents that said they can supervise their children playing while doing other work, so that children can play and fully become sensory explorers while staying in a safe situation at home.

3.2 *Discussion*

Parents have had sensory play activities with their children while at home during this pandemic situation. Sensory play is the first safe choice of play by children to optimally maintain their growth development process. Sensory games are all activities that stimulate the senses, such as touch, smell, taste, movement, balance, vision, and hearing. Research (Sanders 2016) shows that sensory play builds nerve conditions in the brain pathways, which in turn lead to a child's ability to complete more complex learning tasks. This type of game can also help children to develop and improve memory. As a result, the favorite area for playing is the family room; this is consistent with the theory that reveals that living room areas in the middle part of a house are the interaction centers for children with other family members while also allowing for caregiver supervision from various directions (Olds 2002). Most parents agree that their children can get a lot of stimulation from various existing games with this sensory wall in the living room.

4　CONCLUSION

In this pandemic situation, children still need a physical environment that supports their growth and development process. Sensory games that are applied as a treatment of the living room wall are the answer to the busyness of parents and the boredom of children at home. This sensory wall keeps children active while still receiving parental supervision. Because of its application to the wall, the position of the game type applied can be adjusted, including the game of recognizing the texture, shape, and color, as well as drawing it, and moving objects or unloading pairs. The application of sensory games as interior wall treatments in the living room at home is proven to reduce the child's boredom at home and make it easier for parents to watch the children play.

REFERENCES

Choerotunnisa, V. 2018. *Di Tengah Pandemi Covid-19, Kreativitas Pendidik Tetap Dukung Pembelajaran.* Retrieved 2020, from www.siedoo.com: https://siedoo.com/berita-30188-di-tengah-pandemi-covid-19-kreativitas-pendidik-tetap-dukung-pembelajaran/

Galeti, F.S., Arvigo, M.C., Berardineli, F.P., Felippette, T.R.B., and Bordini, D. 2020. *How to Help Children and Adolescents with Austism Sprectrum Disorder during Covid-19 Pandemic.* Journal of Psychology and Neuroscience. Brazil.

Hindiarto, F., Setiawan, A.P., and Kattu, G.S. 2015. *Kajian Terapan Elemen Interior Ruang Pre-School pada Angels n I Children Day Care di Surabaya.* Jurnal Intra 3(2).

Kaiser, C. 2020. *Recommendations for health protection of people with disabilities during outbreaks: Lessons learned from the 2019 Novel Coronavirus.* ONG Inclusiva.

Muljati, S., Triwinarto, A., Utami, N., and Hermina, H. 2016. *Gambaran Median Tinggi Badan Dan Berat Badan Menurut Kelompok Umur Pada Penduduk Indonesia Yang Sehat Berdasarkan Hasil Riskesdas 2013.* Kementerian Kesehatan RI. Jakarta, Indonesia.

Oktaria, R. and Putra, P. 2020. *Child Education in The Family as An Early Childhood Education Strategy During the Covid-19 Pandemic.* Jurnal Ilmiah Pesona PAUD. 7(1).

Olds, Anita, R. 2002. *Child Care Design Guide.* New York: McGraw Hill

Sanders, S. 2016. *Montessori Sensorial Activities: New Montessori Sensorial Activities to Cultivate Learning in the Classroom and the Home.* Iditarod Press.

Vibriyanti, D. 2020. *Work from Home: Cara Bekerja Baru di Masa Pandemi Covid-19.* Pusat Penelitian Kependudukan-LIPI, Jakarta.

Winahyu, A.I. 2020, Maret. *Setumpuk Drama Siswa Saat Belajar Di Rumah.* Retrieved from www.mediaindonesia.com: https://mediaindonesia.com/read/detail/298117-setumpuk-drama-siswa-saat-belajar-di-rumah.

Dynamics of Industrial Revolution 4.0: Digital Technology Transformation and Cultural Evolution –
Wulandari et al (eds)
© 2021 The Author(s), ISBN 978-1-032-04451-4

Literature study on ventilation and Air Conditioning (AC) systems associated with the SARS-CoV-2 pandemic

I. Sudarisman
Universitas Telkom, Bandung, Indonesia

M. Mustafa & M.H.M. Isa
Universiti Sains Malaysia, Penang, Malaysia

F.A. Birwaz
Universitas Telkom, Bandung, Indonesia

ABSTRACT: Based on research on SARS-CoV-2, transmission is generally found to occur in a closed room. The medium through which the virus transmits is droplets. Droplet nuclei can be carried by air flow, causing airborne transmission. Ventilation and air conditioning also play a role in this type of transmission, so it is important to know how it happened and how to deal with it. The study was conducted through the collection of literature related to SARS-CoV-2 and ventilation and air conditioning. The literature data is analyzed and conclusions are drawn. The results obtained are weakness of the ventilation system, improper selection of air conditioners, and poor quality of the indoor environment as a facilitator of transmission. The solution to these problems is the need for careful planning related to building design, ventilation systems, and the right type of air conditioner. All these efforts have consequences in the form of high costs.

Keywords: SARS-CoV-2, airborne, ventilation, air conditioners

1   INTRODUCTION

SARS-CoV-2 (new coronavirus) has caused a global pandemic. This virus can cause deadly pneumonia. About 15% of sufferers require hospital treatment and one third require intensive care (ICU). This virus has a value of R0 (basic reproductive number for infectious diseases) 3.28 or each patient can infect three other people (National Collaborating Centre for Environmental Health 2020). This R0 value can increase sharply (5 to 14) in a closed room (building) (Dietz et al. 2020). The number of infected people in the world has reached 17,660,523 people, with the number of deaths up to 680,894 people, and this virus has entered 216 countries (World Health Organization 2020). Based on SARS-CoV-2 experiments, it can be deactivated at high temperatures, its infectivity decreases at high humidity, and can be removed (disinfection) using UV-C light (National Collaborating Centre for Environmental Health 2020).

1.1   *Conditions that allow for SARS-CoV-2 to occur*

The effectiveness of virus transmission is determined by the number of virus particles that enter the body through breathing and the length of exposure to the virus. The main transmission media of SARS-CoV-2 is through large droplets ($>5\ \mu m$ diameter) resulting from coughing or sneezing from an infected person when making direct contact. In addition, transmission can also occur through droplet nucle/aerosols (diameter $<5\ \mu m$) as a result of breathing, talking, screaming, or singing. This transmission through aerosols occurs when virus particles accumulate in a closed room with poor ventilation that is crowded with people and contact between people occurs for a long time (National Collaborating Centre for Environmental Health 2020).

DOI 10.1201/9781003193241-21

1.2 Cases of transmission of SARS-CoV-2 in confined spaces

Cases of transmission of SARS-CoV-2 occurred in countries all over the world, including China and Singapore. These transmissions took place in public facilities such as schools, sports buildings, bars, shopping, and conferences, with the number of cases reaching between 50 and 100. There was a direct correlation between the transmission rate and how many and how close people are in a closed room the (Leclerc et al. 2020). Another case study of transmission was in Guangzhou, China, which occurred in a restaurant. The restaurant is in the form of a 5-story building, does not have window openings, and fully uses air conditioning (AC) which applies an air recirculation system as a source of air conditioning. The incident involved three families (families A, B, and C) who sat at different tables (next to each other and the position of the family table A was in the middle) and the infected person came from family A. The position of the AC outlet and inlet was above the family table C and air flow flows from family table C to family table A then family table B and back to family table C. The distance of the infected person from family A to family table B and family C > 1 m, but strong AC air flow causes droplet nuclei/aerosols ($< 5 \mu$m) spread to the table of family B and family C. Droplet nuclei can remain in the air for some time and can move far > 1m (Lu et al. 2020).

1.3 The role of ventilation and air conditioning systems in transmission of SARS-CoV-2

In modern times, humans spend most of their time in activities inside buildings, but many buildings are poorly ventilated, have unhygienic conditions, and are overcrowded. The cost factor is more of a priority than the user's health because creating a good environmental condition in the building/room requires high costs. The results showed that the rooms where we live and work are where SARS-CoV-2 is spread. Poor ventilation and AC systems facilitated the distribution (Qian et al. 2020). Therefore, it is important for us to know how the ventilation and air conditioning system facilitates the distribution of SARS-CoV-2 in the room and how we can reduce the risk of such spread through the proper application, operation, and maintenance of ventilation and AC systems.

2 RESEARCH METHODS

The first phase of the study was carried out by gathering various literature on SARS-CoV-2, the spread of SARS-CoV-2, WHO standards, ventilation, and air conditioning systems, as well as the influence of the artificial environment in controlling outbreaks. The second step is to analyze the literature, then make conclusions related to the role of ventilation and AC in transmission and reduce the risk of SARS-CoV-2 transmission. In addition, based on the results of the analysis, conclusions are drawn regarding the application, operation, and maintenance of ventilation systems and ACs that were appropriate during the SARS-CoV-2 pandemic. Data collection was carried out through various literature in the form of guidelines issued by the World Health Organization (WHO) and journals published during the SARS-CoV-2 pandemic since late 2019.

3 RESULTS AND DISCUSSION

3.1 Relationship between ventilation and airborne disease transmission

Based on the results of the study, a link was found between ventilation and transmission of diseases through the air, including WHO (2009):

- Inadequate ventilation and low rates of ventilation through ventilation have an effect on increasing airborne disease transmission.
- The high air exchange through ventilation (ventilation rate) can increase the dilution capability so as to reduce the risk of transmission.

- Air flow from pathogen-contaminated areas (sources of disease) can expand or increase the spread of disease. Conditions that must be met in order to cause the spread of disease due to air flow are high concentrations of pathogens from contaminated areas and low air exchange rates.

3.2 *Relationship between ventilation and airborne disease transmission*

One of the air exchanges in the building can occur through ventilation. Ventilation can be divided into three types: natural, mechanical, and hybrid ventilation (mixed mode). Natural ventilation utilizes openings in buildings and climatic/environmental conditions, mechanical ventilation utilizes technology (e.g., fans and exhaust), while hybrid ventilation combines both (World Health Organization 2009). Natural ventilation has several weaknesses that can be a facilitator of airborne disease transmission, namely (World Health Organization 2009):

- Natural ventilation is very dependent on climatic conditions and the environment around where the building is located, consequently natural ventilation can be optimally applied in one location but is very difficult to apply in other locations.
- It is difficult to obtain a stable air condition inside the building through natural ventilation, for example due to changes in the difference in air pressure between outside and inside the building.
- Natural ventilation can experience various problems such as environmental conditions around buildings that are not conducive, equipment damage (when using technology on hybrid types), poor system planning, poor maintenance, and operation so that it cannot function properly.

3.3 *Contradiction in efforts to maximize room air exchange and its solution*

Utilization of ventilation to obtain high levels of air exchange and regulate the flow of air movement in buildings is very important in reducing the risk of airborne disease transmission. But it can also cause other problems concerning the comfort, health, and safety of humans who are in the building. The first problem, namely natural ventilation through openings in buildings, can cause noise and pollute air quality in the room through pollution from outside the building. The greater or more openings, the greater the risk of noise and pollution. The second problem, in hot and humid climates (such as tropical climates) openings can cause high humidity in the room, which triggers the growth of mold and mildew which endanger human health. The third problem, openings can cause the entry of insects, wild animals, and even increase security risks. The fourth problem, openings that apply the principle of cross-air circulation (continuous opening from one room to another) can cause difficulties in meeting safety standards in the event of a fire (room protection from fire spread) and fire smoke control standards (World Health Organization 2009). Efforts to overcome the problems above can be reached in several ways. First, in the initial stages of planning the site design, building (shape, orientation, and layout) and building envelope must be carefully considered to maximize air exchange in the space but also reduce the risks that may arise due to openings. Second, at the beginning of building design, positioning, magnitude, and type of openings are very important to maximize air exchange. Third, the selection of light barriers outside the building that is right affects the comfort of the temperature inside the room. Fourth, the selection of the right building material (both for exterior and interior) is also important to achieve a comfortable temperature in the room. Fifth, the use of hybrid ventilation can help solve the problem of safety risks and maintain the stability of the exchange rate and the direction of air flow in the building (World Health Organization 2009).

3.4 *Air Conditioning (AC) and its relationship with airborne disease transmission*

Based on research, the AC system can be a facilitator of airborne disease transmission but can also reduce the risk of transmission through (European Centre for Disease Prevention and Control 2020):

- An AC system that uses the right filter can filter droplets and even droplets of the nuclei from SARS-CoV-2.

- ACs can reduce the risk of spreading disease by increasing air exchange (introducing fresh air from outside the building).
- The AC system can be a SARS-CoV-2 transmission medium in buildings if it only uses the air recirculation method.
- Air flow from the air conditioner can expand/increase the range of the droplet (especially the droplet nuclei) from the infected person to its surroundings in the room.

3.5 Strategies for selection and operation of Air Conditioning (AC) during the SARS-CoV-2 pandemic period

The selection of the right system, operation and AC equipment is very important in reducing the risk of SARS-CoV-2 transmission. Based on the following research, several ways that can be taken to reduce these risks, namely the use of proper filtration for air conditioners. SARS-CoV-2 has a size spectrum of 0.25–0.5 μm and thus requires high efficiency filtration to prevent the transmission of SARS-CoV-2 pathogens. Health facilities (for example hospitals) to prevent airborne disease transmission using MERV-13 or higher and combined with HEPA filters to filter out very small pathogens in the air. Setting an air-conditioning system that can maintain room humidity (RH) between 40% and 60% can limit the spread and survival of SARS-CoV-2. Utilizing an air handling unit (AHU) in an AC system to increase room air exchange (taking clean air from outside the building) can help melt contaminants (virus particles) from the air. Based on the results of studies of irradiation for 10 minutes using UV-C light can deactivate (99.999%) SARS-CoV and MERS-CoV, so that the irradiation method using UV germicidal (UVGI) can be applied to the AC system. This irradiation is carried out on a mechanical ventilation duct (ducting) to avoid direct contact with humans (Dietz et al. 2020). The use of a timer or CO_2 detector intended to save energy in an AC system must be avoided because it will reduce the level of air exchange in the room. In addition, the regulation of the air flow direction from the AC outlet must be sought not to lead directly to humans/users of the room, especially those who have long activities in the room and tend to be in a fixed position (not moving much) to prevent the transmission of pathogens directly and continuously through the air flow (European Centre for Disease Prevention and Control 2020). Efforts to reduce the risk of deployment through the selection of systems, operations, and AC equipment also have several consequences, such as increased energy use to increase air exchange through AHU which has an impact on inflated operational costs, increased air exchange (entering air from outside into the room) also impacts filtration requiring maintenance more often, not all AC systems can increase humidity in the room so to realize it requires certain AC equipment and special care in the room to prevent the appearance of mold and mildew due to increased humidity (Dietz et al. 2020).

4 CONCLUSION

Based on the discussion from various literature above, it can be concluded that the ventilation and AC system has a very large influence both on transmission and decreasing the risk of SARS-CoV-2 transmission. Weaknesses in the ventilation and AC systems if not addressed can be a driver of rapid increase in transmission of SARS-CoV-2. This can happen because most of modern human life is spent in buildings and it is certain that it will always come into contact with ventilation and AC which are part of the indoor environment conditioning system. This is exacerbated by the many conditions of modern buildings that do not have good ventilation.

However, efforts to reduce the risk of SARS-CoV-2 transmission through systems, operation, and maintenance of ventilation and air conditioning also have significant consequences in the form of planning costs, supply of equipment, operation, and maintenance, and require intensive maintenance on a regular basis. In addition, professional staff are needed to operate the systems and equipment and to socialize them well to the building users. Not all building owners and operators/managers have the financial ability to meet these standards, so careful analysis and planning are needed to selectively choose the system to be implemented in accordance with the capabilities and field conditions.

Table 1. The factors that need to be considered related to the ventilation and air conditioning systems to reduce the risk of transmission. (Source: personal)

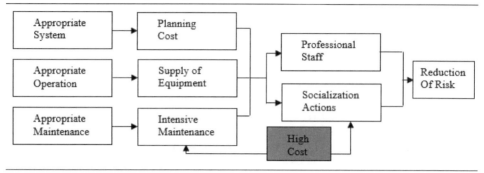

REFERENCES

Dietz, L., Horve, P.F., Coil, D.A., Fretz, M., Eisen, J.A., and Van Den Wymelenberga, K. 2020. 2019 Novel Coronavirus (COVID-19) Pandemic: Built Environment Considerations to Reduce Transmission. Msystems 5(2).

European Centre for Disease Prevention and Control (ECDC). 2020. Heating, ventilation and air-conditioning systems in the context of COVID-19.

Leclerc, Q.J., Fuller, N.M., Knight, L.E., Funk, S., and Knight, G.M. 2020. What settings have been linked to SARS-CoV-2 transmission clusters? Wellcome Open Research 2020 5:83.

Lu, J., Gu, J., Li, K., Xu, C., Su, W., and Lai, Z. 2020. COVID-19 Outbreak Associated with Air Conditioning in Restaurant, Guangzhou, China, 2020. Emerging Infectious Diseases, www.cdc.gov/eid 26 (7):1628–1630.

National Collaborating Centre for Environmental Health (NCCEH). 2020. An Introduction to SARS-CoV-2. Vancouver, BC: NCCEH.

Qian, H., Miao, T., Liu, L., Zheng, X., Luo, D., and Li, Y. 2020. Indoor transmission of SARS-CoV-2. medRxiv preprint doi: https://doi.org/10.1101/2020.04.04.20053058.

World Health Organization (WHO). 2009. Natural Ventilation for Infection Control in Health-Care Settings. Switzerland: WHO Press.

World Health Organization (WHO). 2020. Coronavirus disease (COVID-19) pandemic. [online]. (Last update: August 2, 2020, 07:00 GMT+7). https://www.who.int/emergencies/diseases/novel-coronavirus-2019 (accessed on August 5, 2020).

Dynamics of Industrial Revolution 4.0: Digital Technology Transformation and Cultural Evolution –
Wulandari et al (eds)
© 2021 The Author(s), ISBN 978-1-032-04451-4

Working virtually, exhausting in reality: Virtual cause of burnout in the age of a pandemic

W.T.G. Putra
Telkom University, Bandung, Indonesia

A.L. Hakim
Swasaba Research Initiative, Yogyakarta, Indonesia

T. Kartasudjana
Pasundan University, Bandung, Indonesia

ABSTRACT: Until the middle 2020, the COVID-19 pandemic was still the central point of media conversation. A pandemic such as this one can greatly change human behavior and habis, notably increasing the human–internet interaction through the Work From Home (WFH) phenomena and its consequences. This study uses a digital anthropology approach as one of the strategies and entry points in understanding behavior in the digital world, and techniques for researching social interactions via digital technology. It will be presented in the form of autoethnography to describe and interpret cultural experiences, beliefs, practices, and texts. From the discussion, it shows that virtual and real spaces are connected, and the events between these two different spaces have an impact on each other. Burnout can be seen, not only as an outcome, but also as an indicator of cultural changes and shows the challenges video conferencing platform providers face in presenting experiences that visually and functionally accommodate its users.

Keywords: digital anthropology, work from home, digital culture, autoethnography, COVID-19 pandemic, burnout

1 INTRODUCTION

Until the middle of 2020 the COVID-19 pandemic was still the central point of media conversation. Pandemics can change human behavior and in other perspectives can be seen as a socio-cultural phenomena as infectious disease problems are biological and cultural, historical and contemporary, theoretical, and practical (Inborn & Brown 2013). The handling and spreading of the virus related to the world view of a group of people about the world around them, which then forms a habit in the group. It includes social interactions, transforming the way they act and think.

In this century, regarding this customary negotiation, the pandemic then became central in the discussion of social science, especially anthropology. A 1909 work entitled "Les Rites de Passage" was written about how community groups respond to the presence of new people through habits and create some architecture for quarantine (van Gennep et al. 2013); related to disaster mitigation planning in swine flu (Atlani-Duault & Kendall 2009), human behaviors and its spread (Inborn & Brown 2013); Ebola and its handling related to community habits (Abramowitz 2017); and to discussions related to COVID-19 (Higgins et al. 2020). It also shows that massive pandemics and infectious diseases are part of the dynamics of human civilization and culture. How are the dynamics in Indonesia? This article will try to describe and record the cultural transformation that took place in Indonesia within the COVID-19 pandemic. The focus of this paper is on the Work From Home (WFH) phenomenon as jargon that emerged in Indonesia when the pandemic occurred, increasingly intense virtual interactions with the internet as a medium, and its impact on burnout in tangible forms as a consequence of WFH.

1.1 *Theoretical background*

The government's call for Large-Scale Social Restrictions (PSBB) forced some people in Indonesia to avoid direct physical contact. Due to the restriction of gatherings of humans in places with the potential to spread, some businesses allow workers to work from home, including school students. The transfer of work activities from real space (physical) to virtual space changes the habits of humans who interact in the arena. For example, an increase in internet traffic jumped by up to 20%. This condition is a result of the use of virtual social interaction platforms, ranging from various social media that are commonly used (Facebook, Twitter, Instagram), to those whose interfaces are considered to be more "formal" (Zoom, Webex, Google Meet) as an alternative workspace. The use of the internet is increasingly felt to be a necessity; interaction through this new medium is considered a solution to the limitation of real interaction. The community negotiates itself in two different forms of space, both real and virtual.

Although it is often difficult to distinguish, the boundary between the two becomes vague; virtual phenomena are, of course, real in the sense of belonging to reality, and the words must be understood in the context (Nardi 2015). Despite having vague boundaries, the differences are seen quite sharply through the way they interact and behave in both spaces. Some scholars perceive how they interact in both spaces as cyberculture, a form of a culture focused on how humans create new forms of "technosociality," i.e., social modes of communication and being with others that are mediated by technology, as well as "biosociality," i.e., "A new order for the production of life, nature and body" (Escobar et al. 1994). There are differences in the presence of new forms of technology (in this case, the internet) that mediate human interaction in a new space/environment. Some of the views mentioned above emphasize the presence of new spaces (in the future referred to as virtual spaces) mediated by internet technology, forming specific ways of interacting (distinguishing them from real interactions), to forming ways of thinking of different cultures and having a connection with the real world and space.

The existence of interrelations and vague boundaries between real and virtual space shows that the two impact one another. For example, the presence of alternative spaces in the virtual world serves as a forum for opinion, including various forms of exchange in a broader definition. The effects of this exchange have an impact on real space, as well as virtual burnout, which impacts on real exhaustion.

The term burnout, used as a clinical term, was first proposed in 1974 by Herbert Freudenberger. Burnout refers to the emerging psychological syndrome as a prolonged response to chronic interpersonal stressors on the job (Maslach & Leiter 2016). Burnout is vulnerable in people-oriented professions where work contacts take place both personally and emotionally, the needs of others take precedence over oneself, working hours are long, demands are high, and resources are limited (Maslach & Leiter 2016). Likewise, with changes in the use of technology (mobile phones and computers) in the workplace, it can blur the boundaries between the world of work and home (Peeters et al. 2005). Rapid changes in habit patterns related to the perception of space and time between work and home are prone to lead to conflicting roles of related individuals. Like work–home conflicts that are defined as a form of inter-role conflict in which the role pressures from the work and family domains are mutually incompatible, such participation in one role makes it difficult to participate in the other (Greenhaus & Beutell 1985).

1.2 *Objective*

The purpose of this study then is to: (1) document and show that burnout can occur in real space, as a result of interactions in virtual space; (2) reflect partially, how pandemics force affected communities to transform their habits as a part of a culture, especially a relationship between the working and non-working life in their daily lives; and (3) the existence of other factors—when virtual space is considered a real-world representation—makes this phenomenon so complicated.

2 RESEARCH METHODS

This study uses a digital anthropology approach as one of the strategies and entry points in understanding behaviors in the digital world (Miller & Horst 2012), and as a technique for researching social interaction via digital technology (Boelstorff et al. 2012). Analysis and qualitative data writing will be presented in autoethnography. Differing to other research methods, autoethnography, in its position as a research method, emphasizes the process of writing personal experiences ("auto") to describe and interpret ("graphy") cultural experiences, beliefs, practices, and texts ("ethno") (Ellis 2009; Adams et al., 2017) as a form of self-narrative that places the self within a social context. Here, autoethnographers are scholars that focus on using self as a medium intensely on their life circumstances as a way to understand larger social or cultural phenomena, and those who often uses personal narrative writing as a representational strategy that incorporates effects and emotions into their analysis (Butz & Besio 2009). Autoethnography is a derivative of ethnographic research methods, which is one of the tools used in the field of anthropology, as well as being part of qualitative research methods. In autoethnography, researchers place themselves as insiders and outsiders in a research arena setting. As an insider, it means, researchers are active subjects in a cultural arena. In the context of this study, the researcher was directly and actively involved in a set of events, where he became a part of cultural events that took place during the pandemic. Researchers also create distance from these events. In this section, the researcher places himself as an outsider to write down perspectives and results to other subjects outside the researcher.

2.1 *Data collecting methods*

As previously written, in writing autoethnography and ethnographic writing in general, data is obtained, including through several ways, such as interviews, participant observation field notes, document and artifact analysis, and research diaries (Mayan 2001; Morse & Richards 2002) as a cultural member of several community groups he studied. As part of that society, researchers try to obtain descriptions from several people through: (1) informal interviews to get their perspectives and perspectives on the phenomena they face, in addition to exploring personal memory to get a picture of collective memory when interrelations between data are found and trying to accommodate the views of others; (2) as a cultural member, researchers conduct participatory observation in several event settings in virtual spaces that are considered as "workplaces" as well as being part of them. In this study participatory observation is also used to ensure the involvement of researchers in field activities in everyday life settings and become well known to our informants (Boelstorff et al. 2012); (3) finally, examine a text through video recordings, photographs, and sounds (visual and verbal text), also the archives contained in journals. From the three methods, the researcher then writes his cultural experiences in several settings of events, classrooms, work, various webinars, and meetings outside the field of work (reunions, family gatherings, and limited discussion) in daily data known as fieldnotes. The field here refers to the arena/space of events that occur, in this case, a large part takes place in the virtual realm—some interviews are conducted face-to-face (real)—where humans do not often do face to face, as part of digital ethnography.

3 DISCUSSION AND RESULTS

3.1 *The blurred lines between the workplace and home, the real, and virtual*

On March 2, 2020 in Indonesia, the president announced the presence of patients 01 and 02 infected by this virus (Natalia & Sofya 2020). A few months before, when this virus had only spread in Wuhan, workplaces were still operating as usual, with large numbers of meetings still being held, as other countries in Southeast Asia have begun to close their borders, limit social mobilization, and mitigate disasters related to how people interact. A bit of the story illustrates the initial conditions of this pandemic in Indonesia.

The workplace, as commonly found in Indonesia, is a space where people gather. As the cluster of the spread of this virus before, public places increased awareness, protocols, and new ways of working were implemented. Some offices have a shift system for their employees, to ensure the quota of people who interact within a space is within safe limits. The rest can still work from home, commonly known as Work From Home (WFH), by utilizing a video conference platform.

The habit of working at home is changing human habits in addressing their space, and various adjustments were made. It starts from setting up the room at home as a workplace, so that makes it feasible when displayed on the screen, likewise with interaction patterns that must be adapted to digital "novelty" in this pandemic era. The phenomenon in this WFH condition is that the boundary between the home and office is blurred, so is the boundary between virtual and real spaces, where the need for human interaction through the internet is becoming more intense.

3.2 *A real presence in virtual space*

A few days after the PSBB was carried out, almost simultaneously, various agencies, both public and private, moved their offices into a virtual space. In principle, this virtual space mimics face-to-face interaction in the meeting room in daily practice, where there are people gathered in the same room. The way they communicate can be adjusted by users, using sound, video, both, and deactivating one or all of them. Users can also display photos or names, whether original or disguised as an identity marker that they are present in the room. This phenomenon is known as an avatar, a representation of humans in a virtual world (Boelstorff et al. 2012). The processes of "imagining yourself" in an unknown space (Malinowski 2014), and the embodiment of characters in a virtual world adapted from the Sanskrit language, meaning the embodiment of "God on Earth" (Kerschbaumer 2016).

At the beginning of the use of digital platforms as an alternative to this real space, users are still trying to get used to it. Some of them forget to turn off their microphones when other people are talking, or family members in the background can be seen. The sounds that are considered as interference are often heard. The rest seemed accustomed to turning off the microphone, while their faces seemed to move on the screen, indicating their real presence in the virtual space. Only a few do not turn on the camera and microphone, but there are names as an indicator of their presence. These events color everyday interactions that are slowly trying to be normalized and accustomed, which is how social interaction should be during a pandemic.

The following days, the use of video conferencing platforms became more frequent and intense. Some subjects in this study tell that, often, have to attend this virtual meeting at the same time and with the same priority scale. Usually, they will use more than one gadget to fulfill its role in different spaces. Not infrequently, the meeting lasts into the evening, until finally impacting on the physical fatigue felt by some subjects in real, although this interaction is done virtually. Once at a meeting, a virtual meeting member said, "If someone asks to have a meeting, (using a video conference platform) just serve. What is the difficulty in just turning on the computer and sitting to attend the meeting?"

In practice, working virtually through video conferencing earlier has more or less the same impact felt by some people. Seen in some of the 'mandatory' tasks given by the institutions where they are active, some of them began to outsmart their presence in the virtual space. Seen in the virtual space, some of them began to put photos of their faces in impressive poses, through body language, as if they were in the room. Others use the gif (Graphical Interchange Format) feature to make their presence more visible, with repetitive patterned movements. Similar to the avatar phenomenon described earlier, presence in the virtual realm is only a representation of the presence itself, which manifests in the form of sound, static, and moving images.

3.3 *Intertwined power relations in real and virtual space*

The presence and obligations in the virtual space do not necessarily eliminate the role in the real space, in this case, a house that doubles as a workspace, where individuals also have specific and diverse obligations and roles. In some instances, the writer is faced with the conditions of having to negotiate with other members of the meeting, whether the writer or they are asking permission not to attend the meeting because there are roles/obligations in the real space that must be fulfilled, usually related to family members. At this point, it indicates the presence of virtual space in real life, leading the subject to more complex power relations at the same time. In effect, this power relation is then negotiated, hoping for the discovery of new points of balance in a culture that changes rapidly and in a hurry during this pandemic.

4 CONCLUSION

"I don't know why I feel so tired. I only sit and attend several online meetings a day, both those required by the institution where I work, as well as meetings related to my hobbies and interests. Often, my days end with exhaustion, and even quite often, I find myself easily provoked and angry to yell at other family members at home, hitting the side of the table near me at work, and wanting to sleep all-day, whereas when I was at the office, those are conditions I have never experienced. It feels strange."

The melting of the boundaries between the real and the virtual world through internet interactions, which is getting higher in intensity, has a consequence that humans have to renegotiate their position in the cultural transformation that occurs. The virtual and the real space are interconnected, and the events between these two different spaces impact each other. The Internet, as a medium that forms virtual space, still uses the time and space constraints that apply in their interactions in real space. Burnout, in the end, is not only an outcome, excess, or residue that arises from the presence of the trigger factors previously described. Burnout, in this article, can be seen as an indication of a rapidly transforming culture, requiring humans to impose new standards on themselves—"normal vs new normal"—as well as a sign that humans are faced with an existential crisis that they are still negotiating with. This condition also shows the challenges video conferencing platform providers face in presenting experiences that visually and functionally accommodate its users. At the same time, reconsidering digital technology as a tool, does it make their job easier? Or, do we, as humans, do the job from technology in today's digital era?

REFERENCES

Abramowitz, S. 2017. Epidemics (Especially Ebola), *Annual Review of Anthropology*. doi: 10.1146/annurev-anthro-102116-041616.

Adams, T. E., Ellis, C., and Holman Jones, S. 2017. A brief history of autoethnography, *The International Encyclopedia of Communication Research Methods*, (August). doi: 10.1002/9781118901731.iecrm0011.

Atlani-Duault, L. and Kendall, C. 2009. Influenza, anthropology, and global uncertainties, *Medical Anthropology: Cross Cultural Studies in Health and Illness*. doi: 10.1080/01459740903070519.

Boelstorff, T. et al. 2012. *Ethnography and Virtual Worlds: a handbook of Method*. Princeton, Oxford: Princeton University Press.

Butz, D. and Besio, K. 2009. Autoethnography, *Geography Compass*, 3(5):1660–1674. doi: 10.1111/j.1749-8198.2009.00279.x.

Ellis, C. 2009. *Autoethnography as Method* (review), *Biography*, 32(2):360–363. doi: 10.1353/bio.0.0097.

Escobar, A. et al. 1994. Welcome to Cyberia: Notes on the Anthropology of Cyberculture [and Comments and Reply], *Current Anthropology*. doi: 10.1086/204266.

van Gennep, A., Vizedom, M. B., and Caffee, G. L. 2013. *The rites of passage, The Rites of Passage*. doi: 10.4324/9781315017594.

Greenhaus, J. H. and Beutell, N. J. 1985. Sources of Conflict Between Work and Family Roles, *Academy of Management Review*. doi: 10.5465/amr.1985.4277352.

Higgins, R., Martin, E., and Vesperi, M. D. 2020. An Anthropology of the COVID-19 Pandemic, *Anthropology Now*. Routledge, 12(1):2–6. doi: 10.1080/19428200.2020.1760627.

Inborn, M. C. and Brown, P. J. 2013. The anthropology of infectious disease, in *The Anthropology of Infectious Disease: International Health Perspectives*. doi: 10.4324/9781315078366-10.

Kerschbaumer, L.-M. M. 2016. Anthropology of virtual worlds: history, current debates and future possibilities, *Grafo Working Papers*, 5:95. doi: 10.5565/rev/grafowp.21.

Malinowski, B. 2014. *Argonauts of the western pacific: An account of native enterprise and adventure in the archipelagoes of Melanesian New Guinea, Argonauts of the Western Pacific: An Account of Native Enterprise and Adventure in the Archipelagoes of Melanesian New Guinea.* doi: 10.1017/9781315772158.

Maslach, C. and Leiter, M. P. 2016. Understanding the burnout experience: Recent research and its implications for psychiatry, *World Psychiatry*. doi: 10.1002/wps.20311.

Miller, D. and Horst, H. 2012. *Digital Anthropology, Berg.* Edited by H. A. D. Miller and H. Horst. London, New York: Berg.

Nardi, B. 2015. Virtuality, *Annual Review of Anthropology*, 44(1):15–31. doi: 10.1146/annurev-anthro-102214-014226.

Natalia, D. L. (Antara) and Sofya, H. (Antara). 2020. *Presiden umumkan kasus infeksi corona pertama di Indonesia.* antaranews.com. Available at: https://www.antaranews.com/berita/1329594/presiden-umumkan-kasus-infeksi-corona-pertama-di-indonesia.

Peeters, M. C. W. et al. 2005. Balancing work and home: How job and home demands are related to burnout, *International Journal of Stress Management.* doi: 10.1037/1072-5245.12.1.43.

Dynamics of Industrial Revolution 4.0: Digital Technology Transformation and Cultural Evolution –
Wulandari et al (eds)
© 2021 The Author(s), ISBN 978-1-032-04451-4

Online engagement of Warung Kopi Imah Babaturan's Instagram account during the COVID-19 pandemic

R.Y. Arumsari
Telkom University, Bandung, Indonesia

D. Setiawan
UNIBI, Bandung, Indonesia

ABSTRACT: Bandung, located in West Java, is a city that has many places to eat as well as various types of food. Warung Kopi Imah Babaturan is one of the places to eat that presents the concept of homecooked dishes, and it is never short of customers. However, in early 2020, the COVID-19 pandemic occurred in many countries throughout the world including Indonesia. This caused social activities to be very limited, ultimately resulting in everyone having to stay home. This limitation of social activities has caused many restaurants to stop operating. In order for Imah Babaturan to be able to continue to operate, they started to make use of the social media site Instagram to notify and update new information so that their followers can stay attached to the restaurant. Through descriptive qualitative research methods with interviews, observations, and literature studies, it was concluded that Imah Babaturan managed to make a good online engagement during the pandemic. This was proven by the number of likes and comments obtained from each post. Not only does this form of advertising adhere to health protocols, but it also attracts the attention of their followers by sharing activities for customers and online drivers to increase the number of engagements.

Keywords: online engagement, Instagram, Warung Kopi Imah Babaturan, COVID-19 pandemic

1   INTRODUCTION

Bandung is a city that is famous for its diverse and cheap culinary, therefore, not infrequently, many people from outside the city come to Bandung just to enjoy the food. Warung Kopi Imah Babaturan is one of the best places to visit and eat at as it presents the concept of homecooked dishes and is never empty of customers. However, in early 2020, the COVID-19 pandemic occurred in many countries throughout the world including Indonesia. This has caused social activities to be very limited, which in the end, it is crucial for people to stay at home. They would also prefer to order through deliveries for food to meet their needs.

The impact of the limitation of social activities is that many eating places have had to stop operating because of the pandemic, but this is not the case for Warung Kopi Imah Babaturan. They have continued to operate but only for food deliveries to be sent to customers' homes or ordered through the online motorcycle taxi application. Just like before the COVID-19 pandemic, Imah Babaturan still posts photos of the dishes in their restaurant. But there are unique things that they have done during the COVID-19 pandemic, namely posting items related to COVID-19 such as masks, hand sanitizers, and disinfectants. From these posts, it appears that they have made a move to share with their customers and also the online motorcycle taxi drivers by distributing some masks, hand sanitizers, and disinfectant. Eventually, some people became interested in sharing their products to Imah Babaturan.

Any products that they have received and can be shared will be announced via their posts. Besides, Imah Babaturan has never posted basic food photos that would be given to the online motorcycle taxi drivers who have ordered at their restaurant. In addition, they also made a post describing the COVID-19 health protocol of social distancing by displaying the distances between chairs, or even just one chair, in the restaurant, photos of people wearing masks, and employees who are spraying disinfectant on tables in their stalls.

From these points, the authors want to find out how big the engagement of Imah Babaturan's Instagram account is during the pandemic. Due to the pandemic, the use of social media as a method for media and communication between businesses and their customers grew greatly (De Valck 2020). Brands could deliver messages and engage in conversations that are considered valuable because they provide helpful information and relevant advice and could even simply make you laugh to come out of the crisis stronger.

Online engagement can be defined as the psychological condition of a user, which is categorized by the user's interaction, and co-creative experience with an agent and objects (Bonson & Ratkai 2013). Positive variables that often occur can result in consumer loyalty (Carter 2015). In every Instagram feed post, Imah Babaturan, with the theme of COVID-19, aims to increase engagement with its followers who are facing a pandemic. This can be seen by analyzing the likes and comments on these posts. A post with a lot of likes can indicate that the content is said to be attractive. This increases the likelihood of being liked by someone and leads to the dissemination of information from a brand to potential customers (Moore & McElroy 2012). In this study, the authors want to know the online engagement in the form of positive sentiments from viewers who like and provide comments on the Instagram posts on the theme of COVID-19. This is because the previous research conducted by Santoso et al. did not discuss the positive sentiments on Instagram posts, but instead only discussed the number of likes, comments, and the best schedule for posting. Besides, the object of their research is a women's clothing brand.

2 METHODOLOGY

This study uses the descriptive qualitative method by collecting data through observations, interviews, and literature studies. Observations were made from Imah Babaturan's Instagram account, interviews were conducted with informants who are Imah Babaturan's consumers, and literature studies were done by searching for theories about online engagement.

The authors also analyze the online engagement on the Instagram account of Imah Babaturan, which includes Conversation and Applause (Avinash 2011). On Instagram, what is rated in the conversation category is the comments and, in the applause category, the likes. So, the authors would analyze from the number of likes and comments on each post on their Instagram account from March to July. Not only is it analyzed manually, but the authors also used a kind of social media analytic tool called Keyhole.

3 DISCUSSION

This study discusses the online engagements from Imah Babaturan's Instagram account. The following is the appearance of their Instagram account. As of August 2020, it can be seen that the number of followers of Imah Babaturan is approximately 17,000 with a total of 1,923 posts. Based on the researchers' analysis data using Keyhole, in the period of March to July 2020, Imah Babaturan's Instagram account has increased in number posts, which resulted in an increase in engagement rate. In April, there were 68 Instagram posts with an average engagement of 193.

In March and April 2020, their Instagram account regulates posting photos for their feed, specifically made to campaign for the COVID-19 protocol at a place to eat. This includes spraying disinfectants on each table as well as the completeness of the provisions of the regulation, the distribution of disinfectants free of charge to customers who order food via online food ordering, giving out masks, vitamin C, and other protocols in accordance with the protocol recommended by the government.

Figure 1.   Social media analytic tool for the Instagram account of Imah Babaturan.

In a post made on March 31, 2020, the Instagram account of Imah Babaturan posted a photo of the distribution of cloth masks for drivers delivering food ordered online and received 203 likes from their followers. This is the highest number of likes compared to other posts of the COVID-19 protocol-themed feed. The second most COVID-19 protocol-themed post was on April 21, 2020, where the Instagram account is a chapter posting visual social distancing by photographing a chair with the caption "*Latian buat besok….*" (practice for tomorrow). This caption tells us that they accept consumers who come but still apply the COVID-19 protocol. One of the comments from their followers is "Kangen makan disanah" (I miss eating there). Besides these comments, there are still several other comments that indicate the desire of their followers to enjoy the food there.

3.1   *Characteristics of Instagram posts on Imah Babaturan's account with the theme of the COVID-19 protocol from the aspects of likes and comments.*

Warung Imah Babaturan made posts relating to the COVID19 protocol in the range from March to April 2020, totaling nine posts for their feed with each post displaying different characteristics to reach out or build bonds with their followers.

From Table 1, there are nine Instagram posts made by Imah Babaturan that convey information about the COVID-19 protocol. From the feed, the strategies to get a bond with their followers can be divided into several characteristics. The first characteristic is to connect their feed with the COVID-19 protocol. This is so that their followers can get more information on whether Imah Babaturan has applied the protocol, hence their followers do not have to worry if they want to order food from the restaurant. Additionally, it will generate positive sentiments from their followers. This can be seen from the average engagement that is sufficient both in March and April, which was when Imah Babaturan posted on their feed. The second characteristic is to mention other Instagram accounts that also collaborate and apply the COVID-19 protocol onto their feed. In this post, Imah Babaturan contributes to social activities for online ordering drivers. This also generates positive sentiments from their followers, and this can be seen from the number of likes and comments on the post made on April 24, 2020. The third characteristic is the creation of special hashtags for the COVID-19 protocol made by Imah Babaturan, namely #makandiimah #jangangakmakan. These hashtags are written on the captions of the posts regarding the COVID-19 protocol.

3.2   *Instagram account Imah Babaturan in building of online engagement during the COVID-19 pandemic*

Imah Babaturan's Instagram account strategy in building online engagement can be seen from the number of likes and comments in Table 1, which is a sample representation of the posts related

Table 1. Comparison of engagement between feeds.

Visual	Date	Caption	Like	Comment
	March 23, 2020	imahbabaturan Pentingnya saling menjaga agar kita semua tetap aman... #warungkopiimahbabaturan #jangangamaikan #makandimah	191	7
	March 25, 2020	imahbabaturan Teman-teman tersayang... #warungkopiimahbabaturan #makandimah #jangangamai	99	8
	March 31, 2020	imahbabaturan Hari ini kami ketitipan MASKER KAIN, yang bisa dibeli dan dijualal kembali, titipan temen baik kami yang juga supplier TOKO KUE TEMEN... #warungkopiimahbabaturan #makandimah #jangangamaikan #bersatukitacollab	213	5
	March 6, 2020	imahbabaturan Hari ini warung kami ngedetailin temen-temen DRIVER ONLINE Hand Sanitizer biar higienitas-nya bisa terjaga pas ngater makanan buat temen-temen semua... #warungkopiimahbabaturan #makandimah #jangangamaikan #bersatukitacollab	183	7
	March 13, 2020	imahbabaturan Hari ini kami ketitipan dari @apart_gastronomi dan ini #basicrisu BaKal buat temen-temen driver online... #warungkopi #makandimah	163	5
	April 21, 2020	imahbabaturan Lalan buat besse... #warungkopimahbabaturan #makandimah #jangangamaikan	144	14
	April 22, 2020	imahbabaturan Mari kita mulai PEMBATASAN SOSIAL BERSKALA BESAR dibandung, dan mengikuti semua protokol yang diatur oleh pemerintah supaya berdisa semoga pandemic ini segera berlalu dan kita semua bisa kembali hidup normal... #warungkopiimahbabaturan #makandimah #jangangamaikan	203	4
	April 24, 2020	imahbabaturan Teman baik yang juga bisnis kopi, @kedaikopi_zukasnanahtur kemaren ndijon MASKER banyak... #BUTUH MASKER", biar kita tау. Kalo ada yang perlu masker silang apa	99	0
	April 26, 2020	imahbabaturan Hari ini kami punya HAND SANITIZER buat temen-temen semua, stocknya limpatan banyak jadi bisa buat papa aja yg perlu...	97	0

to the COVID-19 protocol made in March to April 2020. This is also reinforced by the results of interviews with several of their Instagram followers as well as their consumers. The following table contains conclusions from interviews with consumers.

From the interview results above, it shows the positive sentiments of followers and consumers of Imah Babaturan, such as what was stated by Santi Cahya, who expressed positive opinions about

Table 2. The results of interviews with consumers.

Informant	Profile	Interview Conclusion
Lukman Hafidz	27, Teacher,Jakarta	Impressed by the posting made by Imah Babaturan because of their responsiveness of the rules and following trends. Posts that are given a like are posts about additional food needs for online drivers.
Santi Cahya	33, Employee, Bandung	According to Santi, Imah Babaturan made an innovative post so she is often giving likes and also comments on their posts. The most memorable post is of Imah Babaturan giving unexpected gifts to their customers who order online.
Fajar Adi	27, Freelancer, Bandung	Imah Babaturan makes creative and unique posts. Posts that are given a like are posts of when Imah Babaturan helps with the needs of online motorcycle taxi drivers in the form of food or food supplies.

their feed especially with regards to the COVID-19 protocol. Another positive sentiment comes from the comments of their followers in the posts made by Imah Babaturan, which states positive remarks from the comments they convey.

Positive sentiments can be seen from the keywords contained in the comments of followers. For example, comments in some posts consists of the keywords *"ngobrol"* (chat), *"kangen"* (miss), and *"makan"* (eat), which are words often written by their followers. From the interview data and observations on the comments above, it can be concluded that the Instagram account has built a strong online engagement with its followers through posts they have made containing the COVID-19 protocol information.

4 CONCLUSION

Based on the results and discussion described above, it can be concluded that by the way Imah Babaturan makes posts related to COVID-19 not only do they adhere to health protocols, but they also attract the attention of their followers by sharing activities for customers and online drivers. These related posts can receive a large number of likes and comments, which in turn can increase the level of engagement with their customers.

The authors realize that this research is far from perfect because there are still many things that can be studied deeper for this online engagement, such as the number of shares, reaches, profile visits, and website clicks. Therefore, these criteria should be researched further in other sources.

REFERENCES

E. Bonson and M. Ratkai. 2013. A Set of Metrics to Assess Stakeholder Engagement and Social Legitimacy on A Corporate Facebook Page, *Online Information Review,* pp. 787–803.

B. Carter, April 22, 2015. What is The Definition of Customer Engagament? [Online]. Available: http://blog.accessdevelopment.com/what-isthe-definition-of-customer-engagement.

Kaushik, Avinash. 2011. Best Social Media Metrics: Conversation, Amplification, Applause,

Economic Value. https://www.kaushik.net/avinash/best-social-media-metrics-conversation-amplification-applause-economic-value/

D. S. Moore and J. C. McElroy. 2012. The Influence of Personality on Facebook Usage, Wallpostings, and Regret, *Computer in Human Behavior,* pp. 267–274.

De Valck, Kristine. 2020. *What Is The Role of Social Media During the COVID-19 Crisis?* https://www.hec.edu/en/knowledge/instants/what-role-social-media-during-covid-19-crisis-0

Innovation of products, creative industries management and marketing

Dynamics of Industrial Revolution 4.0: Digital Technology Transformation and Cultural Evolution –
Wulandari et al (eds)
© 2021 The Author(s), ISBN 978-1-032-04451-4

Opportunities for the utilization of natural fiber fabrics in home living textile products with the "back to nature" lifestyle trend

R. Febriani
Telkom University, Bandung, Indonesia

W.N.U. Bastaman
Universiti Sains Malaysia, Penang, Malaysia

M. Sutantio
Sekolah Tinggi Desain Indonesia, Bandung, Indonesia

ABSTRACT: The lifestyle trend of "Back to Nature" is widely adopted by the people of Indonesia, especially urban residents who adopt a healthy and practical lifestyle and use natural-based products, one of which are fashion products. Many local brand designers respond to this lifestyle by creating clothing with natural fiber-based ingredients that can be used for daily activities, but this method is seen as not yet widely implemented in home living products. Therefore, the authors see a business opportunity that can be developed in the realm of the creative industries, especially home living products by adding elements of natural fiber fabric utilization and other textile craft techniques to the millennial market. This study uses a qualitative method with a business opportunity planning approach. The biggest reason for this is that the adoption of more environmentally friendly methods for the Indonesian fashion industry can be seen to provide many broad benefits.

Keywords: textile craft products, home living textile, natural fiber, lifestyle, business opportunities

1 INTRODUCTION

The phenomenon of environmentalism is now being carried over into the devleopment of fashion products. Thus, the concept of products being environmentally friendly has evolved into sustainable design and a sustainable fashion concept. The exposure to sustainable fashion was reinforced by Sandy Black, who said that sustainable fashion reflects the interdisciplinary nature of fashion and the complex dimensions between ethics and ecology as it occurs in the production process, consumption, marketing, and representation which often involve the opposition of priorities to be reconciled. (Black 2012). The eco-friendly method currently used by various fashion brands in Indonesia and its trend is the use of natural fiber fabric in the garment production process. Many local brand designers respond to this lifestyle by creating clothing with natural fiber base materials that can be used for daily activities. However, this adaptation is not widely applied to other sub-sectors of the fashion world, such as home living products.

The research problem is based on the conditions in which the development of the fashion industry is growing and becoming one of the country's largest economic resources, but not many designers try to explore the techniques of craft art and natural fiber fabric material when making home living products and combining them with fine art elements. With the innovation seen, there are business opportunities that can be developed and able to compete in the local market. Combining the craft of textile elements, especially in decorative elements, is a type of novelty that can be assessed as

DOI 10.1201/9781003193241-24

differentiator points of the product, so it is necessary to be the more precise business concept to fit the target market. The detail target market will be explained in the discussion section.

The purpose of this research is to create a new concept of business opportunities that maximizes product development with the utilization of natural fiber fabrics using the technique as decorative elements in home living products can be used as a reference for textile craft actors and fashions that will do business to compete with the global market and become a reference for the teaching process of new business management in textile and fashion craft.

2   METHODOLOGY AND DISCUSSION

The research method is carried out using the qualitative method, with data collection methods as follows.

1. Literature or review that is used in books, scientific journals, internet media, and others that discuss the merger of fashion with art, fashion with textile craft design, engineering, and mood board concepts in fashion and business start-ups.
2. Observations relating to the work that was inspired were carried out by conducting a survey.
3. Experimental methods are carried out by exploration using a variety of informal techniques, with mix materials in existing media.

Responding to the needs of the people as consumers, the fashion industry is a creative container for producers and business owners to explore creativity with the value of the beauty of a material that has an element of identical works. The efforts of producers in shaping environmentally friendly products have begun to be seen from the emergence of several brands that use natural materials as a key ingredient in today's fashion products. The effort to fulfill the need for lifestyle also affects the dress trend. People who have an awareness to consider the aspects of quality, safety, and health tend to have an interest in clothing that uses natural fiber fabric material because it is considered more comfortable and "friendly" for body and the environment. However, nowadays the product that carries the concept of eco-friendliness is not found in home living textile products. Products that make use of natural fiber material are not only needed in fashion but on other ready-made products that can be used in the activities of daily life.

Lifestyle depicts the whole self of someone interacting with his environment. According to Kasali, market researchers who embrace lifestyle approaches tend to classify consumers based on AIO concepts, activity, interests, and opinions. In the context of activities, it can refer to areas or places where consumers do, what they buy, and how they spend their time. The community that implements the "Back to Nature" lifestyle is seen as having a fairly unique consumption behavior. Besides being identified as a group with high consumption numbers, this community also can access technology and information that is quite careful. It supports the pattern of activity with no time linkage that can be done even at home though. If further examined in its development, the residence not only serves as a place of residence but also can be a means to realize the wishes of its owners, develop works and creativity and show social status.

The application of lifestyle is not only needed in fashion but can be aligned with all products consumed daily, be it in the form of food or ready-made goods. To support the activities inside the

Table 1. Brand references for home living textile products.

No	Brand	Materials	Technique	Price Range
1	Bermock	Acrylic & Polyester	Woven	IDR 600.000 – IDR 800.000
2	Naratisa	Canvas & Blacu	Pattern Making & Digital Printing	IDR 60.000 – IDR 200.000

Figure 1. Mood board and proof of raw materials.

home, the product must have an environmentally friendly concept according to the pattern of consumer lifestyle. However, home living products are often do not focus on utilizing environmentally friendly materials in their textile materials.

Examples of local brands of home living products that focus on textile products are outlined in Table 1.

From the two local brands outlined in Table 1, it can be seen that the material used has not been utilizing natural fiber fabrics with environmentally friendly processing techniques. Some brands that have implemented this eco-friendly concept are found in international retail brands.

A business opportunity exists for developing home living textile products and then creating a business plan and model to introduce the products to the market. The most important aspect of such a planning step is to determine a specific market. Often, planners have a vague idea of a generalized market that their new venture could appeal to (Janowiak 1976). According to BEKRAF Statistical Data (2015), creative economic contributions are based on subsectors, with fashion ranking as the second highest with a percentage of 18.15% than in the third place in the Occupy by Kriya with a percentage of 15.70%.

From the results of observation and experimentation on the natural fiber fabric material used in this research, produce a prototype of a home living textile product, first in the type of blanket product with a mood board and then detailed product knowledge as follows:

Product Detail:

– Material: 100% Cotton
– Engineering: Woven & Tapestry
– Size: 120 cm x 180 cm
– Style: Natural

CUSTOMER SEGMENT

A. Geographical: Domiciled or working in the city of Bandung, Jakarta, and Surabaya. Residing in a cluster-type residence, townhouse, or apartment, with a high–middle social status environment.

Figure 2. Home living textile prototype on knit blanket.

B. Demographic: Women/men aged 23–35 years (millennials), education level S1 or its level, working in the informal sector (freelancer, entertainer, entrepreneur, and creative industries) with a monthly income equal to management level or socio-economic status, group B and A with the main income per month around Rp. 4.600.000,-up to Rp. 8.000.000,-above.

C. Psychographic: Undergoing a healthy lifestyle or concern about environmentally friendly issues, assess a product based on the value of life in the lifestyle. Tends not to be overly exploratory in style because of the lifestyle factors that are lived, very active in the use of technology-based media.

The value offered from this product is, a local brand with an outdoor textile pricing home Living with a simple design line and natural, using natural fiber fabric material to meet the needs of the people who implement the lifestyle "Back to Nature". Observe the ethics of fashion production by considering the period of work, culture, and philosophy from the place of cloth that became the main material in the pricing is produced. In addition, the manufactured products apply structure textile techniques where similar products are more focused on the processing of color motifs. Figure 3 provides a detail mapping of the concepts of a canvas business model.

In comparison to the price of sale, this product has a selling price in the range of Rp. 600.000 – Rp 1,250,000 which is assessed to be competitive with prices in similar markets. The form of comparative analysis with the products mentioned above can be summarized in the table below:

	Strength	Weakness
Threat	Methods and techniques of natural fiber fabric treatment can be adjusted with materials used to overcome production constraints and get a more harmonious styling	Home living textile products that utilize the natural fiber fabric with the value of product ethics have a limitation of consideration toward the production process to the final stage of the product to attribute the problems of a sumerism
Opportunity	Home living products especially in the field of textiles that utilize natural fiber fabric is still minimal and has not focused on the needs of consumers who apply environmentally friendly lifestyles.	The design of home living textile products that utilize natural fiber fabrics is still limited to several market segmentation, and has not been widely published

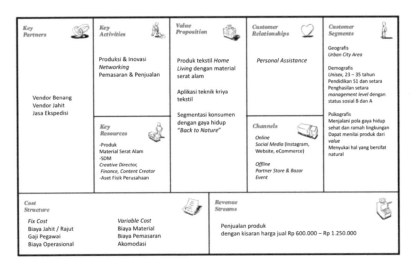

Figure 3. Home living textile products business canvas model.

3 CONCLUSION

The lifestyle trend "Back to Nature" is chosen because it has potential in terms of consumers' need to support an environmentally friendly lifestyle trend that has not been fully touched by most of the fashion manufacturers of home living. The lifestyle trend is applied by women ranges in ages from 23–35. But there are not many home living products that meet some aspects of the "Back to Nature" trend and support the activities of daily life patterns. The use of natural fiber materials can increase consumer interest while answering the needs of people who apply the "Back to Nature" lifestyle pattern especially in the home activities. This business opportunity can be applied to the pattern of micro-enterprises and developed by following consumer needs.

REFERENCES

Arumsari, Arini. 2018. *Pemanfaatan Pewarna Alam Sebagai Trend Baru Pada Fashion Brands di Indonesia.* Jurnal Rupa.
Black, Sandy. 2012. *The Sustainable Fashion Handbook,* London: Thames & Hudson Ltd.
Burke, Sandra. 2013. *Fashion Entrepreneur.* Auckland: Burke Publishing.
David, F. R. 2009. *Manajemen strategi. Edisi Kesepuluh. Jilid 1.* Jakarta: Salemba Empat.
Joyce, A, and Paquin, R.L. 2016. *The triple layered business model canvas: A tool to design more sustainable business models, Journal of Cleaner Production.*
Prihadi, Bambang. 2006. Diktat Mata Kuliah Sejarah Seni Rupa Barat II, FBS Universitas Negeri.
Rogers, Everett M. 2003. *Diffusion of Innovation Fifth Edition.* USA: Free Press.
Rye, D.E. 1996. *Tools For Executives Wirausahawan (Enterpreneur).* Buku Pertama dan Kedua. Edisi Indonesia. Penerbit PT. Prenhalindo, Jakarta.
Yogyakarta Rangkuti, F. 2008. *Analisis SWOT Teknik membedah kasus bisnis,* Jakarta: Gramedia PustakaU-tama.

Dynamics of Industrial Revolution 4.0: Digital Technology Transformation and Cultural Evolution –
Wulandari et al (eds)
© 2021 The Author(s), ISBN 978-1-032-04451-4

Kansei analysis: Motorcycle of choice based on user preferences in the main commercial market area of Gedebage, Bandung

D. Yunidar
Telkom University, Bandung, Indonesia

A.Z.A. Majid
Universiti Sains Malaysia, Malaysia

T.Z. Muttaqien
Telkom University, Bandung, Indonesia

ABSTRACT: Traders in the Gedebage market area often use a motorcycle as a vehicle to support their daily trading efforts. In dealing with the movement of goods with small dimensions, motorbikes are the most feasible modes of transportation to be used in the city of Bandung due to traffic conditions which often experience quite long and time-consuming traffic jams. The purpose of this paper is to present an overview to facilitate how to understand and build products that are consistent with the subjective factors of users in general. By using the Kansei Engineering approach to audit entities in the form of tangible products, and case studies in the form of motorcycle products that are used by traders in the commercial area of Gedebage Market, Bandung, in the end, this paper will provide an overview that can be used by product designers in translating subjective values that determine the user's decision in choosing a product.

Keywords: Kansei, motorcycle, user preferences

1 INTRODUCTION

Based on the 2019 population projection released by the Bandung Central Statistics Agency, Bandung has a population of more than 2.5 million people on workdays that almost doubles on the weekends due to domestic tourists visiting the city of Bandung. Thus it can be said that the city of Bandung is one of the busiest cities in Indonesia.

Judging from the administrative division map of the city of Bandung, the Gedebage area is the most extensive district in the city of Bandung which covers around 9.58 km^2. With a population of around 40,120,000 people and a growth rate of 0.01% per year, the Gedebage area is not the most populous region in the city of Bandung. This area is also passed by two main axes of the streets of Bandung, namely Jl. A.H Nasution, and Jl, Soekarno-Hatta, which makes it a strategic area and a crossing gate for fast access to enter the city of Bandung from the east and south.

Traders in the Gedebage market area often use motorbikes as vehicles to support their daily trading efforts. In dealing with the movement of goods with small dimensions, motorbikes are the most feasible mode of transportation to be used in the city of Bandung due to traffic conditions which often experience quite long and time-consuming traffic jams.

In buying a motorcycle, prospective users usually make their choices based on several common factors such as functional needs, price, engine capacity, maintenance costs, and after-sales prices, but often the potential users decide to buy the motorcycle based on non-technical factors and more on emotional factors such as the shape, color, or even the brand of the motorcycle. There is an interplay between technical factors and non-technical factors that make prospective users decide to choose and buy a particular motorcycle product, and this relationship is meant by subjective factors, where each potential user has a different subjective factor.

DOI 10.1201/9781003193241-25

This paper was made to present a framework to facilitate how to understand the user's subjective factors in general and how the subjective factors are formed.

2 METHODOLOGY

This research is conducted using two method approaches, namely a quantitative approach in the form of a generalization description of the results from the sampled data, and an explorative qualitative approach undertaken to gain a deep understanding of a motivation and reasons that need to be known.

This study was used "random sampling" of type "probability sampling" with the procedure "cluster random sampling", where all members of the population have the same opportunity to be selected as a sample.

Meanwhile, by using the "cluster random sampling" procedure the sampling technique can be carried out based on predetermined criteria, which in this case are motorcycle riders who work as traders, employees, students, and random citizens who are in four locations that are different, namely traditional markets, office areas, campus areas, and residential areas.

The sampling method with the probability sampling method is carried out on the consideration that the source of the sample in this study is homogeneous, where the samples are from the same demographic group (Suprapto 2001).

Based on the calculation, the number of samples used in this study is 40 respondents. This survey was conducted among people in public places, covering both genders (male and female) of various economic levels and ages.

There are six steps taken to audit a product using the Kansei approach in this case. The five steps are as follows:

1. Choice of participant groups
2. Collection of Kansei words
3. Data reduction methods for selection of Kansei words
4. Rating-scaled types used
5. Connecting the Kansei words to product properties

3 ANALYSIS AND RESULTS

From the data obtained through questionnaires and short interviews with respondents in the Gedebage traditional market are, it can be concluded that the results are as follows.

Table 1 indicates that the majority of traders in the area of Gedebage's traditional market feel that family values, social values, and material values are very important in their lives, especially religious values.

Table 2 indicates that the majority of traders in the area of Gedebage's traditional market are the type of people who are realistic in their attitude.

Table 1. Respondents respond to section A (life values) in Gedebage traditional market area.

	N	Range	Minimum	Maximum	Mean	Std. Deviation
Section A1	50	1	2	5	4.48	.863
Section A2	50	1	4	5	4.66	.479
Section A3	50	4	1	5	4.28	.671
Section A4	50	1	4	5	4.92	.274
Section A5	50	3	2	5	4.28	.784
Valid N (listwise)	50					

Table 2. Respondents respond to section B (attitude) in Gedebage's traditional market area.

	N	Range	Minimum	Maximum	Mean	Std. Deviation
Section B1	50	3	2	5	3.86	.857
Section B2	50	3	2	5	3.92	.724
Section B3	50	3	2	5	3.04	.605
Section B4	50	3	2	5	3.96	.832
Section B5	50	4	1	5	2.26	1.291
Valid N (listwise)	50					

Table 3. Respondents respond to section C (interest) in Gedebage's traditional market area.

	N	Range	Minimum	Maximum	Mean	Std. Deviation
Section C1	50	4	1	5	4.20	.808
Section C2	50	4	1	5	3.00	1.370
Section C3	50	4	1	5	3.36	1.241
Section C4	50	4	1	5	2.28	1.230
Section C5	50	4	1	5	3.52	1.446
Valid N (listwise)	50					

Table 4. Respondents respond to section D (lifestyle) in Gedebage's traditional market area.

	N	Range	Minimum	Maximum	Mean	Std. Deviation
Section D1	50	4	1	5	3.48	1.282
Section D2	50	4	1	5	.04	1.384
Section D3	50	4	1	5	3.08	1.353
Section D4	50	4	1	5	2.30	1.182
Section D5	50	4	1	5	3.54	1.249
Valid N (listwise)	50					

Table 5. Kansei words that have been collected.

Ambiance	Fit	Sense of materials
Design image	Shape	New combination
Color	Functionality & convenience	Unexpected application

Table 3 indicates that the majority of traders in the area of Gedebage traditional market are the type of people who are pennywise in the way they spend their money.

Table 4 indicates that the majority of traders in the area of Gedebage's traditional market are a simple type of people with regard to their lifestyle.

In the step of collection of Kansei words, Kansei engineering type I is used to determine consumer preferences for product design elements. At the stage of collecting Kansei's words, nine words are consisting of adjectives and product functions as the first global Kansei words. Table 5 shows a set of Kansei words that has been collected.

Results of the data reduction step, the Kansei words are then grouped based on similarity in the context of their meaning, as shown in Table 6. This stage produces three major groups of Kansei words.

Of the three groups formed, each group is given a naming label and sorted by the level of scale assessment of technical, physical, and emotional aspects, as shown in Table 7. In this stage the names for each group are summarized as follows: emotional factors, interface factors, and basic factors.

Table 6. Kansei words grouped based on similarity in the context of their meaning.

Ambiance				Design image
Color	Fit	Shape	Functionality & convenience	Sense of material
New combination				Unexpected application

Table 7. Labeling the Kansei words grouped.

Emotional factor			Ambience		Design image
Interface factor	Color	Fit	Shape	Functionality & Convenience	Sense of material
Basic factor			New combination		Unexpected application

Data resulting from the "Rating-scaled types used" stage yields the arrangement in Figure 1. Arrangement formed from this stage can be an indication of the stages of prospective users in making decisions to choose or buy motorcycle products offered in the market.

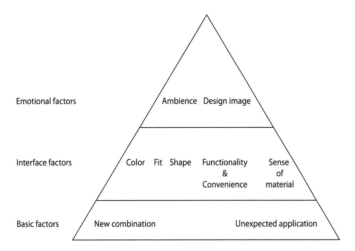

Figure 1. Grouping factors that arise from the participants' chosen opinions.

4 CONCLUSION

In Figure 2, it can be seen that the three groups of factors created influence each other in creating/forming subjective factors of potential users in choosing and deciding to buy certain motorcycle products. Basic factors are usually the most common things that prospective users consider in making their choices, but after the basic factors are felt to be appropriate then the next consideration is interface factors which include the visual appearance of the product such as color, fit, shape, functionality & convenience, and sense of material, whereas emotional factors are very personal in nature and determine the final decision of the prospective user to buy a product even though under certain conditions these emotional factors may not be present in the consideration of prospective users in deciding to buy a particular product. These three factors influence each other and form subjective factors for potential users of the product.

When prospective users discuss a motorcycle model/type, what they will pay attention to and ask first is "what advantages does it offer?" Or "what is the novelty offered by that model/type compared to others?" This is a very basic and hallo-point thing, and if the prospective user feels/finds something interesting in this level then the process of determining the choice will continue to other

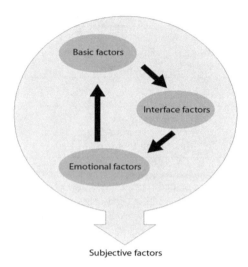

Subjective factors

Figure 2.   Kansei words group relations in the formation of subjective factors.

factors. But for some prospective users and in particular conditions this also could be enough and then they will decide to buy it or not buy it.

In the next stage, prospective users will look for whether a particular model/type has the color, fit, shape, functionality & convenience, and several models/types of motorcycle products on the market. Specifically, for the sense of material prospective users will see whether the products are different from one another in terms of finishing material, and this sense of material will determine that one product is made of higher quality compared to rival products in the view of prospective users.

In the most relaxed conditions where prospective users have more free time and funds, the consideration for choosing and buying a motorcycle product will go to the level of emotional factors, where potential buyers make their choice on the ambiance factors and image design of a motorcycle-like product that will be chosen.

REFERENCES

Goebert, B. and Rosenthal, H. M. 2001. Beyond listening: Learning the secret language of focus groups. New York: J. Wiley. URL for chapter 1: Listening 101: The Value of Focus Groups. http//www.wileyeurope.com/cda/cover/0,,0471395625%7Cexcerpt,00.pdf.

Kunifuji, S. 2013. A Japanese problem-solving approach: the KJ-Ho method. Proceedings of KICSS'2013, pp. 333–338. Progress & Business Publishers, Kraków.

Levy, P., Lee, S., and Yamanaka, T. 2007. On Kansei and Kansei Design a Description of Japanese Design Approach. Proceedings of the 2nd World Conference on Design Research, 1–18.

Norman, D. A. 2004. Emotional Design: Why we love (or hate) everyday things. New York. Basic Books.

Nagasawa, S. 2002. Kansei and Business, Kansei Engineering International Journal, 3:2–12.

Phua, S. J., Keong Ng, W., Liu, H., Song, B., and Li, X. 2007. A Rule Mining Approach To Emotional Design In Mass Customization. International Conference on Engineering Design. ICED.

Schutte, S., Eklund, J., Ishihara, S., and Nagamichi, M. 2008. Affective meaning: The Kansei Engineering Approach. In: Schifferstein, H.N.J., and Hekkert, P. (Editors). 2008. Product Experience. Elsevier.

Scupin, R. 1997. The KJ Method: A Technique for Analyzing Data Derived from Japanese Ethnology. Human Organization, 56(2):233–237.

Tama, I. P., Azlia, W., and Hardiningtyas, D. 2015. Development of Customer-Oriented Product Design using Kansei Engineering and Kano Model: Case Study of Ceramic Souvenir. *Procedia Manufacturing*, 4(Iess):328–335.

Dynamics of Industrial Revolution 4.0: Digital Technology Transformation and Cultural Evolution –
Wulandari et al (eds)
© 2021 The Author(s), ISBN 978-1-032-04451-4

Application of *Soga Tingi* (Ceriops Tagal) as an alternative eco-friendly textile color

A. Hendrawan
Telkom University, Bandung, Indonesia

S. Mohamad
Universiti Sains Malaysia, Pulau Penang, Malaysia

W. Listianingrum
Telkom University, Bandung, Indonesia

ABSTRACT: The negative impact of synthetic dyes caused natural dyes to be widely applied as an alternative method of textile coloring in Indonesia. This matter was supported by the Indonesian government and society, especially the fashion industry, as utilizing natural ingredients is a method for eco-friendly textile coloring. One of the materials that can be used as a natural dye is *soga tingi*. *Soga tingi* contains a natural pigment named tannin that could be produced as a brown coloring extract. This extract can be produced by boiling the bark of the old *soga* tree, in addition to exploring the potency of *soga tingi* as natural dyes using the extraction method. This research aims to find the color variation of *soga tingi* extract using three kinds of mordant: alum, iron, and whiting. The extract can be applied in the textile product as eco-friendly natural dyes.

Keywords: Natural Dye, *Soga Tingi*, Textile Dyes, Eco-friendly, Extraction, Mordant

1   INTRODUCTION

Natural dyes are alternative textile dyes that are non-toxic, can be renewable, are easily degraded, and environmentally friendly (Pujilestari 2015). Using natural materials as textile dyes could preserve natural resources, improve the community's economy, and add cultural value to its products. Natural dyes have great potential to be developed.

The use of natural dyes in textiles has been widely applied in Indonesia. One of the natural ingredients that can be used as a natural dye is *soga tingi*. *Soga tingi*'s bark (*Ceriops tagal*) contains tannins that can produce a reddish-brown color on the fabric. (Jansen et al. in Pujilestari, 2015). This extract is obtained by boiling bark from *soga* trees with air solvent. Natural coloring agents can be obtained by extracting from various parts of the plant using air solvents at high or low temperatures. (Purnomo in Pujilestari, 2015). Based on the description above, the author sees the potential possessed by high-purity *soga* plants to be processed and made as natural dyes. This study found color variations produced by *soga tingi* extract with three types of mordant, namely alum, iron, and whiting using the hot dipping method and six time variations namely 10 minutes, 20 minutes, 30 minutes, 40 minutes, 50 minutes, and 60 minutes.

Data

Natural dyes
We can obtain natural coloring agents for textiles from the extraction of various parts of plants such as roots, stems, leaves, bark, flowers, and fruit. Each plant can be a coloring agent and produce distinct colors, depending on the pigment in it. Some plants have pigments that are naturally formed in them. Some also form during heating, storage, or processing. According to Susanto (1973) in Handayani (2015) some plants that can be used as natural dyes includeL

- Nila Leaf *(Indigofera Sp.)*
- Jelawe Fruit *(Terminalia belerica)*
- *Soga tingi* bark (*Ceriops candolleana arn*)
- *Secang* (*Caesalpinia sappan L*)
- *Tegeran* Wood *(Cudraina javanensis)*
- Turmeric (*Curcuma*)
- Tea (*Tea*)
- Noni Root (*Morinda citrifelia*)
- *Soga jambal's* bark (*Pelthophorum ferruginum*)
- Kesumba *(Bixa orelana)*
- Guava Leaf *(Psidium guajava).*

Soga plants

Soga plants (*Peltophorum pterocarpum*) are a group of plants used as batik dyes whose wood ranges from reddish-brown to black. They can be classified as legumes (Fabaceae or Leguminosae) which spread in Asia. There are three types of *soga* trees that are usually used including Jambal (*Peltophorum pterocarpum*), *Tegeran* (*Cudraina javanensis*), and *Tingi* (*Ceriops Tagal*). Jambal produces a reddish-brown color from the woody trunk, and when the flowers blossom, this tree will be lively with bunches of flowers that appear in unison; that's why this plant is called a yellow flame three or yellow flamboyant. *Tegeran* is a thorny shrub tree that is used as a maker of yellow on fabric. This tree is spread in Java, Kalimantan, and Sulawesi, and when used as a natural coloring agent veteran or yellow wood needs to be extracted and given fixation or reinforcing material. *Tingi* is a clump of shrubs with compound leaves clustered at the ends of the branches. This plant at a glance is similar to mangrove plants but smaller. *Tingi* bark is used as a producer of a dark brownish-red in textiles (Musman and Arini (2011) in Prasetya 2018). *Tingi* bark used as a dye is old bark because young *tingi* bark has an inferior quality with low tannin content (Jansen et al. (2005) in Handayani, 2015).

2   METHOD

This study uses an experimental method in the form of extraction of *soga* bark to become a coloring agent. The material needed is 1 kg of tall wood and 2 L of water which is then boiled for 1 hr, and the tools necessary are pans, stoves, scales, tongs, measuring cups, used cloth, and bottles. The extraction process begins by boiling high wood with a water solvent for 1 hour until the water volume is reduced by half. Then cool the extract before filtering it using a used cloth. The purpose of this filtering is to separate the extract from the dirt in the form of small pieces of wood and powder. Finally, the extract is put into a bottle and stored in the refrigerator where the extract can last for 14 days.

3   RESULTS & DISCUSSION

The dyeing process is carried out on a baby canvas fabric 10 cm x 10 cm in size to get color variations from the three types of mordants used. Immersion is carried out with six time variations: 10 minutes, 20 minutes, 30 minutes, 40 minutes, 50 minutes, and 60 minutes. The results of dyeing using *soga tingi* extract are shown in Table 1.

Table 1.   Dyeing exploration with whiting.

Mordan Akhir Kapur						
Waktu	10 Menit	20 Menit	30 Menit	40 Menit	50 Menit	60 Menit
Hasil						

Dyeing results in 10 minutes produce a peach color (pale pink with a slight mixture of orange). Dyeing results for 20–30 minutes produce a dark peach color with a less significant color difference. After 40–60 minutes, dyeing results produce orange with a mix of a little pastel pink.

Table 2. Dyeing exploration with whiting + alum.

Mordan Akhir Kapur + Tawas						
Waktu	10 Menit	20 Menit	30 Menit	40 Menit	50 Menit	60 Menit
Hasil						

The results of dyeing with whiting fixers and alum produce a dark peach color to brick red. The results of dyeing in 10–20 minutes tend to be the same, as well as color dyeing for 30–50 minutes. In comparison, the 60-minute dyeing results produce a brick red color.

Table 3. Dyeing exploration with alum.

Mordan Akhir Tawas						
Waktu	10 Menit	20 Menit	30 Menit	40 Menit	50 Menit	60 Menit
Hasil						

The results of the dyeing of 10–30 minutes produce a light brick red color. For dyeing results after 40–50 minutes, the resulting color is darker than the dyeing time of 10–30 minutes, but the colors are not mixed evenly, leaving an impression of being faded. As for the 60-minute dyeing result, the resulting color is more balanced.

Table 4. Dyeing exploration with alum + iron.

Mordan Akhir Tawas + Tunjung						
Waktu	10 Menit	20 Menit	30 Menit	40 Menit	50 Menit	60 Menit
Hasil						

The results of dyeing using alum fixation + iron produce a brown wood color. For a result of 10–40 minutes, the color produced tends to be the same as a barely noticeable comparison. As for the results of 50–60 minutes, the color produced is dark brown wood.

Table 5. Dyeing exploration with iron.

Mordan Akhir Tunjung						
Waktu	10 Menit	20 Menit	30 Menit	40 Menit	50 Menit	60 Menit
Hasil						

The color results from the exploration of dyeing by using a fixator tend to be the same as a slight change at any time. However, 60 minutes of dyeing is different as it results in a blackish-brown color.

Table 6. Dyeing exploration with iron + whiting.

Mordan Akhir Tunjung + Kapur						
Waktu	10 Menit	20 Menit	30 Menit	40 Menit	50 Menit	60 Menit
Hasil						

The color produced from exploration with a time of 10–20 minutes produces a light brick red. Dyeing results after 30–40 minutes produce brown with a mixture of brick red and dyeing results for 50–60 minutes produce a dark brown color.

Table 7. Dyeing exploration with iron + whiting + alum.

Mordan Akhir Tunjung + Kapur						
Waktu	10 Menit	20 Menit	30 Menit	40 Menit	50 Menit	60 Menit
Hasil						

The immersion results by combining the three mordants, iron + whiting + alum, produce a color that is almost the same as exploration using alum + iron fixator. The results of the 10–20 minutes color display brown with a mixture of slightly red brick, while for the results of 30–50 minutes produce a wood brown color. For 60 minutes, dyeing results produce colors such as the color of teak wood.

4 CONCLUSION

We can use most plants as coloring agents. This is because the pigment content in them is like tannins, flavonoids, carotene, and anthocyanin which can produce color. The parts of plants that can be extracted as natural dyes include roots, stems, bark, leaves, flowers, and fruit. The extraction method can get natural coloring agents using a water solvent. We can apply the extraction results as textile dyes by hot or cold dyeing methods. Immersion with variations in time and mordant can produce distinct colors. The results of the experiments showed that dyeing for a short time produces a light/pale color while dyeing for a long time can produce dark colors.

REFERENCES

Aini, R. (2017). *Identifikasi Keanekaragaman Pohon Mangrove di Kawasan Wisata Hutan mangrove Teluk Benoa Bali sebagai Dasar Pembuatan Sumber Belajar Biologi.* Universitas Muhammadiyah Malang; Vol. 2.

Alamsyah. (2018). *Kerajinan Batik dan Pewarnaan Alami.* Endogami: Jurnal Ilmiah Kajian Antropologi, *1*(2), 136. https://doi.org/10.14710/endogami.1.2.136-148

Farida. (2016). *Pengaruh Variasi Bahan Pra Mordant pada Pewarnaan Batik Menggunakan Akar Mengkudu (Morinda citrifolia).* Dinamika Kerajinan Dan Batik: Majalah Ilmiah, 32(1), 1. https://doi.org/10.22322/dkb.v32i1.1164

Haffida, A. A. N. (2017). *Ektraksi Zat Tanin Dari Bahan Alami Dengan Metode Steam Extraction. Ektraksi Zat Tanin Dari Bahan Alami Dengan Metode Steam Extraction.* Retrieved from http://repository.its.ac.id/47639/7/2314030091-2314030112-Non-Degree.pdf

Handayani, P. (2015). Jurnal Bahan Alam Terbarukan. *Jurnal Bahan Alam Terbarukan,* 4(1), 14–20. https://doi.org/10.15294/jbat.v4i1.3769

Koswara, S. (2009). *Pewarna Alami: Produksi dan Pengolahannya.* Retrieved from http://tekpan.unimus.ac.id/wp-content/uploads/2013/07/PEWARNAALAMI.pdf

Neraca. (2015). *Kemenperin: Kemenperin Gencar Kembangkan Pewarna Alami.* Retrieved February 17, 2020, from kementrian perindustrian website: https://kemenperin.go.id/artikel/13256/Kemenperin-Gencar-Kembangkan-Pewarna-Alami

Prasetya, G. (2018). *Batik Warna Alam Soga di Home Industry Louby Batik Banyuripan, Bayat, Klaten,* Vol. 10.

Pujilestari, T. (2015). *Review?: Sumber dan Pemanfaatan Zat Warna Alam untuk Keperluan Industri (Review?: Source and Utilization of Natural Dyes for Industrial Use).* Dinamika Kerajinan Dan Batik.

Sulistiami and Fatonah, N. (2013). *Penggunaan Penguat Jenis Mordant dan Daun Jambu terhadap Hasil Pewarnaan Teknik Ikat Celup pada Kain Katun.* Jurnal Buana Pendidikan, 9(13).

Dynamics of Industrial Revolution 4.0: Digital Technology Transformation and Cultural Evolution –
Wulandari et al (eds)
© 2021 The Author(s), ISBN 978-1-032-04451-4

Social media branding on Instagram account @recharge.id

M. Hidayattulloh & F. Maharani
Telkom University, Bandung, Indonesia

ABSTRACT: At present, social media is not only used as personal documentation but also as media branding for businesses in Indonesia. Recharge is an application-based power bank rental service provider company using Instagram in branding through the official account @recharge.id. Through this account, Recharge posts images, videos, and captions that are in accordance with product positioning. This study aims to analyze the form of social media branding that can increase consumer confidence related to a product. Through this study, researchers will analyze social media branding on the official Recharge Instagram account, @recharge.id. This research uses a qualitative method with a case study approach. Apart from that, this research uses social media branding theory which is supported by theories from advertising and visual communication design. In this study, the authors conclude that the use of social media as media branding with product positioning support will foster consumer knowledge and beliefs related to a product.

Keywords: branding, social media branding, Instagram branding, power bank, Recharge

1 INTRODUCTION

The increase in smartphone usage also facilitated the access to social media. The presence of mobile-based social media applications allows smartphone users to access social media anytime and anywhere. Based on data released by We Are Social, there are 160 million active social media users in Indonesia and an increase of 10 million users compared to 2019. Based on this data, the five social media sites that are most often accessed by the Indonesian are YouTube, WhatsApp, Facebook, Instagram, and Twitter (inet.detik.com, accessed July 9, 2020).

From a number of social media sites that exist today, Instagram is a social media app that is often used by various businesses to carry out the branding process. A large number of Instagram users are businesses that cannot be separated from their ability to upload a variety of content such as videos, images, and text and allowed to comment between account holders and the public, making Instagram widely used for promotional and branding purposes (Hidayattuloh & Riandy 2019).

Of the many businesses that use Instagram as media branding, Recharge which is an IoT- (Internet of Things) based company providing application-based power bank rental services in Indonesia, has an official account @recharge.id for conducting promotions and product branding. Looking at the Instagram account owned by Recharge, it emphasizes the functional side of its social media branding activities. Information about the type of service and product function that distinguishes it from other product services becomes quite dominant in the content found on Instagram @recharge.id.

In this study, researchers will carry out social media branding analysis from the functional side found on the Instagram account @recharge.id. This research will emphasize aspects of increasing consumer knowledge about the product being compared. Based on the explanation from Davis (2015), social media branding that puts forward the functional aspects allows consumers to recognize the benefits of the product and understand its functionality.

2 RESEARCH METHODS

The object of this research is the image and text content contained in the social media account @recharge.id. To examine the object of research, researchers use the case study method. Case studies can be specific to a single case and can try to understand the case in a particular context, situation, and time (Raco 2010).

As stated in the previous discussion, this research limits the process of social media branding by prioritizing functional aspects to increase understanding of the functions and benefits of these products. According to Davis (2015), increasing product knowledge by consumers in social media branding can be used as a personal experience to consider before carrying out the purchase process. This cannot be separated from the role of social media in providing offers and understanding regarding the services of a product. Nowadays, social media has become a trend among businesses and has the potential to connect consumers easily (Purwidiantoro et al. 2016). Based on exposure by Davis, social media branding does not mean it is aimed at purchase intentions—bringing brands closer and buying are two different things. In social media branding, consumers are basically more interested in obtaining knowledge about the services and offerings of a product. This is inseparable from the role of social media as a tool for researching a product by consumers.

In this study, in addition to theories about social media branding, researchers also use advertising and visual communication design theory to better understand aspects of persuasion that exist in visual and textual social media accounts @ recharge.id. Apart from that, the authors took three Instagram posts containing images and text as research samples that were compatible with the discussion.

3 RESULT AND DISCUSSION

The information technology that is present at this time makes it easy for businesses to get closer to their consumers. The presence of social media is able to provide product-related information to consumers while allowing consumers to engage directly with brands through various activities that exist on social media and make brands live in the minds of consumers (Yusuf 2016). Apart from that, social media has a considerable impact in establishing a relationship between brands and consumers (Semuel & Setiawan 2018)

As explained in the previous discussion, Recharge is a power bank rental service application that is placed in various places. This service is different from the charging stations that already exist, where consumers are required to bring a personal charger to charge their mobile phones.

Looking at the Instagram posts on @recharge.id, it appears that the emphasis on the position of the product values leads to the ease of making power bank rental through applications that are often conveyed in a number of images and captions. Unique product position and the ability to live in the minds of customers is a form of positioning. By definition, positioning is concerned with how to build trust and confidence in consumers and potential customers. Apart from that, positioning can be said to be a starting point in building product differentiation that can compete with its competitors (Kartajaya 2005)

In conducting this research, researchers examined that Instagram was used as media branding for Recharge in conveying product positioning to differentiate it from competitors as well as providing education to consumers in terms of increasing knowledge and trust in Recharge products.

Looking at the content provided on Instagram @recharge.id, information about the type of product is conveyed through an image that is equipped with information containing an affirmation of the type of product service.

Figure 1 is one of the images contained in the account @recharge.id. It is a visualization that resembles a comic panel with text placed in a speech bubble that reads "hati resah karena nggak bawa charger? Solusinya pakai recharge aja!" In the text, there is an affirmation of the products offered. Apart from that, it seems that the situation formed in the sentence is a decrease in mobile phone battery power which is very commonly experienced by the public at the present time. This

Figure 1. Delivery of product positioning through the comic panel. (Image source: www.instagram.com/recharge.id)

is in line with what is expressed by Davis (2015) wherein social media branding demands to be a problem solver for consumers. The use of the comic style in the delivery of messages makes the information conveyed more attractive. By definition, comics are sequences of images arranged in accordance with the purpose of the message to be conveyed (Gumelar 2011). In addition to communicating through comics, the visual style in the picture is conveyed through cartoons. This is very suitable for Recharge's target audience since the cartoon style is very popular among the younger generation (Artawan et al. 2015).

Information about the type of service is not only shown in the text contained in the picture. It also looks at the caption that supports the image which shows descriptive sentences that state the position of the product as an application-based power bank rental service.

Figure 2. A comparison between recharge and recharging station products. (Image source: www.instagram.com/recharge.id)

Unlike the previous image which emphasizes more on informing the product's position, this picture shows the comparative value where the product compared is to its competitors, in this case the charging station that is often found in public facilities. Unlike charging stations where consumers must carry their own smartphone chargers, Recharge places more emphasis on the practical aspects where consumers just rent and use the power bank provided by Recharge. This is in line with what was expressed by Davis (2015) where the use of social media as a media is used to convey the strength of the product where consumers get a picture of the service/use of a product that is tailored to personal experience before deciding on a purchase.

Comparison is one style of advertising in the delivery of messages. In comparison, product promotion is often positioned as superior compared to competing products and directly emphasizes the value of the main message (Suyanto 2006). The comparison value contained in the picture display is charging the mobile battery with a charging station and recharge product.

Apart from the emphasis on aspects of product positioning, Instagram @recharge.id also displays visualizations related to the use of the product. This is because the use of the Recharge power bank is different from the charging station commonly used by the public.

Figure 3. Demonstration of the use of recharge products. (Image source: www.instagram.com/recharge.id)

Looking at Figure 3, we can see the process of using the Recharge power bank application. The picture is displayed through the slide feature on Instagram where each slide contains steps in the process of borrowing a power bank through the recharge application. From an advertising perspective, instructions for use are included in the demonstration style. The demonstration is an ad style designed to illustrate the advantages of a product. This ad style is very effective in convincing consumers about product quality (Suyanto 2005). The use of a delivery style that is able to convince consumers about the product is in line with positioning in branding that aims to convince consumers about a product.

4 CONCLUSION

As one of the most popular social media sites in Indonesia, Instagram is often used by businesses in branding for a number of products, one of which is Recharge. Various features that are owned by Instagram, such as slides, captions, and other features, make it easy for Recharge to convey messages that are in accordance with product positioning to the public. In use of the product, as well as the procedure for borrowing the product. The message is conveyed through a visual and textual style that is in accordance with the condition of the consumer. This is in line with what Davis (2015) stated that in social media branding, consumers are basically more interested in obtaining knowledge about services and product offerings.

REFERENCES

Artawan, C. A., Ketut, N., and Astuti, R. 2015. *Kartun Sebagai Elemen Visual Media Pembelajaran Lalu Lintas Ditlantas Polda Bali*. Segara Widya, 3(1):418–427.
Davis, R. 2015. *Social Media Branding for Small Business: The 5–Sources Model*. New York: Business Expert Press.
Gumelar, M. 2011. *Cara Membuat Komik*. Jakarta: Indeks.
Hidayattuloh, M. and Riandy, A. 2019. *Digital Brand Building of PT Kereta Api Indonesia Indonesia Through Instagram Account @ KAI121* . 6 Th Bandung Creative Movement International Conference in Creative Industries.
Kartajaya, H. 2005. *Positioning diferensiasi brand*. Jakarta: gramedia pustaka utama.
Purwidiantoro, M. H., Kristanto, D. F., and Hadi, W. 2016. *Pengaruh Penggunaan Media Sosial Terhadap Pengembangan Usaha Kecil Menengah (Ukm)*. Jurnal EKA CIDA, *1*(1):30–39. http://journal.amikomsolo.ac.id/index.php/ekacida/article/view/19/11

Raco, J. R. 2010. *Metode Penelltlan Kualltatlf Jenis, Karakteristik, Dan Keunggulannya*. Jakarta; Grasindo.

Semuel, H. and Setiawan, K. Y. 2018. *Promosi Melalui Sosial Media, Brand Awareness, Purchase Intention Pada Produk Sepatu Olahraga*. Jurnal Manajemen Pemasaran, *12*(1):47–52. https://doi.org/10.9744/pemasaran.12.1.47

Suyanto, M. 2005. *Strategi perancangan iklan televisi perusahaan top dunia*. Yogyakarta: Andi.

Suyanto, M. 2006. *Strategi perancangan iklan outdoor kelas dunia*. Yogyakarta: Andi.

Yusuf, F. 2016. Optimalisasi Program Branding Dan Aktivasi Merek Di Era Digital. Jurnal Komunikasi, *7*(1):7–13. http://ejournal.bsi.ac.id/ejurnal/index.php/jkom/article/view/2169/1531

Dynamics of Industrial Revolution 4.0: Digital Technology Transformation and Cultural Evolution –
Wulandari et al (eds)
© 2021 The Author(s), ISBN 978-1-032-04451-4

The innovation application on Batik craft products in the New Normal Era in Indonesia: Does it have an impact?

F. Ciptandi & M.S. Ramadhan
Telkom University, Bandung, Indonesia

ABSTRACT: The purpose of this study is to find out whether the new normal era set by the Indonesian government has an impact on efforts to apply innovation in handicraft products to batik craftsmen. The traditional batik industry in Tuban, East Java was chosen as an example of a case because it is considered to represent other traditional batik industries in Java Island. In the previous study, the strategy of applying the innovation for batik has been carried out successfully using the diffusion of the innovation theory approach by providing an experimental assignment of the innovation application. This study was conducted by analyzing the factors considered as a source of inhibiting the transfer of innovation and its impact using a combination of the design thinking approach and diffusion of innovation ideas. This is useful as one of the solutions today to prepare for the continuation of innovation in the midst of the post-COVID-19 pandemic.

Keywords: innovation, batik, craft, COVID-19

1 INTRODUCTION

COVID-19 positive patients in Indonesia continue to increase. Responding to this condition, the Indonesian government has implemented several policies to anticipate the wider spread of the virus, ranging from physical distancing, a temporary ban on entry into Indonesia, to large-scale social restrictions.

It was only on May 28, 2020 that the Central Government through the Minister of National Development Planning/Head of Bappenas, in a joint press conference with the Foreign Minister as well as the Task Force Team of experts handling COVID-19, presented the Productive and Safe Community Protocol COVID-19 designed to create a new normal to coexist with COVID-19 (Hadi & Supardi 2020). It also targeted several economic activities that were previously stopped and will begin to be reactivated gradually by following the health protocol requirements. However, this condition still has a significant impact on various economic sectors, including the batik handicraft sector.

Since the implementation of the new normal era in Indonesia, the batik handicraft industry sector can no longer stand by the old patterns that have become a comfort zone. In addition to taking part in thinking about practical steps according to health protocols to reduce the spread of the COVID-19 virus, efforts to innovate quickly and precisely in shaping the craftsmen's new behavior in order to compete and survive also need to be considered (Ciptandi 2020).

Innovations, according to this new vision, have been applied in the traditional batik handicraft industry in Kerek District, Tuban Regency, East Java, which was chosen as an example of a case representing other traditional batik industries on Java Island, Indonesia. In 2018, the strategy of applying innovations in batik handicraft products in Tuban was carried out in the conditions before the COVID-19 pandemic and had obtained results, namely: (1) development of the visual appearance of Tuban batik patterns; (2) application of Tuban batik to the appropriate fashion products; and (3) improvement of creativity and the ability to adapt innovations for batik craftsmen. Based on this study, it has been concluded that the batik handicraft industry in Tuban has the ability

DOI 10.1201/9781003193241-28

to adapt well to innovation and has proven by experimental results to be able to produce several innovative designs (Ciptandi 2018).

There is a problem when innovation is to be given to traditional batik in Tuban continuously, which is currently in a new normal condition. In the protocol set by the government, generally, they still have to pay attention to physical distancing, where people are required to keep a distance from others by at least 1 meter and minimize crowding activities and prioritize activities carried out independently from home. At the same time, one of the stages in the diffusion of the innovation approach is persuasive communication from the innovation provider to the batik craftsmen/innovator. In addition to adjusting to the usual communication patterns in the Tuban environment, the other important step is that communication must be carried out intensively and personally by minimizing the distance between the innovation provider and the innovator, especially when conducting experiments together.

2 METHODOLOGY

This research was conducted by analyzing the factors inhibiting the transfer of innovation and the impact by combining the design thinking approach and the diffusion of innovation theory ideas. The diffusion of innovation is used for analysis in the form of communication channels that can be applied as an alternative to persuasive communication (Roger et al. 2019; Chia &Garrett 2010). Design thinking is used at the same time to analyze the risk factors of implementing an innovation during these new normal conditions.

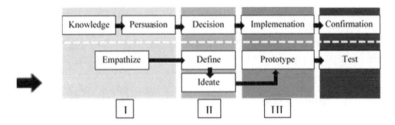

Figure 1. The combination of the design thinking approach and diffusion of innovation idea.

The analysis is done by grouping it into three stages.

1. Stage I: Motivation. It is encouragement that can be a driving force for recipients to accept the challenges of innovation, ranging from the characteristics of the recipient, problems in environmental conditions and social systems, as well as the basic needs of the recipient that must be met and analyzed for the impact of the risks.
2. Stage II: Creativity. It is the origin of ideas and analyzing the impact of the risks so that they are likely to be accepted or rejected.
3. Stage III: Implementation. It is a recommended implementation strategy in the form of a method and prototype, as well as an analysis of the impact of the risks.

3 DISCUSSION

Measuring the extent of the impact of conditions in the new normal era of COVID-19, by the process of applying innovation in the development of motifs on traditional batik crafts in Tuban, was carried out in accordance with Figure 2.

3.1 *Motivation stage*

Motivation factors as a driver for innovation to be possibly carried out, including: (1) recipient characteristics, namely Tuban people; (2) Tuban social system variables; and (3) community needs

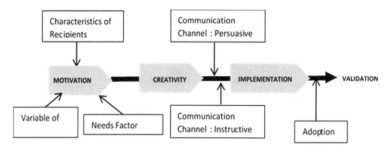

Figure 2. Analysis process of applying innovation of motifs development.

factors. The three motivational factors are analyzed based on the risks that might have an impact due to conditions in the new normal era, including:

1. Problem. In terms of characteristics, Tuban people are generally categorized into three mentality groups: (1) traditional; (2) moderate; and (3) modern. Based on the numbers, it is dominated by groups with moderate mentalities who have problems about how to interact with innovators who represent modern mentalities and traditional craftsmen who represent traditional mentalities. Additionally, the social system also presents problems in the form of interpersonal relationships that are stretched because they are overshadowed by feelings of fear and anxiety by the COVID-19 case. Then, the economic problems were caused by a decrease in market demand, so that production activity declined and product design development activities were stopped.
2. Opportunities. There are still opportunities that can be optimized, namely by targeting Tuban community groups who have a moderate and modern mentality to become open to change again. The attitude of the people with this mentality tends to be open to change and optimistic as proven in previous studies that have succeeded in creating various design developments. In addition, another opportunity is that encouragement to economic needs will force a person to continue to make an effort to continue his/her living.

The motivational stage in the new normal era can be focused on Tuban groups with a moderate mentality. The drive of motivation is supported more by the issue of how the production process does not stop for an economic turnaround.

3.2 Creativity stage

The creativity stage is carried out to develop the design of traditional batik handicraft products starting from the process of identifying, discussing, to prototyping (Tung 2012) and taking into account the conditions in the current new normal era, including the following.

1. Identifying. At the motivation stage, it has been concluded that innovation can be applied to community groups with a moderate mentality with the greatest motivation driven by economic needs. Furthermore, at the identifying stage, it is necessary to make a comprehensive thought process about what can be offered as a solution.
2. Discussing. At this stage, the researcher or designer needs to have a discussion by involving several parties outside himself, to get input for ideas so that the decisions taken will not be subjective.
3. Prototyping. At this stage, the results can be in the form of product prototypes or strategy recommendations in the form of methods that can be done to realize creative ideas that can be applied by craftsmen (Trussler & Beckett 2016), especially under the conditions of (the) new normal era.

At this stage, the biggest challenge is to formulate the problem to come to the right needed solution. The risk of this stage is that the results, offered as a solution, do not have an absolute measure of success. Moreover, especially in the conditions of the new normal era, there are new conditions that have not been experienced before, either by the innovator or the adopters, so that in the identifying stage, it is necessary to conduct research on the characteristics and effects of conditions in this new normal era. The key to success at this stage is an understanding of the characteristics of the conditions of the new normal era and the influence on people's needs.

3.3 *Implementation stage*

The implementation stage is the process of implementing solutions resulted (resulting) from the creativity stage. In the conditions of this new normal era, this implementation stage is closely related to communication channels.

The communication channel consists of two things, the first is persuasion, which is the most influential in transferring innovation to craftsmen, especially because in new normal conditions there are distance restrictions and frequency limits for meetings that are intense. Therefore, with this condition, there is a distance that slows the process of transfer of innovation through communication. This not only happens between innovators to innovator craftsmen but also from innovators to other adopters. Other communication channels are instructive, which is a communication form carried out to provide work instructions in the form of experimental assignments to craftsmen.

The thing that has the most impact on changing conditions entering the new normal era is the communication channel. Communication patterns that were previously intense and personal must be slowly changed with the communication model by involving third parties as a connector of information. These third parties can be selected from the indigenous Tuban community groups who represent a modern mentality that is accustomed to online communication patterns both via mobile phones and other online platforms.

It is also necessary to anticipate the possibility of risks that will arise, one of which is the received information that is misunderstood, so that the resulted (resulting) form of innovation is not achieved. To minimize this condition means to always carry out repeated confirmation processes to ensure the information provided has been received correctly, and to communicate more frequently, at least double the number of common communication frequencies (Fogg 2009).

4 CONCLUSIONS

This study resulted in several considerations in conducting innovation to traditional batik handicraft products in the midst of the new normal era of COVID-19, i.e., first by identifying the factors inhibiting the transfer of innovation and risk factors by using a combined approach of design thinking and diffusion of innovation theory ideas. The results of the analysis include the following.

1. The motivation stage can be focused on the Tuban community group with a moderate mentality and the motivation can be lifted from the issue of economic needs.
2. The creativity stage needs to strengthen the identifying process to understand the characteristics of the conditions of the new normal era and the influence on the needs of the community and be open to receive suggestions and input from parties outside the designer/researcher. This process needs to be done in-depth and not in a hurry so that it can be more precise in continuing the prototyping process.
3. The implementation stage is carried out by changing the communication model with the involvement of third parties as a connector of information from the Tuban native community group that represents a modern mentality and is accustomed to online communication patterns. In this type of online communication, it is also necessary to repeat the confirmation process with more frequencies, at least double from the usual number of communication frequencies.

In the final stage, there is a validation stage which is a process of measuring the level of success in realizing an innovation idea given by the innovator. This stage can be developed in further research.

REFERENCES

Chia, C. F. and Garrett, T. C. 2010. *Diffusion of Innovations Theory*, in Handbook of Research on Contemporary Theoretical Models in Information Systems 242–276. IGI Global.

Ciptandi, F. 2020. Strategies for improving workers' skills through crafts product innovation, *Int. J. Psychosoc. Rehabilitation* 24(7):8295–8301.

Ciptandi, F. 2018. *Transformation on Design of Gedog Weaving and Traditional 'Tuban' Batik Decoration Through Visual Characteristic Experiment*, Institut Teknologi Bandung: Indonesia.

Fogg, B. 2009. A Behavior Model for Persuasive Design, *Proc. Intern. The 4th International Conference on Persuasive Technology – Persuasive 2009*. New York.

Hadi, S. and Supardi. 2020. Revitalization Strategy for Small and Medium Enterprises after Corona Virus Disease Pandemic (Covid-19) in Yogyakarta, *J. XI'AN Univ. Archit. Technol* 12(4).

Rogers, E. M., Singhal, A., and Quinlan, M.M. 2019. *Diffusion of Innovations 1, in An Integrated Approach to Communication Theory and Research*, 3rd ed. 415–434. Routledge.

Trussler, H. S., Sharp, and Beckett, R. 2016. *Innovation through craft: Opportunities for growth*, 1st ed. Craft Council: United Kingdom.

Tung, F. W. 2012. Weaving with rush: Exploring craft-design collaborations in revitalizing a local craft, *Int. J. Des.* 6(3):71–84.

Dynamics of Industrial Revolution 4.0: Digital Technology Transformation and Cultural Evolution –
Wulandari et al (eds)
© 2021 The Author(s), ISBN 978-1-032-04451-4

Package design color preference using eye-tracking technology: Does gender make a difference?

W. Swasty
Telkom University, Bandung, Indonesia

E. Rahmawati
Universiti Sains Malaysia, Pulau Penang, Malaysia

A. Mustikawan & M.I.P. Koesoemadinata
Telkom University, Bandung, Indonesia

ABSTRACT: Studies focusing on gender differences regarding color preferences in the application of package design seems to be scarce. This study aims to reveal the gender differences in
color package design preference and to recommend what color factor to best to apply for package
design using eye-tracking technology. A study of eye-tracking was conducted. T-test and one-way
Anova followed by the Tukey Post Hoc test were used to test if there is a difference in fixation count
based on the colors presented. The study found no difference in color preference between male and
female participants. It revealed that brown, as well as yellow, has no significant difference in color
preferences.

Keywords: Color, Eye-tracking, Gender, Packaging, Preference

1   INTRODUCTION

Most researchers in color used a questionnaire survey (both online and offline) as a method of
investigating color preference (Wei et al. 2008; Ou et al. 2012; Seher et al. 2012; Bakker et al.
2013; Westland and Shin 2015; Yu et al. 2018). However, a study by Bakker et al. (2013) argues that
it is hard to draw valid and reliable conclusions on color responses using questionnaires in color
research. An eye-tracking observation method was used to objectively identify the color preference
of study participants to investigate the feasibility of deriving color preferences by defining fixations
and relevant details (Lee et al. 2005). Other researchers in color used eye-tracking as an investigation
method on color preference (Cho &Suh 2020).

Swasty et al. (2019) used two different methods (questionnaire and eye-tracking) and suggested
that the visual data from the eye-tracking method is more accurate than data from the questionnaire
as a sense of vision is unconscious (Apsari 2012). The main purpose is to find out which areas
attract the most attention (number of fixations) and identify the color and image combination
factors on the packaging that more people preferred. The study revealed that the brown color used
in monster illustrations is the most preferable combination of color and image for the chocolate-
flavored banana chip package design. However, the study results obtained are still general, and did
not show any differences in color preference between male and female respondents.

Eye-tracking is a tool for analyzing the visual attention related to consumers' emotional and
cognitive responses from the neuro-marketing perspective (dos Santos et al. 2015). Eye-tracking
technology can be an effective eye movement measurement tool for saccades (scan paths) and
fixations (pause of the eye movements). It provides objective data on the cognitive processes and
emotion as well as identifies where and how long a viewer looks in the Area of Interest (AOI).
It also indentifies the eye movement time-based sequence to describe the correlation between the
tendency of viewers to gaze at certain stimulus and their preferences (Cho &Suh 2020).

Another study by Husić-Mehmedović et al. (2017) using eye-tracking technology contributes to packaging design studies to explore which package features in the beer category (cans)influence consumer attention and subsequent evaluation packages. The study shows that color might determine—in the category of products that have a standard form (cans)— when color plays an important role.

The relationship between color preference, gender identity, and personality traits was investigated by Bonnardel and Lamming (2010). Making use of 16 stimuli of the D15 color vision panel test displayed in triads on 4x4 cm cards, they argue that gender color preferences deliver the meaning of distinguishing nature. Bonnardel et al. (2018) investigated the gender difference in color preference among British and Indians young adults. Using 16 stimuli based on the Farnsworth D15 test in triads on 4-cm squared cards, they confirmed a gender difference in both cultures. Zhang et al. (2019) investigated the association between age, gender difference, and color preference in Chinese adults by evaluating how much they prefer each of the 31 colors on a 9-point scale to provide color perception in culture-specific characteristics.

The study by Krosse (2018) aims to explore which complementary warm and cold colors males and females prefer the most in a color wheel. Then he investigates whether males and females will give a higher rating for the colors taken from the first study related to their gender than the colors that belonged to the other gender. The results found that both males and females gave higher ratings to the two female colors (derived from the first study). In other words, the result indicates no difference in color preference between males and females.

A pilot study was conducted to reveal the most important color factor to apply for package design. From a questionnaire of 110 respondents, it was revealed that 41% of them mostly agree that color should inform the flavor/variant of the product, followed by brand identity factor (31%), and product category factor (26%), respectively.

Studies focusing on gender differences regarding color preferences for the application in package design seems to be scarce. Most studies focus on gender differences in color preferences in general. Therefore, this study will only focus on color as the extant study pointed out that the most important and attractive factor in packaging is the color element (Babolhavaeji et al. 2015). The objective of this study is to reveal the gender differences in package design color preferences using eye-tracking technology, as the extant study suggests gender differences were discovered and interpreted in terms of visual attention (Cuesta et al. 2018). Another objective is to recommend what color factor best to apply for package design (should it inform the product category or inform flavor/variant).

2 METHOD

2.1 Stimuli

The object of this study is a chocolate-flavored banana chips package design that only focuses on color as a design element. There are four objects with different colors: yellow, brown, white, and purple. The yellow color is associated with the banana product, brown is associated with coco flavor, the white as a neutral color is associated with a private brand, and purple is the contrast color to yellow that is not associated with both product and flavor.

2.2 Subjects

This study was aimed at adolescents and young adults, ages 15–30 based on the classification of Yarlagadda et al. (2015). Forty people participated as respondents who were selected randomly. There were 20 male and 20 female participants. Respondents who participated were required to have normal color vision (as tested by the Ishihara Pseudo-isochromatic Plates) and minimum vision -3D (still clear without using glasses so that the data obtained is valid).

2.3 Procedure

First, participants were given instructions to assess the color of the packaging that was suitable for the packaging of chocolate-flavored banana chips based on their preference. The instructions were delivered in Bahasa. Then they were shown four objects on each slide. Those four objects were displayed four times with the order of color displayed randomly to eliminate the tendency of looking at the central point or from left to right. The four slides were displayed to the respondents for 10 seconds. This is based on the information of Rowan (2010) in Apsari (2012) that buyers generally spend 10 seconds observing a product category in a supermarket display. Data collected were the fixation amounts. Before starting the eye-tracking recording, the calibration was performed on each respondent to detect the position of the user's eye view on the monitor. This is to ensure the data collected are valid.

This eye-tracking study was carried out in the Laboratory of Labor Design Analysis and Ergonomics of the Industrial Engineering Study Program at Parahyangan University, Bandung, Indonesia using hardware and software Tobi X2- 30 from Tobii Studio. The data collected were the fixation counts which were the number of times the eye gaze paused in a spot within the AOI (Bergstrom &Schall 2014) to investigate how often the areas were viewed. The data was then processed by displaying the AOI of each displayed image. The collected data were analyzed concerning the average duration of fixation.

2.4 Data analysis

To analyze data, this study used independent sample T-tests and ANOVA to determine if there were any differences in the color preference of a particular grouping variable, i.e., gender.

3 RESULT & DISCUSSION

3.1 Eye-tracking study

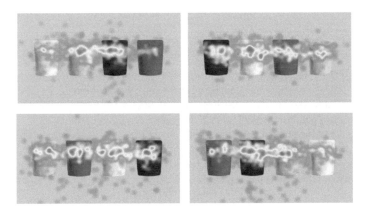

Figure 1. Heatmap results of four display slides based on fixation count.

Figure 1 illustrates that the heat map uses different colors to show the participant fixation count and the length of time they spent looking at the areas (Bergstrom &Schall 2014). The red color indicates the highest fixation count or the longest time, while green indicates the least. Zero fixation count means that the participant has not fixated on the AOI by the end of the recording (Tobii Technology AB 2012).

3.2 The analysis of gender differences in fixation count

A T-test was performed to confirm if the eye movements were influenced by color preference. On the average condition, there is no difference infixation count between males and females on the four colors presented. Details of the difference analysis results are presented in Table 1.

One-way ANOVA followed by the Tukey Post Hoc test was used to test if there was a difference in fixation count based on the colors presented. In short, this test was performed to see which

Table 1. Comparison analysis results of the mean fixation based on gender.

No	Color	t	p	Mean		SEM	
				Male	Female	Male	Female
1	Brown	−0.500	0.621	5.050	5.513	0.455	0.805
2	Yellow	0.238	0.813	4.588	4.425	0.439	0.524
3	White	.031	0.975	3.975	2.153	0.482	0.648
4	Purple	.457	0.650	3.638	3.338	0.410	0.513

Table 2. Analysis results of the comparison of mean fixation by color.

No	Color	p
1	Brown*Yellow	.194
2	Brown*White	.047
3	Brown*Purple	.004
4	Yellow*White	.252
5	Yellow*Purple	.011
6	White*Purple	.313

Table 3. Mean value and standard deviation of the four colors presented.

No	Color	Mean	SD
1	Brown	5.28	2.89
2	Yellow	4.51	2.14
3	White	3.96	2.52
4	Purple	3.49	2.06

color of the four the participants most preferred. The results of the analysis showed there was a significant difference in the fixation count between the four given colors ($F_{(3.117)} = 4.23$, $p < 0.05$). The subjects tended to see brown and yellow more than other colors. A detailed analysis of the difference in fixation count on the colors displayed is presented in Table 2.

From the results of the signification test (Table 3), there was no significant difference between yellow and brown. The highest rating was given to the brown color (5.28), but it makes no difference from yellow. It can be concluded that these two colors can be alternative options in designing chocolate-flavored banana chips packaging.

4 CONCLUSION

This study utilized eye-tracking technology as color preference can be denoted by people's eye movements (Babolhavaeji et al. 2015). The objective of this study was to reveal the gender differences in color package design preference and to recommend what color factor best to apply for package design using eye-tracking technology. The results confirmed a study by Krosse (2018) that found no difference in color preference between male and female participants. From the study, it revealed that brown, as well as yellow, has no significant difference in color preference for chocolate-flavored banana chips package design. Thus, for practical implication, designers or brand owners can use color that informs the flavor/variant of the product (as suggested from the pilot study), as well as color that indicates the product category for alternative color.

Furthermore, the results would allow the brand owner to develop relationships with customers when packaging can be generated according to the expectations of each consumer gender group and thus make the visual elements of packaging more appealing to them. However, this study is limited to the same age group (adolescents and young adults between 15 and 30 years-old) and country (Bandung-Indonesia). Further studies could also compare the gender contrast between different ages, cultures, and countries.

REFERENCES

Apsari, S. 2012. *Analisis kombinasi faktor pada packaging produk shampoo dengan menggunakan metode eye-tracking skripsi.* Universitas Indonesia.

Babolhavaeji, M., Vakilian, M. A., and Slambolchi, A. 2015. The role of product color in consumer behavior. *Advanced Social Humanities and Management*, 2(1), pp. 9–15.

Bakker, I. et al. 2013 The use of questionnaires in color research in real-life settings: in search of validity and methodological pitfalls. *Theoretical Issues in Ergonomics Science.* Taylor & Francis, pp. 1–15. doi: 10.1080/1463922X.2013.815287.

Bergstrom, J. R. and Schall, A. J. 2014. *Eye Tracking in User Experience Design.* Massachusetts: Morgan Kaufmann–Elsevier.

Bonnardel, V. et al. 2018. Gender difference in color preference across cultures: An archetypal pattern modulated by a female cultural stereotype. *Color Research and Application*, 43(2), pp. 209–223. doi: 10.1002/col.22188.

Bonnardel, V. and Lamming, L. 2010. Gender differences in color preference: personality and gender schemata factors., in *The 2nd CIE Expert Symposium on Appearance.* The University of Winchester.

Cho, J. Y. and Suh, J. 2020. Spatial color efficacy in perceived luxury and preference to stay: an eye-tracking study of retail interior environment. *Frontiers in Psychology*, 11, pp. 1–15. doi: 10.3389/fpsyg.2020.00296.

Cuesta, U., Niño, J. I., and Martínez, L. 2018. Neuromarketing: Analysis of Packaging Using Gsr, Eye-Tracking and Facial Expression, in *The European Conference on Media, Communication & Film*, The International Academic Forum. Available at: www.iafor.org.

De Krosse, D. 2018. *Fifty shades of web design: A study on gender differences in color preferences regarding perceived aesthetics and usability in web design.* Utrecht University.

dos Santos, R. D. O. J. et al. 2015. Eye tracking in neuromarketing: a research agenda for marketing studies. *International Journal of Psychological Studies*, 7(1), pp. 32–42. doi: 10.5539/ijps.v7n1p32.

Husić-Mehmedović, M. et al. 2017. Seeing is not necessarily liking: Advancing research on package design with eye-tracking. *Journal of Business Research*, Elsevier Inc., 80, pp. 145–154. doi: 10.1016/j.jbusres.2017.04.019.

Lee, T.-R., Tang, D., and Tsai, C.-M. 2005. Exploring color preference through eye tracking. *AIC Color 05 - 10th Congress of the International Color Association*, pp. 333–336.

Ou, L. C. et al. 2012. Age effects on color emotion, preference, and harmony. *Color Research and Application*, 37(2), pp. 92–105. doi: 10.1002/col.20672.

Seher, T. et al. 2012. Impact of colors on advertisement and packaging on buying behavior. *Management Science Letters*, 2(6), pp. 2085–2096. doi: 10.5267/j.msl.2012.06.011.

Swasty, W., Mustikawan, A., and Koesoemadinata, M. I. P. 2019. Kajian Warna & Ilustrasi Primary Display Panel Kemasan menggunakan Metode Kuesioner dan Eye-Tracking. *Jurnal Manajemen Teknologi*, 18(1), pp. 38–53. doi: 10.12695/jmt.2019.18.1.3.

Tobii Technology AB. 2012. *User Manual — Tobii Studio Version 3.2.* Danderyd: Tobii Technology AB.

Wei, S. T., Ou, L. C., and Luo, M. R. 2008. Color design for carton-packed fruit juice packages, in *Undisciplined! Design Research Society Conference 2008.* Sheffield, UK: Sheffield Hallam University, pp. 1–13. Available at: http://shura.shu.ac.uk/499/.

Westland, S. and Shin, M. J. 2015. The relationship between consumer color preferences and product-color choices. *Journal of the International Color Association*, 14, pp. 47–56. Available at: http://www.aic-color-journal.org/.

Yarlagadda, A., Murthy, J. V. R., and Prasad, K. 2015. A novel method for human age group classification-based on correlation fractal dimension of facial edges. *Journal of King Saud University - Computer and Information Sciences*, 27(4), pp. 468–476.

Yu, L. et al. 2018. The role of individual color preferences in consumer purchase decisions. *Color Research and Application*, 43(2), pp. 258–267. doi: 10.1002/col.22180.

Zhang, Y. et al. (2019) Hue, chroma, and lightness preference in Chinese adults: Age and gender differences. *Color Research and Application*, 44(6), pp. 967–980. doi: 10.1002/col.22426.

Dynamics of Industrial Revolution 4.0: Digital Technology Transformation and Cultural Evolution –
Wulandari et al (eds)
© 2021 The Author(s), ISBN 978-1-032-04451-4

Theory of consumption value in identifying the role of color in product labeling

W. Swasty & M. Mustafa
Universiti Sains Malaysia, Pulau Penang, Malaysia

ABSTRACT: Consumption Value Theory constructs that color is one of the packaging elements that affects the assessment of food products. This theory argues over the causal effect of functional vs. emotional value in product labeling. The main limitation of using colors in product labeling is that it helps with brand identification but fails to provide functional value when its consumers are seen to be driven by emotional value in choosing the product. Previous studies on Consumption Value Theory focus mostly on luxury products but not much is discussed on small medium enterprise (SME) products. Therefore, this study will provide information on the functional and emotional value of color in food product labeling in the SME industry. This study uses a mix-mode approach to investigate the Consumption Value Theory to explain the role of color and design and employ the theory of consumption value to help explain the role of color in the product labeling of food packaging.

Keywords: Consumption Value Theory, product labeling, color, SME product, packaging

1 INTRODUCTION

Product labeling and packaging are the most visible aspects at the point of purchase. While color is the most visual cue of product packaging since it is the first factor to be noticed by the consumer. Color selection in packaging plays an important role and has a significant impact in attracting consumers attention as it stimulates different aspects of emotional arousal (Beneke et al. 2015). Designers can utilize the use of color as a visual sign for product decisions by understanding how consumers interpret single-cue representations (Kauppinen-Räisänen & Jauffret 2018).

Many other elements of packaging, such as color, shape, material, and aesthetic appeal may also potentially influence product consumption value (Silayoi & Speece 2007). However, the main limitation of using colors in product labeling is that even though it helps with brand identification it fails to provide functional value when consumers are driven by emotional value in product selection. This research examines the emerging role of color as value creation in the context of product labeling. There are two primary aims of this study: (1) to examine the importance of colors and their role within branding and value creation; and (2) to map the effect of colors with functional and emotional value and their causal effects on branding. Hence, this paper attempts to address the research question by investigating the theory of consumption value to help explain the role of color in product labeling in packaging.

1.1 *Working definition*

This study will look at and employ certain terms based upon the Consumption Value Theories and other significant design theories to help uncover and explain the issue within the scope of the research. A number of working definitions were identified specifically for the research. The phrase "consumption value" will be used in this study to describe the consumer or customer value as a basis in a marketing perspective. The theory of consumption value is a famous theoretical

DOI 10.1201/9781003193241-30

framework to understand the various dimensions that can make preference judgments of a product type or brand choice (Lin et al. 2020), influence purchase decision (Dhir et al. 2020), and motivate the consumers' post-purchase behavior, i.e., loyalty (Poushneh & Vasquez-Parraga 2019). While a variety of definitions of the term consumption value have been suggested, this paper will use the definition first proposed by Sheth et al. (1991) who saw that brand, product type, and buying decision within a single product category can be determined by different consumption values.

Presently, existing studies on consumption value theory have identified several contexts that affect consumers' intention to buy. These are functional, emotional, social, conditional, and epistemic (Sheth et al. 1991). Functional value is defined as the perception of the consumer of product performance based on durability, reliability, dependability, price, and other physical quality which is expected to be the main driver of the consumer's decision (Sheth et al. 1991; Qasim et al. 2019). Social value is a different approach that acquires social meaning by associating demographic, socioeconomic, and ethnic groups with positive or negative stereotypes. Emotional value is the perceived utility from the potential of an alternative to elicit feelings or affective conditions. Aesthetic options are often associated with emotional meaning. Epistemic value is the perceived utility derived from the possibility of an alternative to arouse curiosity, generate news, or fulfill the desire for knowledge. Conditional value is the perceived utility of an option due to the specific situation, or circumstances of the decision-maker often depends on the condition (Sheth et al. 1991).

2 METHOD

This study uses a mix-mode approach to investigate the consumption value theory to help explain the role of color in product labeling in food packaging. The first step in this analysis is to identify and compile secondary sources from papers through the online journal database related to research topics, specifically on color psychology in branding/packaging and labeling in food products/SME products. This study is later cross-referenced to the Consumption Value Theory, which employs specific values: consumption value, functional value, and emotional value. The criteria of the sources are peer-reviewed scholarly papers (journal and proceeding articles) from 1990–2020. The time frame is chosen to reflect Seth et al.'s conceptual framework of consumption value theory published in 1991 and this would allow for comprehensive mapping of changes in design trend and style in packaging design specifically on the usage of colors in labeling. Input from the secondary sources will also inform the next stage of the research which will help frame the case study (which will include product comparison and eye-tracking experiment), survey, and interviews.

3 RESULT & DISCUSSION

3.1 *Previous works*

The color-product meanings interpretation reveals that color has the potential to convey sensory (taste), functional (relief or calmness), hedonic (medicinal cures), and even situational (strong medicine that cures immediately) meanings (Kauppinen-Räisänen & Jauffret 2018). Another study by Chaouali et al. (2020) suggests that functional value, emotional value, social value, and epistemic value mediate the influence of design esthetics. The current research by Lee et al. (2019) suggests that hedonic value plays an important part in promoting a positive attitude and intention to buy rather than utilitarian value. Moharana and Pradhan (2020) suggest three shopping values, i.e., utilitarian, hedonic, and social value, to build more considerable consumer loyalty, and both marketers and designers need to formulate distinction approaches. Chen and Peng (2018) examine how the consumption value impacts consumers' attitudes and suggest that consumption value can influence the attitudes of the customer, which in turn may affect their behavioral intentions. The prior literature has used the theory of consumption value for examining consumers' decisions as compiled and summarized in Table 1 below.

Table 1. Prior research related to consumption value.

Author(s) & Year of Publication	Research Context	Values
Sheth et al. (1991)	Cigarettes	functional, conditional, social, emotional, epistemic
Holbrook (2005)	photograph	economic, social, hedonic, and altruistic value
Smith and Colgate (2007)	Framework for marketing strategy	symbolic/expressive, experiential/hedonic, functional/instrumental, and cost/sacrifice value
Tynan et al. (2010)	Luxury brand	symbolic/expressive, experiential/hedonic, functional, utilitarian, cost/sacrifice, and rational value.
Choo et al. (2012)	Luxury fashion product	symbolic value, hedonic value, utilitarian value, and economic value
Ramayah et al. (2018)	Online shopping	functional, social value, emotional value, epistemic value, conditional value
Kirillova and Chan (2018)	Hotels' visual appeal	aesthetic value (classic and expressive) functional value (amenities)
Chen and Peng (2018)	Luxury restaurant	functional, financial, hedonic, and symbolic/expressive
Eren-Erdogmus et al. (2018)	Luxury fashion brand extensions	functional, hedonic/experiential, and symbolic
Wiedmann et al. (2018)	Luxury hotel industry	financial, functional, social, and individual
Qasim et al. (2019)	organic food behavior	functional (price and quality), social, conditional, epistemic, and emotional
Cha and Seo (2019)	eating-out consumption	hedonic value, utilitarian value
Ali et al. (2019)	Green IT product	functional, social, epistemic, emotional, conditional, and religious value
Jan et al. (2019)	Green product	ecological, economic, health and safety value
Poushneh and Vasquez-Parraga (2019)	smartphone as a smart product	emotional, functional, social, conditional, and epistemic, + monetary value
Carlson et al. (2019)	social media retail brand communities	functional, emotional, relational, and entativity value
Amalia et al. (2019)	luxury brand	functional, symbolic, and experiential values
Zhang and Zhao (2019)	luxury fashion product	personal value and luxury value: symbolic, experiential value and functional value
Lee et al. (2019)	study on cosmetic packaging	social, emotional, quality value
Krey et al. (2019)	Smartwatch advertising strategy	functional and ergonomic value, hedonic and symbolic
Huang et al. (2019)	Mobile marketing (WeChat)	emotional, functional value, monetary value, guarantee value, social value, design value
Rantala et al. (2019)	Digital business	service process-, product-, and cost-related value
de Klerk et al. (2019)	Luxury genuine leather products	financial, functional, individual, and social
Diallo et al. (2020)	Luxury brand	the functional, social, symbolic value
Lin et al. (2020)	Organic Food	functional and emotional
Moharana and Pradhan (2020)	hypermarket context (retail)	two dimensions (hedonic and utilitarian) and three dimensions (hedonic, utilitarian, and social)
Lim and Kim (2020)	Online shopping	utilitarian and hedonic value
Jung et al. (2020)	Sustainable Apparel Products	aesthetic consumption, conspicuous consumption, and utilitarian consumption
Omigie et al. (2020)	Mobile Financial Services	utilitarian, hedonic, and personal
Chaouali et al. 2020	Mobile banking	functional, emotional, social, epistemic
Dhir et al. (2020)	Mobile instant messaging apps	functional and social

164

3.2 *Finding*

In this study, two consumption values will be addressed, i.e., functional and emotional values. The multidimensional approach to the consumption value takes two basic dimensions into account: functional (utilitarian or cognitive value) and emotional (hedonic or affective value) (Lee et al. 2019). They were emphasized by Lin et al. (2020), and the results indicated that both functional and emotional value has an important impact on buying intention. Table 1 does not document all research related to consumption value/customer value yet. However, from Table 1, it can be concluded that functional or utilitarian value and emotional or hedonic value have been used mostly in prior studies which are 29 and 24 number of studies, respectively.

Functional value refers to the product or service design or functions; which is cognitive because it is connected with utility and usability whereas the emotional value is more effective because it is linked to pleasure, entertainment, and interest-based on personal identification of consumers to the brands (Tian et al. 2018; Lim & Kim 2020). For food product packaging, the functional value can indicate values of the product either perishable or non-perishable products, besides a reflection on the price and quality of the product. Throughout this paper, the term "functional value" refers to utilitarian or cognitive value, while "emotional value" refers to the hedonic or affective value.

This study helps to identify the difference between perceived functional and emotional values and how it influences customers decisions. When launching a new product, designers should pay attention to customers' functional needs and emotional desires (Poushneh and Vasquez-Parraga 2019). A study by Ramayah et al. (2018) indicates that, along with functional value, emotional value plays an instrumental role in online purchase intention. Functional value (especially price and service quality) has the best positive relation to customers' intention to use the internet as a retail platform. Emotional value influences consumers' willingness to buy products online. The subdimensions of consumption values used in past studies in research contexts are slightly different (Jung et al. 2020).

Several previous studies address Consumption Value Theory are mostly on luxury products. Therefore, this study wants to fill in the gap by providing knowledge in functional and personal value of color in food product labeling in the SME context. In addition, the need to strengthen the competitiveness of SMEs in Indonesia is crucial in the global competition era as the ASEAN economic community, as they have a great contribution to national economic growth and lead to improving the Gross Domestic Products (Darwanto et al. 2018).

4 CONCLUSION

This study is designed to address a research question and framework on employing the theory of consumption value to explain the role of color in product labeling. Selected studies concerning the theory of consumption value are summarized in Table 1. It may be noted that the consumption value literature from 1990–2020 highlights the functional and emotional value as the key factor in a consumer's decision and the key indicator for a consumer's brand loyalty. As customers perceive functional value, strong emotional links with brands are generated for products (Poushneh and Vasquez-Parraga 2019).

Previous studies address Consumption Value Theory mostly on luxury products. This study clearly highlights the need for further research in the role of color in product labeling in the SME context. The findings described above enhance our understanding and serve as the basis for a research question in color as value creation. This study would benefit from the further emphasis placed on the complexity of contextual usability and answering such research questions as follows.

RQ1. Why is the use of colors important within branding and value creation in SME products in Bandung?

RQ2. What is the effect of colors in the creation of functional and personal value for branding?

The elaborate scope of the research framework outlined above highlights the importance and potential of consumption value in color research. This research-in-progress pioneers analyzing consumers' value published to-date.

REFERENCES

Beneke, J. et al. 2015. The role of package color in influencing purchase intent of bottled water Implications for SMEs and entrepreneurs, *Journal of Research in Marketing and Entrepreneurship*, 17(2):165–192. doi: 10.1108/JRME-05-2015-0030.

Chaouali, W. et al. 2020. Design aesthetics as drivers of value in mobile banking: does customer happiness matter?, *International Journal of Bank Marketing*, 38(1): 219–241. doi: 10.1108/IJBM-03-2019-0100.

Chen, A. and Peng, N. 2018. Examining consumers' intentions to dine at luxury restaurants while traveling, *International Journal of Hospitality Management*. Elsevier, 71:59–67. doi: 10.1016/j.ijhm.2017.11.009.

Darwanto, D. et al. 2018. Designing model and strategy for strengthening the competitiveness of small medium enterprises, *Etikonomi*, 17(1): 69–92. doi: 10.15408/etk.v17i1.6826.

Dhir, A., Kaur, P., and Rajala, R. 2020. Continued use of mobile instant messaging apps: a new perspective on theories of consumption, flow, and planned behavior. *Social Science Computer Review*, 38(2):147–169. doi: 10.1177/0894439318806853.

Jung, H. J., Choi, Y.J., and Oh, K.W. 2020. Influencing factors of chinese consumers' purchase intention to sustainable apparel products: exploring consumer "attitude–behavioral intention" gap, *Sustainability*. MDPI AG, 12(5): 1–14. doi: 10.3390/su12051770.

Kauppinen-Räisänen, H. and Jauffret, M. N. 2018 Using color semiotics to explore color meanings, *Qualitative Market Research*, 21(1): 101–117. doi: 10.1108/QMR-03-2016-0033.

Lee, S. et al. 2019. Communicating authenticity in packaging of Korean cosmetics, *Journal of Retailing and Consumer Services*. Elsevier Ltd, 48:202–214. doi: 10.1016/j.jretconser.2019.02.011.

Lim, S. H. and Kim, D. J. 2020 Does emotional intelligence of online shoppers affect their shopping behavior? From a cognitive- affective-conative framework perspective, *International Journal of Human–Computer Interaction*. Taylor & Francis, pp. 1–10. doi: 10.1080/10447318.2020.1739882.

Lin, J. et al. 2020. Purchasing organic food with social commerce: An integrated food- technology consumption values perspective, *International Journal of Information Management*. Elsevier, 51. doi: 10.1016/j.ijinfomgt.2019.11.001.

Moharana, T. R. and Pradhan, D. 2020. Shopping value and patronage: when satisfaction and crowding count, *Marketing Intelligence & Planning*, 38(2):137–150. doi: 10.1108/MIP-07-2018-0264.

Poushneh, A. and Vasquez-Parraga, A. Z. 2019. Emotional bonds with technology: the impact of customer readiness on upgrade intention, brand loyalty, and affective commitment through mediation impact of customer value, *Journal of Theoretical and Applied Electronic Commerce Research*, 14(2):90–105. doi: 10.4067/s0718-18762019000200108.

Qasim, H. et al. 2019. The defining role of environmental self-identity among consumption values and behavioral intention to consume organic food, *International Journal of Environmental Research and Public Health*, 16:1–22. doi: 10.3390/ijerph16071106.

Ramayah, T., Rahman, S. A., and Ling, N. C. 2018. How do consumption values influence online purchase intention among school leavers in Malaysia?, *Revista Brasileira de Gestao de Negocios*. Fundacao Escola de Comercio Alvares Penteado, 20(4):638–654. doi: 10.7819/rbgn.v0i0.3139.

Sheth, J. N., Newman, B. I., and Gross, B. L. 1991. Why we buy what we buy: a theory of consumption values, *Journal of Business Research*, 22(2): 159–170. doi: 10.1016/0148-2963(91)90050-8.

Silayoi, P. and Speece, M. 2007. The importance of packaging attributes: A conjoint analysis approach, *European Journal of Marketing*, 41(11–12):1495–1517. doi: 10.1108/03090560710821279.

Tian, G. et al. 2018. Old names meet the new market: an ethnographic study of classic brands in the foodservice industry in Shantou, China, *Human Organization*, 77(1):52–63. doi: 10.17730/1938-3525.77.1.52.

Dynamics of Industrial Revolution 4.0: Digital Technology Transformation and Cultural Evolution –
Wulandari et al (eds)
© 2021 The Author(s), ISBN 978-1-032-04451-4

Digital board game design for an English vocabulary learning tool while learning from home

D.K. Aditya, I.N. Kusmayanti, R. Hendryanti & P.F. Alam
Telkom University, Bandung, West Java, Indonesia

ABSTRACT: English language learners often comment that learning English vocabulary is a challenge due to spelling, pronunciation, parts of speech, and a variety of meanings. Over the years, using educational games for classroom activities has been a popular and effective way to teach since it brings fun and relaxation, creates a friendly environment for competition, and keeps learners interested in learning. Therefore, this research aims to develop a digital learning tool called SQUARE TALKS!, a digital board game for English vocabulary learning focusing on the design phase involving language experts, game designers, and software developers. This current research explores the design phase from the game designers' perspectives. Qualitative methods are used in this research since the research does some observations and content analysis for data collecting. The results of the game development phase covered four aspects: narration, mechanic, aesthetics, and technology. The digital game prototype is envisioned to be an alternative learning tool to use game-based learning to assist learners and teachers during the recent COVID-19 pandemic situation.

Keywords: Digital board game, English vocabulary learning, game-based learning

1 INTRODUCTION

English is important to learn as an international communication language. This makes the teaching of speaking skills and mastery of vocabulary important to facilitate the communication process. Most of the students in the world learn English to develop their abilities and proficiency in speaking. However, this vocabulary learning must be supported by the use of good grammar and pronunciation (Marzban & Firoozjahantigh 2017). The problem that arises is that most students who study English have difficulty with learning vocabulary (Rohmatillah 2014). Other problems arise from the vocabulary learning material itself, such as: (1) the difference between written and oral forms of words; (2) the very large amount of vocabulary; and (3) differences in pronunciation of vocabulary by native speakers and English as a Foreign Language (EFL) teachers. Seeing this situation, we need learning instruments that can provide encouragement and motivation in developing the ability to learn English vocabulary, because vocabulary is the center of language learning (Zimmerman 2012). One learning instrument that can attract the attention of students is to use games, especially games that are classified as edutainment games. By using the play method, the hope is that students can hone and improve their vocabulary memorization skills, improve their interaction and communication skills using vocabulary, and at the same time motivate students to learn (Derakhshan & Davoodi Khatir 2015).

Board games are the media chosen by the research team as a medium for learning English vocabulary. There are many traditional board games used in order to learn English in fun ways, such as Scrabble. The first digital prototype developed to teach English numbers to Telkom University students was SPEAK UP!, a learning media based on Game Based Learning (GBL), a learning method which uses playing and games as learning media. The learning materials within such a process and the results have been determined first, before they apply into the game's gameplay

(Shaffer et al. 2005). The game SPEAK UP! was intended to assist beginner to low-intermediate learners in learning vocabulary to recognize parts of speech and use words. At the first test, the game successfully helped the students understand the vocabulary. After the first test play, SPEAK UP! was introduced to high school English teachers in a community service program, however the COVID-19 pandemic forced the teachers to learn how to use SPEAK UP! in an online meeting.

The conditions brought on by the COVID-19 pandemic made the researchers wants to develop SPEAK UP! into a digital version that could be easily accessed using portable gadgets. The first prototype had a very simple and plain interface design that needed to be enhanced further so as to attract the target audience of the game: junior high students. To simplify the game's physical devices, reproduce and update content, facilitate access and expand users, the offline or table-top version of the game was developed into an online game. SPEAK UP! developed into a web-based and mobile online version under the name SQUARE TALKS! As a consequence, this new version needed more advanced visual enhancements in order to bring the attractive visual interface for the players. Until now, SQUARE TALKS! was still under development.

2 METHODS

2.1 *Research methods*

The research uses the qualitative research method to analyze the visual needs for the game's prototype. The research did some observations for data collecting in order to figure out what must be added or removed from the first prototype by running some play tests and interviewing the players about how they experience the game, what they want to see and play in the game, and their feedback about the game. Observation was used for understanding the subjects from the curriculum for making a good game play based on what the subjects teach the students and the visualizations that are close to the students' taste. The research also made some comparisons with other games that were close to this project and in the same genre. Observation was also used for making a good game play (Aditya et al. 2019). The research learned from some similar words and language board game's rules and some board games assets in order to develop board game concepts not only the suitable in visual language but also for designing the game's aesthetics and also its dramatic elements in digital ways.

2.2 *Subjects*

Initially, the board game SPEAK UP! had been tested to 30 students of Telkom University in 2019. After playing SPEAK UP! twice, there was a significant difference between pre-test and post-test vocabulary scores. Thus, SPEAK UP! had a positive influence on improving the vocabulary score and speaking ability of its players. Feedback from students who played SPEAK UP! is that the game has a variety of challenges such as variations of the types of questions on the game card.

On April 23, 2020, SPEAK UP! was briefly introduced to some teachers from different schools in community service activities. Initially, these community service programs would take the form of a workshop, but due to the social and psychical distance required as a result of the COVID-19 pandemic in the Bandung Region, the program later became an online knowledge-sharing session, so that new teachers were given examples of syllabi or lesson plans where SPEAK UP! was used in classroom learning activities. The response from them was very positive and they were curious to use SPEAK UP! in learning activities in their classrooms. However, due to the Covid-19 pandemic, the research team agreed to made "SPEAK UP!" become more advanced as a digital platform that could be accessed easily by the audience.

2.3 *Data analysis*

Feedback from teachers joining the community service programs had been followed up by the research team to bring SPEAK UP! online, in order to reach other students to experience the media as learning instruments. Using content analysis, the research realizes that although the board game/table-top version is successful in helping the students raise their vocabulary skills, the game still has much weakness with regard to language learning instruments, such as sounds. Therefore, the research team recruited the visual communication advisor and designers to simplify the table-top game to more compact physical devices, reproduce it as digital game, and update the contents so as to facilitate access for an expanded user base.

3 RESULT & DISCUSSIONS

3.1 *Early prototype*

SPEAK UP! was first introduced to high school English teachers in a community service program, however the COVID-19 pandemic forced teachers to learn the uses of SPEAK UP! in an online meeting. This conditions made the researchers want to develop SPEAK UP! into adigital version that could be easily accessed using gadgets. To simplify the game's physical devices, reproduce and update content, facilitate access and expand users, the offline or table-top version of the game was developed into an online game. SPEAK UP! developed into a web-based and mobile online version under the name SQUARE TALKS!

3.2 *New mock up and product development*

Since the research focused on the game's visualizations, this research will use the aesthetics aspect from four basic elements in game design: mechanics, stories, aesthetics, and technologies. These four elements couldn't stand alone to create a good game; they must work as a unity. A game must have a good narration where the world's buildings and characters make the game come to life by using a mechanics that allows the players to interact with their technologies. These aspects must have the aesthetics touch and also the instruments to play with (Aditya & Febrina, 2019). The research is focusing on aesthetic aspects, which give the game looks, sounds, and feels that have the direct relationship to players' experience and Technologies Aspects, as the medium in which the aesthetics take place and produced (Schell 2019). Other opinions that support the statements above are visual aesthetics such as the overall looks, feel of the game, and the character of the game. Visual aesthetics appearance must have a cognitive function and aesthetic function (Plass et al. 2010). Art and design in a game determines how the tools and functions of game mechanics are visualized, how rules are conveyed, and how feedback is displayed. SQUARE TALKS! was developed based on SPEAK UP!, the previous table-top version, that become the mock four or the digital versions. The research discovered that a game design development using a table-top mock up is much more effective for digital game's design, especially for the words and language games. One of several benefits of using the table top mock up is that the games are directly easy to modify

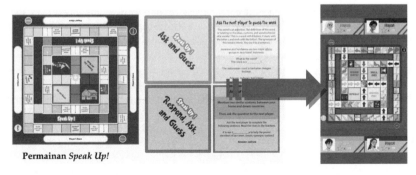

Figure 1. The first SPEAK UP! compared to SQUARE TALKS! Applications appearance (Source Ima Normalia 2019 and Aditya 2020).

Figure 2. The final interface design for SQUARE TALKS! for the Web and applications (Source Ima Normalia 2019 and Aditya 2020).

in its table top mock up manually (Pulsipher 2013). Tracy Fulteron describes that it's important for a game designer and developer to build a board game/table-top prototype as a mock up at first, in order to review the effectiveness and efficiency and make any necessary changes or modifications easily (Fullerton 2008).

3.3 The final prototype descriptions

SPEAK UP! thus upgraded into SQUARE TALKS! The name of SQUARE TALKS! itself was taken from the squares shapes on the board game's tracks and the cards as its assets and activities in the game mechanics, talk and find the answers of the quiz than embed in the game. The research finds that to compete with other words games in the genre of the internet, the game must have its own unique identity. There are several visual modifications that are used in SQUARE TALKS!: (1) the flat and general tracks design in SPEAK UP! are filled up with more artistic typography and illustrated with the map of the big islands in Indonesia; (2) he animated effect for cards in digital version; (3) the additional redesign quiz cards and questionnaires from two types of cards, expanded to four types of cards; (4) the sounds enhancements that will help the students with input of the the pronunciations and listening features, greatly helping the player to learn the vocabulary within the game; (5) players could choose whether they could use their photo or use the character's avatars; (6) there were 8–12 avatar characters that could be used in the game; and (7) there are several costumes including traditional costumes for the characters to wear that will open after a player reaches a certain score.

4 CONCLUSIONS

Although the research was still developing on SQUARE TALKS! by the time this paper was written, the research team optimized the aesthetics in digital enhancements to the game that will make it more attractive. (You can, however, try the early access version by downloading it from the Google Play store). With the digital upgrades in visualizations, the researchers hope that SQUARE TALKS! could help students learn and use vocabulary in a fun way without being worried about making mistakes or feeling nervous. The research is also open to the critics and input and suggestions from others in order to do more fine tuning of the prototype especially with regard to aesthetics. New media such as digital board games are a great way to help students learn English vocabulary in fun and easily accessible ways, especially during the challenging times of the COVID-19 pandemic era.

ACKNOWLEDGEMENTS

The research team would like to thank Telkom University for funding the development of Square Talks! Moreover, we also would like to thank the game illustrators Dissa Mirai Aoi and Muflih Rabbani Tampubolon.

REFERENCES

Aditya, Dimas Krisna and Febrina, A. K. (2019) Digital game prototyping using board game/table top as it's mock up case study: Taman Putroe Phang game project, in *6th Bandung Creative Movement International Conference in Creative Industries 2019 (6th BCM 2019)*. Available at: https://www.neliti.com/publications/302034/digital-game-prototyping-using-board-gametable-top-as-its-mock-up-case-study-tam.

Aditya, D. K. et al. (2019) Sangkan Hurip, a board game design project based on Kolenjer Astrological math narratives, in *5th Bandung Creative Movement International Conference on Creative Industries 2018 (5th BCM 2018)*, pp. 179–186. Available at: https://www.atlantis-press.com/proceedings/bcm-18/125910932.

Derakhshan, A. and Davoodi Khatir, E. (2015) The effects of using games on english vocabulary learning, *Journal of Applied Linguistics and Language Research*, 2(3), pp. 39–47. Available at: www.jallr.ir.

Fullerton, T. (2008) *Game Design Workshop: A Playcentric Approach to Creating Innovative Games, Technology*. doi: 10.1007/s13398-014-0173-7.2.

Marzban, A. and Firoozjahantigh, M. (2017) The relationship between willingness to communicate and vocabulary learning strategies among Iranian EFL learners, *Theory and Practice in Language Studies*, 7(11), p. 1119. doi: 10.17507/tpls.0711.22.

Plass, J. L., Perlin, K. and Nordlinger, J. (2010) The games for learning institute: Research on design patterns for effective educational games, Game Developers Conference, San Francisco. Available at: http://dev.gamesandimpact.org/wp-content/uploads/2012/09/PlassNYU-Ideas-for-Impact-Games-2.pdf.

Pulsipher, L. (2013) Game design: how to create video and tabletop games, start to finish, Choice Reviews Online. McFarland & Company, Inc., Publishers,. doi: 10.5860/choice.50-3897.

Rohmatillah, R. (2014) A study on students' difficulties in learning vocabulary, *English Education: Jurnal Tadris Bahasa Inggris IAIN Raden Intan*, 6(1), pp. 75–93.

Schell, J. (2019) *The Art of Game Design: A Book of Lenses, 3rd Edition*. doi: 10.1201/b22101.

Shaffer, D. W. et al. (2005) Video games and the future of learning, *Phi Delta Kappan*, 87(2), pp. 105–111. doi: 10.1177/003172170508700205.

Zimmerman, C. B. (2012) *Historical Trends in Second Language Vocabulary Instruction, Second Language Vocabulary Acquisition*. Edited by J. Coady and T. Huckin. Cambridge: Cambridge University Press. doi: 10.1017/cbo9781139524643.003.

Dynamics of Industrial Revolution 4.0: Digital Technology Transformation and Cultural Evolution –
Wulandari et al (eds)
© 2021 The Author(s), ISBN 978-1-032-04451-4

Engineered print for zero waste fashion design

F. Nursari & A. Nabila
Telkom University, Bandung, Indonesia

ABSTRACT: Generally, a garment produced using the zero-waste fashion design method focuses on implementing various manipulations of fashion patterns or cutting patterns. The surface design on fabric has not been optimally implemented as a part of the garment because the process of manipulating the clothing pattern is the focus of the design process. The engineered print is one of the surface design techniques used on garments designed with the zero-waste concept. The purpose of this research is to apply the concept of zero waste fashion design to the process of making ready-to-wear clothes in the production process to make it more environmentally friendly and sustainable. The end result is a recommendation on how the basic application of engineered print on the zero-waste garment can lead to a better design process and production.

Keywords: Engineered Print, Zero Waste, Fashion Design

1 INTRODUCTION

Since 2008, the zero-waste fashion design method, or better known as the abbreviation ZWFD, has been widely studied and practiced by students, academics, and practitioners in the fashion sector who have an interest in the issue of pre-production waste and its effects on the environment. ZWFD itself is a design process that refers to steps in producing clothing with minimum pre-production waste. Pre-production waste itself is waste generated in the process of making clothing, and in the ZWFD process, this waste generally comes from the process of cutting clothing materials.

Generally, clothing that is produced by the zero-waste fashion design method focuses on the implementation of various manipulations of fashion patterns or pattern cutting. Surface or background engineering techniques have not been implemented optimally as one part of fashion is due to the process of manipulating fashion patterns that are the focus of the design process. The engineered print is one of the surface designs utilized in clothing designed with the zero-waste fashion design method. This engineering technique is the development of digital textile printing, which is one of the techniques of digital printing into textile media using printers with a process that is more effective and efficient (Bowles 2012).

In the engineered print technique, fashion patterns can be engineered and arranged precisely with digital software. The motives can be adjusted so that it can produce a seamless visual effect. Garments designed with zero waste fashion design method has a lot of design lines and manipulation of shapes and lines. The application of engineered print techniques can provide a more attractive visual form because of its ability to optimize the motifs used in clothing. The application of engineered print techniques in garments designed with the zero-waste fashion design method has the potential to be implemented for the ready to wear fashion industry. The method is also providing more efficient production time. By applying technology for designing fashion with the zero-waste method, designers can contribute to the fashion industry in order to produce clothing in an environmentally friendly, sustainable, and quality way. Sustainability is a factor that is currently considered by most designers globally due to the many environmental issues that occur due to the impact of the fashion industry waste (Gwilt 2012).

This research begins by reviewing the literature related to the zero-waste fashion design method, the fashion production process, and engineered print technology so that it can be implemented

DOI 10.1201/9781003193241-32

precisely in the experimental process. There are two experimental processes in this research, namely, to adopt the manufacturing process in the zero-waste fashion design method and implement engineered print with the help of digital software in generating zero-waste fashion patterns. The result of this research is the evaluation and conclusion of the research and fashion prototype.

1.1 *Zero waste fashion design*

In the fashion industry, two types of waste are produced in the process of producing a garment. First is waste produced by industry, and second is waste produced by consumers. Zero waste fashion design focuses on reducing waste generated during the production process of textile materials and products, also known as pre-consumption waste (Mcquillan 2011). The integration of pattern cutting techniques in the zero-waste concept can optimize the design process. In addition to pattern cutting techniques, there are alternative other techniques that can be applied to produce clothing without pre-consumption waste such as digital printing and draping techniques. The application of the concept of zero waste has been and unwittingly, practiced in traditional clothing in the world (Rissanen & Mcquillan 2016). The limitation of raw materials and the prolonged fabric production process made people in the past more respectful of material to make clothes so that in every process of making clothes, the material was used entirely without residue.

The practice of zero-waste fashion design methods starts from various forms of traditional clothing. One of the applications of zero-waste fashion design is seen in the form of traditional clothing in Indonesia that utilizes basic geometric shapes in its clothing patterns. Geometric shapes used are generally square, because the fabric material for clothing is made by weaving or felting techniques so that the dimensions of the material produced depend on the size of the loom. Due to the time-consuming and challenging process of making materials, traditional communities will try to optimize the materials available for fashion. Furthermore, because of this tendency, generally, clothing that has passed its lifetime will be reconstructed so that it can extend the wear life of the clothing. The application of the zero-waste fashion design concept seen no change in the optimization of material dimension. However, the resulting clothing designs can be adapted to the tastes, functions, and needs of modern society for fashion at this time. The technique used has evolved and not only focused on the process of utilizing geometric shapes to create clothing patterns but was more explorative with variations in the shape of the design lines and motifs on the material used.

1.2 *Garment production*

There are two different categories in the production process of garment, namely ready-to-wear garments and those according to specific sizes and orders. Some factors that distinguish between the two categories are the stages in the process of clothing production, the process of design considerations, and consideration of the ability to be mass-produced (Onuma 2009).

In the process of producing ready-to-wear clothing or known as ready-to-wear, design considerations that do not only refer to the public who are consumers but need consider several factors such as function, price of production, purchasing power, and sustainability. However, this does not make the ready-to-wear process more time consuming than individual clothing. Due to the dynamic fashion trends, the ready-to-wear fashion industry is more active in producing clothing with different designs. The production process carried out in ready-made clothing can be said to be more modern than clothing for individuals.

Material knowledge is not only limited to the type but can include how the material is following the function of the clothes designed. Making fashion patterns, still through the process of prototyping or making samples of clothing, but at the time the embodiment was carried out on an industrial scale. Furthermore, the process of quality control or inspection of the final product is an important step to ensure product quality.

1.3 *Engineered print*

Engineered printing is one of the engineering techniques that developed along with the development of computer technology and the fashion production process. The engineered printing technique is a technique that allows applying motifs to a clothing pattern and printed directly onto a plain cloth so that when the motifs are put together in a seam form, it connects according to the shape of the clothing without being seamless. The use of engineered print is also to add the shape effect of a garment or to accent specific parts of clothing such as cuffs, collars or other specific parts of clothing. One example of using this technique is the work of Alexander McQueen in 2012, where the motif was applied to the pattern to produce a seamless effect.

In using the Engineered Printing application, the conventional method used is scanning flat pattern paper or draping patterns and digital manipulation. As in the work of Hussein Chalayan in 2007 in which Chalayan scanned patterns and then performed digital manipulations to apply motifs to fashion patterns. Digitally compiled patterns applied with motifs using software before finally being printed directly on the surface of plain cloth (Bowles 2012).

2   METHOD

Based on the qualitative research method, the experiment carried in this research refers to theories and results from the literature or previous research that supported the topic. Furthermore, conducting the analysis and evaluation process from the experiment results to produce proto- types following the research objectives. The literature study used as a reference for this research is the literature on zero waste fashion design methods, clothing production, and engineered print techniques used as a basis for understanding and limitations in conducting experiments.

The scope of this research is how to apply the zero-waste fashion design method to produce ready to wear clothing. The limitation is narrowed to the application of engineering techniques in the form of engineered print applied to digital patterns of zero-waste garments. The material used is adjusted to the ideal specifications for digital textile printing by utilizing geometric formations in zero waste clothing patterns.

2.1   Zero waste patterns and engineered print

The process of obtaining data was carried out by reviewing the literature on various ways of applying zero-waste methods to optimize the cloth dimension with fabric waste below 15% for a garment. A geometric pattern is one of the basic techniques used in the development of clothes with fabric waste less than 15%. Geometric shapes are also proven to be versatile in flat pattern making with many possibilities of variations depends on the characteristic of the fabric, cutting process, and the position or direction of the pattern on the fabric itself (Nursari & Djamal 2019). Historically, geometric shapes exist in most traditional garment shape namely kimono, baju kurung, and is the basic shape of ancient Greek and Roman costumes.

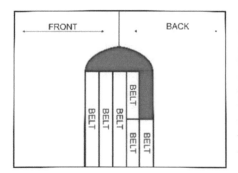
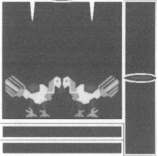

Figure 1.   Pattern draft. Source: Nabila, Annisa (2019)

This is the basic geometric pattern plot for a dress with long sleeves. The length is equipped with a ribbon collar and an outer garment in one-shoulder style completed with several belts. The belts are part of the design to optimize the fabric width and length and to achieve less than 15% fabric waste. The overall fabric waste in this design is 3,7%.

Geometric shapes are manipulated in width and length according to the dimension of the fabric used in printing. Corel is used for drafting the patterns instead of paper. The drafting of patterns did not use a specific formula for a basic bodice and sleeve as a foundation pattern. Instead, the designer used the basic measurements of the model to determine the length and width of a few parts of the garment such as sleeve, belt, and dress. The pattern drafting process is done by constructing a rectangular shape with the obtained measurements and adapting the basic details on a foundation pattern such as darts, collar length, and depth. In this process, the designer should have a clear view of how the shape will hold. The main idea is derived from the basic tubular shape of ancient Greek costumes which is well known for its fabric optimization.

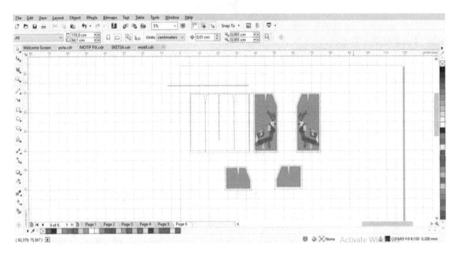

Figure 2.   Pattern plot on Corel Draw. Source: Nabila, Annisa (2019)

After the final pattern is constructed in adobe illustrator according to its original measurements, it is manipulated further by deleting unnecessary seams such as side seams and center seams. The elimination of seam will provide a better canvas for the printed motif and ease the assembly process after it is print and cut. When the pattern is set, the last stage is to position the motifs on the garment patterns and adjusting the position accordingly. Seam allowance is then added to the final stage before printing.

2.2   Producing a garment

Printing the final garment patterns with the applied motifs is done in the actual fabric dimension due to efficiency and practical reasons in the assembly process. After the printing is done, the fabric is cut out according to its seam allowance and hand-sewn to match the motifs. The hand- sewn garment is inspected for shape and alterations are made during this process. Because of its basic shape, major adjustments are not required for this design. The last stage in production is machine sewing and final inspection of the garment quality.

3   RESULT

The result of this research is a dress with long sleeves with a ribbon collar and an outer garment in a one-shoulder style completed with several belts. By using Corel draw as software to draft and manipulate patterns, the designer can effectively produce patterns that are ready to print and sew without wasting paper.

Figure 3. Final design. Source: Nabila, Annisa (2019)

Furthermore, it is possible to reduce fabric waste by 3,7% by adapting geometric shapes in the design. At the final production stage, the designer used vinyl instead of polyester for the outer garment to achieve a modern and fun look. Although the decision was made in the last stage in the production, it did not have any specific effect on the waste or shape of the garment.

4   CONCLUSION

To design a zero-waste fashion collection, having less waste is not only the main concern. The conventional process of drafting garment patterns can lead to the accumulation of pre-consumption waste other than leftover fabrics. To address this issue, the use of digital technology is one of the solutions proposed for designers to create a zero-waste ready-to-wear garment. Industrial pattern making software such as Lectra or Gerber is a few examples where technology is applied to efficiently ease the manufacturing process of a garment. However, each software is expensive for students or independent designers to operate, hence, it is better to send the designs off to be manufactured outside the design studio. This could be difficult if the designer has a specific design process, concept, or other sustainable goals in mind. In this research, such ideas and goals are abled by the simple use of everyday design software such as Corel Draw or Adobe Illustrator. However, the designer should be knowledgeable enough in the foundation of garment construction and software use. This will not only lead to more efficient ways in designing fashion but also create the opportunity for the designer to explore other creative techniques to work with in the future.

REFERENCES

Bowles, M. (2012). *Digital Textile Design Second Edition.* London: Lauren King Publishing. ISBN: 978 1 78067 002 7
Gwilt, A. (2012). Integrating sustainable strategies in the fashion design process: A conceptual model of the fashion designer in haute couture. School of Architecture + Design College of Design and Social Context. Melbourne: RMIT University Press.
Nabila, Annisa. (2019). Penerapan Metode Zero Waste Fashion Design Deangan Teknik Geometric Cutting Pada Busana Wanita. Bandung(ID): Universitas Telkom.
Nursari, Faradillah, and Fathia H. Djamal. "Implementing Zero Waste Fashion in Apparel Design." *6th Bandung Creative Movement 2019, Bandung, Indonesia, October 2019.* Telkom University, 2019, pp. 98-104.
Onuma, S. (2009). Fundamentals of Garment Design. Tokyo: Bunka Publishing Bureau.
Rissanen, T., & Mcquillan, H. (2016). *Zero Waste Fashion Design.* London: Bloomsbury.

Dynamics of Industrial Revolution 4.0: Digital Technology Transformation and Cultural Evolution –
Wulandari et al (eds)
© 2021 The Author(s), ISBN 978-1-032-04451-4

Fabric effectiveness on a batik shirt through design motifs

S. Yuningsih & E.P. Hokianti
Telkom University, Bandung, Indonesia

C. Puspitasari
Universiti Sains Malaysia, Penang, Malaysia

ABSTRACT: The development of batik-patterned shirts presents various forms and visualizations of various motifs, although the shirts' silhouettes do not show much change. The diversity of motif compositions on the batik-patterned shirts provides attractiveness and value. On the other hand, it has an impact, one of which is the production waste from batik cloth processing into clothing products. Seeing these problems, it is necessary to have a formulation or reference that underlies the design of an effective batik-patterned shirt product. The results of the literature study show that strategies for the effectiveness of use in the shirt production process can be carried out with a zero-waste approach that emphasizes the optimization and effectiveness of the material design process through an exploration of fabric dimensions and motif dimensions as well as synchronization of patterns and clothing design designs.

Keywords: effectiveness, batik, design, motif

1 INTRODUCTION

The fashion industry's development, especially apparel, is very rapid, marked by the emergence of innovative products and new fashion businesses that offer various products for consumer needs. The apparel industry is built on the participation of other industries moving from upstream to downstream. Ernawati (2015) states that the upstream apparel industry includes the fiber, spinning and yarn industry, knitting, printing, and finishing, and downstream the textile and textile products industry includes the apparel industry. In line with Ernawati et al. (2015) explained that there are three sectors of the textile industry: the upstream sector, which includes the fiber and yarn industry; the intermediate sector, which includes the fabric industry; and the downstream sector, which includes the apparel industry and the textile article industry. For this reason, the apparel industry is one of the mainstay commodities to drive the economy.

The apparel industry products are very diverse; one of the interesting ones is the batik shirt industry. Batik shirts have been around for a long time, around 1972, during Governor Ali Sadikin (Doellah 2002), and up to now can still survive through various obstacles and challenges of the times. Batik shirt now comes with a variety of creations in terms of diverse motifs and details, not even rare, unique, and unusual motifs are found (Yuningsih 2018). Basically, a batik-patterned shirt is product development in the batik-patterned fabric that adapts to modern needs (Suryana 2013). Batik cloth as the main raw material in batik shirt products, processed by designers to produce various shirt creations, both motifs, and details. However, the development of batik-patterned shirt products currently does not significantly change the shape and construction details of the shirt, so it can be said that the changes are very slight and do not change the shirt silhouette in general (Yuningsih 2018).

These conditions and the exploration of massive motifs on batik cloth material need to be responded positively. On the other hand, with the composition and dimensions of the increasingly diverse motifs on the fabric surface, new problems will arise, one of which is the synchronization of motifs on the shirt and the amount of fabric waste causing inefficient use of fabric raw materials. With the explanation above, the processing of apparel products in shirts with batik motifs can still be made efficient to reduce the amount of waste produced, one of which is through the design of efficient motif designs. For this reason, this research will discuss the efficiency of motif dimensions for batik shirts, so that the results of this study can reveal the composition and dimensions of motifs that are effective for production in the batik shirt industry. After this research is completed, it is expected that there is an efficient design or recommendation of motif dimensions and can be used as a reference in designing the development of motifs for apparel products, especially men's shirts made from batik motifs.

2 METHOD

In the above explanation, it was stated that the condition of the production design of a garment has potential waste, one of which is in the form of fabric leftover. Not all of these wastes can be utilized into products of economic value; for that, it is necessary to improve production material efficiency starting from the initial production process. This study aims to find the dimensions of motives effective in the production of men's batik-patterned shirts. In achieving this research, the authors researched qualitative methods through literature studies to find opportunities for effectiveness in clothing production and map the composition of the batik pattern in the shirt production process.

3 RESULT AND DISCUSIONS

As previously stated, the apparel industry has a broad scope of the industry, including the fiber and yarn processing industry, fabric processing, and apparel manufacturing (Zamroni and Ernawati 2015). Businesses in the field of apparel are owned by large-scale businesses and owned by businesses with small and medium scale. The batik shirt business can be mostly in the classification of Small and Medium Enterprises (SMEs) where the management is very diverse. The search for batik business constraints is known to be one of the big challenges in developing batik products related to the production costs and the differentiation of alternative products (Mangifera 2016). It was also conveyed by Nurainun and Rasyimah (2008), which explains that some things weaken the batik industry, namely high production costs, diminishing human resources, difficulties in obtaining raw materials at affordable prices, and the security situation.

Following the explanation above, a strategy is needed for the development of efficient batik products. In this research, the product is focused on batik shirts, so the production process does not stop only with batik cloth, but its processing to become ready-made clothing products. In this case, Fletcher (2008) explains in his book sustainability fashion, to start the production of ready to wear clothing starting from the time of processing the fiber to be marketed to consumers. This is related to the apparel production chain relating to broad industrial processes. To focus this research on achieving the formulation of the batik shirt production process's effectiveness, an approach is needed to obtain the effective formula in the production of batik patterned shirts, one of which is the concept of zero waste fashion.

Zero waste fashion is a method that aims to minimize waste and optimize fabric dimensions. According to Risannen and Almond (2013), the concept of minimizing waste in the production process can be done effectively by optimizing fabric dimensions. To optimize the fabric, it is necessary to design clothing patterns and design materials that are designed from the beginning effectively. This is far different from the concept of conventional clothing design, which still tends to emphasize the production process that stands alone in each process. In Risannen's explanation, most of the research was conducted on plain or striped cloth. In research, batik cloth has a pattern and structure of distinctive and unique motifs, so of course, a deep design and analysis process is needed.

With the above concept, the effectiveness of batik shirt production can be achieved through the design's effectiveness at the material design stage, where the fabric is planned to be more

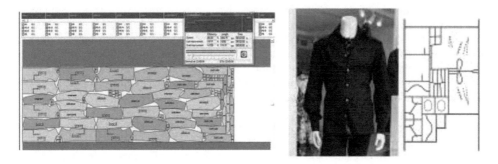

Figure 1. Layout design process (left: computerized system, right: zero waste method). (Source: Risannen and Almond 2013).

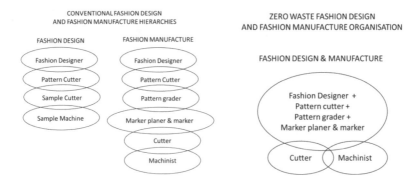

Figure 2. Comparison between conventional hierarchies and a new possibility for industry organization. (Source: Risannen and Almond 2013).

effective and still maintain the decorative elements of batik as its main characteristics. With this, it is necessary to experiment with placing the shirt pattern on batik cloth. Batik motifs with various visual dimensions and dimensions of different dimensions need to be analyzed to map the pattern of motifs on the fabric when the material design process can be known as effective dimensions of motifs for batik-patterned shirt products.

Batik shirts are familiar to people in Indonesia and even globally. For men, a batik shirt has become one of the dress choices in everyday life, both for formal or informal events. Basically, this patterned shirt is produced with the main material of the batik-patterned fabric; then it is produced into ready to wear clothing in the form of a shirt. To determine the effectiveness of this batik-patterned shirt, it is necessary to be traced through the pattern of developing batik motifs as the main material for shirt production.

One of the traditional fabrics known for their motive characteristics is batik; the unique technique and composition and its philosophical value make batik a traditional fabric that has distinctive characteristics compared to other traditional fabrics. The specificity of batik motifs can be known as one of them through the development of the motif. Batik motifs can be said as a framework of images that will realize batik as a whole (Susanto 1973).

To describe and map the patterns of developing batik motifs, it is necessary to know how the batik motifs are made and patterned in a fabric field. In this case, it is generally known that, based on Susanto (1973), it is also known that batik has a classification to distinguish the arrangement patterns, namely groups of geometric and non-geometric motifs. Geometric motifs are groups of motifs arranged with geometric forms or arranged in sloping lines that form rhombic lines. Examples of motifs classified in the geometric classification with a class of geometry are *banji, ceplok*, *ganggong*, and *kawung*, while the batik group with slanted lines, namely *semen* and *udan liris*. In this geometric group, the term *raport* is known, which is a part of the repeated motif vertically, horizontally, and diagonally in a field of batik cloth; in general, these report cards are rhombic or square in shape. Unlike geometric motifs, non-geometric motifs are groups of motifs arranged based on the forms of plants, animals, or nature. Even though this non-geometric pattern tends to be free, it still has a repetition of motifs in the fabric field. Examples of non-geometric motifs are found in *semen* and *buketan terang bulan*.

In his book, Susanto also explained the pattern of the development of geometric motifs consisting of four repetition patterns: (1) *Tubruk*, this pattern is a simple pattern where *raport* are arranged vertically and horizontally by shifting one step; (2) *Onda-ende*, this development pattern is arranged in a horizontal direction (left-to-right) shifted one step and vertically (face-to-back) shifted one step; (3) *parang*, *raport* arranged in an oblique direction in one direction, either just left or right only one step; and (4) *Tubruk miring*, this pattern is arranged in the direction of a slash, to the right or left by shifting one step. For non-geometric motifs in general, the arrangement patterns consist of batik motifs consisting of three parts: the main decorative motifs, fillers, and *isen-isen* (Doellah, 2002; Susanto, 1973). The motif patterns are arranged repeatedly in certain patterns in the fabric field so that the shape of the raport pattern is very dynamic in shape.

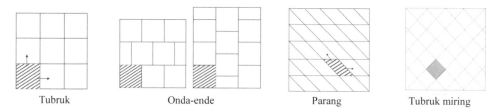

Tubruk   Onda-ende   Parang   Tubruk miring

Figure 3.   Raport/repetition of batik pattern. (Source: Susanto 1973)

In different literature also explained the pattern of repetition in the design of a motif. This was explained by Wilson (2001) and Kight (2011) that the basic structure of the repetition motif consists of (1) Straight repeat. This repetition pattern is the simplest repetition pattern, where the motif pattern is repeated to the top or bottom section repeatedly. (2) Half drop: For this repetition pattern, the vertical column's repetition pattern shifts half of the part to the bottom repeatedly. (3) Tile (or brick) repeat: This pattern of repetitive motifs is as simple as a brick placement pattern, where the motif is repeated half or one part in a horizontal direction. (4) Repeat mirrored vertically and horizontally: this motif is repeated by placing a mirror-like motif or facing off, repeated vertically and horizontally.

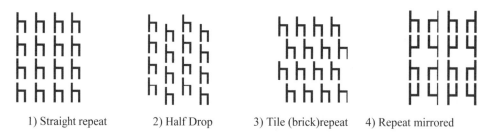

1) Straight repeat   2) Half Drop   3) Tile (brick)repeat   4) Repeat mirrored

Figure 4.   Basic repeat structures. (Source: Wilson 2001).

With the description of the motif patterns above, the analysis of batik motifs in this study can be done by outlining the motifs' dimensions through the patterns of its development. For this reason,

Table 1. Analysis of the batik motifs component.

Analysis of batik motif patterns	Motif classification	Type of motif	Batik motif forms (raport pattern)	Raport system of the motif	Raport dimension
Classification of motif types	a. Geometric	*Banji* *Ceplok* *Ganggong* *Kawung*	Rhomb Square	*Tubruk* *Onda-ende* *Parang/ miring* *Tubruk miring* atau	In centimeter or inches
	b. Non-Geometric	*Semen* *Buketan*	In accordance with prepared rapot cards	Straight repeat Half drop Tile (or brick) repeat Repeat mirrored	

the formulation of the analysis of the development of batik motifs in the fabric field in this study refers to the above literature; see Table 1.

With the analysis above, the pattern of developing batik motifs can be known and mapped by elaborating the motifs, such as the classification of motifs, types of motifs, and the basic forms of motif patterns (report cards) developed. The basis of the compilation is the basis in preparing batik fabric motifs; if it refers to making clothes, the pattern of motif development is one part of the consideration in the effectiveness of the material when it will be produced.

4 CONCLUSIONS

After the analysis above, the fabric's effectiveness in the production of batik shirts can be achieved with a zero-waste fashion approach that emphasizes the effectiveness of fabric dimensions through clothing patterns on the fabric. In its application in the production of batik motifs, it is necessary to pay attention to the decorative elements of the batik motif based on consideration so that it requires an analysis of the composition and dimensions of the motif map motif patterns in the fabric field. Analysis of these motifs' composition or development can be done by classifying the motives, types of motives, report cards, repetition patterns, and report card dimensions. After knowing the formulation above, the next stage in the research still requires exploration and application of batik motifs in the field of fabric that is synchronized with clothing patterns through the material design process. This will be done in subsequent research reports to find out potential patterns and dimensions of motifs to be developed as a reference in designing efficient batik motif shirts.

REFERENCES

Doellah, H. Santosa. 2002. *Batik Pengaruh Zaman Dan Lingkungan*. Solo: Danar Hadi.
Fletcher, Kate. 2008. Earthscan *Sustainable Fashion & Textile: Design Journeys*. UK: Earthscan.
Mangifera, Liana. 2016. Pengembangan Industri Kreatif Produk Batik Tulis Melalui Value Chain Analysis. *The 3rd University Research Colloquium*: 157–66.
Nurainun, Oleh, and Heriyana Rasyimah. 2008. Analisis Industri Batik di Indonesia Oleh: Nurainun, Heriyana Dan Rasyimah Fakultas Ekonomi Universitas Malikussaleh Banda Aceh. *Fokus Ekonomi*.
Risannen, Timo, and Kevin Almond. 2013. Zero-Waste Fashion Design: A Study at the Intersection of Cloth, Fashion Design and Pattern Cutting. *Fashion Practice*.
Suryana, Yan Yan. 2013. ITB *Batik Digitalisasi Kreatif Motif Dalam Gaya Desain Dunia*. Bandung: ITB.

Susanto, S.K Sewan. 1973. *Seni Kerajinan Batik Indonesia*. Yogyakarta: Balai Pelatihan Batik dan Kerajinan Lembaga Penelitian dan Pendidikan Industri Departemen Perindustrian.

Wilson, Jacquie. 2001. Handbook of textile design *Handbook of Textile Design*. New York: Woodhead Publishing Ltd. & CRC Press LLC.

Yuningsih, Sari. 2018. *Kajian Elemen Estetik Kemeja Bermotif Batik Kontemporer (Studi Kasus Pada Desain Kemeja Bermotif Batik Danar Hadi)*. Bandung.

Zamroni, Salim, and Ernawati. 2015. Info Komoditi Pakaian Jadi *Info Komoditi Pakaian Jadi*. Jakarta: Badan pengkajian dan Pengembangan Kebijakan Perdagangan Kementrian Perdagangan RI dan Al Mawardi Prima.

Dynamics of Industrial Revolution 4.0: Digital Technology Transformation and Cultural Evolution –
Wulandari et al (eds)
© 2021 The Author(s), ISBN 978-1-032-04451-4

Replacement of Public Area with Service Area as a COVID-19 Safety House Design

S. Rahardjo, M.K.A. Rahman & A. Safinatunnajah
Telkom University, Bandung, Indonesia

ABSTRACT: The existence of COVID-19 has created many safety procedures when people enter their homes. The need for immediate handwashing or spraying disinfectant has turned the public area of a house into a crucial place for filtering unwanted viruses. An adjustment to the house situation then becomes necessary, but hard to achieve especially in smaller houses. As a response to this current situation, this article proposes a recommendation in the form of rearrangement design. Data collection through questionnaires were perfomed to discover the habits that create the new flow of activities and the design is explored by taking samples from small houses that only have one access point. In conclusion, it was found that bringing the service area closer to the main entrance at the front of the house can accommodate the flow of activities that support COVID-19 safety procedures.

Keywords: small house design, house layout, COVID safety, service area

1   INTRODUCTION

1.1   *Residential Re-layout as a COVID-19 Prevention Method*

Since early 2020, the world has been facing a pandemic from Coronavirus disease (COVID-19). The disease and threat to public health is so prevalent in all populations that cleanliness in the home has become one of the major concerns in COVID-19 prevention as the virus might persist on surfaces for several days (Kampf et al., 2020). As the primary habitat for human beings, a residence needs to meet the criteria of comfort, safety, and health to support its occupants (Munif, 2009). As a result of that, the government through the Ministry of Health of the Republic of Indonesia (Kemenkes RI) encouraged citizens to comply with policies to prevent transmission of the COVID-19 virus from residential areas.

Nowadays, Indonesian houses generally start with a sitting area, a living room, or a common room that accommodates the whole family as well as a location to welcome guests. Before COVID-19, house occupants could place their belongings anywhere and directly lay down on the sofa without worrying about being contaminated with viruses. Now, we prefer washing hands before anything else and choose to change our clothes or take a shower before relaxing on the sofa. Thus, some modifications are required to adjust to the new flow of activity, mainly in the form of rearranging residential spaces and furniture.

Layout changes may not be a major problem for houses with spacious areas as there are flexible options for rearranging the furniture. However, even a minor furniture change could be difficult to apply in small-sized houses due to limited space that needs to be spared for movement and circulation. However, new safety and hygiene habits since COVID-19 have increased certain activities in the home regardless of the size of the house. This is a specific challenge for smaller houses since there isn't as much availability of space in which to accommodate those new activities (Schmidt, 2011). Room adaptation must be supported by the design of room layout in accordance with the needs and activities of these new habits. Therefore, layout changes are very important to support new habits during and after this pandemic to maintain the health of the house's occupants and prevent the spread of the COVID-19 virus. Responding to this phenomenon, this paper proposes ideas for layout modifications for small-sized houses based on the COVID-19 safety protocols for the flow of activity.

1.2 *Layout*

Designing a layout is one of the most fundamental parts of interior design which takes a lot of analysis (White, 1983). In residential design, the number of occupants, space needs, space function, comfort, and safety are aspects to consider alongside aesthetic value (Simbolon and Nasution, 2017). The user aspect is a basic factor in designing a room—the concept of the room always adjusts to user activity. This activity will influence the sequence of space and affect the zoning area (Karlen and Fleming, 2016). The space planning process usually begins with defining the problems and is then translated into bubble diagrams of activity flow, followed by block plans, finally ending with layout design. The zoning area itself usually begins with a public space that is considered a free space where everyone can pass through (Snyder, 1979). In a level of a private house, that area can be the outdoor space, carport, terrace, or the sitting area after the main entrance that welcomes visitors. However, a public area does not mean that anyone is free to pass through or get in, but rather to separate the character of the space with more private areas, such as family room or bedrooms;; service areas contain spaces such as storage and a kitchen. Thus, the re-layout proposal in this article is designed following this method with a consideration that the zonation of a house is categorized into public, private, and service areas.

2 METHOD

This research is conducted in mixed quantitative and qualitative methods. The quantitative method is performed through a Google Form questionnaire of which there were over 240 respondents spread out from Sumatra, Java, and West Nusa Tenggara who shared their new household cleanliness procedures to prevent COVID-19 as well as difficulties with areas in their homes still in need of some adjustments. The next method is qualitative where we formulate the flow of activity based on the data collection through questionnaires and apply it to the layout samples taken from the smallest sized houses offered by real estate developers in the Podomoro Park Residence of Bandung and PIK 2 Residence by Agung Sedayu Group in Jakarta. Those home sizes were Akasha Type at 66 m², Asoka Type at 36 m², and PIK 2 Millennial Type at 60 m². Since the problem exists only in the public area of a house or in the transition space from public to private areas, the redesign experiment was only performed on the first floor, and the second floor remains unchanged as the whole area is private and already filtered by the floor below.

3 RESULT

3.1 *A new flow of activity inside houses post COVID-19*

The questionnaires collected information from respondents contained a variety of answer selections. First, we aimed to find out as many new safety and hayiene habits as possible as well as many obstacles as possible for implementing those habits in their houses. Four of possible selectable habits featured on the questionnaire are: (1) increasing the frequency of handwashing (91.3%), (2) changing clothes after outdoor activities (73%), (3) cleanse luggage or belongings after travel (57.7%), and (4) cleanse household surfaces that are exposed to physical contact, such as the floor, chair, doorknobs, etc. (50.2%). As for the obstacles, the most distinguished problems were (1) the lack of space for changing outfits near the house's entrance (91.3%), (2) the lack of a proper area for sorting items especially after a grocery trip (36.5%), followed by (3) the lack of space to store disinfectant products near the entrance (27%).

The second type of question was given in multiple choice format where respondents have to choose only the first activity they do when they first arrive at home: getting into the house, handling groceries, or receiving a delivery package. When respondents arrive without carrying a specific item in their hands, it is discovered that handwashing was the most common activity (66.4%) followed by directly taking a shower (16.2%). For the question about handling groceries and receiving delivery packages, the answer choices are in the form of several activities in different sequences and cases. The result shows that 55.6% still choose washing hands first before sorting groceries, but 34.9% choose to sort groceries first and then wash hands. For the case when they received a delivery package, 50.2% of the respondents choose to spray disinfectant first and 27% choose to directly open the package and then wash their hands.

There were also some unique habits found in the questionnaire. Whenever possible, several respondents chose to let the package sit for several days before opening it to ensure that any virus was inactive. Several respondents also show a better concern regarding natural daylight in their houses as a means of maintaining health.

The last type of question as given in the form of a short sentence where respondents were asked whether there is another habit or need regarding COVID-19 safety procedures at home that wase not mentioned in the previous questions. Unexpectedly, there were such mentions of unresolved needs or items of concern that they wish to have in their houses, such as a dedicated quarantine area for an occupant who is sick, a place to store disinfecting products, and a designated spot to place their linen masks for reuse.

3.2 Re-layout design

Based on the flow of activity, it was seen that what is needed is a transitional space between public and private areas a home to filter unwanted particles that may harm the occupant's health. When the house has two accesses, usually one connects to the living room and the other one connects to the service area through the garage. Occupants can choose to use the service access to get into the house and keep the common and private areas of the house clean. Unfortunately, small houses with single entrances do not have this opportunity. To respond to this necessity in the era of COVID-19, we propose the idea of bringing the service area to the front of the house, as described in the samples below.

Sample 1 (Figure 1) shows that the first area of access is the living room (1a). With this situation, the occupants will need to trespass the living room with their possibly contaminated outfit and belongings before finding the closest access to wash their hands at the sink (1b). Thus, we

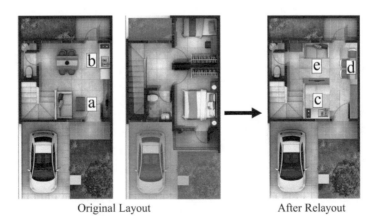

Original Layout   After Relayout

Figure 1.   Rearrangement recommendation from Sample 1.
(Source. https://podomoroparkbandung.id/padmagriya/, modified by authors)

recommend replacing the area of the living room with a kitchen and storage area (1c). This replacement will enable the occupants to wash their hands, place their items, spray them with disinfectant or sort, and store them directly immediately when they get into the house. The dining area (1d) is placed right after the kitchen and still has close access to the living room (1e).

Sample 2 (Figure 2) shows that the first area to access is the living room (2a) where there is no designated furniture to place storage facilities near the main access, but the access to the bathroom is close to the entrance (2b). Another problem that might occur is when the occupants need to sort items in the kitchen pantry (2c). Most likely, they will use the dining table (2d) that is supposed to be hygienic to place their groceries. To resolve the conflict, we recommend replacing the living room with a kitchen and storage area (2e) where occupants can wash their hands, place their items, spray them with disinfectant, or sort and store them directly once they get into the house. The new dining area (Figure 2f) is placed side by side with the kitchen and the living room (2g) is located at the corner with the orientation for space under the stairs that can be used for the TV and other electronic devices for family entertainment.

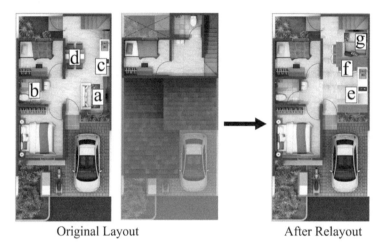

Original Layout   After Relayout

Figure 2.   Rearrangement recommendation from Sample 2.
(Source. https://podomoroparkbandung.id/padmagriya/, modified by authors).

Sample 3 (Figure 3) has a different situation as the service area is already set at the back of the house and linked to the maid or house helper's room. This house also has a spacious area on the first floor where the addition of furniture is possible. The problem is that the living room (3a) blocks

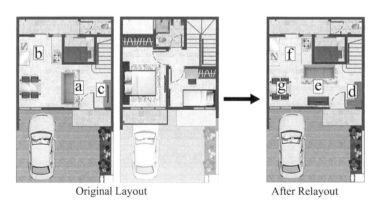

Original Layout   After Relayout

Figure 3.   Rearrangement recommendation from Sample 3.
(Source: https://www.sedayuindocity.com/p/rumah-milenial-pik-2.html, modified by authors).

the main access to the kitchen area (3b). Thus, we recommend replacing the television table (3c) with storage facilities (3d), rotate the orientation of the living room (3e) to widen the circulation width into the kitchen area (3f), and apply a small change in the kitchen which is moving the stove to the corner to keep the distance from the sofa.

4   DISCUSSIONS AND CONCLUSION

From the three samples provided, it is seen that preventing the spread of COVID-19 in small-sized houses is applicable by flipping the public areas and service area. The result from the re-layout design may not seem convenient for the flow of activity that we are accustomed to, but small houses with only a single entrance should not compromise the hygiene of the private area, especially in this era when we might have to live side by the side with the virus for the foreseeable future. Nevertheless, the proposed design comes as a result to the response to the new flow of household activities, where most occupants prefer to wash their hands before doing anything else and therefore need the shortest access from the entrance to running water, such as at the kitchen sink or bathroom.

However, the COVID-19 strategy that can be applied in small-sized houses where the limited dimensions of the home act as a hurdle. Even though the service area can be brought near to the entrance, the size cannot accommodate all the activities required to prevent the spread of COVID-19, such as providing an area to change clothes or having a designated spot for spraying disinfectant. In a small house, spraying disinfectant indoors may create another issue since the particles can spread to the adjacent area and intoxicate the occupants. Therefore, not only is prioritizing the service area essential, but interventions from the government might also be necessary to ensure that small-sized houses meet the standards of health and safety for residential buildings.

REFERENCES

Kampf,. G., Todt, D., Pfaender, S., and Steinmann, E. (2020) Persistence of Coronaviruses on Inanimate Surfaces and Their Inactivation with Biocidal Agents. *J Hosp Infect.* 104(3):246–51. doi:10.1016/j.jhin. 2020.01.022./,2020.

Karlen, M. and Fleming, R. (2016) *Space Planning Basics Fourth Edition,* p. 1, Hoboken, New Jersey.

Munif, A. 2009. *Perumahan Sehat* (Lumajang, East Java, 2009). Available on https://dhanwaode.wordpress. com/2011/01/26/sanitasi-perumahan/.

Schmidt III, R., Deamer, J., and Austin, S. (2011) Understanding Adaptability Through Layer Dependencies. *International Conference on Engineering Design, ICED11.* Technical University of Denmark, Kongens Lyngby, 2011.

Simbolon, H. and Nasution, I. N. (2017) Desain Rumah Tinggal yang Ramah Lingkungan untuk Iklim Tropis, *J Education Building* 3(1):46–59.

Synder, J.C. (1979) *Introduction To Urban Planning,* p. 212. New York.

White, E.T. (1983) *Site Diagramming Information for Architectural Design Analysis,* Florida A&M University, Florida.

Dynamics of Industrial Revolution 4.0: Digital Technology Transformation and Cultural Evolution –
Wulandari et al (eds)
© 2021 The Author(s), ISBN 978-1-032-04451-4

Electric kick bike design for a recreational vehicle

T.S. Pambudi, A.W. Heru, A. Deefinpramasya & V.R. Ramdhan
Telkom University, Bandung, Indonesia

ABSTRACT: Amusement parks are a popular tourist destinations. Usually, in the amusement park there is a relaxing area, a natural landscape, as well as a playground with various entertainment attractions. There are several modes of transportation available to accommodate user access to all areas or just admiring the beautiful scenery. One alternative is the kick bike with additional electric power to make it easier for users and not get tired when driving around in an amusement park, especially the uphill area. An electric kick bike was chosen as an alternative to attract young adult visitors to visit the amusement park. The research to be conducted is qualitative. Qualitative research is a method for exploring and understanding the activities and needs of amusement park visitors. Based on this potential, this research will design an electric kick bike for a recreational vehicle. The aim of this research is how to create an environmentally friendly vehicle as transportation as well as a recreational vehicle for amusement park visitors

Keywords: vehicle, kick bike, design, environmentally friendly

1 INTRODUCTION

The amusement park is a trendy tourist place, which not only offers beautiful natural attractions but also provides a variety of attractions for family games available in the amusement park area. The amusement park provides transportation facilities, both mass transportation and personal transportation, as well as recreational vehicles. One alternative for individual vehicles, as well as amusement park attractions, is the kick bike. The kick bike itself is a kind of scooter vehicle with a larger dimension on the wheels and frame compared with a conventional scooter. This vehicle (is) also an answer to accommodate the needs of attraction vehicles for young adults. Besides, this kick bike will be equipped with an additional electric engine to add power to facilitate users when going through the uphill terrain in the amusement park area.

The choice of kick bike with the addition of electric power is to create environmentally friendly transportation. By using an electric motor that does not produce carbon residues will help reduce environmental pollution. Based on the previous explanation, this research will design a kick bike with the addition of electric power. The goal is to provide modes of transportation and attractions for amusement park visitors that are environmentally friendly, based on the activities and needs of young adult visitors.

1.1 Sustainable design

In the early 1990s, the concepts of eco-design and green product design had emerged, which were a company's strategy to reduce the negative impact on the environment from the results of their industrial production activities. Until 1997, UNEP announced a statement on eco-design: "the concept of eco-design was an agreement to create sustainable products and consumption" (UNEP 2009).

This statement is the beginning of today's concept of sustainable design. As the issue of global environmental damage is increasingly visible, this forces the global industrial community to focus

DOI 10.1201/9781003193241-35

more on the environmental impacts of their production waste. This motivates companies to be more innovative in the activities of the production process and create better products, so as to balance the development of industrial speed with the environment. Also, environmental groups have broadened their scope by including social, economic, and environmental issues in the concept of sustainable design.

1.2 *Kick bike*

Kick bikes are human-powered road vehicles with handlebars, a deck, and wheels driven by being pushed using feet on the ground. Material that are used to make these vehicles are aluminum and steel. The significant difference between conventional scooters is the dimensions of the frame and wheels. On kick bikes, the frame dimensions are more extensive, with sizes based on the standard geometry of the bike. The large frame size is because the targeted kick bike users are adults. Also, the size of the wheels on the kick bike is more significant than the wheels on the scooter. The goal is with large wheels, creating a more massive wheel rotation and making it easier for kick bikes to pass various terrain or road types. A kick bike that will be designed is a combination of the form of a bicycle and a scooter. Where this vehicle has large bicycle tires that are driven by being pushed with legs like a scooter, this kick bike has dimensions according to the ergonomics of adults.

1.3 *Electric motor*

The electric motor is a tool to convert electrical energy into mechanical energy. Tools that function in reverse, converting mechanical energy into electrical energy, are called generators or dynamos. Electric motors are in every household appliance such as fans, washing machines, water pumps, and vacuum cleaners.

Today, the typical electric motor used for a modern electric bike is (a) BLDC or Brushless DC motor drive. BLDC moto(r) drive is commonly used because it is easy to apply to the bike and also more efficient (Ohio Electric Motors 2012). There are two models of BLDC motor drive: the first BLDC mid-drive and the second, more popular one, are BLDC hub drives. BLDC hub drives are made by putting the electricity into the wheel hub itself, while the stator is fixed solidly to the axle. The bicycle wheel hub is the motor; the result is more powerful (and) more efficient.

1.4 *Bike geometry*

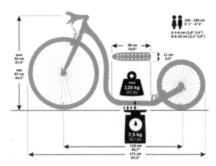

Figure 1.   Geometry Info Race Max 20. (source: www.kickbike.com)

Vehicle geometry is the dimension of the vehicle and the driver's position based on the concept of ergonomics. The geometry is fundamental because it affects the comfort, safety, and handling of the vehicle. The following is the kick bike geometry that will be the basis of the design; the geometry refers to products from the kick bike (Kickbike.com)

2 METHOD

The research to be conducted is qualitative. Qualitative research is the method for exploring and understanding the meaning of individuals or groups of people ascribed to social or humanitarian problems. This process requires essential efforts, such as asking questions to collect specific data from participants, analyzing data inductively, and interpreting the meaning of the data obtained. The results of this study are usually flexible (Creswell 2010).

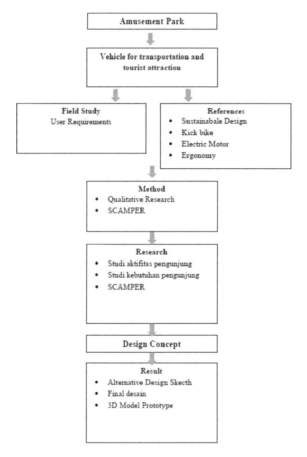

Figure 2.   Research flowchart.

The qualitative research strategy applied in this design is a study approach to the activities and needs of users for the basis of product design. The design process then uses the SCAMPER technique based on similar products on the market.

SCAMPER stands for Substitute, Combine, Adapt, Modify, Put to another use, Eliminate, and Reverse. Therefore, this technique is a collection of creative problem-solving methods based on design thinking methods. In use, we can choose one or several existing methods to use. The following ways will carry the data collection process:

1. observe the activities and needs of amusement park visitors,
2. study of literature on sustainable design and vehicles that has a sustainable design concept, and
3. study existing products in the market to guiding for (guide) the design process using the SCAMPER technique.

2.1 User requirements study

The process of obtaining data was carried out by interviewing several park visitors whose ages ranged from 14–26 years. In the interview conducted, an alternative kick bike as a vehicle is offered based on what visitors desire. From the results of the interviews conducted there are several important points, one of which is the ease of use. According to most visitors, they want a vehicle that is easy to use for various things while driving around the park, e.g., safety of goods carried by visitors, when visitors use vehicles, and carrying luggage safely without having to store it.

The conclusion from the study of end requirements is that vehicles needed by park visitors are vehicles that make are (that are) easy for visitors to use or at least not difficult, as well as having a place to carry goods in the vehicle.

2.2 Design aspect: SCAMPER

The first SCAMPER method used for finding the design aspect is Substitute. Replace the wheels on conventional scooters with bicycle wheels (16" in diameter), because the size of the wheels on a conventional scooter are too small. With a larger wheel diameter, the bike will be able to be easily pushed using the feet lightly and be able to cross the terrain with different contours.

The second is Combine—combine human power with an electric motor on a kick bike. The use of an electric motor is to help move the kick bike when used for transportation around an amusement park. It is also to help tourists when passing the uphill area. The choice of an electric motor is also one of implementation on (of) the concept of sustainable design, which is one of the recommendations for environmentally friendly vehicles is to use electric motor power. Electric motors produce no waste and have a lower carbon footprint. Electric motors also have a more compact size and are easier to install in vehicles.

The third SCAMPER method that we used is Adapt. For reasons of driver safety, it is necessary to have adequate brakes to support safety when driving the kick bike. When using the vehicle in areas with varying contours, and crowded by people passing by, it needs a brake that reliably controls the speed. Based on these needs, the kick bike adopts the braking system of the bicycle, the dual-pivot calliper brake type. This type of brake is commonly used for braking systems on daily use bicycles in urban areas. Also, the dual-pivot calliper brake is easy to install and maintain. Adding a basket to the back of the kick bike accommodates the need to carry bags or goods when using the vehicle. With this additional back basket, the tourist who uses this vehicle will be able to carry their bags safely.

3 RESULT

3.1 Concept design

The electric kick bike design aims to be a mode of transportation and attraction in amusement parks. Kick bikes are designed for adults based on ergonomy and bike geometry. This vehicle also uses a large wheel diameter so that it is easier to use in various types of areas. It has the addition of an electric motor for driving power to help the driver when traveling uphill. In this vehicle, there is also a luggage basket located at the back of the kick bike. Due to its simple and functional design, the kick bike is expected to attract riders, both for transportation around the park as well as a vehicle for visitor attractions.

3.2 Term of reference

1. Design Considerations: The design must meet the needs of the amusement park. First, the vehicle must attract the interest of visitors. Second, there is a container to carry luggage on the vehicle so that luggage remains safe when driving. Third, the addition of an electric motor helps the vehicle when traveling uphill. Finally, it (is) is more environmentally friendly and energy efficient.
2. Design Limits: The construction and material used must be sturdy to withstand shocks when used in areas with rough terrain. The BLDC type of electric motor comes with a rechargeable battery

so usage time is limited. The dimensions of the kick bike are based only on adult geometry. Kick bikes are specifically designed for use in amusement parks.

3. Design Description: The product designed is a kick bike using an electric motor as additional power. It is for transportation around an amusement park. This vehicle is also equipped with a basket as a place for visitors' luggage when driving. The kick bike target users are teenagers and adults.

3.3 *Product visualization (visualization)*

Figure 3.   A 3D model rendering of an electric kick bike.

4 CONCLUSION

The conclusion of this research is that the electric kick bike is one of the solutions that we choose to accommodate the need for transportation and attraction in an amusement park. The electric motor drive chosen to be added on the kick bike provides more power that can help tourists efficiently drive the vehicle uphill. An additional feature that adds function to the kick bike is the rear basket for carrying luggage safely. Furthermore, the electric kick bike will become one of the choice ways for young-adult tourists to enjoy the amusement park. The next step is to figure out how to apply the design concept and product visualization to the scaled model and so that it can become a product prototype.

REFERENCES

Creswell, John W. 2010. *Research Design: Pendekatan Kualitatif, Kuantitatif, dan Mixed*. (diterjemahkan oleh: Achmad Fawaid). Yogyakarta: Pustaka Pelajar.

Eberle, Bob. 1996. *Scamper: Games for Imagination Development*. Prufrock Press Inc.

KickBike. 2018. *Geometry Info Race Max 20*. https://kickbike.com/showroom_en/product-race-max-20.html

McLennan, J. F. 2004. *The Philosophy of Sustainable Design: The Future of Architecture*. Kansas City: Ecotone LLC.

Ohio Electric Motors. 2012. *Brushless DC Motors Used in Industrial Applications*. http://www.ohio electricmotors.com.

Swifty Scooters. 2020. SwiftyOne MK3. www.swiftyscooters.com

UNEP. 2009. *UNEP Year Book 2009: New Science and Developments in Our Changing Environment*. United Nations Environment Programme, Kenya

Walker, Stuart. 2006. *Sustainable by Design: Explorations in Theory and Practice*. Earthscan: London.

Dynamics of Industrial Revolution 4.0: Digital Technology Transformation and Cultural Evolution –
Wulandari et al (eds)
© 2021 The Author(s), ISBN 978-1-032-04451-4

Mahogany fruit material exploration for an essential oil nebulizer in the new normal adaptation

H. Azhar, A.S.M. Atamtajani & Andrianto
Telkom University, Bandung, Indonesia

ABSTRACT: The material investigation strategy in product design advancement may be a typical methodology that results in numerous unusual chances. Our examination centers around the investigation of material use from Swietenia macrophylla, usually known as mahogany, a local South American plant that is commonly naturalized in south-east Asian nations. This plant is regularly developed in estates since it yields veritable mahogany lumber which is very popular for making furniture. The plant delivers a gigantic measure of side natural product, its fruit, that tragically can't be improved upon at this point in society. In light of the perception and test result, its fruit can be utilized as elective specialty materials that advance the item's esteem with the aesthetical eco-plan approach. A viable cycle must be applied to treat the natural product fittingly with an appropriate pressed wood blend. This test method is applied to the essential oil nebulizer, one of the most popular items in this area of new normal. The correct treatment of this mahogany organic product is expected to be a future elective material for wood mix in making a wide scope of specialty products.

Keywords: Kata Kunci: material, exploration, mahogany, nebulizer, new normal

1 INTRODUCTION

The issue of national wood deficit demand drove the researcher to find wood-alternative materials for crafts and furniture manufacturing. According to Pengkajian and Perdagangan (2017) Badan Pengkajian dan Pengembangan Perdagangan (2017), the national wood demand has reached 57–58 million m^3/year while the production capacity of natural forests and plantations is around 45.8 million m^3/year. This means Indonesia still has a wood deficit of around 11 million m^3/year.

The Forest Management Center (2017) reported that mahogany (*Swietenia macrophylla*) is one of the easiest solid woods to cultivate with the plantation reaching 54,000 ha in Indonesia. However, the mahogany plantation has a plentifully discarded side product, its fruit. The abundant mahogany fruit reaches 216 tons/year and is still not used properly.

This fact inspires the author to explore the mahogany fruit material for wood combination in developing a new product. The main purpose of utilizing the mahogany fruit material is to create an aesthetical wood combination alternative material for making crafts and furniture. The research focuses on the utilization of mahogany fruit for creating an essential oil nebulizer design, a relaxing product for helping people in the new normal adaptation. An essential oil nebulizer was chosen to be developed with this wood combination material to develop one of the most wanted products during the pandemic into a brand new product with an eco-design approach.

2 RESEARCH METHOD

2.1 *Research approach*

The research method for this material exploration and design process was a qualitative approach. This qualitative method uses visual strategies as study material to process the research object. The study can be categorized as an entrenched case study (Flick, 2014).

2.2 Data collection techniques

The empirical data collection was gathered from archival information and semi-structured interviews from the wood crafters in Banyuwangi, East Java, Indonesia. Furthermore, the author also conducted field observations about the utilization of mahogany fruit in the plantation area.

2.3 Design method

The design method for this research focuses on the interchangeable method by making an adjustment or removing the visual element parts of the essential oil nebulizer. Hence, the author focuses on the remaking process of the visual appearance from the existing product, an essential oil nebulizer. According to Masry (2010), the visual strategy can be an added value for an object's visual quality based on the impact of the visual elements on human perception.

3 DISCUSSION AND RESULT

3.1 Mahogany fruit utilization

Forest Management (2017) reported that mahogany fruit production has reached 216 tons/year and has not been utilized yet for craft or mass furniture production. However, some studies revealed that mahogany fruit has many uses for antiseptics and plantation. Gultom et al. (2014) discovered that the mahogany fruit, actually its seeds, are useful as an insecticide to control soybean plant pests. Another study by Koneri (2016) proved that the mahogany fruit can be applied for *Aedes aegypti* larvae insecticide, as well as various traditional medicinal herbs. To optimize the abundant mahogany fruit that is treated like trash, the author focuses on research to make a combination of material products from the fruit.

3.2 Essential oil nebulizer and new normal adaptation

The World Health Organization (WHO) declared a pandemic caused by the SARS-CoV-2 on March 11, 2020. Since then, the virus that was first seen in Wuhan, China, has subsequently appeared in many countries around the world. Regarding this pandemic, the world is now facing a new normal adaptation such as physical distancing, masking for all, and the way people work and learn. Working from home is a new culture and there is no longer a need for frequent face-to-face meetings. The author focuses on assisting productive ambient working from home.

According to Lehrner et al. (2005) and Goes et al. (2012), the study determined that particular ambient odors can reduce anxiety and improve a worker's mood in the office. The evidence clearly proves that it is effective to manage symptoms like stress, anxiety, and insomnia. It makes the demand for essential oil diffusers and nebulizers raise significantly in the global market during a pandemic.

Essential oils considered to be "antiviral" are not universal virus killers. One virus that can be tackled by essential oil is influenza (Wu et al., 2012). However, there is no research on essential oil and SARS-CoV-2 at present that acclaimed any essential oils as antiviral for people with COVID-19. Therefore, the use of aromatherapy focuses on reducing anxiety and improving mood.

3.3 Material exploration

Mahogany plants only bloom after the age of 7 years. When the fruit is still young, it is green and becomes brown after it is ripe. There are flat-shaped seeds with a rather thick tip and blackish-brown winged colors inside the fruit. This material experiment uses the half-ripe mahogany fruit, so its fruit and seeds were still strongly fused. It will be dried in the sun to brown.

Figure 1.   The dried mahogany fruit. (Source: personal documentation, 2020)

After the mahogany fruit is dried, it is cut flat with the same thickness. The pieces will be shaped like a pentagon following the natural shape of mahogany.

Figure 2.   The cut-flat mahogany fruit.(Source: personal documentation, 2020)

The mahogany fruit that has been cut flat will be manually trimmed to be the same size. This measure aims to make mahogany fruit easily combined with the other material, plywood.

Figure 3.   The size standardization process.(Source: personal documentation, 2020)

The sorted size of mahogany fruits will be arranged in an aesthetic order with plywood as its material combination. Pieces of mahogany fruit are neatly arranged and glued together with plywood. After it sticks to plywood tightly, wait for it until dry and then tidy up with electric sandpaper.

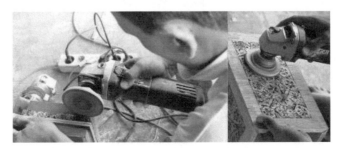

Figure 4.   The sanding fragment activity. (Source: personal documentation, 2020)

The results of sanding material combination between mahogany fruit and plywood can be used as an alternative material combination with added aesthetic value. This result can be used to create any kind of craft and wood furniture.

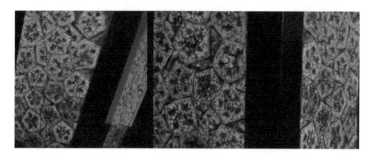

Figure 5.   The completed combination material of mahogany fruit. (Source: personal documentation, 2020)

3.4   *Term of references*

Term of reference serves as design limitation so the author can create the expected design:

1. Product Considerations. The product has a simple form and focuses on its function with an aesthetic combination material of mahogany fruit and plywood.
2. Product Limitation. The product uses the existing applied technology of an essential oil nebulizer on the market. So, the design will be adjusted to the nebulizer that already exists. Besides, this product can spread the aromatherapy odor only in one room.
3. Product Description. The target users are people who hardly manage symptoms like stress, anxiety, and insomnia. During the so-called new normal adaptation in the COVID-19 pandemic, people are forced to stay at home. Some people are struggling with the pandemic situation and cannot go outside for months. The essential oil nebulizer will help people reduce anxiety and improve their mood while working from home.

3.5   *Final design*

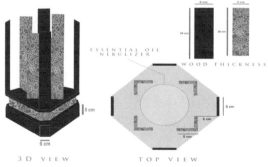
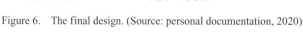

Figure 6.   The final design. (Source: personal documentation, 2020)

4 CONCLUSION

The national issue of a wood deficit has driven researchers to explore alternative materials for crafting and furniture products. The material exploration research of mahogany fruit revealed that the fruit which is treated like trash actually can be used as an alternative combination material to craft diverse creations. With the mahogany fruit combination, an applied product, such as an essential oil nebulizer in this research, becomes more attractive with a natural classic appearance. To create this combination of alternative material, the author must apply the proper treatment for the fruit. This research result can be used to develop other products from a combination of material exploration.

REFERENCES

Balai Pengelola Hutan Lebak. 2017. *Budidaya Mahoni (Swietenia Macrophylla King)*.

Flick, U. 2014. *Introducing Research Methods*. Sage, London.

Goes, T., Antunes, F., Alves, P., and Teixeira-Silva, F. 2012. *Effect of sweet orange aroma on experimental anxiety in humans*. Journal of alternative and complementary medicine. 18(8):798–804.

Gultom, R.M., Pangestiningsih, Y., and Lubis, L. 2014. *Pengaruh Beberapa Insektisida Terhadap Hama Lamprosema Indicata F. dan Spodoptera Litura F. Pada Tanaman Kedelai*. Jurnal Online Agroekoteknologi 2(3):1159–1164

Koneri, R. 2016. *Uji Ekstrak Biji Mahoni (Swietenia Macrophylla) terhadap Larva Aedes Aegypti*. JURNAL MKMI 12(4):2016–223

Krisnawati, H., Kallio, M., and Kanninen, M. 2011. *Swietenia macrophylla King*. Ecology, Silviculture and Productivity. CIFOR, Bogor.

Lehrner, J., Marwinski, G., Lehr, S., Johren, P., and Deecke, L. 2005. *Ambient odors of orange and lavender reduce anxiety and improve mood in a dental office*. Physiology & Behavior 86.

Masri, A. 2010. *Strategi Visual, Formalistik dan Semiotik*. Bantul: Jalasutra

Pengkajian, B. and Perdagangan, P. 2017. *Info Komoditi Furnitur*. Kementerian Perdagangan Republik Indonesia.

Wu, Q., Wang, W., Dai, X., Wang, Z., Shen, Z., Ying, H., and Yu, C. 2012. *Chemical compositions and anti-influenza activities of essential oils from Mosla dianthera*. Journal of Ethnopharmacology 139(2): 668–671.

Dynamics of Industrial Revolution 4.0: Digital Technology Transformation and Cultural Evolution –
Wulandari et al (eds)
© 2021 The Author(s), ISBN 978-1-032-04451-4

Design environment analysis on a portable handwash station: A case study in Lengkong sub-district, Bandung

S. Salayanti & W. Prihantoro
School of Creative Industries, Telkom University, Bandung, West Java, Indonesia

L.H. Penta
Sekolah Tinggi Desain Indonesia, Bandung, West Java, Indonesia

ABSTRACT: The Lengkong Sub-District, located on the south side of Bandung, is a very crowded sub-district. With how dense the population of it, the people in Lengkong have the indirect responsibility of keeping themselves and others safe amid the COVID-19 pandemic. Notably, this applies to those who work in the Sub-District Office, as well as those whose work involves going in and out of the Sub-District Office building. To prevent further spreading of the virus, the writer intends to provide the necessary facility for people to wash their hands, as well as to create a campaign icon/symbol to encourage people to wash their hands diligently. This campaign is directed not only to the people who work in the Sub-District Office, but also to all the citizens of Lengkong. The design of this portable handwashing station is made to be as attractive as possible for whoever passes by. The hope is that if they see it, they will have the urge and motivation to wash their hands. The design is also made with the health protocol in mind, with necessary features added to minimalize contamination.

Keywords: COVID-19, Lengkong Sub-District Office, portable handwash

1 INTRODUCTION

The Lengkong Sub-District office is located at Talaga Bodas Street No. 35, Malabar, Lengkong, Bandung City, West Java. In addition to the workers working in the office, Lengkong citizens also come to the office for several administration services, making it a high traffic location, in which virus spread is especially vulnerable. In this trying time of the COVID-19 pandemic, places like this should have the appropriate facility to accommodate the prevention of virus spread in order to protect not only those who work in the office, but also the civilians coming to the area for the governmental administration services.

One of the simplest facilities supporting the prevention of the virus spread is a place for people to wash their hands. Although they can do this in the washroom in regular circumstances, more facilities are needed in more places to encourage easier access to more frequent handwashing. In this special circumstance, the design of these handwashing posts should be adjusted to fit in the requirements for the purpose to be fulfilled.

Design environment is a systematic approach to evaluate the environmental consequences of a product and its processes, as well as the impact of said product to human engineering and environment (Calori & Vanden-Eynden 2015). Based on the understanding of what is needed, option analysis, and the available resources for a fast production that also considers the product handling and a cradle-to-grave production. The main focus is the content identification and the environmental implication of the product's development and the life cycle towards the environment (Fiksel 1996).

The purpose of design environment is to create a healthier environment for the worker, the civilians, and also the ecosystem. This program fulfills this purpose by promoting a change of

DOI 10.1201/9781003193241-37

technique in how the company manages environmental awareness. The fundamentals of design environments are:

1. fixing the safety of the workers, civilians, and the environment while maintaining the performance and the quality of the product. Another way to put it is to lessen the risk on the workers, civilians, and the environment;
2. using the resources responsibly; and
3. merging the environmental considerations into a product design, product redesign, process, and management.

With the fundamentals of the design environment listed above, there are some examples that can be done to fix a design to be more environmentally aware. The first example is the use of environmentally friendly materials. Be it materials with low use of energy, non-toxic materials, ozone-friendly materials, or a recycled material obtained from the waste of other manufacture process. The second is to use a recyclable resource. Plant and animal produce-based materials is a great example for that, with the provision that these resources should be extracted with conservation in mind. The third example is to use materials with minimal energy and water input, the fourth is to minimalize distribution impact by reducing the product's size and weight, the fifth being the minimalization of resource output like energy and water that will be used by the product during its life, and the sixth and final example is to maximize the durability and longevity of the final product, making parts that could be fixed without scraping everything and making them as recyclable parts.

With the efforts of making a product using the design environment approach gives both the manufacturing process and the final products some advantages. Some of these advantages include not only a product that is environmentally friendly, but also that the final products tend to be a better quality and to add to that, the price of manufacturing could be reduced significantly if the designer choose to use recycled material and/or use reasonable transport option, given the reduced size and weight. It will also appeal to a more environmentally conscious community as well as encourage other to be more conscious of it.

The most common applications of design environment are:

1. recyclable design,
2. knock-down design,
3. energy efficient design,
4. remanufactured design,
5. disposability design, and
6. minimalization of hazardous materials.

Other than the effect on the ecosystem, the design should also mind the effect on the users as members of society. Supporting the main function of the product and beyond, or in this case to promote the habit of handwashing beyond the main function of merely being a facility to do it. Educating the users to a better habit for the sake of not only the user's, but especially in this pandemic, the health of other people who have to make physical contact with the user.

2   METHOD

The execution of this research was done with the academic procedure generally applicable in this field of study, which is a qualitative method by observation and literature study about design environment. Although, due to the circumstances of this COVID-19 pandemic, all steps are done online to obey the current health protocol by the time this research was conducted.

Observations and interviews are directed toward the members of the local government institution and to the targeted local civilians. These data were then analyzed to design and produce the proper portable handwashing station.

3 RESULTS AND DISCUSSION

With the condition of the COVID -19 pandemic, this portable handwashing station should comply with the health department's protocol in order to support it, although at the same time, it needs to give the impression that is representative of the local environment without losing its main purpose. To educate the society of the healthy habit of frequent proper handwashing, it is also important to not only put an educational poster near it to display the diagram of proper handwashing, but to also put the supporting facility to act it out.

Figure 1.   The old portable handwashing station.

The old portable handwashing station prior to this research was placed too far from the main entrance. Not only that, but the overall shape and design weren't very representative of the Lengkong Sub-District office. Moreover, the shape, function, and implemented material did not correspond to the health protocol, the faucet required physical contact to turn the water on, the soap dispenser also required physical contact to pump it out, and there also weren't any hand drying facilities in sight, making the surrounding ground wet with puddles from a lot of people's wet hands.

After analyzing the problems found by observing and giving interviews to the users, the new and improved handwashing station was made with supporting components like the multifunction rack with two separate water storage inside, one for clean water and the other for used dirty water. The zinc sink basin is equipped with a sensor-activated faucet, and on the side is a storage space for a soap dispenser, hand dryer, thermometer, and hand sanitizer dispenser. The design was made with the user target physics in mind, making it as ergonomic as possible for every age, gender, character, and everyday activity. Other than the ergonomic design for the users, this portable handwash also functions as a campaign tool to encourage people to wash their hands. The infographic design is made to appeal to wondering eyes even from afar. It is made so that even people from 5 meters away could see the information educating them of how important it is to wash their hands constantly to prevent the spread of COVID-19. The circulation problem is also fixed by putting the station nearer to the entrance, making the space for a queue longer so that the visitors have more space to follow the health protocol and avoid physical touch against each other.

Figure 2.   The new portable handwash station.

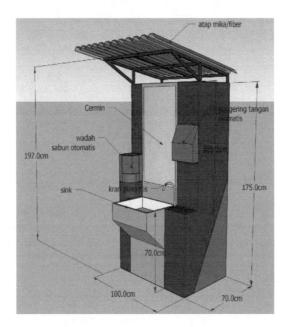

Figure 3.   3D visual of the new handwash station design.

The automatic touchless faucet, soap dispenser, and hand dryer minimizes, if not completely eliminates, cross contamination. Significantly improving the previous condition where everything needs physical contact to work. The roof is designed to keep the station shielded from direct rain, making it more sustainable for durability. Although even if it doesn't keep all the rain water away, the materials used are mostly rust-free recyclable stainless steel, and melamine-finished steel pipe, making it as water resistant as possible as an insurance for risks of being placed outdoor, exposed to the tropical rain and humidity of Indonesia. These materials are the most sustainable, considering all aspects like recyclability, transportability, durability, and functionality.

Figures 4 and 5.   The touchless sensor activated water faucet and hand dryer.

Figure 6.   The design of the infographic diagram used in the campaign.

An infographic diagram is conveniently placed on the mirror, making it easy for the user to see so that it can serve its purpose to educate them about the proper way of handwashing. This way, the *"The Cuci Tangan Biar Aman"* campaign could be spread more effectively as the viewer of the infographic diagram could try the steps with the provided facility as they see it.

4   CONCLUSION

In an effort to stop the spread of the COVID-19 virus in the Lengkong Sub-District as well as to raise the awareness of the local people, the redesign of the portable handwashing station is in order. Coming from the characters of the product's users, the new product is made to be as efficiently functional as possible. Not only that, but the new product has several new modifications to minimize cross contamination from physical contact, it is also designed to be ergonomic for the local people, and after considering every aspects of sustainability, also the best material for this case of circumstance.

These improvements are proved to be more efficient than the old portable handwashing station. By considering its environmental character, it achieves beyond the original function of the hand-washing station by also educating and encouraging the local people's awareness of the COVID-19 pandemic and how serious it is. The product also gives a passive imposing encouragement for its target users to use it without physically forcing anything. The obvious image of the campaign on this product could potentially make passerbys feel obligated to wash their hands, which is a good thing for society to be better handle the current pandemic.

REFERENCES

Calori, C. and Vanden-Eynden, D. 2015. *Signage and Wayfinding Design*: A Complete Guide to Creating Environmental Graphic Design Systems.
Fiksel, J. 1996. *Design for Environment, Creating Eco-Efficient Products and Process*, McGraw-Hill.

Tanudireja, O. and Solahuddin, M. 2013. Ergonomics Viewed from Anthropometry at the Interior of Pizza-Hut Restaurant in East Surabaya. *Journal of Intra.* 1(2).

Teladan WargaNet. 2017. Design for Environment. https://warganetteladan.wordpress.com. (diakses tanggal Januari 2, 2021)

Ulrich, R.S., Zimring, C., Zhu, X., DuBose, J., Seo, H.B., Choi, Y.S., Quan, X., and Joseph, A. 2018. A review of the research literature on evidence-based healthcare design. *Herd*, 1(3): 61–125.

Zahra, Maysitha Fitri Az and Salayanti, S. 2016. Analysis of Visitor Circulation Patterns at Celebrity Fitness Transtudio Mall Bandung. *Idealog: Indonesian Design Ideas and Dialogues* 1.3:257–270.

Dynamics of Industrial Revolution 4.0: Digital Technology Transformation and Cultural Evolution –
Wulandari et al (eds)
© 2021 The Author(s), ISBN 978-1-032-04451-4

The potential to revitalize *Sasirangan* fabric using natural dyes

A. Salsabillah & A. Arumsari
Telkom University, Bandung, Indonesia

ABSTRACT: The fashion industry in Indonesia is increasingly developing with the demand for various fashion products that always follow fashion trends. Along with the increasing demand, *Sasirangan* fabrics began to lose their identity by dyeing using synthetic dyes. This is because synthetic dyes, which are relatively stable, are firmly attached to the fabric and the manufacturing process, which tends to be faster and cheaper. *Sasirangan* fabric production activities always produce a large amount of liquid waste, especially synthetic dyes that cannot decompose naturally. The liquid waste is directly disposed into the surrounding environment without going through any processing process, so that it has great potential for environmental pollution, especially in Kalimantan waters. Therefore, it is necessary to revitalize *Sasirangan* fabric coloring by using natural dyes. In addition to restoring the identity of the *Sasirangan* fabric, which is believed to be a "medicine" with various natural motifs and colors, it is also hoped that the selling value and creativity of *Sasirangan* fabric products will increase so that it can realize sustainable fashion and the 8th sustainable development goal, for the sake of ensuring the sustainability of a prosperous life on earth.

Keywords: *Sasirangan* fabric, fashion industry, natural dyes, sustainable fashion

1 INTRODUCTION

Population growth in Indonesia has increased every year, which is directly proportional to the development and progress of the country's industry. However, industry's progress is not balanced between the processes contained and the waste produced, resulting in environmental pollution that threatens the survival of humans and the ecosystem on Earth. One of the industries in Indonesia that is growing rapidly is the fashion industry, as evidenced by the statement put forward by the Creative Economy Agency (BEKRAF) in the OPUS – Creative Economy Outlook 2017 that fashion is the largest sub-sector of the 15 sub-sectors in Indonesia's creative industry which accounts for 56% of country's products in the creative industry. Also, 24% of the workforce is in the fashion sub-sector.

The phenomenon of the rapid development of the fashion industry also has an impact on the growing *Sasirangan* fabric industry. *Sasirangan* fabric is one of the traditional fabrics of the Banjar tribe from South Kalimantan Province which has been passed down from generation to generation from the 12th to the 14th centuries when Lambung Mangkurat became Patih Negara Dipa. Based on the story that developed, the *Sasirangan* fabric was first made by Patih Lambung Mangkurat after he was meditating for 40 days and 40 nights on a raft (Andriani 2018). According to Kholis (2016), *Sasirangan* fabric was originally known by the people of South Kalimantan as *Pamintan* fabric, which in the Banjar language means request, the function of the *Sasirangan* fabric being if someone is being treated for a pingitan disease. Seclusion disease is a disease that originates from the spirits of ancestors who are aristocrats, said to have lived in the pantheon or the spirit realm. At this time, *Pamintan* fabric is better known as *Sasirangan* fabric. The word *Sasirangan* is literally not a noun: "*Sa*" means one and "*Sirangan*" means baste or sewn (Wijaya et al. 2015). This refers to the process of making the *Sasirangan* fabric itself which has a sewing process or baste and then dipped in dye.

DOI 10.1201/9781003193241-38

According to data from the South Kalimantan Industry and Trade Service, the total *Sasirangan* home industry is 103 units. An important part of making *Sasirangan* fabric is making the motif by coloring the finished fabric using synthetic dyes, which are relatively stable and firmly attached to the fabric. *Sasirangan* fabric production activities always produce large amounts of liquid waste. The liquid waste is disposed of directly to the surrounding environment without going through any treatment process. The *Sasirangan* industry in the fabric processing process includes several stages: watering the fabric, preparing dyes, coloring, washing, drying, and ironing. The production stages that produce waste come from the dyeing and washing processes. In the coloring stage, the dyes used are synthetic dyes and dyes derived from plants and roots from forests in Kalimantan. As auxiliary materials to create and strengthen the color, other things are used, e.g., lime, lemon, vinegar, saltpeter, alum, lime water, terusi, diazonium salt, NaOH, spirits, sulfuric acid, etc., for washing detergents (Nora 2000).

Sasirangan liquid waste that is disposed of generally comes from the dyeing process, either from the residue of immersion or the washing process. *Sasirangan* industrial wastewater generally contains contaminants whose amounts exceed the Liquid Waste Quality Standard for the Textile Industry Number: KEP51/MENLH/10/1995 (Imoco & Irman 2003). These contaminants are TSS (total suspended solid) and chromium metal with amounts above 50 ppm and 1 ppm as well as organic materials which cause high COD (chemical oxygen demand) and BOD (biochemical oxygen demand) values. Therefore, if they are not handled properly they can disturb the surrounding environment (Hartanto et al. 1993).

The negative impact generated from the fashion industry is not only from *Sasirangan* fabrics, making this a trigger for the eco-friendly, green fashion, or sustainable fashion movement. According to Kaikobad (2015), sustainable fashion is part of a larger trend of sustainable design where the products produced have social and environmental considerations that impact all aspects of life from these products, including the carbon footprint. The development of sustainable fashion in Indonesia is marked by the holding of the Indonesian Fashion Week (IFW) in 2015, which carried the theme "Fashionable People Sustainable Planet".

One of the implementations of sustainable fashion is the use of natural dyes as textile dyes that are environmentally friendly and can experience natural decay. They can also be used as a countermeasure for liquid waste produced by *Sasirangan* fabric. Andriani (2018) states that long ago, *Sasirangan* fabric used natural dyes such as seeds, fruit, leaves, skin, or tubers. Natural dyes are considered to be able to cure various diseases, and it is believed that the motifs displayed are also capable of healing diseases. In addition, natural dyes have an advantage in terms of color that synthetic dyes cannot imitate. So, this can be done by revitalizing *Sasirangan* fabrics using natural dyes in order to create a sustainable fashion. The existence of sustainable fashion can also help realize SDG (Sustainable Development Goal) #8 (ensuring the availability and management of sustainable clean water and sanitation for all) to reduce waterwaste in rivers in South Kalimantan. Also, #12 (ensuring sustainable consumption and production patterns) reduces the consumption of products that are not environmentally friendly.

2 RESEARCH METHOD

The method used in this research is qualitative. The first step is to base the phenomenon of shifting the use of natural dyes to synthetic fabrics in *Sasirangan* by using the data collection method in literature studies. In addition, data collection on the use of natural dyes in brands in Indonesia was carried out. Furthermore, the analysis of the revitalization potential of *Sasirangan* fabrics uses natural dyes. Therefore, the results of this study are the conclusion of the author's analysis regarding the object of the study raised.

3 RESULT AND ANALYSIS

Sasirangan fabric is a traditional fabric originating from South Kalimantan, also called *Pamintan* fabric, which means "request". Initially, *Sasirangan* fabric only used natural dyes, which also

Table 1. Functions and symbolic meanings of the various colors of *Sasirangan* fabric.

No	*Sasirangan* fabric	Symbolic Functions and Meanings
1.	Yellow	symbolizes that the wearer is in the process of healing from jaundice (*kana wisa* in Banjar language)
2.	Green	symbolizes that the wearer is in the process of healing from a paralyzed disease (stroke),
3.	Purple	symbolizes that the wearer is in the process of healing from stomach ailments (diarrhea, dysentery, and cholera),
4.	Red	symbolizes that the wearer is in the process of healing from headaches, and difficulty sleeping (insomnia),
5.	Black	symbolizes that the wearer is in the process of healing from fever and itchy skin,
6.	Brown	symbolizes that the wearer is in the process of healing from a mental illness (stress).

strengthened the public's belief in the ability of *Sasirangan* fabric as a medicine that could cure various diseases.

However, the increase in market demand and the intense competition among artisans have caused artisans to start using synthetic dyes. Synthetic dyes are more widely used because the coloring process is faster than natural dyes and is also easier to obtain and use. *Sasirangan* fabric market demand also prefers striking colors, which can only be obtained from synthetic dyes.

At this time, natural dyes are only used in *Pamintan* fabrics, even though there are only a few enthusiasts. *Sasirangan* fabrics that use natural dyes can be found in Hulu Sungai Tengah Regency and are produced in limited quantities (Andriani 2018). The origin of synthetic dyes replacing natural dyes in the *Sasirangan* fabric production process in South Kalimantan is uncertain. However, compared to fabric production in other regions in Indonesia, namely in Bali, based on historical records, in woven fabrics on the island of Bali, synthetic dyes began to enter the market around 1908 (Wronska 2015).

The symbolic meanings previously possessed by the *Sasirangan* fabric based on the natural dyes used have now shifted. The healing ability of the *Sasirangan* fabric is now only considered a gimmick. The colors used in *Sasirangan* fabrics are now only limited to market demands.

Behind the many advantages that synthetic dyes have, it turns out that synthetic dyes also have a negative impact due to the use of dangerous substances of synthetic organic compounds, heavy metals, and phenols. This threatens the sustainability of rivers in South Kalimantan. The liquid waste has a big influence on the ecological life of the Martapura River, Banjarmasin City, located in three locations, namely Sungai Jingah Village, Surgi Mufti Village, and Seberang Masjid Village, where the Martapura River is one of the rivers that has a major function in the life of the people of Banjarmasin City, as a medium for river transportation, tourism assets to a source of drinking water managed by PDAM Kota Banjarmasin. (Isnasyauqiah. 2018).

However, in recent years, public awareness about the dangers of synthetic dye waste for the environment has led to a trend of revitalizing natural dyes for various products. Therefore, the Provincial Government of South Kalimantan held training on the use of natural dyes. The dyes used are rambutan leaves, mahogany tree bark, noni root, ironwood sawn powder, ketapang leaves, mango leaves, daughter shame leaves, and guava leaves.

In addition to increasing public awareness, it turns out that the market for the use of natural dyes is increasing because the colors produced have their own characteristics, such as the resulting colors will be softer, and this is preferred by foreign markets and those outside South Kalimantan. According to Setiawan in Andriani (2018), natural dyes produce beautiful and distinctive colors, which synthetic dyes will find difficult to imitate.

However, the manufacturing process is complicated and takes a long time. Therefore, the price for products using natural dyes will be relatively higher than using synthetic dyes. Apart from the complicated and time-consuming production process, the availability of natural dyes is already limited. One of them is ironwood, which is now limited in number due to forest exploitation in Kalimantan, where ironwood grows and is replaced by oil palm plantations, resulting in the availability of ironwood being scarce. Ironwood, which is now used for dyeing *Sasirangan* fabric, results from waste from ironwood processing artisans.

In recent years, local brands have offered products made from natural ingredients with exclusive product designs. The purpose of these brands is to remind and raise awareness that the fashion industry has the potential for adverse impacts on the environment. Based on the phenomenon of natural pollution, many parties, individuals and communities, and organizations have developed an environmentally friendly fashion. The method used is the use of natural fibers and dyes.

The use of natural dyes for the fashion industry is becoming a trend marked by the increasing number of brands using natural dyes. The brands in question are Kana Goods, Jarit, Manungs, Javanese Batik Gallery, Nurzahra, Bluesville, Tarum, Imaji Studio, Kembang Tjelup, Osem, and Seratus Kapas (Arumsari et al. 2018). In addition, there are Sasirangan fabric products that use natural dyes. The color of natural coloring tends to be more in demand by markets overseas and outside South Kalimantan. Currently, a local brand uses *Sasirangan* fabric products that use natural dyes with exclusive designs, namely Halomasin, which was founded by Santika Syaravina and Yuri Alfa Centauri in collaboration with IKKON. Also, there is the Assalam Sasirangan brand, which was founded by Muhammad Redho in 2009.

Figure 1.   Product of fashion brand named Halomasin, made from *Sasirangan* fabric.

The use of natural dyes in *Sasirangan* fabric products has the potential to help realize the SDGs (Sustainable Development Goals) in 2030, as for SDG #8 (ensuring the availability and management of clean, sustainable water and sanitation for all) to reduce waterwaste in rivers in South Kalimantan due to the river in Banjarmasin being the main function as a medium for river transportation and tourism assets to a source of drinking water managed by PDAM Banjarmasin City. Also, #12 (ensuring sustainable consumption and production patterns) reduces the consumption of products that are not environmentally friendly and maximize ironwood waste for natural coloring so that there is no side/waste from ironwood.

Apart from realizing the SDGs, revitalizing *Sasirangan* fabrics using natural dyes will add to these products' aesthetic value because the colors produced have their own characteristics such as the resulting colors being softer, and this is preferred by foreign and outside of South Kalimantan markets. In addition to adding aesthetic value, there will be an increase in the selling value of these products, and this is because the results of products that use natural dyes will be more expensive than using synthetic dyes and increase the philosophical value of *Sasirangan* fabric, which is a fabric for treating, although, this is only a gimmick.

4   CONCLUSION

Based on the data above, it can be concluded that *Sasirangan* fabric can be revitalized using natural dyes. The advantage of revitalizing using natural dyes is as prevention against the pollution that endangers nature and can help realize the SDGs. Although producing *Sasirangan* fabrics using natural dyes is much longer and more complicated, this can be handled by an increase in market production with the latest designs and motifs that can reach all circles so that it can increase the selling value and creativity of these *Sasirangan* fabrics. The sustainable fashion market develops over time and increases along with human awareness of the sustainability of nature, so that *Sasirangan* fabrics with natural dyes can be a solution in realizing sustainable fashion.

ACKNOWLEDGMENT

Thank you to the research team for collecting data and working with one other. It is hoped that this research can be developed further in the implementation stage of processing natural dyes on *Sasirangan* Fabric.

REFERENCES

Andriana, Yunita Fitri. 2018. *Pergeseran Fungsi dan Makna Simbolis Kain Sasirangan.* Jurnal Rupa Vol. 03. Edisi 2 No. 01:77–92. Jakarta: Indonesia.

Arumsari, Arini. Agus Sachari., Andyanto Rikrik Kusmara. 2018. *Pemanfaatan Pewarna Alam sebagai Trend Baru pada Fashion Brands di Indonesia.* Jurnal Rupa 03. Edisi 2 No. 03:115–129. Bandung: Indonesia

Hartanto, E.S., Syarif, B., and Padmono, C. 1993. *Pengaruh Penambahan Khitosan dan Lama Pengendapan terhadap Hasil Penanganan Limbah Cair Industri Penyamakan Kulit.* Warta IHP/J.of Agro-based Industri, 10(1–2):14–17.

Imoco, B. and Irman. 2003. *Penghilangan Warna Limbah Cair Industri Kain Batik Sasirangan dengan Proses Koagulasi. Buletin BIMADA Departemen Perindustrian dan Perdagangan.* Samarinda. 15(11):8–14.

Isnasyauqiah. 2018. "Potensi Limbah Cair Zat Pewarna Sasirangan Terhadap Pencemaran Di Kota Banjarmasin. Kota Banjarmasin: Lembaga Penelitian dan Pengabdian Masyarakat Universitas Lambung Mangkurat.

Kaikobad, Najmul Kadir dkk. 2015. *Sustainable and Ethical Fashion: The Environmental and Morality Issues.* IOSR Journal Of Humanities And Social Science (IOSR-JHSS) Volume 20, Issue 8, Ver. I), 17–22.

Kholis, N. 2016. *Kain Tradisional Sasirangan "Irma Sasirangan.* Kampung Melayu Kalimantan Selatan. Skripsi Program Studi Pendidikan Seni Rupa Fakultas Bahasa dan Seni Universitas Yogyakarta.

Nora, S. 2000. *Pertumbuhan Vegetatif Tanaman Kangkung (Ipomoea reptans Foir Var. Grand) pada Pemberian Limbah Sasirangan.* Banjarmasin: Skripsi P. S. Pend. Biologi. FKIP UNLAM.

Wijaya, Fianto, Dan Hidayat. 2015. *Penciptaan Buku Ilustrasi Kain Sasirangan Sebagai Upaya Promosi Seni Budaya Banjarmasin kepada Remaja.* Surabaya: Jurnal DKV STIKOM.

Wronska, Maria. 2015. *Balinese Textile For Gods and People. Poland: Central Museum of Textilein Lodz.* https://www.sdg2030indonesia.org/ accessed October 2, 2020.

Dynamics of Industrial Revolution 4.0: Digital Technology Transformation and Cultural Evolution –
Wulandari et al (eds)
© 2021 The Author(s), ISBN 978-1-032-04451-4

Calligraphy crafts made from waste: A case study on Sawdust

M.N. Hadiansyah
Telkom University, Bandung, Indonesia

P.S.T. Dewi
Bali Design & Business Institute, Bali, Indonesia

P. Adinata & F. Syaban
Telkom University, Bandung, Indonesia

ABSTRACT: The problem raised in this study is wood waste from the wood industry. This industry produces building accessories such as doors, windows, and frames that are considered very useless and has a bad impact on the environment. Calligraphy craftsmen see an opportunity from this wood waste. Through the creativity of craftsmen, wood waste can be used as a craft that has a sale value. They chose sawdust as a material for making calligraphy crafts. This study aims to know how calligraphy craftsmen take advantage of furniture industry waste, namely sawdust, in order to increase the selling value so that it has an impact on increasing their economy. Through the method of the qualitative approach with a comparative method, it can be traced how the process of increasing the sale value of crafts made from sawdust by craftsmen is found in two techniques of making: molding and sticking. Both can increase the sale value of wood waste with multiple benefits. The results of the comparison show that the molding technique is more profitable in time, process, and cost.

Keywords: calligraphy, craft, wood waste, sawdust

1 INTRODUCTION

The definition of wood waste is the result of the remnants of human activity in making some products made from wood that have no economic value (Purwanto 2009). The production process in the craft industry of wooden furniture at the initial stage is in the form of raw material, that is raw wood in the form of spindles or pieces. In the next stage, the raw wood is processed with the latest technologies and certain equipment by the needs so that it becomes a product. The process that can't be avoided is the existence of waste from the production such as shavings, pieces of wood, and sawdust created by equipment and cutting tools such as hand saws, table saws, and other equipment used to produce wood waste in the form of powder (Sumarno 2015). The existence of mishandling wood waste has a negative impact on the environment and the community, so there is a need to think continuously about the waste material (Sutarman 2016).

Previous research on sawdust did not concentrate on its commercial value. Such sawdust was used as a medium for growing mushrooms (Taskirawati 2018), and in the study of Purba and Lubis (2018), sawdust was used as a mixture of light bricks, while Salman (2020) examined sawdust which can be made into compost for soil fertilizers.

Lately, creativity appears that changing the sawdust into a craft has a high sale value. It is a given that many people are aware of the importance of maintaining the environment so that many people are interested in crafts made from waste. One of the popular crafts in Muslim community is the sawdust calligraphy crafts. In this craft, sawdust is highlighted as the main material that can look aesthetic. Sawdust calligraphy reads *Asmaul Husna*, *Kursi* verse, *Shalawat*, and *Tauhid* sentences loved by most Muslim people, because this craft can be hanging on the wall and can fill the emptiness in a room (Rofiq 2019). Based on observations, there are two techniques in making sawdust calligraphy, namely molding and sticking. This study focuses on how calligraphy craftsmen take the advantage of furniture industry waste, namely sawdust in order to increase the selling value so that it has an impact on increasing their economy. Besides, it aims to find out whether the molding or the sticking that provides greater benefits for the craftsmen.

2 RESEARCH METHOD

The method used in this study is a qualitative approach with a comparative method. A qualitative approach is an approach based on a researcher's experience in producing a thinking perspective that is conveyed in descriptions (Creswell 2003). While the comparative method is used to compare two variables (Sugiyono 2010), in this study the variables are molding and sticking in the technique of making sawdust calligraphy.

2.1 Data collection

The data collection method used is the descriptive qualitative data collection method. Qualitative research is used to produce detailed data because the data comes from interviews and direct observation (Poerwandari 2007). The stages of data collection are made through observation and interviews with five manufacturers of calligraphy made from sawdust. Among them, three of them use the molding technique, while two of them use the sticking technique. During the observation, the process documentation of each technique was also carried out to support the results of the interview. Besides, data collection through a reference is also carried out to obtain data on the method of processing sawdust.

2.2 Data analysis

This study used a comparative method to analyze the data. Based on observations, there are two techniques in making sawdust calligraphy, namely molding and sticking. Each technique is observed for the detail of the process and the cost of production so that the differences from each technique are known. The last stage is comparing both to find out which one has the greatest benefit.

3 RESULT AND DISCUSSION

3.1 Result

Waste from the furniture industry can be categorized into a few kinds, namely: shavings, pieces of wood, sawdust, and dust. Waste like that is very difficult to reduce in the furniture industry. In the process of making the craft of calligraphy, the type of waste selected is sawdust, because sawdust has a particle size smaller than some other types of wood waste.

Sawdust calligraphy can be done using two techniques: sticking and molding. The technique of sticking is the technique of twisting sawdust dough then sticks one by one to follow the shape of the pattern on the surface of the flat field. The making of sawdust calligraphy with the sticking technique requires a few tools and materials: sawdust, wood board, wood glue, and a palette knife.

Based on Figure 1, the initial technique of making sawdust and wood glue mixed on the board and then mixed evenly using a palette knife (1). Furthermore, make a mixture of sawdust and wood glue into the dough (2), and round the dough to an elongated shape for easy to form the calligraphy on the continued process (3). Sticking a dough of sawdust round elongated shape to follow the pattern sketch on the plywood (4), using a palette knife to form the composite powder of the wood neatly and to follow the shape of the pattern. After all the patterns are covered by sawdust dough, hereinafter closing the part out of the pattern that is still empty, use the wood glue and sawdust (5).

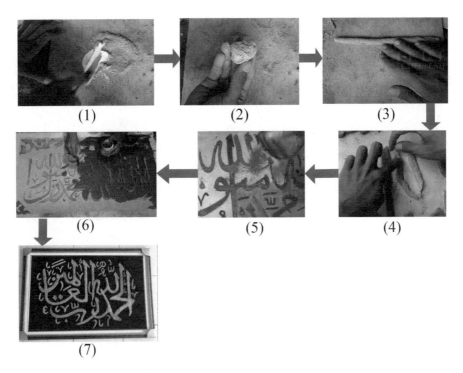

Figure 1. The stages of the sticking technique.

The next step is waiting for it to dry completely, which takes 4–5 days. After the entire surface is dried, the next step is finishing using wall paint with a different color between the background and the calligraphy (6). The goal is to make it look more colorful and interesting (7).

The molding technique in the manufacturing of calligraphy sawdust still uses glue as a mixture for sticking. Sawdust is not strong enough to withstand stretches that are elongated and needs another mixture as the adhesive. The technique of making the calligraphy crafts made from sawdust with the molding technique requires a variety of tools and materials such as electric soldering, styrofoam, wood glue, sawdust, paper, pencil, and cutter.

Based on Figure 2, the initial technique is to draw the shape of the pattern calligraphy on paper, and then patterned paper is hollowed to follow the pattern using the cutter (1). Paper that has been hollowed out and then taped on the styrofoam. After the paper is tacked, the styrofoam is hollowed to follow the pattern of the calligraphy contained in the paper using electric soldering (2). Mix the sawdust and wood glue evenly and then fill in the molding made from styrofoam that has been made (3). After the styrofoam is filled, the next step is to dry it using sunlight (4). This process of drying takes 4–5 days depending on the weather. The last stage is framing the calligraphy so it can be hung on the wall (5).

3.2 Discussion

From the comparison conducted, it was found that each technique is different. The comparison can be seen in Table 1.

The results of the comparison Table 1 show that the technique of molding is faster with a higher price than the technique of sticking. The molding technique does not use synthetic dyes. It only relies on the natural color of the sawdust that is friendly to the environment. If the sticking technique, the advantage obtained is the other result of the craft having different looks. Because the process of the sticking technique is handmade from the start to the end, it certainly is a different result.

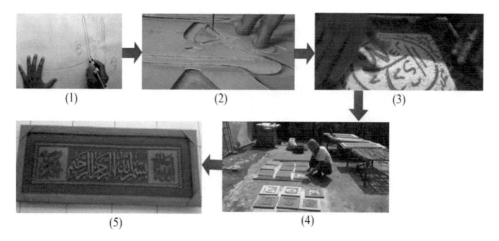

Figure 2. The stages of the molding technique.

Table 1. Comparison of sticking and molding technique.

Sticking Technique	Molding Technique
The sticking process following the pattern in the sketch calligraphy on the wood board takes up a lot of time because one should be careful and follow the shape of the pattern manually.	The process of punching holes in paper and styrofoam to be the main focus. Because if the process is not neat, the result of moldings is not neat either. The advantage of the molding technique is relatively short and does not take much time.
After the annealing process is completed enter the process of drying after that is painted using wall paint and given a layer of spray paint clear.	The molding technique does not need finishing using paint, it just needs to follow the original color on the wood so that is friendly for the environment.
The calculations of profit earned by size 1125 square inch (in IDR): Production Cost: 147,500 Selling Price: 450,000 Profit: (selling price – production cost) 450,000 – 147,500 = 343,500 Percentage of profit: (302,500:450,000) x 100% = 67.22%	The calculations of profit earned from each craft by size 1125 square inch (in IDR): Production cost: 141,500 Selling Price: 485,000 Profit: (selling price – production cost) 485,000 – 141,500 = 343,500 Percentage of profit: (343,500:485,000) x 100% = 70.82%
The percentage of profit earned by size 1125 square inch is 67.22%.	The percentage of profit earned from each craft by size 1125 square inch is 70.82%.

4 CONCLUSION

The type of wood industry waste chosen by calligraphy craftsmen is sawdust. Sawdust was chosen because it hasit a smooth texture and easy to shape. There are two techniques to be used in making sawdust calligraphy, namely molding and sticking. The molding technique is more profitable and faster both in terms of time and production process as well as the percentage of profit on the selling price. Comparison between the molding and the sticking with the same size, the profit of the molding is 70.82% while the sticking technique is 67.22%. From these results, it can be seen that the function of sawdust can be increased through skill and creativity to make calligraphy crafts. Besides, the crafts made from waste can increase the selling value of the craft so that it is profitable and of course has an impact on improving the economy of craftsmen.

ACKNOWLEDGMENTS

The authors gratefully acknowledge the support for this research provided by the School of the Creative Industries, Telkom University. The authors also wish to thank all colleagues and the community of craftsmen, especially wood waste craftsmen in East Java, who have contributed to this research. Thank you for all the support.

REFERENCES

Creswell, J. W. 2003. Research design: Qualitative, quantitative, and mixed methods approach (2nd ed.). *Thousand Oaks, CA: Sage.*

Poerwandari, K. 2007. Pendekatan Kualitatif untuk Penelitian Perilaku Manusia. *Universitas Indonesia: Jakarta.*

Purba, R.E.S. and Lubis, K. 2018. Pemanfaatan Limbah Serbuk Gergaji Kayu Sebagai Subtitusi Campuran Bata Ringan Kedap Suara. Buletin Utama Teknik UISU Medan (Vol. 13) https://jurnal.uisu.ac.id/index.php/but/article/view/277/298

Purwanto, D. 2009. Analisa Jenis Limbah Kayu pada Industri Pengolahan Kayu di Kalimantan Selatan. *Jurnal Riset Industri Hasil Hutan* (Vol. 1). http://dx.doi.org/10.24111/jrihh.v1i1.864

Rofiq, M. 2019. Berkah Ramadhan, Seni Kaligrafi Serbuk Kayu di Probolinggo Laris Manis. Retrieved from https://news.detik.com/berita-jawa-timur/d-4554434/berkah-ramadhan-seni-kaligrafi-serbuk-kayu-di-probolinggo-laris-manis. 2020

Salman, N. 2020. Potensi Serbuk Gergaji Sebagai Bahan Pupuk Kompos. *Jurnal Komposit* (Vol. 4) http://dx.doi.org/10.32832/komposit.v4i1.3695

Sugiyono. 2010. Metode Penelitian Kuantitatif Kualitatif dan R&D. *Álfabeta: Bandung.*

Sumarno. 2015. Inovasi Produk Kerajinan Melalui Limbah Padat (Recycle) Industri Pengolahan Kayu Jati. *Jurnal Pengabdian Masyarakat Kewirausahaan Indonesia* (Vol. 1). https://doi.org/10.36600/.v1i1.38

Sutarman, I.W. 2016. Pemanfaatan Limbah industri Pengolahan Kayu di Kota Denpasar (Studi Kasus pada CV Aditya). *Jurnal PASTI* (Vol. 10). https://publikasi.mercubuana.ac.id/index.php/pasti/article/view/668/571

Taskirawati, I. 2018. Pemanfaatan Limbah Serbuk Kayu Jati (Tectona Grandis) Sebagai Media Tumbuh Jamur Tiram (Pleurotus Ostreotus). *Journal Perennial* (Vol. 14) https://doi.org/10.24259/perennial.v14i2.5642

Dynamics of Industrial Revolution 4.0: Digital Technology Transformation and Cultural Evolution –
Wulandari et al (eds)
© 2021 The Author(s), ISBN 978-1-032-04451-4

The packaging structure exploration of ready-to-eat kebab products for street vendors (Case Study: Royal Kebab, Kebab Franchise)

S.A. Putri, A.S. Pawestri & A.N. Hutami
Telkom University, Bandung, Indonesia

ABSTRACT: Market competition is growing rapidly especially in the field of food, and many producers are competing with each other to grab the attention of potential consumers, as has been done by kebab street vendors. Therefore, it is necessary to explore new packaging design as a recommendation for ready-to-eat kebab products sold by street vendor. In the packaging design process, it is necessary to analyze the products that need to be packaged. This analysis is conducted to determine the product character and design requirements as a reference in the packaging design process. This needs to be done so that the resulting packaging design recommendations match the packaging needs of Kebab products. This packaging design recommendation aims to achieve the ideal packaging character, namely packaging that can increase the attractiveness of the products being sold, make it easier for consumers to consume the products contained therein, and can facilitate the packaging process.

Keywords: packaging, packaging system, design exploration, street vendor packaging, kebab packaging

1 INTRODUCTION

Fast food has long been recognized by the Indonesian people. The need for a food serving system that does not take time, both in the processing process and the consumption of the product, has led to innovations in fast food outlets that offer increasingly diverse product variants with competitive quality and prices. One of the most popular fast-food products is the kebab. This type of food originating from the Middle East is quite popular in Indonesia, of course, by adjusting the original taste to the tastes of the Indonesian people. This kebab product has been circulating with various brands in the market, ranging from restaurant class to street food vendors. One of the street kebab brands is Royal Kebab. Royal Kebab is a kebab franchise, specialized in street food-style kebabs and sold out of a cart.

Like any other street kebab vendors, owners of Royal Kebab reduce packaging costs by using simple packaging to make their products affordable for their customers. This is why the packaging that they are using right now still has room for developments, especially since the competition among similar brands and products is tight. packaging development is not only about protecting the product but also plays an important role in increasing the selling value of the product. In the packaging design process, it is necessary to analyze the products to be packaged. This analysis is carried out to determine the character of the product and design needs as a reference in the packaging design process. This needs to be done so that the resulting packaging design recommendations match the packaging needs of Kebab products. This packaging design recommendation aims to achieve the ideal packaging character, which is packaging that can increase the attractiveness of the products being sold, make it easier for consumers to consume the products contained therein, and can facilitate the packaging process.

DOI 10.1201/9781003193241-40

2 RESEARCH METHOD

According to Klimchuk and Krasovec (2012), the packaging design's function is to visually communicate product differences. Packaging design becomes a brand's promotional vehicle, highlighting its position on the shelf. Therefore, a well-designed packaging informed the consumer about the product, increasing product value (especially from visual aspects), and also influencing consumers to buy. Packaging design can be done through several systematic arrangements. Klimchuk and Krasovec (2012) also describes the seven phases of the packaging design process as follows:

Phase 1: Research and analysis (or observation, immersion, and discovery)
Phase 2: Preliminary design (or design strategy)
Phase 3: Design development (or creative development)
Phase 4: Design refinement
Phase 5: Design finalization and preproduction
Phase 6: Production
Phase 7: Brand activation

In this paper, the phases to be applied are Phases 1–3 with the assumption that the design made is a concept that has not been realized in physical form.

The research process begins by collecting data about the character of kebab products. In this research, the street vendor used as a case study is Royal Kebab. Located on Jalan Sukabirus, Telkom University Area, Royal Kebab has been operating since 2017 with non-franchise ownership status. The data is then analyzed and supported by literature studies, seen from the material and packaging structure aspects. The results of the analysis in the form of design requirements (design requirements) are then used as the basis for designing kebab packaging. The alternative design is then supported by material exploration and a packaging prototype is made. The results of the design and exploration are then used as packaging recommendations.

3 RESULT AND DISCUSSION

The first phase in packaging design is research and analysis (or observation, immersion, and discovery). In this study, research and analysis were carried out to obtain an overview of packaging needs and the possible materials that will be used in the packaging. Sources of field information are obtained from Royal Kebab products. The products in "Royal Kebab" are packaged using oil paper that has been printed with the words "Royal Kebab". The kebab that has been packaged using wax paper is then given adhesive in several parts to prevent it from falling apart. The kebab which has been wrapped in wax paper is then put into a paper bag. The wrapping process is done in a folded manner, so it takes quite a while when there are quite a lot of orders.

The kebabs in "Royal Kebab" come in various sizes, from jumbo to small. All kebabs are packaged using the same size wax paper and paper bag. For kebab products with additional toppings such as eggs and cheese, use extra wax paper to ensure that the oil does not leak out. To enjoy the product, the packaging is torn randomly to release the product. There are no guidelines to open the product.

The next phase in packaging design is the preliminary design (or design strategy). Based on the findings from the character of the existing "Royal Kebab" packaging, packaging development must be able to meet the following needs:

1. Packaging that can speed up the seller during the packaging process.
2. Packaging that can facilitate consumers when consuming these kebabs.
3. Packaging that no longer produces a lot of waste.

This strategy is then used as the basis for Phase 3: Design development (or creative development). To facilitate the packaging process, the new packaging design must be able to lock the product

Figure 1.   Current packaging of Royal Kebab (2019).

securely even without the folding process as has been done with the existing product. In the new packaging design, the shape chosen is a hexagon or hexagon as the main shape.

The choice of this shape is so that it has a better grip than the curved and flat surface of the existing packaging. For the bottom of the package, a fold lock system is used at the bottom of the package. This lock system is easy to open, but it can hold the product in the package. The lock on the top is tied using a rope as shown below. This lock can also act as a temporary handle of the packaging. The selection of a strap in the form of a strap is used to give a personal impression while making it easier to attach the tag label if needed.

For the second packaging strategy point, a product opening mechanism is created that helps consumers to open packages neatly. A neat packaging opening not only supports the aesthetics of the product when it is enjoyed by consumers but also allows the product brand to be better displayed. In the new packaging design results, the product operational mechanism is carried out by opening

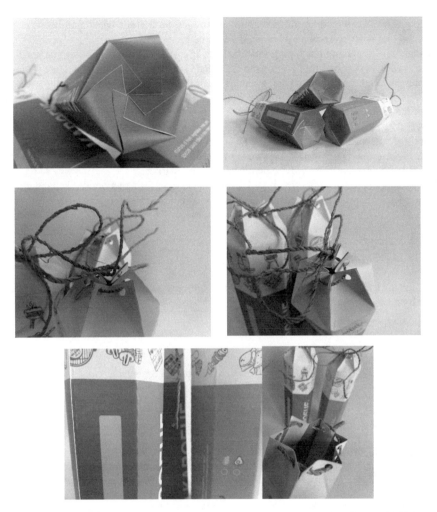

Figure 2. Kebab packaging system exploration result. (Source: Putri, Prawestri, and Hutami 2020).

the rope on the top of the package. After opening, the package can be torn according to the dotted line provided. Then kebab will immediately be enjoyed by consumers.

To minimize additional paper layers that have the potential to leave more waste, the packaging material uses laminated food-grade paper which is able to withstand oil.

The way the packaging works is as follows. The kebab that will be packed will be directly put into the package through the top, without being coated with warp paper anymore, because this package has been laminated so that it is oil resistant. The shape and appearance of the packaging will remain intact and maintain its freshness even if the kebab is not coated with additional wrapping paper.

However, further studies and research are needed to test this design result in its actual purposes. The design needs to proceed further through Phase 4: Design refinement, Phase 5: Design finalization and preproduction, Phase 6: Production, until Phase 7: Brand activation.

4 CONCLUSION

Packaging is a container to protect an item in order to keep it safe, intact, and also attract potential customers. Packaging can also be a medium of communication between producers and potential consumers as well as a medium for promoting a product. So that the packaging needs to include information that must be known by potential consumers.

The material for making packaging must be safe. It is safe to protect goods when sending it to the hands of consumers and safe for consumers when consuming a food product. By re-designing this kebab package, we improved a few things from the previous kebab packaging. We tried to solve the problems in kebab packaging, such as the difficulty of consumers enjoying kebabs, the length of the kebab packaging process, to the less attractive form of kebab packaging.

However, further studies are needed to make sure the newly designed packaging is suitable for the market. These further studies include the street vendor experiences using the new packaging and how the consumers respond to the packaging. The result will be determined if the packaging still needs to be developed or ready to be released in the market.

This re-design process, hopefully, it will inspire packaging for street vendor kebabs, help overcome the packaging problems faced, and of course, it can make consumer appeal to kebab products increase.

ACKNOWLEDGMENT

Special acknowledgments for royal kebab owners who are willing to cooperate during the data collection process.

REFERENCES

Creswell, John W. 2010. *Research Design: Pendekatan Kualitatif, Kuantitatif, dan Mixed.* (diterjemahkan oleh: Achmad Fawaid). Yogyakarta: Pustaka Pelajar.

Cuffaro, Daniel. 2006. *The Industrial Design.* Rockport Publishers: Beverly. Mayall, William H. (1979). *Principles In Design.* Design Council: London.

Ellicot, C. and Roncarelli, S. 2010. *Packaging Essentials.* Massachusetts: Rockport.

Klimchuk, M. R. and Krasovec, S. A. 2012. *Packaging design: Successful product branding from concept to shelf (second edition).* Hoboken, NJ: J. Wiley & Sons.

Moleong, Lexy J. 2007. *Metode Penelitian Kualitatif.* PT Remaja Rosdakarya: Bandung.

Purwandi, Lilik. 2016. *INDONESIA 2020:The Urban Middle-Class Millennials.* Avara research center: Indonesia.

Sugiyono. 2015. *Metode Penelitian dan Pengembangan.* Penerbit Alfabeta: Bandung.

Ulrich, Karl T. Eppinger, Steven, D. 1995. *Product Design and Development.* McGraw-Hill Book Co.: Singapore.

Dynamics of Industrial Revolution 4.0: Digital Technology Transformation and Cultural Evolution –
Wulandari et al (eds)
© 2021 The Author(s), ISBN 978-1-032-04451-4

Musculoskeletal analysis of a stand screen-printing table design using the nordic body map questionnaire

Y. Herlambang
Telkom University, Bandung, Indonesia

ABSTRACT: In the screen-printing process the factor of dependence on operators is very high. However, there are a variety of problems such as decreased body resistance or fatigue to potential musculoskeletal injuries or complaints that can make the process difficult. The research method used is the ergonomics approach using the Checklist measurement in the form of the Nordic Body Map Questionnaire to interpret musculoskeletal complaints. The data obtained will be used for the preparation of formulas that are suitable for the development of a new screen-printing table design that is in accordance with the characteristics of small industries and has better comfort with low levels of physical complaints. The most common complaints were in the lower body region, such as calves and ankles due to frequent standing and walking in the printing process. Development of a new work equipment design is needed by considering the unbalanced load reduction on the operator's body, and the development of the temporary transport system when the operator moves from the work point.

Keywords: printing table, musculoskeletal, Nordic body map questionnaire, stand work posture

1   INTRODUCTION

Screen-printing techniques in Indonesia have been widely used by the public (Bandi 2004) including various creative industries such as the fashion industry, publishing and printing, advertising, crafts, and design. This research is expected to explore the role of the operator in the production process that can affect the level of productivity. The design has advantages in the simplicity and visibility of the work system, however the shortcomings surround a guide system that does not have good accuracy, a calibration and registration process that still relies on operator feeling, low efficiency of transportation distance, set-up time efficiency, and efficient use of space. Fatigue, potential musculoskeletal injuries, or physical complaints are all possible negative characteristics of using screen-printing equipment.

The method used tried to understand the role of the operator in the production process that can affect the level of productivity and kind of work posture and body parts that interact when using an existing design. This was analyzed using the ergonomics study approach with the Nordic Body Map to assess which parts of the body have complaints when using the existing design so that later designs would have a low level of human error and can be mastered easily, quickly, and well by other screen-printing operators. The data to be obtained is whether the design of this standing screen-printing operator is ergonomic enough so that it can increase productivity or would it illuminate the primary physical problems that inhibit productivity.

2   METHOD

2.1   *Research method*

The research to be conducted is qualitative research. Qualitative research is a method for exploring and understanding the meaning of individuals or groups of people ascribed to social or humanitarian problems. This process requires important efforts, such as asking questions to collect specific data from participants, analyzing data inductively, and interpreting the meaning of the data obtained. The results of this study are usually flexible (Creswell 2010).

The qualitative research strategy to be used is the case study approach: the research strategy carefully investigates a program, event, activity, process, or group of individuals. Cases are limited by time and activity, and researchers gather complete information using various data collection procedures based on a predetermined time (Stake in Creswell 2010).

The objective type of this research is explanatory, trying to explain the effect the different screen-printing table designs used by operators had on the level of fatigue or physical complaints. It is expected that this research will explain the effectiveness of screen-printing design when used by several operators with different competencies and different work pose habits, related to musculoskeletal complaints and the quality of printing results. The approach taken is to use an experiment with a quasi-experimental design type, where the control group in the form of non-equivalent is determined based on the competence of the operator and puts forward a screen-printing table design factor.

2.2 Nordic Body Map

The Nordic Body Map is a tool in the form of a questionnaire that is most often used to find discomfort or pain in the body (Kroemer et al. 2001). This questionnaire was developed by Kourinka in 1987, then in 1992 Dickinson modified it. Respondents who filled out the questionnaire were asked to give a sign of the presence or absence of disturbance in the body area (Kroemer et al. 2001). The Nordic Body Map is intended to find out in more detail the parts of the body that experience interference or pain when working. Although this questionnaire is subjective (Santoso et al. 2014), it is standardized and valid enough to be used.

2.3 Posture of work

Work pose is human posture when interacting with work tools/equipment. A good work pose is one that makes it possible to carry out work effectively and with minimal muscle effort. The posture of not doing movement or work is standing, lying down, squatting, and sitting (Pheasant 1991). Workers' positions and work poses when carrying out activities in the workplace affect the physiological response of the workers. An unnatural/physiological work pose is the cause of various disorders in the musculoskeletal system (Manuaba 1998). To overcome these problems, it is necessary to know the criteria for an ideal work pose in carrying out an activity or work, such as muscles that work statically or very little (Pheasant 1991; Palilingan et al. 2012b). In carrying out tasks, using one's hands is carried out easily and naturally. Changing or dynamic work poses are better than relaxed static work poses, and a relaxed static work pose is better than a tense static work pose.

According to Pheasant (1991), there are seven basic principles in overcoming posture while working: prevent forward inclination of the neck and head; prevent forward inclination in the body; prevent the use of upper limbs in a raised state; prevent body rotations in an asymmetrical (twisted) pose; joints should be in the range of one-third of the maximum movement; and if you use muscle power, it should be in a position that results in maximum strength.

2.4 Data procedures

The data collection process will be carried out in the following ways:

1. Literature Study
2. Interview
3. Observation of activities
4. Questionnaire

Data collection used a questionnaire and the interview method to obtain data about complaints when using a screen-printing table design and then measuring the dimensions of the product and the dimensions of the user's body with the anthropometric measurement method with sitting work attitude and reach of the hands and feet when in a standing position.

3 RESULT AND DISCUSSION

3.1 Modular table design data

The design of the modular table with a permanent guide system commonly called the banting table system is the development of a long table system. The printing table generally uses a wooden frame (the) with a length of 200 cm, width of 70 cm, and height of 80 cm, and table surface uses 6 mm plywood, equipped with a drying rack at the bottom table.

The base material is in the form of sheets of boards in the form of smaller pieces with a size of about 50 x 40; generally, the ratio is one sheet of wide board cut into 16 parts, with each board having a permanently attached guide system, having a thickness of boards 6–10 mm, and a gluing system to the base of the material using table glue or glue sticker.

This table has a screen registration system that is permanently installed with wood material attached to the rail as well as the frame which is also with wood material, the register system uses two earring screws that refer to the stopper with wooden frame rails as a support on the base of the material.

Figure 1.   Modular table workstation.

3.2 Modular table activity

In the flow diagram map, it can be seen how the trajectory used in the production process uses a unit board table, the design of the fixed unit table requires the operator to walk from one material to the next and rotate again to do the next process, even though the distance is closer than the long table design.

3.3 Nordic Body Map data

Assessment of musculoskeletal complaints with the Nordic Body Map questionnaire four Likert scale. The assessment steps are as follows.

1. Preparation
2. Procedures

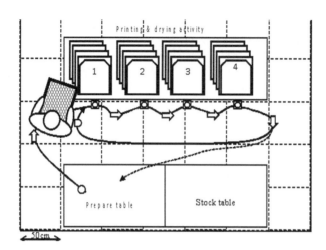

Figure 2.   Modular table activity.

a. Before starting the work each subject was given a Nordic Body Map questionnaire and subjects were asked to fill in themselves by putting grass marks (√), on items that corresponded to the perceived complaint, then the results were collected.

b. After finishing work, each subject was given a Nordic Body Map questionnaire again and the subjects were asked to fill in themselves by giving a sign of grass (√), on items that corresponded to the perceived complaint, then the results were collected.

3. Recording

4. The data collection that is processed consists of six respondents using the Nordic Body Map technique, and the data obtained are arranged into a table to see the level of complaints. Explanation of the level of complaints is classified into 4 options: the body part that has been given the number does not hurt (choose 1), a little sick (choose 2), sick (choose 3), and very sick (choose 4).

5. The number of samples measured is as many as six people, the data taken is the data after the sample is finished working for one working day or eight working hours by using a standing desk.

If seen from Table 1, the average score for complaints is 76, with the highest score with a score of 84 originating from operator V, and the lowest score being 65 derived from operator W. There are 3 operators with a score above 80 and 3 with a below average score, so the range from lowest to highest is 17.

When viewed from the score per skeletal muscle obtained, an average score of the total per body part is 16.3, with the lowest score of 9 and with the highest score of 21, and there are 15 body parts with complaints above the average, namely: Left Upper Arm, Back, Right Upper Arm, Right Wrist, Right Hand, Left Thigh, Left Foot, Right Leg, Waist, Left Wrist, Right Thigh, Left Calf, Right Calf, Left Ankle, and Right Ankle.

Then if we filter again, there are 7 parts of the body with the highest score of 3 complaints, totaling a total of 20 and/or more, namely: Waist, Left Wrist, Right Thigh, Left Calf, Right Calf, Left Ankle, and Right Ankle.

Some of them have complaints about the thigh because they use thigh pressure toward the front in the print process to press the screen to hold the register, then complain of the waist due to standing too long for many processes, and some complain of the left wrist because of the registration process and the movement of their boards supporting the screen with the left hand dominant because the right hand holds the squeegee.

222

Table 1. Nordic body map data.

NO	OTOT SKELETAL	SKOR PER OPERATOR					
		Z	Y	X	W	V	U
0	Leher atas	2	3	2	2	3	3
1	Tengkuk	2	2	2	2	3	2
2	Bahu kiri	2	3	2	2	2	2
3	Bahu Kanan	2	3	2	2	2	2
4	Lengan Atas Kiri	3	3	3	2	3	3
5	Punggung	3	4	3	2	4	2
6	Lengan Atas Kanan	3	3	3	2	3	3
7	Pinggang	3	3	4	3	3	4
8	Pinggul	2	2	2	1	2	2
9	Pantat	1	2	2	1	2	2
10	Siku Kiri	2	2	1	1	2	1
11	Siku Kanan	2	2	1	1	2	1
12	Lengan Bawah Kiri	2	2	3	2	3	3
13	Lengan Bawah Kanan	2	2	3	2	3	3
14	Pergelangan Tangan Kiri	3	3	4	4	3	3
15	Pergelangan Tangan Kanan	3	3	3	3	3	3
16	Tangan Kiri	2	3	3	2	2	3
17	Tangan Kanan	3	3	3	2	3	3
18	Paha Kiri	3	3	3	3	4	3
19	Paha Kanan	4	3	3	4	4	3
20	Lutut Kiri	3	3	3	2	3	2
21	Lutut Kanan	3	3	3	2	3	2
22	Betis Kiri	3	4	4	3	4	3
23	Betis Kanan	3	4	4	3	4	3
24	Pergelangan Kaki Kiri	3	4	3	3	4	3
25	Pergelangan Kaki Kanan	3	4	3	3	4	3
26	Kaki Kiri	3	3	4	3	3	3
27	Kaki Kanan	3	3	4	3	3	3
	TOTAL SKOR PER-OPERATOR	73	82	80	65	84	72
	RATA-RATA SKOR OPERATOR			76			

Generally, it is seen that there are more body parts that are in pain compared to those that are not sick. Most complaints are on the lower body such as calves and ankles due to frequent standing and walking back and forth in the printing processing (process) to each board, drying, and collecting printed materials. Some have complaints about their thighs because they use high pressure toward the front in the printing process to press the screen so that it meets the register; some complain about the waist due to standing for too long in a standing position in many processes, and some complain about the left wrist because of the registration process and the displacement of their boards supporting the screen with the dominant left hand because the right hand holds the racket.

4 CONCLUSION

There are limitations of Small and medium-sized enterprises (SMEs) in filter printing in the mastery of simple technology, one of which is using a type of unit board table with a standing work position. This position causes musculoskeletal complaints when working against the operator. In the production process, there are two processes that require a major operator role, namely the process set-up and printing process, starting from the preparation of paint, installation of printing materials, printing of basic colors, second layer/subsequent layers, drying, walking to the storage of printed materials, all mostly done while standing or running 8 hours each day.

The priority in the development of this proposed design is to reduce musculoskeletal complaints in the body with regard to Waist, Left Wrist, Right Thigh, Left Calf, Right Calf, Left Ankle, and Right Ankle. Development of a new work equipment design is needed to consider the unbalanced load reduction on the operator's body, and the development of the temporary transport system when the operator moves the work point so that it does not have an ill impact especially on the operator's hand. In addition, this new design attempts to reduce the standing required in the printing process thereby lessening the stress on the operator's body.

REFERENCES

Creswell, J.W. 2010. *Research Design: Pendekatan Kualitatif, Kuantitatif, dan Mixed*. (diterjemahkan oleh: Achmad Fawaid). Yogyakarta: Pustaka Pelajar.

Herlambang, Y. et al. 2015. *Penerapan Micromotion Study Dalam Analisis Produktivitas Desain Peralatan Kerja Cetak Saring*. Jurnal Teknologi Informasi dan Komunikasi (Tematik) PPM PLB. Bandung, 2:26–34.

Kroemer, K. et al. 2001. *Ergonomic, how to design for ease and efficiency*. 2nd edition. Prentice Hall, New Jersey.

Pheasant, S. 1991. *Ergonomics, Work and Health*. London: Macmillan AcademicProfesional Ltd.

Manuaba, I.B.G. 1998. *Ilmu Kebidanan, Penyakit Kandungan dan KB*. EGC. Jakarta.

Santoso, et al. 2014. *Perancangan Metode Kerja untuk Mengurangi Kelelahan Kerja pada Aktivitas Mesin Bor di Workshop Bubut PT. Cahaya Samudra Shipyard*. Profesiensi, 2(2):155–164.

Sobandi, B. 2004. *Model Pembelajaran Kewirausahaan Sablon dalam Menumbuhkan Minat Wirausaha Santri di Kecamatan Cisalak Kabupaten Subang*. Bandung: Universitas Pendidikan Indonesia.

Tusianti, E. et al. 2019. *Analisis Hasil SE2016 Lanjutan Potensi Peningkatan Kinerja Usaha Mikro Kecil*. Jakarta. Badan Pusat Statistik.

Dynamics of Industrial Revolution 4.0: Digital Technology Transformation and Cultural Evolution –
Wulandari et al (eds)
© 2021 The Author(s), ISBN 978-1-032-04451-4

Protective pants design for skaters to be analyzed by divergent and convergent thinking concepts

D. Yudiarti & I. Khofiani
Telkom University, Bandung, Indonesia

ABSTRACT: Extreme sports are sports that have challenges that must be faced with a high level of difficulty with a greater risk of accidents than sports in general. Skateboard is one of the extreme sports groups that are currently developing among teenagers. Skateboarding actually has the risk of fatal injuries to the limbs for skaters. They must give up their bodies which often fall during each exercise. Departing from this phenomenon, this study is interested in designing the design of user safety when skateboarding by combining apparel products with existing protectors to overcome minor injuries due to collisions while skateboarding to make it more practical and easier to use. This research conducted a case study method and analyzed by Divergent (analyzed Divergent) and Convergent Thinking Concepts, thus the design is delivered using the SCAMPER design method. The product designed (design) contains a safety function in the knees that assists the skateboarding activity and is applicable to the trends of the skater lifestyle.

Keywords: safety equipment, deckers, safety pants, skateboard, skaters

1 INTRODUCTION

Sports activities are a necessity of human life and an effective way to improve physical health and physical fitness which thereby improves the quality of human life. The development of extreme sports may still be less popular but it (is) still very attractive to young people today. Extreme sports are sports that are more directed toward a modern style and are more individualistic, with challenges that must be faced with a high level of difficulty (and) a greater risk of accidents than sports in general. Skateboarding is one such extreme sport that is currently developing among teenagers.

Factors that influence the rapid growth of skateboarding in young people and teenagers are the ability to freely express themselves and do anything in the form of movements or tricks on a skateboard (Ace 2006). That is because teenagers have a desire for freedom and enthusiasm. The development of skateboarding can be seen from the emergence of several skateboard communities in every city in Indonesia. Many skateboarders argue that skateboarding is not only a sport but also a lifestyle (Kolinug 2017). This is indicated by the activities carried out intensively by individuals, giving them meaning.

Skateboarding actually comes with a risk of fatality or limb injuries. They must give up their bodies which often fall during each exercise. Departing from this phenomenon, the authors are interested in creating a design of user safety when skateboarding by combining apparel products with existing protectors to overcome minor injuries due to collisions. There are two choices of opportunity, namely the elbows in clothes/jackets or in the knee area. The design is adapted to fashion trends for skaters related to the lifestyle and needs of users. It should also be noted that the design must meet the needs required by the target market of this product so as not to impede the activities being carried out.

2 METHODOLOGY

2.1 *Research method*

In this study, the authors conducted a case study on one of the skateboarding communities in Bandung, precisely in the Pasupati Skatepark area. The area is a gathering place for several skateboarding communities in Bandung that are interconnected. In this design, the authors conducted research with observation and interview techniques.

2.2 *Design strategies*

1. Divergent and convergent thinking analysis were used in managing design problems both in process and practice, which is the decision-making conduct of the event of specifying design materials, working relationships, and ethical responsibilities (Best 2006). Designers are required to narrow the problem space to solve the problem, and there are four basic cognitive steps: generation, exploration, comparison, and selection (Stempfle & Badke-Schaub 2002).

Considerable imagination is required by designers and can often be unpredictable in its outcome, hence the creative process to manage design problem enhances the Divergent and Convergent Thinking, which are the most crucial things in brainstorming (Yudiarti & Lantu 2017).

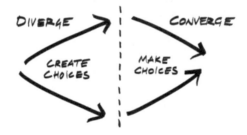

Figure 1.   Divergent and convergent thinking. (Source: Brown 2009).

2. SCAMPER analysis

SCAMPER is a technique that can be used to develop creativity in a different way from existing ones to trigger and generate new ideas. It can help overcome any challenge that might be encountered in a design (Michalko 2006).

Figure 2.   SCAMPER diagram. (Source: Human Resources-UWA).

Figure 3. SCAMPER application while analyzing on cargo (analyzing cargo)pants.

SCAMPER is based on the idea that everything new is a modification of something that already exists. SCAMPER is an acronym that stands for

Substitute (Replacing), Combine, Adapt (Adapting), Magnify, Put to Other Use, Eliminate, and Rearrange/Reverse (Michalko 2006).

3 DISCUSSION OF ANALYSIS

3.1 *Functional aspects (safety and secure)*

This design process uses the SCAMPER analysis technique. It combines the function of the safety cushion (decker) with the pants or trousers. Based on the functional aspect, the design requirements are pants that are comfortable to use and also serve or provide safety when skateboarding. This product is designed by adjusting (Adapt) existing components on pants and knee pads as the Combine method. The product must be able to contain safety functions in the knees of pants or in areas that assist with the extreme activities. Substitute the pocket functions on the pants, thus the users could put the safety pad inside.

To become a multipurpose product by placing different functions (Put to Another Use), the design requirement needed is the application of the bearing function in certain areas that experience direct impact with the surface when the player falls. Table 1 describes the needs of the activities carried out on the product:

Table 1. Product activity needs.

ACTIVITIES	FACILITIES	DESCRIPTIONS
Users' movement when doing extreme sports	Adequate pants size	Pant size ratio must adjust to the range of activities
User position when performing trick moves	Comfortable pants material	The material requirements used, must be comfortable and not hamper all the activities
Idle moment of users between activities	Casual design	The pants designed could be used and applied in any situation
Users' positions when falling	Safety pad	Product application is suitable and the materials are easy to find

Cargo pants have a slightly complex component that can be dealt with by a little extra design that doesn't really change the overall appearance. By inserting these bearing components, it becomes as if a new bag is in the cargo pants. To place the position of these bearings, analysis is needed on what areas need the most function. Table 2 details the various injury positions in the foot area when skateboarding.

Table 2. Indicator type of injury positions when falling in the leg area.

Indicator	hip	knee	buttocks	tibia
Intensity occurred	✓	✓	✓	✓
Fit dimensions	✓	✓	–	✓
Materials easy to find	–	✓	–	✓
Easy and applicable design	✓	✓	✓	✓

From the analysis of the user's injury positions during falls, it was concluded that this design implements safety equipment that protect the knee and tibia areas. The sections are adjusted to the cargo pants which are designed to be comfortable for the user during extreme activities.

3.2 *Terms of Reference (TOR)*

1. Design Description
   a. The main function of the product is to enable users to have more practical equipment without interfering with their activities.
   b. These pants are made with the aim that the user has a new alternative to safety equipment products that accommodate users while skateboarding. This product is expected to overcome the injury problems that arise when skateboarding.

2. Design Requirements
   a. The function needed is the addition of a safety pad in the knee area to the tibia as a component in the pants.
   b. The type of pants designed are cargo pants so that the bearing components are easily applied.

3. Design Limits
   a. The safety cushion feature to be applied only focuses on the knee and shin area based on the results of the analysis.
   b. Products are designed only for types of cargo pants.
   c. Bearing components only serve as a barrier to injury because the impact is not for blisters or damage due to surface friction.

4 VISUALIZATION AND FINAL DESIGN

4.1 *Styleboard*

The mood board concept created in Figure 4 refers to the old-school fashion style theme which is a trend among skaters. The style board shows various mix and match outfits that are used as a source of ideas in the design process.

4.2 *Final design*

Each element of the selected alternative sketches is combined into a new final design. The pockets in the thigh area are taken from the concept of the alternative sketch, and the final design has a simpler appearance with no collision between components. The pockets area of the safety pad on the knee area is structured, so it is easy to operate. There is an elastic part above the knee to facilitate user movements, and on the top of that part is a zipper applied as an additional option so that the pants can be changed into shorts.

Figure 4.   Style board users.

Figure 5.   Final design detailing.

Figure 6.   Operational product.

5 CONCLUSION

These protective pants for skaters are designed with an additional pocket for safety pads on the knee area that serves as a barrier to injury due to impact, but not for blisters or damage due to surface friction. The material used is twill which has a texture of fabric fibers that form diagonal lines. The choice of material is because the twill material has the advantages of being durable, strong, and not rigid. This product is equipped with supporting components of the model on cargo pants in general, such as the number of dominant pockets and loose size. For the next design development, the application of a safety system can be replaced or re-developed with a design that is more complex in function not only to withstand collisions. The need for further exploration is related to the trends and lifestyles of target users (skaters) that adjust to the activities carried out more broadly. The design exploration can be even more varied with the addition of other supporting compartments or different fashion styles. In addition, there is a need for a deeper study of the bearings to be used in order to save learning production costs in a more interesting form.

REFERENCES

Ace. 2006. *Speed & light: Indonesian skateboarding*. Jakarta: GagasMedia.

Best, K. 2006. Design Management: Managing Design Strategy, Process and Implementation. AVA Publishing.

Brown, T. 2009. Change by Design: How Design Thinking Transforms Organizations and Inspires Innovation. Harper Collins Publisher.

Kolinug, A. A. 2017. Eksistensi Komunitas Skateboard Di Kota Manado. *Holistik, Journal Of Social and Culture*. https://ejournal.unsrat.ac.id/index.php/holistik/article/viewFile/17448/16981, Retrieved Februari 24, 2020.

Michalko, M. 2006. Thinkertoys: A Handbook of Creative-Thinking Techniques.

Nurpramadya, A. and Irawan, A. H. 2012. Perancangan Buku Visual Skateboard Untuk Remaja Indonesia. *Jurnal Sains dan Seni ITS*, *1*(1):F17–F21. http://ejurnal.its.ac.id/index.php/sains_seni/article/view/502, downloaded at 27 Februari 2020.

Stempfle, J. and Badke-Schaub, P. 2002. Thinking in Design Teams: An Analysis of Team Communication. Design Studies, 23:473–496.

Yudiarti, D. and Lantu, D.C. 2017. Implementation Creative Thinking for Undergraduate Student: A Case Study of First Year Student in Business School. Advanced Science Letters, 23(8):7254–7257.

Dynamics of Industrial Revolution 4.0: Digital Technology Transformation and Cultural Evolution –
Wulandari et al (eds)
© *2021 The Author(s), ISBN 978-1-032-04451-4*

Designing advertising strategies for the Armenti Coffee House

I. Sumargono & A.P. Ayu
Telkom University, Bandung, Indonesia

ABSTRACT: The Armenti Coffee House is one of the coffee shops in Bandung that has the vision to make its coffee shop educational. Here, customers can deepen their insight into the coffee as well as have the unique experience of making their own coffee while learning about coffee processing. Based on the results of the interview analysis, the lack of maximum branding activity makes the target audience unable to recognize Armenti as an educational coffee shop. Also, many consumers want to learn about coffee, but Armenti is not their choice of places to study. This research uses qualitative methods in collecting data, in the form of observation, interviews, and literature study. The data obtained were analyzed using SWOT, AIO, and AISAS. The author makes a series of branding and promotions with the theme "Ragam Literasi Rasa," with the goal of increasing awareness and recognition of The Armenti Coffee House.

Keywords: Armenti, branding, educative, promotion

1 INTRODUCTION

The Armenti Coffee House, established in Bandung in September 2018, is one of the small- and medium-sized companies engaged in the coffee industry. Besides selling coffee, Armenti also has a pleasant cafe atmosphere, a spacious, clean, and comfortable environment, excellent coffee quality, and adequate coffee equipment, ranging from manual coffee machines to automatic ones. Along with it serving third-wave coffee (high-quality coffee elevated to an art form) and supported by its facilities, Armenti also hopes to create a coffee shop that is well known in the community as an educational coffee shop.

Compared to other coffee shops, the Armenti Coffee House provides more experiences with which customers can learn about the coffee-making process. It aims to educate the public to know more about coffee. This unique experience is also supported by visual brand activation, including logos and colors, as well as communication and non-visual behavior (Pamungkas 2018). Unfortunately, due to lack of visual marketing such as slogans and mascots, the image of Armenti's coffee shop as an educative coffee shop is not yet formed. At the same time, according to Judisseno (2019), creating good branding for consumers must be a provider of ideas and inspiration, as well as a provider of experience. Besides, the existing brand strategy is still not optimal, so it does not build a unique and valuable position in the minds of consumers. This is proved by the lack of association of the Armenti Coffee House in the minds of consumers as an educative coffee shop.

Based on the results of the questionnaire and interview, many of the target audience of the Armenti Coffee House cannot associate Armenti with being an educational coffee shop. This is unfortunate, considering that many of the target audience want to learn and deepen their insights about coffee, but do not know where to go, however Armenti is not a choice in their minds for that.

In designing this advertising strategy, maximum branding and promotion activations will be carried out to increase brand equity in the category of the Armenti Coffee House brand association and create a unique position in the minds of consumers.

Based on the background, the problem was formulated on how to design the right branding strategy and promotion for the Armenti Coffee House. Issues that will be discussed in the design of advertising strategies for the Armenti Coffee House will go through a series of branding and promotional activities, with a creative strategy approach and the media. The AISAS method is believed to be the most appropriate to carry out this activation because this method was created effectively by observing the behavior of the target audience (Sugiyama & Andree 2011).

2 RESEARCH METHODS

The methodology used in this study was the qualitative data approach utilizing observation activities by making observations to gain empirical experience, understand the context of the data, and discover the situations that occur in the field. First, such observations were done by visiting the Armenti Coffee House which is located on Jl. Reog No.6A, Turangga, Bandung, to meet staff and observe the situation in the café. Second, interviews are conducted to obtain information or ideas to gain deeper understanding. In this interview method, the writer interviewed the Head of the Business Unit at the Armenti Coffee House, Mr. Dwi Anggiadi. Finally, method was literature study. The authors used book sources, journals and other sources for reference.

3 RESULT AND DISCUSSION

In the creative strategy, the authors first analyze the brand value using the SWOT matrix. After analyzing the matrix, the authors use the strength and opportunity matrix to enhance the chances to compete with other competitors. In the media strategy, the author uses the AISAS method to project the effective media to approach the target audience.

As stated by Kotler et al. (2016), branding is a process of providing brand strength or value to products and services. This is to facilitate the identification and make a difference in the product. So, branding needs to be done so that Armenti has brand strength and a striking difference compared to its competitors through its messaging and visual aspects.

Tagline. The authors designed the tagline for the Armenti Coffee House based on the analysis of the S-O strategy. This tagline is useful for influencing customer buying behavior by evoking an emotional response. Also, the tagline contains the positioning of the company, thus differentiating it from its competitors (Swasty 2016). The tagline for Armenti is "Ragam Literasi Rasa."

Logo. In the process of activating branding conducted for the Armenti Coffee House, a new logo is formed to facilitate the delivery of messages to be conveyed by Armenti. The logo itself is the character or identity of a product or service (Pratiwi & Sumargono 2019). The formation of a new logo helps to make Armenti a cultural icon, participate in building ownership, and value development (Budeimann 2010).

Figure 1. Armenti's new logo. (Source: Personal).

Mascot. The mascot was formed on the branding strategy to facilitate the target audience to associate the Armenti Coffee House. Besides, according to Delbare in Hoolwerff (2014), the formation of a mascot can bring brand attributes or the value of the Armenti itself.

Promotion. Regarding the concept of promotion, Armenti has to communicate with its target audience to inform, persuade, and remind consumers about the products and brands they sell. The authors use the AISAS method to adequately influence the target audience.

Figure 2. Armenti mascot. (Source: Personal).

Attention. To attract the attention of Armenti consumers and increase awareness of brand activation carried out by the Armenti Coffee House, digital poster media, Instagram filters, and Instastory advertisements were created.

Interest. In the interest stage, the main media becomes the advertising strategy of the Armenti Coffee House. At this stage, the main media is in the form of advertisements with video formats. They contain a message about the advantages that exist in the Armenti Coffee House.

Search. The media search stage used aims to support awareness of the attention and interest stages using an informative and persuasive communication strategy through explanatory content on social media, while still selling their products through the website.

Action. The activity carried out was organizing a coffee class where the event contained a brewing competition, cupping session, and a seminar. This is to support the tagline "Ragam Literasi Rasa," which aims to increase the target audience's literacy toward coffee. There is also a social media challenge called "Doodle Your Cup" to help increase Armenti sales shares. In addition to using hashtags that will be included in all media, the use of Instagram templates in Instastory also facilitates the activation of the Armenti brand to be distributed to a wider target audience.

On the attention stage poster, visuals related to coffee will be displayed, such as barista activities, coffee beans, and latte art. As for the advertising poster, it contains provocative writing which will be related to a video in the interest stage.

Figure 3. Armenti Coffee House digital poster. (Source: Personal).

The video advertisement becomes the main media in the advertising strategy of the Armenti Coffee House. At this stage, the main media in the form of advertisements with video formats and contains a message about the advantages that exist at the Armenti Coffee House.

Figure 4.   Armenti Coffe House video ad. (Source: Personal).

To gain a wider audience, Armenti uses contents on their social media.

a. Instagram Filter

Figure 5.   Armenti Instagram filter (Source: Personal).

b. Instagram Explanatory Content

Figure 6.   Instagram explanatory content. (Source: Personal).

The website will be a bridge for the target audience who want to find more information about the process of making coffee. On the website, there is also information on class schedules, as well as testimonies from people who have taken classes at the Armenti Coffee House.

There are two events that will be held in the activation of the Armenti Coffee House branding. The first is the coffee class event, which will be held to coincide with International Coffee Day. This activity will be broadcast live on Armenti's social media. In addition, before welcoming the Coffee Class and International Coffee Day, a social media challenge will take place with the concept of

Figure 7.   Website. (Source: Personal).

Figure 8.   Event at the Armenti Coffee House. (Source: Personal).

"Doodle Your Cup." The winner of the competition will be announced on Coffee Day and receive merchandise from Armenti as a prize.

4   CONCLUSION

Based on the results of observations, interviews, and data processing, the authors can conclude that the Armenti Coffee House is still not optimal in carrying out a series of branding and promotional activities. This can be seen from the non-maximum brand identity and promotion in order to communicate the strengths of Armenti. Customers still don't associate Armenti with an educative coffee shop.Through designing this advertising strategy, the authors create a series of brand activations in the form of brand identity, and a series of promotions as a medium to communicate with the target audience. This is considered appropriate as a solution to the problem of the Armenti Coffee House.

ACKNOWLEDGMENT

Thank you to the resource person, Armenti Coffee House, and also the Head of the Business Unit at the Armenti Coffee House, Mr. Dwi Anggiadi. Thank you to PPM Telkom University for providing internal funding for this research.

REFERENCES

Hoolwerff, D. Van. 2014. *Does Your Mascot Match Your Brand Personality?* University of Twente.
Judisseno, R. K. 2019. *Aktivitas dan Kompleksitas Kepariwisataan.* Jakarta: PT. Gramedia Pustaka Utama.

Kotler, Philip and Keller, K. L. 2016. *Marketing Management*. Global. Essex, England: Peason Education.

Kusrianto, A. 2009. *Desain Komunikasi Visual*. Yogyakarta: Andi Offset.

Moriarty, Sandra, Mitchell, Nancy, and Wells, W. 2012. *Advertising & IMC*. principles. New Jersey: Peason Education.

Pratiwi, G. and Sumargono, I. 2019. Designing Campaign of Speech Delayed to the Children for Parents in Bandung.

Sugiyama, K. and Andree, T. 2011. *The Dentsu Way*, *Journal of Chemical Information and Modeling*. doi: 10.1017/CBO9781107415324.004.

Swasty, W. 2016. *Branding*. Memahami d. Bandung: PT. Remaja Rodakarya Offset.

Dynamics of Industrial Revolution 4.0: Digital Technology Transformation and Cultural Evolution –
Wulandari et al (eds)
© 2021 The Author(s), ISBN 978-1-032-04451-4

Decorative elements in muslim fashion product: A case study using macrame technique

C. Puspitasari
Universiti Sains Malaysia, Penang, Malaysia

A.S. Pakpahan
Telkom University, Bandung, Indonesia

J. Dolah
Universiti Sains Malaysia, Malaysia

S. Yuningsih
Telkom University, Bandung, Indonesia

ABSTRACT: The research's problem is the limitation in using structure design techniques, especially macrame in Muslim fashion. Based on the observation and interview, decorative elements in Muslim fashion dominated by surface textile techniques, such as embroidery, both by machine or hand embroidery and beads embellishment. Whereas, besides there are opportunities for structural textile design applied to Muslim fashion as decorative elements. The previous study used basic knot patterns and minimal exploration of its concepts, shapes, materials, and color combination. This research aims to develop a decorative element in Muslim fashion products by utilizing the potential of macrame. The experiments were carried out in stages, including the macrame knot pattern experiment and the 3D module experiment using the macrame technique. This study's output is the implementation of Macrame experiments on Muslim fashion products, which could be a reference for further Muslim fashion research.

Keywords: Decorative Element, Macrame, Muslim Fashion, Structure Textile

1 INTRODUCTION

The development of Muslim fashion trends in Indonesia increased significantly due to several things: developing technology and information, the growth of the Islamic community, and the rise of Muslim fashion shows and trade exhibitions (Puspitasari & Dolah 2017). Other than that, Hijrah's phenomenon on Indonesian Muslim - celebrities since 2018 has played a role in increasing people's interest in Muslim fashion and wearing fashionable products. (Puspitasari & Dolah 2018).

For those people who work in fashion design, to answer the potential things of this phenomenon, they need to be creative and innovative (Fan & Zhou 2020). Therefore, in the opportunity to offer alternative designs in Muslim fashion products. The decoration on fashion makes fashion development more dynamic, considering the silhouette or design of the basic forms of fashion generally does not change at once but evolves gradually from one to another through changes in detail (Udale 2014). Decorative elements can function as an effort to improve the quality and attractiveness of a product. Based on the previous study, the decorative elements in Indonesian Muslim fashion products most widely use the surface technique textile, such as painting, embroidery, and beads embellishment (Puspitasari et al. 2019).

Macrame, one kind of structure textile technique, is not common in Muslim fashion, but it can actually be applied as decorative elements. This is because the macrame technique's basic knot patterns can be combined and modified so it can produce an unlimited variety of knot shapes (Rizani 2018).

DOI 10.1201/9781003193241-44

237

2 METHOD

Based on the design process, there are three steps, as shown in the research method phase (Wang et al. 2013)

1. Identification: in this stage, extracting features from an original object,
2. Translation: in this stage, transforming object elements into design elements, principles, technique
3. Implementation: in the last stage, designing the product

2.1 Data collection

The data collection method in this study is observation and experiment. Through the direct field observation method to the Muslim fashion events or Muslim market place in Indonesia both online and on-site, the focus was on how decorative elements in Muslim fashion products were made. Using visual references to generate ideas is a way to get source information, and it is not the same as copying. It is important to take the information and develop and transform it (Purcell 2005). Based on the Hijrah phenomenon, Muslim celebrities and Indonesian Muslim fashion designers play a role in increasing public interest in using fashionable products. Therefore, the design process begins with the determination of fashion icons and determining the inspiration derived from the form of flower (Gaimster 2011). The determination of the inspiration at this stage is based on observations made other than that flower has a symbolic and meaningful relation to the women (Brown 2020). Another data collection method in this study is the experiment. The experiment gained data about the knot variation for decorative elements that appropriate with the objective of this study to offer an alternative design of decorative elements in Muslim fashion products.

2.2 Data analysis

To analyze the data, this study used a sample of macrame technique experimental results and combined it with the composition of the placement of decorative elements in Muslim fashion products.

3 RESULT AND DISCUSSION

3.1 The analysis of decorative elements in Muslim fashion product using macrame technique

Figure 1. The stages of experiment - macrame application in Muslim fashion product.

From the experiments conducted, it was found that the combination of several basic macrame knots can produce new shape variations. The figure above showed the result of macramé application in Muslim Fashion products. Starting in the IDENTIFICATION stage, using visual inspiration in the form of a mood board containing a collection of picture collages consisting of pencil orchids, basic macrame patterns, and fashion icons related to the product(A). Then, for the TRANSLATION stage (B), adapting the idea from the mood board and transforming it into a fabric experiment sheet. The macramé experiment was carried out in two stages, starting from making an exploration using basic macrame, then doing 3D modules, and making the combined 3D modules' combined composition. After getting the fabric composition containing the macramé technique, the IMPLEMENTATION stage (C) applies it to the Muslim fashion product.

The macramé technique is a structured textile that requires the maker or the designer; therefore, the determination of Muslim fashion products must be following the experimental stage's efforts and the character of the experimental results themselves. Also, based on the observations made, it was concluded that the type of Muslim fashion products that are suitable for the experiment results is a party dress. The form of clothing is a dress with a basic A-line shape with a decorative macramé element as the center of attention. The macrame experiment's fabric is treated in a similar way to the lace that generally dangles over the clothing. Then the 3D module, which has the form of an orchid, was repetitively applied so that a harmonious and orderly composition of decorative elements was obtained.

Overall, after adding decorative elements, the dress has a Y silhouette where the top looks wider, and the lower part looks smaller. This is due to the addition of a robe inspired by the shape of orchid flower petals. On the body part of the dress is presented a tube shape based on a pencil's shape. According to the pencil orchid flowers, the color shades used in the dress are mostly white and purple gradations. The composition of the color between the dress and the macrame's decorative elements is used as accents in the outfit. This outfit also has asymmetrical balance in terms of distance and layout from the left and left sides.

4 CONCLUSION

This research discusses the macrame technique's advantages to create an alternative decorative element design for Muslim fashion. Based on the process, it can be concluded that the pattern structure and aesthetic impression formed from the composition of the experimental results on the product are proof that gradually through the process of identification, transformation, and implementation, the design process that occurs will be clear and directed.

Based on observations and experiments that have been carried out in this study, the macrame technique is included in the slow design technique because it requires good skills to produce explorative modules and sheets. Therefore, the appropriate types of Muslim fashion products following this character are the clothes aimed at special events. This is in line with the value of textile craftsmanship, which wants to expose.

Design concepts can support optimization macramé as a technique to make a decorative element in Muslim fashion. In this research, the concept is carried out in Indonesia's local content, namely the Pencil Orchid flower. This flower is an endemic flora of Indonesia and can function as an inspiration because a macrame combination knot pattern can form its appearance and physique. This inspiration is related to the segmentation of Muslim fashion products that are made, namely women with grace and femininity.

For further studies, some opportunities can be developed. In this study, the macrame technique was applied as a decorative element in Muslim fashion products, and the portion amount was less than 50%. In the next study, it can make product development using the macrame technique with more than 50%. Also, using other concepts besides flowers will be able to produce more varied designs.

ACKNOWLEDGEMENT

I gratefully acknowledge the support for this research provided by School of the Creative Industries, Telkom University and School of the Art, Universiti Sains Malaysia. The author also wishes to thank all colleagues in the Textile & Fashion Department, Telkom University who have contributed to this study. Thank you for all the support.

REFERENCES

Brown, M. L. (2020). Representing the Modified Body. In *In The International Encyclopedia of Gender, Media, and Communication (eds K. Ross, I. Bachmann, V. Cardo, S. Moorti and M. Scarcelli).* https://doi.org/doi:10.1002/9781119429128.iegmc310

Fan, K. K., & Zhou, Y. (2020). The influence of traditional cultural resources (TCRs) on the communication of clothing brands. *Sustainability (Switzerland), 12*(6), 1–19. https://doi.org/10.3390/su12062379

Gaimster, J. (2011). *Visual Research Methods in Fashion.* Berg Publisher.

Purcell, P. (2005). How designers think. In *Design Studies* (Vol. 2). https://doi.org/10.1016/0142-694x(81)90033-8

Puspitasari, C., & Dolah, J. (2017). Hijab Design and Style in Indonesia which Influenced by. *SSPIS 2017 Proceedings*, 201–212. Retrieved from http://eprints.usm.my/40509/1/ART_27.pdf

Puspitasari, C., & Dolah, J. (2018). The Analysis of Integration between Hijab Concept and Fashion in Indonesia. *Proceedings of the 3rd International Conference on Creative Media, Design and Technology (REKA 2018)*, 325–328. https://doi.org/https://doi.org/10.2991/reka-18.2018.71

Puspitasari, C., Wulan, D. A., & Dolah, J. (2019). Designing " Culture " Into Modern Product – A Case Study Of Bengkulu ' S Ark Festival As An Inspiration In Muslim Fashion Product. *Proceeding of the International Conference on Local Knowledge (ICLK) 2019*, 1–4. Kuala Lumpur: USM.

Rizani, H. (2018). *Aplikasi teknik makrame pada produk aksesoris fesyen untuk remaja perempuan* (Telkom University). Retrieved from https://openlibrary.telkomuniversity.ac.id/home/catalog/id/147623/slug/aplikasi-teknik-makrame-pada-produk-aksesoris-fesyen-untuk-remaja-perempuan.html

Udale, J. (2014). *Basic Fashion Design 02: Textiles and Fashion.* Switzerland: AVA Publishing.

Wang, Y., Qin, S. F., & Harrison, D. (2013). Culture-inspired design principles , methods and tools in current products. *The 5th Intl Congress of the Intl Association of Societies of Design Research*, 1–12. Tokyo: Chiba Univrsity.

Aesthetic evolution in digital era

Dynamics of Industrial Revolution 4.0: Digital Technology Transformation and Cultural Evolution –
Wulandari et al (eds)
© 2021 The Author(s), ISBN 978-1-032-04451-4

Indonesian gestures on the cover of fashion magazines

D.W. Soewardikoen & M. Tohir
Telkom University, Bandung, Indonesia

ABSTRACT: Fashion magazines published in Indonesia were initially influenced by the local culture with regard to race, gestures, and modest clothing. Nowadays, both domestic and foreign magazines are published in Indonesia. There are many similar cover designs especially in relation to layout, typography, colors, illustrations, and in the way models are displayed. This similarity is the result of globalization that continues to grow, especially ideology in the field of fashion that has been disseminated through magazines from international publishers who have contributed to the changing views and values of Indonesian society. The research question was whether there are magazine covers that still feature Indonesian gestures. The research was done through observations, literature studies, interviews, and questionnaires, looking at the origin of magazine publishing and the visual elements displayed. It was found that gestures have been influenced by norms and fashion developments. Foreign magazine covers are very influential in the development of magazine covers in Indonesia.

Keywords: Indonesian, gestures, fashion, magazines

1 INTRODUCTION

Various magazines published in Indonesia have been hit by media disturbances, marked by a decrease in sales turnover and a decrease in advertising revenue, especially in print media. The digital revolution gives users previously unimaginable access to new products and ideas (Cooper 2017). Publishers started to build communities to maintain their audience, and online media and social media became alternatives so that magazine publishing would not disappear altogether (Bachdar 2018). There are several foreign fashion magazines still present on the market, featured in the general magazine sales area. Domestic publishers no longer have a monopoly on fashion magazines. In fact, international publishers have begun to dominate magazine display racks in supermarkets. Transnational corporations, cyber technology, and electronic mass media have given birth to a network of closely related networks that are covering the world (Rabine 2016). Fashion has become an arbitrary force because it can determine which clothes are still suitable for use and which are out of fashion. Fashion magazines are important reading for fashion followers or the middle class who don't want to be considered out of date.

The magazine cover plays an important role for potential readers because the outermost appearance of a magazine contains headlines, body copies, and captions of images or photos, which play a role in persuading prospective magazine buyers. Cover images carry values that shape the tastes and insights of consumers. Persuasion occurs when there is a relationship between the appearance of the cover and the consumer's insight. Circulation of well-known fashion magazines from foreign publications, that carry the values of their home countries, will influence readers' tastes and insights. Consumption is not only done by buying clothes in stores but also by reading fashion magazines (Alexandersson & Matlak 2017). Continuous development, especially ideology in the field of fashion, which is disseminated through international publications helps change the views and values of Indonesian people. This research questioned the presence of magazine covers in Indonesia that still display Indonesian gestures.

Two similar writings on magazine covers have been published in 2018. The first publication titled *Desain Cover Majalah Cosmogirl Indonesia* was written by Thalia and Franzia (2018). Their focus were on the covers of *Cosmogirl Indonesia Magazine* published between 2015–2017. The aim of the writing was to find out the meaning contained in the cover of a Cosmogirl Indonesia magazine in informing the lifestyle of adolescent girls. Analysis of the data in the study used the Roland Barthes semiotic analysis model. The second publication titled *Representasi Model Remaja Wanita dan Interaksinya dengan Model Remaja Pria pada Cover Majalah Gadis* was written by Sunyoto et al. (2018). The research looked at aspects of the trick effect, pose, object, and linguistic meanings behind the sentences on the cover. The data was also analyzed using the Barthes semiotic analysis model. The two publications aimed to find out the visual meanings contained in the covers of magazines and rubrics by using a semiotic analysis approach.

Visual representation (illustration or photography) has the power to attract attention directly and has a large influence on the role of persuasion, compared to just relying on the strength of the text (Soewardikoen 2015). Gestures are a form of nonverbal communication carried out with the attitude of the body and limbs. Movements, made by body parts to express meaning, emotion, or communicate instructions, are actions aimed at expressing feelings or emphases (Navarro 2014). Body language makes observers able to see far beyond the words spoken and understand the message without hidden words conveyed. In summary, body language speaks louder than words (Borg 2009). Visual elements are focused on the models who are being displayed. There are several elements' categories, namely race, clothing, and gestures. In terms of race, it is divided into three categories: namely European, Indonesian, and Malay (Suwardikun 2017). In Indonesia, there is also Law number 44/2008 which regulates pornography and the appearance of clothing openness. The percentage of openness is categorized as follows: if the entire body is not covered then the clothes are included in the 100% openness category; if the body is closed only in vital parts such as the breasts and genitals, it is included in the 75% openness; if the body is covered in the breast, abdomen, and genitals, it is included in the 50% openness; and finally, if the body is covered from the breasts to the knee, it is included in the 25% openness (Apsari & Widiatmoko 2010). The openness of clothing is important to discuss, because open clothing or minimal clothing is a Western habit, while Indonesian women's clothing nowadays tend to be covered.

2 RESEARCH METHODS

This research used visual communication research methodology (Soewardikoen 2019), with the conceptual approach of a visual work consisting of three aspects: the visual work itself, the aspect of the creator's work, and the aspect of the viewer. Each aspect used a separate data collection instrument. Data from the aspect of visual works used observation instruments, data from aspects of the work of the creator used interview instruments, and data from aspects of the viewer used a questionnaire. Data analysis used matrix comparison analysis and a conclusion drawing matrix. The object sampled in this study was the cover of fashion magazines published in Indonesia on the magazine display racks in both supermarkets and train stations. Five samples were selected, namely *Femina*, *Kartini*, *Bazaar*, *Vogue*, and *Cosmopolitan*. The visual sampling for the magazines were carried out in 2017. Observations, in this case, are studies and records of magazine cover samples carried out with the theory of visual communication design. The photo aspect of the model was analyzed using gesture theory, clothing openness, and racial stereotypes. The distribution of questionnaires with random sampling criteria to 100 respondents was done through online Google Forms to female viewers as young adult magazine readers between the ages of 20–30 years. Interviews were conducted with magazine designers and fashion designers. The analysis was done by comparison matrix analysis.

3 RESULT AND DISCUSSION

The aspect of visual work, as mentioned above, were visual samples from covers of fashion magazines circulating in Indonesia in 2017 presented on the display racks of magazine sellers, both in supermarkets and train stations. The magazines analyzed were *Femina*, *Kartini*, *Bazaar*, *Vogue*, and *Cosmopolitan*. The covers of the Indonesian-language Kartini magazine featured models of the Malay race with light brown skin and a pose that tended to be formal with faces looking straight head and smiling. The models wore clothes with openness of less than 25%. The cover of the Indonesian-language *Femina* magazine featured a model of the Malay race with light brown skin, a face looking straight ahead and smiling with formal body posture, and although the model wore shorts her thighs were hidden. The cover of a mixed Indonesian language *Cosmopolitan* magazine featured a European race model with white skin, a charming attitude with a straddling thigh position, with 50% openness of clothes, no smiling face, sharp eyes, and a slightly sloping face. Another cover featured a model with shorts showing her thighs, facing forward, with lips slightly open but not smiling. *Bazaar* magazine featured a European race model with pink hair, a seductive face, no smile, being embraced by another model with 50% open clothes. Another *Bazaar* cover showed a European race model dressed in fancy clothing with a body posture showing off her armpits. The cover of the English-language Indonesian *Vogue* magazine featured a European race model in a standing position pulling on a belt, unsmiling face with lips slightly open, and transparent clothing that was at 40% of openness. Another *Vogue* cover featured an Asian model who was swaying, and even though she was fully dressed up top, her thighs were expose. The findings from the five magazines, specifically those displayed on magazine shelves, were their font headlines used modern serifs, with only one still using special Indonesian-style fonts. Three of the five magazines displayed more than 50% clothing openness, three magazines featured attractive model poses, and three magazines used Indonesian–English mixed languages. Two magazines originating from Indonesia still used Indonesian models. One featured a model with polite gestures, of the Malay race, and an openness of less than 25%. They also still use Indonesian visual elements, while Western magazines used Western visual elements and Western gestures.

Figure 1. Cover samples of fashions magazines—*Kartini*, *Femina*, *Cosmopolitan*, *Bazaar*, and *Vogue*. (Source: Laporan Penelitian *Unsur Visual Indonesia dalam Sampul Majalah Mode* ; Suwardikun and Tohir 2019).

The following discussion is on the aspect of a creator's work. To understand how magazines make cover designs, data is required from the aspect of the creator, in this case represented by graphic designers and fashion designers. Eka Audria Wulandari is a graphic designer who worked in magazine publishing. According to interview with her, it was revealed that the cover of the magazines reflected the content and acted as the main attraction to potential consumers who might want to buy the magazines. Colors for the fashion magazine were not always the same because they were usually adjusted to what the magazine wanted to expose. Usually, every magazinehad its own concept so that there were no colors that were identical to other magazines. The differences in cover design depends on the desired age of the consumers; if adults like *Cosmopolitan*, the model would look sexy, but for teenagers the model usually stood in a normal pose. Foreign magazines are still influential but only as a reference and as examples of magazine designs in Indonesia. Faradillah Nursari, a fashion designer and lecturer in crafts and fashion, s that the gesture of her magazines usually highlighted on the body to the head. The development of fashion magazine covers has changed for several decades. Gestures are influenced by norms and the development of fashion in that respective era. The cover of foreign magazines is very influential in the development of magazine covers in Indonesia. It is for the reason that there are several foreign fashion magazine franchises that are usually given a template from the magazine's central company. This trend is also very influential because foreign trends are still a benchmark for trends in Indonesia.

The next aspect is aspect of the viewer. The questionnaire used for this research was distributed to 100 respondents, especially women with age ranges between 20 and 30 years old from middle- and upper-middle socioeconomic status. The results obtained are as follows—the first thing noticed when seeing the magazine cover: 42.7% model; brand magazine 17%; magazine content 14.6%; illustration 13.4%; typography 6.1%; and other 2.4%. Cover magazines that look more attractive: foreign magazine covers 90.2%; and Indonesia magazine cover 9.8%. Cover design affects the interest to buy: Yes 84.1%; No 15.9% (Suwardikun and Tohir 2019). Some takeaways from this data are: the cover model more of a significant attraction than magazine content; foreign magazine covers are more interesting than Indonesian magazine covers; and a magazine cover affects the interest to buy.

A summary of three aspects are discussed next. On the aspects of model's race, *Kartini* and *Femina* magazines always feature Malay race models. In the meantime, *Cosmopolitan*, *Bazaar*, and *Vogue* magazines use European models and text with European typography. On the aspects of gesture, *Kartini* magazine displays models with formal gestures, *Femina* magazine displays models with semi-formal gestures, while other magazines from abroad display models with alluring gestures. On the clothing aspect, *Kartini* and *Femina* magazine models wear clothing with only 25% openness, while *Vogue* magazine displays models with about 50% openness, and *Cosmopolitan* and *Bazaar* magazines display models with open fragments greater than 50%. On the aspects of language, *Kartini* and *Femina* magazines always use Indonesian, while other magazines use mixed languages, Indonesian and English. Based on the assessment, *Kartini* magazine has the most visual element of Indonesia. *Femina* appears to be influenced by outside magazines but is still of great value. *Cosmopolitan* and *Bazaar* magazines use visual elements that are lacking in Indonesia. The cover of foreign magazines as a world trend is used as an example of magazine designs in Indonesia. Franchise magazines use original visual standards from their place of origin. Foreign magazine covers are more attractive than Indonesian magazine covers, and magazine covers affect buying interest.

4 CONCLUSION

The world of fashion is a Western cultural industry which is disseminated through various media, as a result of global values that ultimately shift local values. Indonesian fashion tastes have influenced visual magazines since the circulation of Western fashion magazines in Indonesia. Even though Indonesian magazines have tried to maintain their existence, they are already exhausted. This is seen by the Indonesian fashion magazines that have gone out of business, while Western magazines are still circulating in Indonesia. Magazines originating from Indonesia still use some visual elements of Indonesia, while Western magazines use Western visual elements and Western-style gestures. The covers of foreign magazines are very influential in the development of magazine covers in Indonesia.

5 ACKNOWLEDGMENT

Thank you to the resource person, Ms. Eka Audria Wulandari, and Ms. Faradillah Nursari for providing useful data. Thanks to PPM Telkom University for providing internal funding for this research.

REFERENCES

Alexandersson E. and Matlak R. 2017. *Cultural Differences in Fashion Magazines: Targeting Vogue*. University of Boras. Available at: https://www.diva-portal.org/smash/get/diva2:1143856/FULLTEXT01.pdf.

Apsari, D. and Widiatmoko, D. 2010. Visualisasi Wanita Indonesia dalam Majalah Pria Dewasa. *Visual Communication Journal Wimba*. Available at: http://journals.itb.ac.id/index.php/wimba/article/download/10885/4071 (Accessed November 11, 2019).

Bachdar, S. 2018. Bagaimana Femina bertahan ditengah disrupsi media. *http://marketeers.com/*. Available at: http://marketeers.com/bagaimana-femina-bertahan-di-tengah-disrupsi-media/.

Borg, J. 2009. *Buku Pintar Memahami Bahasa Tubuh*. Think. Available at: https://books.google.co.id/books/about/Buku_pintar_memahami_bahasa_tubuh.html?id=ts67YgEACAAJ&redir_esc=y.

Cooper, L. 2017. '00s at FASHION: How Globalization Changed Fashion. Available at: https://fashionmagazine.com/style/00s-fashion/.

Navarro, J. 2014. *Cara Cepat Membaca Bahasa Tubuh*. Change Publication.

Rabine, L. W. 2016. Globalization and the Fashion Industry. *fashion-history.lovetoknow.com*. Available at: https://fashion-history.lovetoknow.com/fashion-clothing-industry/globalization-fashion-industry.

Soewardikoen, D. W. 2015. *Visualisasi Iklan Indonesia Era 1950-1957 Edisi 2*. 1st edn. Yogyakarta: Calpulis. Available at: http://calpulis.com/index.php/products/978-602-73097-0-8/.

Soewardikoen, D. W. 2019. *Metodologi Penelitian Desain Komunikasi Visual*. Yogyakarta: PT. Kanisius.

Sunyoto, F.W., Natadjaja, L., and Yuwono, E. 2018. Representasi model remaja wanita dan interaksinya dengan model remaja pria pada cover majalah gadis. *Jurnal DKV Adiwarna* 1(6):14. Available at: http://publication.petra.ac.id/index.php/dkv/article/view/3185.

Suwardikun, D. W. and Tohir, M. 2019. *Laporan Penelitian: Unsur Visual Indonesia dalam Sampul Majalah Mode*. Bandung.

Suwardikun, D. W. 2017. Wajah Indo dalam Iklan Tahun 1950an. *Panggung*. doi: 10.26742/panggung.v26i2.171.

Thalia, R. P. and Franzia, E. 2018. Desain cover Majalah Cosmogirl Indonesia. *Jurnal Dimensi DKV Seni Rupa Dan Desain* 3(1):15–30. doi: 10.25105/JDD.V3I1.2845.

Dynamics of Industrial Revolution 4.0: Digital Technology Transformation and Cultural Evolution –
Wulandari et al (eds)
© 2021 The Author(s), ISBN 978-1-032-04451-4

The value of heterotopia space constructed by the hybridity of physical and digital interior design

J. Hidayat
Universitas Pelita Harapan, Tangerang, Indonesia

C. Dharmawan
Universitas Komputer Indonesia, Bandung, Indonesia

ABSTRACT: Heterotopia is a theoretical concept referring to real space comprising character-istics such as ambiguous, temporary, contextual, personal, and illusive. It unveils the contradictive hidden meaning. The advance of digital technology in design brings forth the hybridity that delivers a spatial aesthetic experience in the form of an intervention space between the physical element with its constant trait and the digital space that is temporary; between a more objective construction of meaning and contextual or personal. The case study method was used in this study with objects from the Museum of the Bible, the Vuitton store, and the Miguel Chevalier Digital Art Installation. The result is that the value of heterotopia was used as a critique space and a representation of identity crisis precipitated by the encounter between physical and digital space. It in turn stipulates interior design to redefine the understanding of space. The meaning of space is a value which will always be present in a process of negotiating and reinterpreting.

Keywords: heterotopia, hybrid, digital, interior, illusive

1   INTRODUCTION

Digital art was first introduced by Harold Cohen (1928–2016), a British painter and academic who had been in the United States since 1968. In 1971, he published a drawing machine controlled by a computer. Cohen then developed a computer program for the drawing composition of lines, surfaces, and colors. The abstract drawing produced by this computer-controlled drawing machine was brought to the public at the Los Angeles County Museum of Air (1972), La Jolla Museum of Air in San Diego (1973), and the "Documenta" art exhibition in Kassel, Germany (1977). Cohen subsequently enhanced a more elaborate computer program which enabled the drawing machine to develop into a painting-fabricator machine that could produce figurative paintings such as floras, human paintings, as well as making simulations of colors decided upon by an artist. In the 1990s, this painting fabricator machine lost the competition to the printing machine which can produce a replica of a colored picture on large-sized paper, including canvas for paintings who also had unlimited opportunities for artists to create visual collages by combining images originating from photos, videos, and computer paintings, turning them into new works of art. The artificial intelligence, used to create paintings and the strategy of combining physical and digital images to generate a novelty, merged into the design world including interior design.

The first application of computer technology in interior design occurred in the making of design drawing, working drawing, and presentation drawing by using computer software such as AutoCAD since 1982, 3D Max Animation since 2005, Adobe Illustrator since 1986, and Adobe Photoshop since 1990, followed by design softwares for 2D and 3D drawings, such as SketchUp, TurboCad, Revit, Archicad, Infurnia, and Live Home 3D. Computer technology was also used on 3D printing machines to translate the 2D drawings into 3D models, in calculating the energy efficiency on

DOI 10.1201/9781003193241-46

the green designs and in the making of green construction (ConstructionSuite since 1999, Green Wizard, Autodesk Green Building Studio and Greengrade), and to create animated images, moving objects, simulations, and hyperreal spaces utilizing virtual reality. This study reviewed the combination of physical and digital elements in interior design to learn the values of hybrid space created when users experienced the mixture of static stable image and the constantly moving/changing image. The physical space has the temporary, ambiguous, dual coding (physical-digital) characteristics, which in turn generates the problem of representation referred to as Heteropia space by Michel Foucault in 1967.

2 METHOD

This study's question was how the value of Heterotopia space was created by the hybridity of physical and digital space elements. This research used the case study method with two bases as follows: (1) as a method that can be used to deepen a theory and its implementation in various cases and (2) to put theories into tests as well as enriching them to modify it and broadening the readers' horizon on contextual truth. The chosen cases were the Museum of the Bible in Washington, DC, the Luis Vuitton Store at Changi Airport, Singapore, and the Miguel Chevalier Digital Art Installation at Cathedral Notre-Dame, Rodez, France. They were chosen for the accessibility and capability in illustrating the theory to show Heterotopia space and the aesthetic experience created by it.

Based on Robert K. Yin's theory on Case Study Research (Yin 2014), the applied method of data collecting and analysis were (1) exploration of Heterotopia theory to generate the Heterotopia space characteristic analysis variable, (2) selection of cases and data collection through literature study and survey, (3) cases analysis, and (4) modification and implication of theory on the understanding and meaning of space.

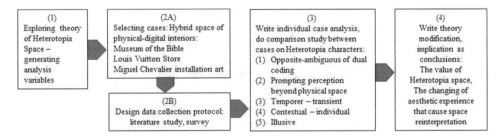

Figure 1.   Adaptation on the Yin Model of the case study research method.

3 RESULT

3.1 *Heterotopia space*

Heterotopia space is a real space with tangible physical elements, and a theoretical concept developed by Foucault (1967), with characteristics: (1) opposite and ambiguous character of double coding (physical and digital elements of space); (2) prompting perception beyond physical space; (3) temporary and transient; (4) contextual and individual; and (5) illusive (Hidayat 2005).

The first characteristic is the existence of opposing traits creating ambiguous meaning of the space. For that, the space meaning can be re-interpreted by different users. Within the hybridity between the physical and digital space, disparity emerges when the static physical element encounters the dynamic digital element having different concepts of form and significance.

The second characteristic is the appearance of spatial perception that goes beyond the boundaries of three-dimensional physical elements. The existence of tangible and measured Heterotopia is categorized as a real space, although it is beyond sensorial perception. It can occur when a space has a meaning related to the user's spirituality. When the appreciator experiences the space, he put(s) himself in the present as well as the past (nostalgia) on the same function or type of space.

The third characteristic is that Heterotopia space does not have a universal and consistent form, aside from having a different shape. Heterotopia also has various functions of space, depending on the context of time and space. In the traditional (in traditional) culture, a church has a sacred function as a place for worship. However, in the postmodern culture, it is possible to use a church as an art exhibition space, as exemplified by Chevalier's digital installation art. Within this context, two opposing characters present together: the sacred and the profane. The existence of a digital element enables the image in the space to continuously shift. It delivers various performances that are estranged from one another with different meanings that makes the visitors feel like being in a temporary transit area. Heterotopia professes a continuum characteristic toward the changing dimension of space and time. The metaphor uttered by Foucault is a sailing ship on the ocean, where a ship has no absolute space reference. The ship's space is an individual solitary space, but it is a part of a universal space with no boundaries (Mirzoeff 1998).

The fourth characteristic is that perception produced is contextual toward the user's cultural space. Different cultural backgrounds of users produce different engagement between users and the space. It happens when space has a digital element with changing images. In the time of advances of (in) information, communication, and modern transportation technology, people can swiftly move from one cultural space to another, and connect with people from various cultural spaces regardless (of) geographic and institutional barriers. The perception generated within a space may even become individual, unmapped, such as the ethnic culture.

The fifth characteristic is illusive. The function of Heterotopia space is creating an illusional space contesting the real. It puts boundaries on human life and generates human values that become the representation of artificial or superficial culture. Therefore, Heterotopia space has a critique function toward diverse ideology, social, and cultural problems.

3.2 *The heterotopia space characteristic of the Museum of the Bible*

Figure 2.   Entrance, lobby, and World Stage Theatre of the Museum of the Bible (entrance, lobby photos were taken on October 2018 survey, World Stage Theatre image is courtesy of the Museum of the Bible).

The Museum of the Bible in Washington, DC, has been open to the public since 2017. This museum's design uses a narrative approach in delivering visual language through storytelling. The implemented narrative design strategy is to create a multi-sensory perception by stimulating sensorials and movement using digital technology. The space chosen to represent physical and digital hybridity is the lobby, virtual reality area, and World Stage Theatre. The ceiling on the lobby corridor is a LED (Light Emitting Diode) digital screen panel with a projector connected to the computer, presenting different images. It enables visitors to experience spatial images that changes (change) as they walk through the corridor, creating a continuum of time-space accordance. It differs from the traditional design where a designer created one image concept for one space.

The dual coding within the space not only exists through the divergence between the static elements of floor, wall, and column to the temporary-dynamic images of the digital ceiling, but also happens due to differences in concept, content, and style of the image itself. The ceiling image is a limitless visual collage, starting from Middle Age classical, to Renaissance, to the Modern era, delivered by the computer screen on the ceiling that can be shifted anytime by the programmer following the content provided by the museum curator. This virtual reality (VR) area is a Heterotopia space because in this empty physical space, by using VR glasses, the visitors experience a VR tour of cultural spaces within the Bible. When experiencing the virtual space, it is as if visitors have traveled through the past time-space dimension, deriving a hyper-reality.

Hyper-reality is a spatial experience generated through simulation. Here, metaphysic representation, the vanishing of reality ideology, duplication of nostalgic, and fantasy world replaces the form-meaning (Piliang 1999, 2004). Digital technology was also applied in the World Stage Theatre, where walls and ceilings were covered by digital screens. This condition resulted in a continuously changing spatial image adjusting with the presentation currently displayed on the front screen, creating a 360° virtual perception.

3.3 *Heterotopia space characteristic of a Louis Vuitton Store*

Figure 3. Louis Vuitton Store, Changi Airport, Singapore. (Photos were taken on December 2017 survey).

At Changi Airport, the Louis Vuitton Store has a storefront display different from the window displays found in traditional stores. Space hybridity occurs between the door as a physical element placed alongside a digital LED panel, creating a dynamic facade with its shifting images. The image displayed has no direct correlation with the store's product, rather representing the characteristic of a Louis Vuitton's product. The temporary and transient characteristics exist in this space, where visitors feel like taking a journey transiting from one fantasy realm to another.

Users experience individual illusions following the cultural context in constructing meaning. The hybrid space gave a less (gave less) of an intense effect since the digital element only of one (had one) visual panel. The design combination was still dominated by physical elements making the digital only as decorative for its monumental size, while the designer tried to create the illusion of fantasy-like space dimension to visitors.

3.4 *Heterotopia characteristic of the Chevalier installation art at The Notre-Dame Cathedral*

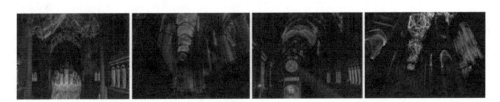

Figure 4. Digital Supernova Installation Art by Miguel Chevalier, Cathedral Notre-Dame, August 2019. (source: designboom.com, accessed July 2020).

Installation art by Miguel Chevalier at The Cathedral Notre-Dame in Rodez, France, in 2019 was presented during the evenings. The chosen time added a contrast to the characteristic and affected visitors' perception. This dual-coding happened in the church came from the physical material, digital characteristics, shape, color, and composition.

The church has a gothic style with natural and monotonous colors. The digital art installation delivered a modern style with abstract forms and gleaming bright colors. The creation of the installation generated a novelty surfacing the form, due to high contrast expression came (coming) from the shape and color substance. This novelty also happened at the level of meaning.

In a church, light is a symbolic representation of God's presence. The darkroom symbolized the sinned human since sins are identical to miseries and despair. When a human repents, he feels God's presence and guidance within himself, like the light that comes into the darkroom. The light in a gothic church comes from the stained-glass composition.

In the Chevalier installation, the installation art's lines, surfaces, and colors produced luminescence that replaced the divine light. In this case, the light had no spiritual meaning, but a profane frenetic world of material. It is like congregations worship in a church while their minds are not on God but on their agendas, business, and worldly pleasures. Their body is in the church, but they have their mind on other places. This fractured-identity characteristic represented by the dual-coding existed within the art installation.

4 DISCUSSION

The digital element in a Heterotopia space takes part as an open variable. It delivers a continuously changing image causing the whole image of space unclear due to its dynamic. Basically, form and space's meanings have a singular and static relation, because the image and meaning narration are statics. The digital element makes the image of space temporary, as well as the perception it generates. Thus, space becomes transitional. When the floor, walls, and ceiling elements come in the form of a digital screen or panel, what is space?

Interior design's discipline understands space as a physical element consisting of tangible and measurable elements of floor, walls, and ceiling. This discipline also gives a comprehension of interiority seeing space in a more fluid understanding. It considers the imaginary space that does not always have complete physical components, but proffers the feeling of being sheltered, protected, and surrounded like being under a tree or walk in a narrow roofless corridor between buildings. What if the floor, wall, and ceiling elements can no longer be clearly defined when meaning has no longer become important compared to the shifting space image itself? The physical-digital hybrid space phenomenon brings back the space theory to the Lao Tzu philosophy that things always change and one remains unchanged is the way of becoming (Ven 1995).

Space is organic and existential because space is formed from the inside out, starting from imaginary personal space to hybrid physical and digital space. However, the interpretation of space is existential, depending on the context of being and time of humans who experience it. According to Heidegger, the spatial experience is phenomenological as Das sein is spatial and Das sein spatiality or lived spatiality or place is a representation of being in the world (Wollan 2003). When the meaning of space becomes unstable and unclear, it leads to a paradox. However, space becomes a medium to reflect or critic (criticize) when the meaning displayed on the surface differs from the one existing within the user's perception. When the museum users experience the historical space, not all of them treat it as a learning space, but as a background visual collage for self-existence in the social media, a space for spiritual pilgrimage, a space for dating, a pre-wedding photoshoot space, or a space for a fashion show. The same thing when a church is enabled as an art piece display space. The real space that is paradox like a utopian at the real–physical site, contested and inverted, is a Heterotopia space (Sajjad 2019).

5 CONCLUSION

The users obtain the ambiguous, temporary, transient, and illusive values of a Heterotopia space when they understand that those characteristics represent the actual reality of space as a unity of opposing characteristics. The being and not-being, static and dynamic, superficial and hidden meaning, explicit and implicit, those are the characteristics that represent the dynamic balance. This study confirms Cornelis van de Ven's articulation about Tao space theory (Ven 1995), that intervention between two opposing characteristics is the essential structure of temporary space aesthetic. The same goes for Deleuze and Guattari's viewpoint (Deleuze & Guattari, 1994) that limitation is an illusion and determination is a negation unless if there is a relation between the determined and the one that is not; hybridity between physical and digital space.

REFERENCES

Deleuze, G. and Guattari, F. 1994. *What is Philosophy?* New York: Columbia University Press.

Hidayat, J. 2005. Bahasa Estetik Skizofrenia dalam Ruang Heterotopia: Studi Kasus Area Natah dalam Sintaks Tradisional Bali. *Jurnal 2d3d*. Tangerang, Banten: Fakultas Desain, Universitas Pelita Harapan.

Mirzoeff, N. 1998. *Michel Foucault of other Spaces.* New York: Routledge.

Piliang, Y.A. 1999. *Hiper-realitas Kebudayaan.* Yogyakarta: LKiS.

Piliang, Y.A. 2004. *Posrealitas: Realitas Kebudayaan dalam Era Posmetafisika.* Yogyakarta: Jalasutra.

Sajjad, N.u.A. 2019. Private Heterotopia and the Public Space: An Incongruity Explored through Orhan Pamuk's My Name is Red. *Sage Open Journal* 9(1). New York: Sage Publishing.

Ven, C.v.d. 1995. *Ruang dalam Arsitektur (3rd Edition).* Jakarta: Gramedia.

Wollan, G. 2003. Heidegger's Philosophy of Space and Place. *Journal Norsk Geografisk Tidsskrift – Norwegian Journal of Geography* 57(1): 31-39. Taylor & Francis.

Yin, R.K. 2014. *Case Study Research Design and Methods (5 Edition).* Thousand Oaks, CA: Sage.

Dynamics of Industrial Revolution 4.0: Digital Technology Transformation and Cultural Evolution –
Wulandari et al (eds)
© 2021 The Author(s), ISBN 978-1-032-04451-4

The metaphor of micin generation in an MSG product commercial

R. Belasunda, M. Tohir & T. Hendiawan
Telkom University, Bandung, Indonesia

ABSTRACT: Advertising, as a persuasive social strategy, is inseparable from the cultural context that surrounds it. The controversy that developed in the community surrounds the use of flavoring ingredients, or *micin*, and the *micin* generation that is assumed to be a presentation of the side effects caused by the product. The problems in the advertisement itself are related to the strategy of delivering the message, in this case it is about what is to be conveyed and how the message is interpreted by consumers or viewers of the commercial. Roland Barthes' semiotics with its order of the stages of meaning, i.e., denotation, connotation, myth, and ideology, were used as research methods in this study. The purpose of this research was to find out, through academic studies, how consumers or viewers comprehend and interpret the ideas and messages in commercials.

Keywords: commercial, micin, idea, message, micin generation

1 INTRODUCTION

The messages in commercials are a persuasive social strategy that intends to influence the way people perceive the purchase and consumption of certain goods. It is often interpreted differently by consumers or viewers. It relates to the cultural context behind them.

The commercial about *Sasa* food flavoring (*micin*) as a research object was chosen due to the television commercial some time ago that became a concern on social media (Sasa Melezatkan 2020). This commercial is considered as a breakthrough against the negative stigma of society toward *micin* (food flavoring) consumption and the *micin generation*.

2 THEORETICAL BACKGROUND

Advertising is a commercial and impersonal way an organization can communicate with consumers and advertise its products to the target audience through mass media (Lee & Johnson 2018). In its development, advertising evolved into a form of a persuasive social strategy that intends to influence the way people perceive the purchase and consumption of certain goods. Positioning and creating images are the main techniques in producing a strong commercial. Advertisers emphasize not only the product, but also the social significance that is expected to be materialized from purchasing the product (Danesi 2010). Metaphor as a rhetorical strategy used in advertising to provide meaning to a certain product. In context of television, in which advertising serves as a communication media, advertisement creators serve as senders of messages or ideas; advertisement viewers serve as readers of ideas; and an advertisement serves as the medium through which the ideas are being conveyed. As the result of the relations between the verbal and symbolic elements in the advertisement structure, the message in the advertisement is conveyed in a narrative. Advertising on the television media has similar characteristics as film, consisting of its physical structure and constituent elements. The structure of the film consists of shots, scenes, and sequences. The constituent elements consist of narrative elements (story and plot, characterization, main elements, space, time, and story

DOI 10.1201/9781003193241-47

information) and cinematic elements (mise-en-scene, cinematography, editing, and sound) (Pratista 2008).

The message in advertising is the main element as object of research in semiotics. A commercial contains three elements: (1) a sign (text), the entity (object) being advertised; (2) context in the form of environment, people or other beings giving meaning to objects; and (3) text (in the form of writing) which strengthens the meaning (anchoring) (Piliang 2010). In the text significance, Barthes in Thwaites and Davis (2009) divided it into denotation and connotation order. Denotation appears to be something after true meaning, with a strong relationship between the signifier and the signified. The connotation, as the second order of significance of the text or signifier, appears as a rather less tangible, imaginary, or illusory meaning. Next, is the myth—the second stage of signification—which constitutes of a way of thinking of a particular culture toward some matters, a manner to conceptualize or comprehend matters (Fiske 2007), and ideology as an illusionary belief in the form of pseudo-ideas and pseudo-awareness (Fiske 2007).

3 RESULT AND DISCUSSION

The television advertisement *Welcome Back Micin SWAG Generation* was the object of the research conducted by the author. This is a commercial for an MSG (Monosodium Glutamate) product from the *Sasa* brand from *PT Sasa Inti*, the commercial has been broadcasted on television since early 2020, lasting for 59 seconds of duration (Sasa Melezatkan 2020). The analysis of MSG Sasa's commercial text was carried out toward the narrative and cinematic elements as a sign and sign systems. Text analysis was performed based on narrative, text elements, and cinematic elements.

The results of the text analysis denotatively showed that these commercials used the personification metaphor, wherein the Sasa's food flavoring product (MSG) was represented as *micin swag generation's* people. MSG which stands for Monosodium Glutamate is identified with *Micin Swag Generation*. The text element and narrative construction of the commercial were used to build the new comprehension and significance about the product.

Table 1. Text analysis: visual, film semantics, and meaning units.

No	Visual Narrative	Narrative and Text Element (*Object, Context, Anchoring*)	Cinematic Elements and Meaning Units
1		*Object:* a group of people in the room. *Context:* swag generation's socializing space	Subjective camera *angle*, *straight camera angle* viewpoint. The swag generation's closeness and relaxed atmosphere
2		*Object:* two swag generation girls holding a flag outside the room. *Context:* swag generation's socializing space *Anchoring:* We are MSG	Subjective camera *angle*, *straight camera angle* viewpoint, and it used symmetric composition. The MSG group's liberty and identity.
3		*Object:* a girl holding a megaphone *Context:* a room with a plastic background *Anchoring: We speak outloud.*	Subjective camera *angle*, *straight angle* camera viewpoint, and using symmetric composition. The declaration of identity and existence.

4		*Object:* a young man in a room *Context:* a closed room *Anchoring:* the Sasa's product *banding*	Subjective camera *angle, straight angle, close-up* camera viewpoint The declaration of identity.
5		*Object:* a young man walks upon the wall *Context:* doing *parkour*	Subjective camera *angle, low angle* camera viewpoint Traversing the obstacles efficiently and as quickly as possible
6		*Object:* a group of young men jumped and broke through the lettering *Context:* outdoor *Anchoring: We break boundaries*	Subjective camera *angle, straight angle* camera viewpoint, and using symmetric composition. Breaking through the boundary together.
7		*Object:* a woman slicing vegetables *Context:* moving from the kitchen to an open space	Subjective camera *angle, high angle* camera viewpoint, and using *over shoulder* Routine
8		*Object:* a woman in thekitchen *Context:* moving from the kitchen to an open space and the costume changed. *Anchoring: We live the life*	Subjective camera *angle, low angle* camera viewpoint Breaking through the boundary
9		*Object:* white text *Context:* a dark lane in a building *Anchoring: We follow our passion*	Subjective camera *angle, straight angle* camera viewpoint, and using symmetric composition. Moving, affirmation.
10		*Object:* two young women confidently crossing the road *Context:* public space *Anchoring: We are confident*	Subjective camera *angle, straight angle* camera viewpoint, and using symmetric composition. Confident.
11		*Object:* a group of people in a room *Context: swag* generation's socializing space *Anchoring:* the Sasa's product *banding*	Subjective camera *angle, low angle* camera viewpoint, dynamic, neutral *screen direction.* The swag generation's closeness and relaxed atmosphere with the product's identity.

12		*Object:* a young woman walks in front of three old men *Context:* in the office space *Anchoring:* We lead the way	Subjective camera *angle*, *straight angle* camera viewpoint. *Leader.*
13		*Object:* a text in front of a fast moving background *Context:* outdoor, evening *Anchoring:* Welcome Micin SWAG Generation	Subjective camera *angle*, *straight angle* camera viewpoint. The brisk change in welcoming the Micin Swag Generation.
14		*Object:* a group of young people of swag generation walking together *Context:* outdoor *Anchoring:* #EnjoyLifeFully and We are MSG	Subjective camera *angle*, *high angle* camera viewpoint. The declaration and identity of Micin Swag Generation
15		Narrative: MSG made of the molasses that fit for human consumption *Object:* text, packaging, and *product brand* *Anchoring:* We are MSG dan brand product	Subjective camera *angle*, *straight angle* and symmetrical camera viewpoint. Declaration and product's identity.
16		Narrative: …As long as the wrapper isn't eaten. *Object:* text *Anchoring:* MSG made of the molasses that fit for human consumption, as long as the wrapper isn't eaten.	Subjective camera *angle*, *straight angle* and symmetrical camera viewpoint. Declaration and product's identity.
17		*Object:* text *Anchoring:* PDGKI (Indonesian Clinical Nutrition Doctors Association): the subtle consumption of seasoning is not harmful to health.	Subjective camera *angle*, *straight angle* and symmetrical camera viewpoint. The statement of authorized institution.

Meanwhile, connotatively it opened up possibilities for dialectical interpretation of messages related to the use of the *Micin Swag Generation* tagline. *Micin* generation and *swag* generation are included in Generation Z, whose characteristics are varied. The *swag* generation is more likely to be considered to have positive values, while the micin generation was given a negative stigma. The word *swag* is another word for *cool* or *gangster fashion style*. *Swag* is assumed as an acronym of "*style with a little bit gangsta*". The *micin* generation, however, is used to judge the strange, unearthly, unreasonable, difficult to understand, love to show off on social media, and oblivious behavior. The *micin* generation is assumed to be a generation that has consumed too much *micin* or MSG, as if their level of intelligence is decreased.

The results of the myth analysis relating to the positive values in the Generation Z characteristics are: (a) confidence in expressing opinions; (b) mastering technology and having the potential to lead in the future; and (c) like social activities and enjoy life. Sasa's MSG products delivered an ideology of pseudo-awareness through a metaphorical narrative that represents the positive values of *micin swag generation* through the products offered.

4 CONCLUSION

Based on the results, it can be concluded that there is a mythical dialectic of positive values in the cultural system and values represented in the advertisement of Sasa's MSG products. Through the narrative of personification and metaphor, the commercial of the very product offers an ideology of pseudo-awareness to the consumers, wherein the product is a representation and is only identified by positive values of the *micin swag generation*. These commercials formalize a pseudo-awareness that by consuming the product, people can obtain (only) the positive values of the *micin swag generation*, and put aside the negative stigma of society toward the *micin generation*.

REFERENCES

Danesi, M. 2010. *Pesan, Tanda, dan Makna*. Yogyakarta: Jalasutra.
Fiske, J. 2007. *Cultural and Communication Studies*. Yogyakarta: Jalasutra.
Lee, M. and Johnson, C. 2018. *Prinsip-Prinsip Pokok Periklanan Dalam Perspektif Global*. Jakarta: Kencana Prenada Media Group.
Melezatkan, S. 2020. *Welcome Back Micin Swag Generation*, *Youtube*.
Piliang, Y.A. 2010. *Hipersemiotika: Tafsir Cultural Studies Atas Matinya Makna*. Yogyakarta: Jalasutra.
Pratista, H. 2008. *Memahami Film*. Yogyakarta: Homerian Pustaka.
Thwaites, T. and Lloyd Davis, W.M. 2009. *Introducing Cultural And Media Studies*. Yogyakarta: Jalasutra.

Dynamics of Industrial Revolution 4.0: Digital Technology Transformation and Cultural Evolution –
Wulandari et al (eds)
© 2021 The Author(s), ISBN 978-1-032-04451-4

Garudayana comic adaptation of the Mahabharata story series in the millennial era

I.D.A.D. Putra
Telkom University, Bandung, Indonesia

ABSTRACT: Mahabharata comics, once popular in the 1950s–1970s, receded and sank in popularity because of the development of Japanese comics in the globalization era. During the sinking of Indonesian comics, the comic *Garudayana* emerged as a popular Mahabharata series among millennials. The success of these comics was due to the author's creative process in dealing with changes and challenges of the times. Reinterpretation and reduction of the Mahabharata story can be accepted and represent the tastes of readers of his era. Changes that were made, such as storyline, new characters, drawing style, and the right promotional strategies as keys to the success of the comic. This research used a qualitative method with data collection techniques through observation and literature study, as well as visual analysis to position the comic that can show the Mahabhatara story values and Indonesian identity.

Keywords: comics, Mahabharata, millennial

1 INTRODUCTION

Indonesian comics triumphed in the 1950s–1970s in various genres including the puppet genre with a comic artist named R.A. Kosasih. Kosasih was later considered the father of Indonesian *wayang* comics. Visualization or character figures in the Mahabharata comic created by R.A. Kosasih used the classic West Java Sundanese puppetry form approach, namely "*wayang golek*", "*wayang wong*", and ballet. The comic artist succeeded in merging puppet comics and Indonesian identity, which at that time were heavily influenced by American comics, with Western superhero characters. Even so, in Indonesia at that time there were already superhero comics, such as "Sri Asih", which was made by R.A. Kosasih who was influenced by the American comic "Wonder Woman" and "Garuda Putih" made by John Lo (Irena & Andri 2017).

Entering the era of globalization in Indonesia, puppet comics are no longer known. Indonesia was flooded by the Japanese comic with its manga style. Japanese comics flooded Indonesia both physically, in the form of books, and digitally. Manga visualization was not only popular in the form of comics, but also in the form of animation, films, games, and other social media. This makes the millennial generation only recognize manga visuals. The millennial generation, born at that time, were crammed with manga visuals. They were also used to draw people at school, at home—everywhere was manga. Manga has become a meat in their minds, who shifted the visuals of American and European comics with their superheroes.

This development makes it appear that Indonesian comics have lost their identity and do not have reliable comic artists. In addition, the Indonesian people themselves have underestimated Indonesian comic artists. In 2009, the comic puppet Garudayana by comic artist Is Yuniarto appeared. It adopted the classic Mahabharata puppetry story from the first series, Adi Parwa. The story of Garuda in its classic version was changed through a contemporary approach with a simpler storytelling style by applying manga as a visual approach.

The Garudayana comic created by Is Yuniarto still can be said to be a success for a millennial version of the puppet comic with various publishing media. The success of this comic artist is the study in this paper. The aim of this paper was to see how the adaptation process of the Mahabharata story affected the comic industry, especially the first Parwa series, Adi Parwa, by Is Yuniarto in his Garudayana comic. It attemped to see if the adaptation of new characters and the creative process and strategy in introducing the comics made them become popular among millennial Indonesian youth.

2 METHOD

The research of this paper was a study of the comic Garudayana by Is Yuniarto. Comics are one of the most popular visual-based information media in the millennial generation. This study used qualitative methods through data collection techniques such as observation, literature study, and visual analysis. The qualitative method according to Bogdan and Taylor in Ratna (2016) does not merely describe, but more importantly find, the results and meanings contained behind them, as hidden meanings or intentionally hidden.

The qualitative method in turn produces descriptive data in the form of words, both written and oral. Furthermore, this method is used to explore and express the behavior or characteristics of millennial society, because the comics created by the comic artist were born in that era. Strengthening the background and any phenomena contained in the change in Garudayana comics can be done through literature study, by observing objects in the form of a Garudayana comic book series that has been made, and by analyzing visuals, especially classical puppets and new characters as well as aspects and rules contained in comic theory.

The description of the Garudayana comic was done by taking some of the visuals in the comic, from the creation process, as well as in terms of the promotion strategy in making this comic popular among millennial generation. The visualization of the Garudayana comics included aspects of general comic principles and particularly manga comics principles, story problems, and setting that makes the comic unique from other comics.

3 RESULT AND DISCUSSION

Comics as a medium of information and entertainment are closely related to the readers' tastes. The taste or interest in comics in each era or generation are different. Interest or taste in reading comics cannot be separated from the development of scientific and technological advances, which can change readers' behavior as consumers. In the development of comics in Indonesia, a trend in visualization style will emerge that also adapts to the current tastes preferred by the market. The flow of the market tastes always depends on the genre of interest, and the genre that is in demand by the market is always changing in every decade or era. The fate of this reading depends on the readers' temporary fondness for a genre (Boneff 1998). This statement proves that the trend of comics development in Indonesia fluctuates. Readers' tastes are strongly influenced by a trend of the genre that they are interested in and are also influenced by the comic industry which is stronger and has a wider market.

The millennial generation is a generation term that is currently being discussed by many people in the world in various fields. Millennials are also known as the Millennial Generation or Generation Y as a demographic group after Generation X. Social researchers often classify generations born between the 1980s and 2000s as millennials (Naldo & Satria 2018). Compared to the previous generation, Generation X, the millennial generation is indeed unique. The research results released by the Pew Research Center in 2010, for example, in detail explain the uniqueness of the millennial generation compared to the previous generation, namely in the use of technology, pop culture, and music.

The life of the millennial generation cannot be separated from technology, especially the internet, or entertainment which has become a necessity for this generation. The birth process of the millennial generation has given birth to the generation of gadgets, a term used to mark the emergence of the millennial generation. Gadgets are more appropriate to be interpreted as equipment, where the generation of gadgets is meant to be the generation in life that has always been in contact with something called equipment containing elements of information technology. Various pieces of equipment including high-technology tools are an inseparable and important part of their lives (Wahana 2015).

The situation above explains the characteristics of the millennial generation, where the comic artist Garudayana is part of that generation. Is Yuniarto, born on June 22, 1981, certainly understands the world of millennials as he has been connected to the world of the internet from a young age. Visual pop culture such as manga in various media such as films, games, webtoons, comics, and animation became the author's aesthetic experience. These conditions and situations gave Is Yuniarto an advantage, in addition to his natural talent for drawing.

The Mahabharata puppet comic has also been popularized by R.A. Kosasih and several Indonesian comic artists such as S. Ardisoma, Oerip, Suherlan, N. A. Giok Lan, and others. R. A. Kosasih created 22 volumes of Mahabharata, 5 volumes of Bharatayudha, 4 volumes of Pandawa Seda, and 4 volumes of Parikesit. Ardisoma created Wayang Purwa which explained the initial story of the gods and the Bharata family in 22 volumes. He also created the story of the beginning of the Ramayana and Arjuna Sasrabahu and other stories (Sunarto 2013). These two comic artists created the basic understanding of Mahabharata and Ramayana and are used as references by other comic artists.

The Garudayana comic made by Is Yuniarto only used the background of the classic Mahabharata story and modified it into a new version tailored to the needs of the millennial generation. The Garuda comic story is not made like the classic story of the great epic. The comic artist is more generalized in essence; it is about heroism, about good and evil. The story in the comics was made simpler in several book series with smaller page counts, considering that millennials like practical and short things.

The story of the Garudayana puppet comic created by Is Yuniarto tells the story of Garuda, out of Adi Parwa's standard. The comic artist preferred to make his own story line as well as create new characters such as "Kinara" and "Garu" which are not found in the classic version. In addition, the author also made a new background setting that is closer to the places in Indonesia. All aspects in the Garudayana comic follow the comic aspects in the Japanese manga.

The contribution of Japanese popular culture such as manga to Indonesian comics began to appear in the 1980s and have increasingly dominated it since the 1990s. Comic artists who were born in the 1980s–2000s made manga the main reference which eventually gave birth to Indonesian comics in today's manga style. The influx of manga influences in Indonesia was also strengthened by the entry of the Japanese animation industry which is commonly known as anime. Is Yuniarto is very familiar with his socio-culture as well as his drawing talents that represent his era.

The Mahabharata story in the Garudayana comic is only the trigger for the story. The comic artist takes the general philosophy of the Mahabharata story that tells good and evil or "Dharma" versus "A-Dharma". The stories and characters that are presented tell more about how to struggle and fight against monsters, as well as other evil characters. The comic artist Is Yuniarto has successfully interpreted and reduced the Mahabharata story to get closer to the tastes of millennial readers. The story is simple and does not raise the value of the puppet philosophy, which makes it easier for Generation Y to digest.

Reinterpretation and reduction of the understanding of the classic Mahabharata story through comics is accompanied by a superficiality of meaning, compared to the shadow puppets show where the puppeteer can play with, using nuance, one word to broach complex problems. Shadows display the mysteries and complexities of life, inviting people to go beyond the limits of appearance. While the lines in the comics stop the movement of the soul, it is impossible to rival the mastermind. The comic artist made something that is realistic, the comic artist's clear 'imagination' (Boneff 1998). The weakness of a comic can be described properly. Images can inform something imaginary or dreamy. The reader's power of the imagination is lost.

Figure 1. The new character of the creation "Kinara" by Is Yuniarto. (Source: deviantart.com/vanguard-zero/art/Garudayana-Comic-Cover).

The comic artist had Garudayana's foresight toward female teenage millennial readers and created a character in the form of "Kinara". This character was made in an effort by the comic artist to attract female teenage millenial readers. "Kinara" is a new character created by Is Yuniarto, as he is very familiar with the stories and characters in the Mahabharata. The character "Kinara" was made by combining several elements contained in the female shadow puppet (putri) figure such as *kamben*, necklaces (*badong*), bracelets, ear ornaments, etc., while maintaining a manga-style depiction. Then the image of the weapon used by the "Kinara" character is heavily influenced by games and movies (see Figure 1).

The Garudayana comic also uses references to other characters in the style of shadow puppets, as well as page decorations using traditional decorative elements, in an effort to elevate the multi-cultural nature of Indonesian culture. In making the background, the comic artist includes several cultural houses in Indonesia. Like the shape of the Gadang house, and the shape of the Toraja house in Indonesia. This effort was made in addition to introducing Indonesian culture, as well as promoting comics for having Indonesian identity.

4 CONCLUSION

Garudayana comics made by Is Yuniarto are popular among millennial adolescents. It has lifted the Indonesian comic industry during the onslaught of the Japanese comic industry with its anime. Many Indonesian millennials did not know and weren't familiar with the puppetry comics that told the story of Mahabharata; they were more familiar with stories and characters in manga comics, as well as other entertainment media such as games, films, and music.

Garudayana comics can give readers a comic that is in line with the behavior or the habits of millennials with aspects that exist in manga which has been the trend of the decade. The Mahabrataha story interpreted and reduced by Is Yuniarto can provide a story that represents the comic trend of the era and lift the image of puppetry that gives identity to Indonesian comics.

Is Yuniarto is a comic artist who was born and grew up in the millennial era which resulted in his being able to cope with its development. Besides being a comic artist, he is also an entrepreneur who can read the market's tastes. Utilizing the effectiveness and efficiency of digital media, the promotion carried out succeeded in making the Garudayana comics favored by the millennial generation.

ACKNOWLEDGMENTS

The author would like to greatly thank PPM Telkom University for granting this research in basic and applied research programs.

REFERENCES

Boneff, Marcel. 1998. *Indonesian comics* (translation of Rahayu S. Hidayat). Jakarta: Gramedia's Popular Library.

Irena and Andri. 2017. Effects of Foreign Comics on Visualization of the Development of Comics in Indonesia. *Journalof Magenta, STMK Trisakti* 1(01).

Naldo Satria, Hardika Widi. 2018. Observation Study of the Use of Line Applications by Millennials. *Journal of Social Applied Humanities* 1(1).

Ratna, Nyoman Kutha. 2016. *Research Methodology Cultural Studies and Social Sciences Humanities in General*. Yogaykarta: Student Library (Matter II).

Sunarto, Wagiono, 2013. Visual Transformation of Mahabharata Figure. *Journal of Stage Arts & Culture* 23(1).

Wahana, Heru Dwi. 2015. The Effect of Millennial Generation Cultural Values and School Culture on Individual Resilience (Study at SMA Negeri 39, Cijantung, Jakarta). *Journal of National Resilience* XXI(1):14–22

Dynamics of Industrial Revolution 4.0: Digital Technology Transformation and Cultural Evolution –
Wulandari et al (eds)
© 2021 The Author(s), ISBN 978-1-032-04451-4

Defamiliarization of video clips and aesthetic value in the "Lathi" song from weird genius

T. Hendiawan & Y.A. Barlian
Telkom University, Bandung, Indonesia

ABSTRACT: Video clips, as a medium of communication, have begun to use narrative and experimental cinema styles in conveying their messages and meanings. However, the video clip entitled "Lathi" from Weird Genius has problems when it is interpreted by the audience. There are those who consider it as creative or novel through its aesthetic value and those who criticize it as something that is misleading. The purpose of this study was to understand how visual defamiliarization changes the aesthetic value in terms of expression and position related to the experience of the aesthetic subject in interpreting Lathi's video clips. The study was conducted using Peirce's trichotomy semiotic research method with interpretive descriptive techniques through stages of understanding: representamen, objects (icon, symbol, index), and interpretants. The main purpose of this research is to increase the understanding of the audience in interpreting, understanding, and appreciating the work of video clips.

Keywords: defamiliarization, visuals, aesthetic values, video clips

1 INTRODUCTION

Video clips are mediums of expression to deliver messages and the meaning of a song so that the audience can better understand it. One of these cultural products has its own narrative structure and character, both related to the lyrics, visuals, aesthetics, meanings, symbols, movements, sounds, and visual language styles that are displayed. From each structure, it can be explored or exploited for the sake of conveying the meaning of song lyrics through visual construction.

This research revealed what was constructed in a part of the "Lathi" video clip from Weird Genius, an Indonesian EDM and synth-pop music group pioneered by 2 YouTubers and a DJ (Eka Gustiwana, Reza Arap, and Gerald Liu) featuring a rapper from Surabaya, Sara Fajira, as vocalist. Lathi's song was chosen because of its viral phenomenon since it was uploaded on YouTube in March 26, 2020. In just three months, this song reached more than 50 million viewers and is still increasing up to the moment of this research. Surprisingly, its popularity is not only in Indonesia, but also worldwide which is indicated by various Lathi Challenge made by influencers and also the song reviews made by YouTubers. As a result, this music group can prove its existence with their poster establishment in Times Square, New York.

There must be ways for how this Indonesian music group gained their noteriety. The song and video clip "Lathi" (meaning "tongue" and symbolically "utterance" in Javanese) has the theme about a toxic relationship. The theme is quite popular and one of the phenomena that currently exists in social relationships. Yet, what makes it interesting was the visual narrative construction which was packaged with a new form so that it becomes something unfamiliar/unusual, but very aesthetic, making the purpose of this work to be more "visible" to public which was achieved. This is called the defamiliarization technique (Fiske 2007).

The concept of defamiliarization has been applied in various disciplines, including in domestic technology which presents "novelty" in designing residence and furniture (Bell et al. 2005). In several pedagogical studies, defamiliarization in music was also used to provide students with new

DOI 10.1201/9781003193241-49

insights, knowledge, and writing skills in the teaching process. The defamiliarization approach was carried out in many literary studies such as research on novels and songs by Toni Morrison which were rich in metaphor and symbolism (Vegge 2000). Even the technique of defamiliarization was juxtaposed with software for creating creative writing (Gabriel 2012).

The application of the defamiliarization concept changes the aesthetic value of each audience because the audience has a different worldview depending on the culture they have. In the context of position, aesthetic values that are not tied to other values are classified as independent values. On the contrary, aesthetic values associated with other values are called dependent aesthetic values (Junaedi 2016).

In this research, the authors explored techniques of defamiliarization and aesthetic values contained in the "Lathi" video clip. It was interesting to observe it to discover the aesthetical value and the perspective/point of view of the spectators appreciating it. This research can provide an alternative interpretation in watching the video clip of "Lathi"s" song from Weird Genius, along with accusations of some people who think that "Lathi" is closely related to mystical nuances considered as one of the rituals to summon spirits.

2 THEORETICAL BACKGROUND

This research used the qualitative method, a study that uses interpretation through various methods, which aims to obtain a holistic understanding (Mulyana 2006).

In collecting data, the literature study and observation methods were used. Observation was made on the object of research ("Lathi" video clips) taken from YouTube, as well as observations on other media, such as "Lathi" challenges and various "Lathi" video clip reviews. In addition, data collection was also taken through literature study to gain the theories needed.

Data analysis was conducted to examine the defamiliarization techniques and aesthetic value of video clips through the selection of scenes needed in research based on Todorov's five-step narrative theory: (1) equilibrium which is the beginning of a narrative; (2) disequilibrium is a scene where problems begin to occur; (3) recognition of the disequilibrium is a scene where the protagonist and other characters are aware of the problem; (4) attempt to restore the equilibrium is a scene where the problem is resolved or usually in a video clip depicting emotional support between characters; and (5) new equilibrium, usually at the end of the narrative, the protagonist will build a new equilibrium to make this video clip more interesting (Ward 2019). The scene taken is the fourth scene from the narrative video clip.

To analyze the scene, this study also used Peirce's trichotomy semiotic research method with interpretive descriptive techniques through stages of understanding; representamen, objects, and interpretants to determine whether the existing aesthetic value is universal/general (independent value) or other factors that determine, for example "world view", or the aesthetic subject's view of life (spectators and creators) about the phenomena around, or it can also be cultural values that are the pride of the nation (Junaedi 2016).

3 RESULT AND DISCUSSION

Based on the observations of the video clip, the scene was taken using the defamiliarization technique. The refrain scene uses the Javanese language and some Javanese cultural rites. The use of Javanese language lyrics "*Kowe ra iso mlayu saka error Ajining diri ana ing lathi*" means "You cannot run away from mistakes because your pride lies in your tongue/utterance". Analyzing the microstructure, the discourse element of "Lathi" is an expression which means "one's self-esteem is determined by his words". This is an ancient Javanese language expression.

The use of Javanese lyrics is a referential function associated with names or objects and ideas that are represented in the world around them, that is, speech or in one of the proverbs is "untrustworthy words", which means that humans are very easy to lie or make promises. Effectively, the lyrics link who can have "rights" to say "what", which is very closely related to power and social status.

Analysis related to the technique of defamiliarization was also conducted through visuals that multiply the perspectives of meaning in the "Lathi" video clip. The following is the analysis of the visual text of "Lathi"'s video clip.

Table 1. Visual Text Analysis Table: Visual, Index, Icon, and Symbol

No	Visual	Index and Icon	Symbol
1	*Kowe ra iso mlayu saka kesalahan. Ajining diri ana ing lathi 1*	*Index: Black smoke billowing around a woman's body* *Icon: A woman in anger*	*Displeasure*
2		*Index: Scattered dry leaves and gray background* *Icon: Three modern dancers dancing fast, full of energy*	*Confusion*
3		*Index: Scattered dry leaves and gray background* *Icon: A traditional dancer dancing fast, energetic, and full of strength*	*Resistance*
4		*Index: Scattered dry leaves and gray background* *Icon: A lumping horse artist spitting fire from his mouth*	*Anger*
5		*Index: White background with silhouette of a mastermind and Rahwana skin pup* *Icon: A puppeteer playing the character of Ravana puppet*	*Antagonists*
6		*Index: Scattered dry leaves and gray background Context: outdoor* *Icon: A lumping horse artist playing his whip*	*Violence*

The results of the visual text analysis on this representamen showed a paradox through denialor resistance, to the powerlessness of women who try to maintain their existence to become authentic human beings. The object presented was a technique of defamiliarization, namely, the power of women who are transformed into a new force that is not necessary or ordinary automation that is understood by the general public. Paradoxically in humans, in female souls, there is also a male soul and vice versa. In the visuals, it can be seen how Javanese female dancers who are supposed to dance smoothly and gently turn into fast, energetic, and full of strength. Then it is depicted by a *lumping* horse male artist with magical powers, namely the symbol of the fire, that represents the

266

anger and whip as the strength, and the character of the Ravana shadow puppet as an antagonistic symbol.

The concept in the lyrics "your self-esteem lies in your mouth/utterance" is inseparable from the self-concept as an awareness that is continuously involved in reality. In fact, the self is constructed by someone else or the other, both in person, culture, experience, religion, and others. Hence, to be true or authentic you need to have a moment of vision. In the video clip, "Lathi" shows the "existential anxiety" of a woman who strives to become an authentic human being.

Changes in visual defamiliarization formed aesthetic values associated with the expression and position of the audience. The aesthetic value position in the clip is an aesthetic-dependent value, an association with Javanese cultural values. While the expression of aesthetic value uses chaos, providing surprises both in lyrics and visuals, as a form of creativity, as well as the musical disharmony in the major-minor and *pelog* barrel as a form of aesthetic values resulting from cultural blending.

4 CONCLUSION

It is concluded that defamiliarization techniques were used in forming aesthetic values. The aesthetic value will certainly be interpreted differently by the audience because each audience has a different worldview. The concept of defamiliarization as a strategy and form of cultural dialogue is an effort to establish relationality in modern-western and eastern-traditional thinking.

REFERENCES

Bell, G., Blythe, M., and Sengers, P. 2005. Making by making strange. *ACM Transactions on Computer-Human Interaction* 12(2):149–173. doi: 10.1145/1067860.1067862.

Fiske, J. 2007. *Cultural and Communication Studies*. Yogyakarta: Jalasutra.

Gabriel, R. P. 2012. Defamiliarization: Flarf, conceptual writing, and using flawed software tools as creative partners. *Knowledge Management & E-Learning: An International Journal* 4(2):134–145. doi: 10.34105/j.kmel.2012.04.013.

Junaedi, D. 2016. *Estetika: jalinan subjek, objek, dan nilaI*. Edited by B. I. Yogyakarta.

Mulyana, D. 2006. *Metodologi penelitian kualitatif: paradigma baru ilmu komunikasi dan ilmu sosial lainnya*. Bandung: PT Remaja Rosdakarya.

Vegge, T. 2000. *Toni Morrison: Defamiliarization and Metaphor in Song of Solomon and Beloved*. University of Oslo. Available at: https://www.duo.uio.no/bitstream/handle/10852/25163/Hovedoppgave-Tolli-Vegge.pdf?sequence=2&isAllowed=y.

Ward, A.B. 2019. *Popular Song and Narratology: Exploring the Relationship between Narrative Theory and Song Lyrics through Creative Practice*. Queensland University of Technology. doi: 10.5204/thesis.eprints.134488.

Dynamics of Industrial Revolution 4.0: Digital Technology Transformation and Cultural Evolution –
Wulandari et al (eds)
© 2021 The Author(s), ISBN 978-1-032-04451-4

Expression and message style in Indonesian television advertising during the month of Ramadhan in the time of the COVID-19 pandemic period

M. Tohir, T. Hendiawan & R. Belasunda
Telkom University, Bandung, Indonesia

ABSTRACT: Advertising on television in the 2020 Ramadan in Indonesia developed in various styles and became a specific phenomenon. Several issues arise including in the way ideas and messages were conveyed in the work of television advertisements, especially in the month of Ramadan during the COVID-19 pandemic. Further efforts are needed to be able to understand, interpret, and appreciate the text of television advertisements. The purpose of this study was to understand the way form and style of television advertising is revealed and where ideas and messages from creators were conveyed. The study was conducted using the Barthes semiotic research method and interpretative descriptive techniques based on the stages of understanding, denotation, connotation, myth, and ideology. The main objective of this research was to support the increasingly active and productive role of television viewers to understand, interpret, and appreciate television commercials through academic studies.

Keywords: TV ads, ideas, messages, Ramadan, pandemic covid-19

1 INTRODUCTION

Advertisement is one of the cultural products that reflects the lives of its people into an inevitable part of human life. Advertising as a messenger informs us about something and asks us to buy it, the information it conveys (often) is incorrect, or even if it is true the content is a persuasion to buy products that we do not need.

Television as a medium for delivering messages has its own character. Many things can be exploited using this form of media, ranging from conversation, movement, and sounds. Television with a variety of advantages eventually became a favorite medium to deliver advertisements.

This paper tried to explore what is presented in advertising through a case study on television advertisements that aired during Ramadan 2020 which coincidentally happened during the COVID-19 pandemic. It was designed to understand the kind of messages that would be conveyed besides the normative product messages that would be linked to the cultural background of making television commercials. This is because the presence of advertisements is strongly influenced by the social and cultural life of its people.

2 METHOD

Advertising is a form of paid communication that uses mass media and interactive media to reach a broad audience to connect clear sponsors with buyers (target audience) and provide information about products, whether in the form of goods, services, or ideas (Moriarty et al. 2018).

Television is one of the advertising media that is still the backbone of advertisers because almost every household in Indonesia has a television. Advertising on television media has various advantages compared to other media. Lee and Johnson (2011) said that television media has

DOI 10.1201/9781003193241-50

several advantages: television allows for product or service demonstration, it is easy to adapt, is cost-efficient, and attracts the attention of viewers.

Advertising on television media is a film work which is a series of images projected on the screen with the appropriate speed aimed at creating the illusion of continuous motion (Danesi 2010). Film as a medium aims to convey cultural events/practices and social phenomena to a wide audience with mass communication through the mass media system. In the context of film as a medium of communication, and creators act as senders of messages or ideas, ad viewers as readers of ideas, and the ads themselves as the media through which the ideas are conveyed.

Film as an object/artifact consists of the physical structure and its constituent elements. The structure of the film consists of shots, scenes, and sequences. The constituent elements consist of narrative elements (story and plot, characterization, main elements, space, time, and story information) and cinematic elements (*mise-en-scene*, cinematography, editing, and sound) (Pratista 2008).

Semiotics generally talks about signs. Signs are described as anything that produces meaning. They can represent/reflect things that are in/about the world, more specifically in the social world. Signs not only convey meaning but also produce meaning; even one sign can have multiple meanings.

Ferdinand de Saussure, a linguist (Fiske 2007) said that a sign is a physical object with meaning, or, to use the term, a sign consisting of a marker. Markers are images of signs as we perceive them, such as writings on paper or sounds in the air. A sign is a mental concept that is referred to by it. This mental concept is broadly the same in all members of the same culture who use the same language. In line with that, Williamson (2007) said that a sign is something (a thought) that can be an object, word, or picture that has a certain meaning for a person or group of people. A sign is not just a thing and not just a meaning but both at once.

Many definitions of the meaning offered by linguists and philosophers, but for the study of television advertising the author refers to the method that was stated by Barthes (Fiske 2007), which divides meaning into two domains: denotation, which is something (words) which does not contain additional meanings or feelings, and connotation, which is something (words) that contains additional meanings, certain feelings, or certain taste values besides general basic meanings. This will illustrate how an advertisement is denoted and then get its meaning after interacting with the audience. And then it continues to the concept of myth as a way of thinking, conceptualizing, and understanding about culture, and the concept of ideology as a false beliefs.

3 RESULT AND DISCUSSION

Based on observations of television advertisements during Ramadan 2020, there were 20 television commercials that had a high broadcast frequency and can be grouped into 2 categories: products and services. Product categories consisted of brands: Khong Guan, Teh Botol Sosro, Mc. Donald, Enervon C, Nutricake, Top Coffee, Ciptadent Herbal, Milo, Pocky, Esemag, Dancow, Indofood Bumbu Racik, HerbaKof, Kraft Cheddar, Brightgas Pertamina, Indomie, and Bejo Jahe Merah. The service category consisted of brands: Roma Festive, Shopee, and Blibli.

In general, the messages conveyed in these advertisements were: (a) benefits and product positioning; and/or (b) how the product relates to the current conditions of Ramadan and the COVID-19 pandemic. From the available data, the Teh Botol Sosro product (Ramadan 2020 edition, 60 sec, Flock Creative Network) was interesting to be used as a sample for further research because it had a way of conveying messages (styling) that was relatively different from other products advertised on television during Ramadan 2020.

What follows is the analysis of Teh Botol Sosro ad text on narrative and cinematic elements as a sign and sign system.

The results of the analysis are that many of the cinematics' style uses subjective camera angles in an effort to bring the audience closer to the subject or object in the ad. Narrative construction emphasizes semiotic, semantic, and cinematic elements. These elements are used to build the empathy and sympathy of the audience.

Table 1. Text analysis: visual and semantic films

No	Visual Narration	Verbal Narration	Cinematic Elements
1		*Ramadhan kali ini terasa sedikit berbeda*	The camera angle is subjective, its angle is low. The object of the bridge is silhouetted against the background of the mosque from the green. Ramadan is a special month for Muslims to get closer to the almighty. The visuals displayed are a limitation, distance, and silence.
2			Subjective camera angles; a straight angle was used on the camera and it uses symmetric compositions. The object of focus is someone praying inside the mosque. Closed, trapped, and alienation of someone who worships in the mosque.
3		*Hari demi hari ada yang setia berdiri demi semua kebutuhan terpenuhi*	Subjective camera angles; a straight angle is used on the camera and it uses a symmetrical composition with neutral screen direction. The object of focus is a security person standing under the bridge. Interpreted as protection and hope.
4			Subjective camera angles; a straight angle is used on the camera and it uses a symmetrical composition with neutral screen direction. The object of focus is a policeman standing on the side of the road. Interpreted as charm, protection, and hope.
5		*Ada yang turun kejalan, sukarela menambah beban demi kurangi beban sekitar*	Subjective camera angles; a straight angle is used on the camera and it uses a symmetrical composition with neutral screen direction. The object of focus is a nurse walking on the side of the road. Interpreted as caring and togetherness.
6			Subjective camera angles; a straight angle is used on the camera and it uses a symmetrical composition with contrasting screen direction. The object of focus is someone ordering MC D. Interpreted as caring and togetherness
7		*Saat jumpa bukan menjadi pilihan*	Subjective camera angles; a high camera angle is used, and using over-shoulder withn neutral screen direction. The object of focus is a person having an online interaction. Interpreted as search and happiness
8		*Ada yang ikhlas menyambung ikatan*	Subjective camera angle; a high camera angle is used, the object of focus is two children interacting, but separated by a windowpane between them. Interpreted as breaking the line, subordinate

(Continued)

9		*Mereka terus berdiri digaris depan*	Subjective camera angles; high camera angle is used. The object of focus is a military patient who is being taken care by a nurse. Interpreted as concern, togetherness, and hope.
10		*Memberi harapan untuk bersama mencapai kemenangan*	Subjective camera angle; high camera angle is used. The object of focus is a nurse examining a patient. Interpreted as responsibility and sincerity.
11		*Karena mereka tahu*	Subjective camera angle; low camera angle is used with neutral screen direction. The object of focus is two nurses delivering a message. Interpreted as courage, humanity, and struggle.
12		*Memberikan kebahagiaan adalah kebahagiaan*	Subjective camera angle; straight camera angle. The object of focus is someone drinking TehBotol. Interpreted as equality and equal rights.
13			Subjective camera angle; high camera angle. The object focuses on a family eating together. Interpreted as sharing and togetherness.

Visual analysis of the first myth: Eid is a sacred thing and important in achieving happiness for every Muslim. The word "happiness" is a modern myth that must be achieved after a full month of fasting. However, during this COVID-19 pandemic, the meaning of happiness has changed. Second, Teh Botol Sosro product tried to instill an ideology of false consciousness through poetic narratives to build the connotation of "happiness" through its product as a metaphorical truth.

4 CONCLUSION

It could be concluded that there is a mythical battle about "happiness" between cultural systems (thinking) with materials or products (having) through social systems (doing) that cause ideological problems. Ideological problems and representations in the Teh Botol Sosro advertisement (Ramadan 2020 edition) form ideological awareness and representation.

The ideological status is related to awareness, beliefs, and concepts of the value system. Ideology has a fundamental connotation, so that the advertisement is a false awareness and there is an effort of idealization in cultural systems toward individuals and society. This is "emotional hypnotism", meaning that individuals and the community will always need or require these products to achieve happiness.

The representation contains the purpose of describing the reality as it is in the form of facts and current conditions. In the meanwhile, the imitation of reality is related to Teh Botol Sosro products about false consciousness and questions the reality of happiness itself.

REFERENCES

Danesi, M. 2010. *Pesan, Tanda, dan Makna: Buku Teks Dasar Mengenai Semiotika dan Teori Komunikasi.* A. Adlin (Ed). Yogyakarta: Jalasutra.

Fiske, J. 2007. *Cultural and Communication Studies*. Yogyakarta: Jalasutra.

Kumpulan Iklan Edisi Bulan Ramadhan #22 https://www.youtube.com/channel/UCBTqzsrxGdTRAmWg0F2 bcoQ (7-8-2020)

Lee, M. and Johnson, C. 2011. Prinsip-prinsip Pokok Periklanan Dalam Perspektif Global Cetakan ke-3. *Penerjemah: Haris Munandar, Dudi Priatna.* Jakarta: Kencana.

Moriarty, S., Mitchell, N., and Wells, W. 2018. *Advertising*. Jakarta: Prenadamedia Group.

Pratista, H. 2008. *Memahami Film*. E. Damayati (Ed). Yogyakarta: Homerian Pustaka.

Williamson, J. 2007. Decoding Advertisements: Membedah Ideologi dan Makna dalam Periklanan. *Penerjemah: Saleh Rahmana. Editor: Alfatri Adlin.* Yogyakarta: Jalasutra. https://swa.co.id/swa/business-update/tehbotol-sosro-dan-flock-creative-network-apresiasi-garda-terdepan-di-tengah-covid-19 (7-10-2020)

Dynamics of Industrial Revolution 4.0: Digital Technology Transformation and Cultural Evolution –
Wulandari et al (eds)
© 2021 The Author(s), ISBN 978-1-032-04451-4

Motion graphics as first aid information medium for early childhood diseases

Z.V. Rahmallah & Y. Rahman
Telkom University, Bandung, Indonesia

ABSTRACT: Parents are the first doctors for their children, so it is essential that they know about children's health in general. In this regard, there is much information available on the internet displayed in the forms of text, audio, video, and other media such as animation. This study aimed to optimize motion graphics, a form of video, as a first-aid informational tool for dealing with a variety of illnesses that children might develop. The methods used in this study were observation, literature review, interviews, questionnaires, and matrix analysis. These motion graphics contain information about various types of children's illnesses including how to provide the optimal first aid which will be disseminated through social media so parents can more easily learn about it through their gadgets.

Keywords: animation, childhood, diseases, first aid, motion graphics, social media

1 INTRODUCTION

Along with current conditions, parents typically tend to have dual roles, especially those living in big cities: acting as parents who take care of their children and workers who support the family. At home, parents play a role as the first doctor for their children. Therefore, it is crucial for parents to have basic technical knowledge and understanding of children's health, especially about illnesses that are often faced by children at a young age, such as fever, cough, flu, vomiting, asthma, diarrhea, etc. Without this knowledge, parents will most likely panic when their children suffer from one of these illnesses.

In this era of internet access, it is very easy to get information about anything, including health. Some of them are presented with text, others are presented through audio and video. As Edgar Dale said in the Cone of Experience in Sari (2019), if the information is presented in a visual form, then the possibility of remembering will be greater than that which is only presented in the form of text. Mayer and Moreno in Sukiyasa and Sukoco (2013) said that animation can improve memory absorption if used consistently by the cognitive principles of multimedia learning. Multimedia and technology can be sources that help teachers to facilitate student learning, and motion graphics animation is one such form (Amali et al. 2020). In this context, motion graphics can be a medium for conveying information about various types of illnesses and first aid that can be done by parents at home.

2 RESEARCH METHODS

This study was developed through literature review on instructional media, interviews with medical experts and motion graphic designers, observations at home and hospitals, and observations on interactions with motion graphics that contain educational context.

2.1 Literature review

According to Nazir in Miranti et al. (2017), a literature study is not done just to look for secondary data to support the research, but also to understand how far the relevant knowledge we have goes and conclude what further is needed. In a multimedia context, Lancien in Surasmi (2016) said that multimedia in this era refers to the incorporation and integration of media, such as text, animation, graphics, sound, and video into a computer system. The illustrations used in multimedia can communicate messages in a better way.

In a similar opinion, Whardani argues that motion graphics are graphs that use video or animation to create the illusion of movement or transformation. Motion graphics can help simplify messages from content carried out by databases by using interesting ways to present information (Miranti et al. 2017). For this reason, according to Miarso, it is important to create well-designed and attractive visual media to stimulate internal dialogue in students, in other words, communication between students and the media or between students and message sources. For example, the instructor is said to be successful if there is an improvement in the student (Agustina 2015).

One of the most popular and easy-to-understand media across generations is animation because it is one of the most interesting forms of illustrative representation that illustrates the movement of an object. Animation in the learning process can help raise the effectiveness and efficiency of the learning process and boost study results. Besides that, it can also raise a student's desire and motivation to keep up with the learning process (Sukiyasa & Sukoco 2013).

In the context of the learning process, Dale said that when someone studies, the results obtained by firsthand experience are concrete. They are as real as things that happened in someone's environment, replicas of something, and verbal symbols (abstract). Getting up to the top of the cone, the media of message delivery is becoming more abstract. The learning process and teaching interaction doesn't need first-hand experience anymore; they can start from the type of experience that is most appropriate with the student's skills and depends on the learning situation (Sari 2019).

2.2 Interview and observation

Interviews were performed with medical experts and motion graphic designers. It aimed to get insights and explanations from the experts. According to the experts' interviews, parents need to learn about first aid information for young children because they are their children's first guardians. Experts have explained the kind of illnesses that are more likely to happen to children and how to give them first aid for each illness. The next step was observations done in the hospital to get information about the effective steps to treat those diseases.

2.3 Matrix analysis

Matrix analysis was made to measure and find the best elements from comparing several references, because according to Rohidi 2011 in Miranti et al. 2017, matrix analysis is the best tool for managing information or analyzing objects. Matrix analysis is a column and row which is shown in two different dimensions, a concept or data reference to identify the data's similarities and differences in that research (Miranti et al. 2017). In this study, two motion graphics videos were compared in terms of duration, final resolution, color nuances, movement patterns, voice-over, information displayed, and effects used. Then, the right elements were taken to be displayed for the target audience who are young parents that are active in social media. These elements were then used as the main reference in making motion graphics, with the theme of first aid for children.

3 RESULT AND DISCUSSION

Visual media can help us in the learning process. One such medium is motion graphics that can be used to present information in an interesting way for a short time. According to observations and interviews, motion graphics with simple and informative concepts are suitable for young parents to obtain information and knowledge about children's health, as well as how to do the proper first aid effectively.

The illustration reference that will be used is a simple line art illustration style with shades of peach and yellow, adjusted to the colors of femininity. Flower-themed graphics will also be used in this video to raise the female-oriented character. The character used in this motion graphic is a young woman, to represent young parents. This character will present information in an interesting way in a short time.

3.1 The message

The message expected to convey in this work is information about the types of diseases that are often hit children and how to do the right first aid. The main goal is to keep the child safe with the right help.

3.2 Creative concept

Based on the data that has been obtained, the main viewers of this motion graphic are women, so the creative concept exhibits femininity, calmness, and intelligence, to convey the impression of a flexible, gentle, and intelligent woman.

3.3 Visual concept

The visual concept that was used in this motion graphic will be divided into soft nuances of typography, with a yellow and peach color palette. Graphic elements such as red and yellow flowers, and character designs that feature figures, that have been described in creative concepts, also used.

3.4 Media concept

These motion graphic viewers are parents who have toddlers. According to the data already obtained, parents often use the internet as a source of information. Therefore, the media that were used to spread the motion design was a platform on the internet that is often seen by these parents, especially Instagram and YouTube.

3.5 Final art work (artwork)

The main typography used for the title has a dynamic character and is shaped like handwriting, to strengthen the impression of womanhood, and to be more familiar to first-time viewers.

Figure 1.   Typography in title design.

The color spectrum used is warm shades, such as yellow, peach, pink, and red brick. These colors are also implemented in the colors of the figure which represent a graceful and intelligent woman. This color depicts the warmth of parents who care for and love their children.

As a result, portrayals of the figure explaining various children's illnesses and how they are treated are displayed as simply as possible so that information is focused and reaches the audience quickly. The duration used is also quite proportional, between 30–60 minutes, depending on the medium.

Figure 2.   Color implementation in the design.

Figure 3.   Motion graphic scene.

4   CONCLUSION

Based on observations, suggestions, and input after the post-test to the audience, it is concluded that motion graphics videos can be used to relay information on first aid for young children's diseases effectively. However, there was a suggestion of adding some more descriptive illustrations to make the information clearer and easier to understand quickly. Other functions of this motion graphic are also expected to help parents have a better understanding of various types of children's illnesses and make them more able to inform others about the knowledge of these illnesses.

ACKNOWLEDGEMENTS

We would like to thank all those who were involved in supporting this research: resource personnel, collaborators, audiences, reviewers, mentors, and several others who cannot be mentioned. This research still has the potential to be developed in different contexts, and for a wider audience. Hopefully, this research can be useful for many people.

REFERENCES

Agustina, L. 2015. Pengaruh Penggunaan Media Visual dan Minat Belajar Siswa terhadap Hasil Belajar Matematika. *Formatif: Jurnal Ilmiah Pendidikan MIPA* 1(3). doi: 10.30998/formatif.v1i3.74.

Amali, L. N., Zees, N., and Suhada, S. 2020. Motion Graphic Animation Video as Alternative Learning Media. *Jambura Journal of Informatics* 2(1). doi: 10.37905/jji.v2i1.4640.

Miranti, G. D., Putra, I. D. A. D., and Komariah, S. H. 2017. Perancangan Animated Motion Graphic Sebagai Media Alternatif Pembelajaran Anak Tunagrahita. *E-Proceeding of Art & Design* 4(3):634–643.

Sari, P. 2019. Analisis Terhadap Kerucut Pengalaman Edgar Dale dan Keragaman Gaya Belajar untuk Memilih Media yang Tepat dalam Pembelajaran. *Mudir: Jurnal Manajemen Pendidikan* 1(1):58.

Sukiyasa, K. and Sukoco, S. 2013. Pengaruh Media Animasi Terhadap Hasil Belajar dan Motivasi Belajar Siswa Materi Sistem Kelistrikan Otomotif. *Jurnal Pendidikan Vokasi* 3(1). doi: 10.21831/jpv.v3i1.1588.

Surasmi, W. A. 2016. Pemanfaatan Multimedia Untuk Mendukung Kualitas Pembelajaran. *Temu Ilmiah Nasional Guru VIII Tahun 2016: Tantangan Profesionalisme Guru di Era Digital*, 1595. Jakarta. Available at: http://repository.ut.ac.id/6555/.

Dynamics of Industrial Revolution 4.0: Digital Technology Transformation and Cultural Evolution –
Wulandari et al (eds)
© 2021 The Author(s), ISBN 978-1-032-04451-4

Exploring Sumba woven textile motifs through a digital technique using the Escher method

M. Rosandini & J. Samuel
Telkom University, Bandung, Indonesia

ABSTRACT: East Sumba traditional woven textiles are East Indonesian textile artifacts. They have considerable visual potential because of their ornaments and motif patterns. This article explores the transformation of the East Sumba motif pattern through digital art techniques. Using digital experimentation with the Escher-types repeats method, innovative and varied new patterns were produced to meet the fashion industry's needs. As a result, four new digital patterns were created. The most effective Escher techniques for exploring non-geometric forms are translation, reflection, and glide reflection. The further development of the East Sumba–Escher digital motif will enhance the various artwork on surface pattern textiles and fashion designs.

Keywords: digital art, Escher, exploration, motif, Sumba

1 THEORETICAL BACKGROUND

1.1 *Introduction*

Sumba woven motif patterns are inspired by the Sumba community and its environment, which are then distilled into decorative ornaments. Stilation is a changing the shape of an object in nature into an artistic form or a particular style (Nizam 2019). The characteristics of Sumba weaving motif patterns are geometric and non-geometric shapes. The ornaments on the East Sumba Ikat woven fabric are dynamic with their inspiration coming from natural, non-geometric decoration in the form of humans, flora, and fauna. According to Kartiwa (2007), Sumba ornaments are inspired by nature, and are usually in the form of animals such as horses and chickens.

The horse ornament symbolizes courage, unity, authority, and the nature of a noble. The horse's motif on Sumba's ikat weaving is often depicted by the horse's character swinging its legs back and forth, where this pose symbolizes the courage and nature of a warrior (Kartiwa 2007). The ornamental chicken variety is used in Sumba ikat because these animals are often used in ritual ceremonies to tell fortune. Therefore, chicken represents leadership and unity. Chicken motifs are usually in the form of male roosters with the comb's characteristic that symbolizes virility (Kartiwa 2007). From that explanation, we can see the enormous potential of Sumba woven ornaments from their decorative shapes and the value of meaning that lies within them.

Figure 1. East Sumba Ikat woven textile.

DOI 10.1201/9781003193241-52

However, despite its great potential, many designers and researchers utilize the Sumba woven textile to develop and use its decorative shapes as the inspiration for products, especially for the surface motif patterns in digital techniques.

Some research that leads us to the utilization of East Sumba woven textiles was conducted by Ningsih (2019) that wrote about the utilization of the textiles through fashion for urban people. Ningsih (2019) used natural woven textiles. The innovation appeared on the function and form of its original woven textile, the result of which was a collection of fashion wear. On the other hand, Indonesian surface pattern designer Fika Julia, with her brand *byfikajulia* in 2016, produced textile printing inspired by motif patterns from East Sumba woven textiles. The textiles were then applied to ready-to-wear fashion. She used a digital technique to compose the shapes of Sumba motifs, with some simple repeat patterns. The motifs that Julia produced has a more modern-pop look because she was targeting young people. Based on Julia's motif pattern observation, it was discovered that she was using simple, seamless, repeat patterns, such as half-drop and brick repeat patterns (Kight 2011). However, to make motifs, there are many ways to create innovation. Therefore, digital techniques for developing patterns utilizing Sumba ornaments still need to be developed to produce a greater variety of forms.

1.2 *Initial conceptual framework*

Chun (2011) said that digital technology development is rapidly exercising influence across all fields, including contemporary art. He applied new concepts, values, tools, and methods. Based on the authors' observation, research of traditional motif pattern development using advanced techniques is limited. In fact, some of artists are still using conventional repeat pattern techniques, such as square repeat or half-way repeat (half-drop and brick repeat pattern) (Kight 2011), which therefore brings out the usual pattern composition. There is a potential repeat pattern technique, the Escher Repeat Type, which could be applied to any non-geometric form to make an innovative composition. The Escher Repeat Type is usually used for artwork, considering its original form was from M.C. Escher's graphic art masterpiece, but the principle of making the composition could be applied to digital surface pattern design as well.

M.C. Escher was a graphic designer who used mathematics in the making of his works. The tessellation technique that Escher introduced, or commonly called the Escher technique, was inspired by the beautiful and intricate arrangement of tiles in architecture in Alhambra, Spain. However, the elements forming its patterns were only limited to geometric shapes, so Escher tried to make tessellation using living objects such as birds, fish, and horses. One of Escher's works that used tessellation techniques is "The Horseman" with its constituent element being a man who is riding a horse (Taschen 2009).

Figure 2.   "The Horseman", Escher's masterpiece.

Between the Sumba motif and Escher artwork, similarities were found in their characteristics. Both process non-geometric shapes and have mathematical elements, so there is good potential that can be developed by combining them. The form of non-geometry in the variety of Sumba ikat weaving is another potential source of inspiration for developing motif patterns using the Escher technique. Therefore, it is possible to create an innovative motif form, inspired by the variety of ornamental Sumba woven textiles, using the Escher-Repeat technique with digital work, to be applied to fashion products. This digital method was included in the characteristic of digital art, *perfectly duplicability* (Chun 2011), in which all substances abstracted into "bits" in the digital world, making it possible to create a perfect and infinite duplication of the original product/artwork.

2 METHOD

2.1 *Quantitative method*

The method used in this study was a mixed-method, namely qualitative and quantitative. The quantitative method was used because in processing motifs using Escher techniques, some calculations were needed since Escher techniques are mathematics. Literature study was done to collect information on the Escher-Repeat types from various sources including books and journals.

2.2 *Qualitative method*

The qualitative method was used because this research focused on exploring the techniques used. In terms of finding out the motif patterns' characteristics, the observations on the Sumba woven textile and Escher's artwork and techniques were done. The visual observation was done by seeing each motif's details and comparing the design elements of both objects. To make the new form of motifs, some digital explorations were undertaken to find the innovative structure. The digital experimentation method, applying the Escher technique using the graphic software design, consists of four methods: translation, reflection, rotation, and glide reflection, inspired by Sumba ikat weaving patterns such as chickens, horses, deer, and dragons. This visual exploration aimed to find new advanced form of motif pattern. There were three steps of exploration: (1) Initial exploration: specify the shapes from East Sumba ornaments. In this step, the chicken and horse forms were chosen since they are common, and the Escher-Repeat technique was mastered.

(2) Advanced experiment: applying East Sumba ornament with Escher-Repeat by producing modules.

(3) Arranging the modules into seamless repeating composition.

3 RESULTS

3.1 *Initial and advanced exploration results*

Initial exploration was carried out to understand the Escher technique. The experiments applied were translation, reflection, rotation, and glide reflection. The four methods used objects found in the ornamental variety of Sumba ornament shapes. The result of the process was the motif modules. In advanced exploration, colors and more detailed elements were added into the motif modules. The use of virtual texture elements (invented texture) was done by making a square geometrical arrangement in the coloring process and providing details that aimed to imitate the actual texture inspiration (real texture) on Sumba woven textiles because of the intersection points of warp and weft. By using contrasting colors, it became more dynamic and brought up the harmony and balance patterns. The best results were presented on the table below. The translation and glide-reflection method are the most optimal form and produce the best visual from this experiment. The advanced exploration was aimed to create the tessellation formed composition from the motif modules, then it automatically seamlessly repeats.

Table 1. Results of initial and advanced exploration.

Visual inspiration	Initial exploration module	Advanced exploration
		 Translation Method
		 Glide-Reflection Method
		 Translation Method
		 Glide-Reflection Method

3.2 *Digital seamless Escher-repeat of sumba woven textile*

The next step after the tessellation module formed was making a seamless composition. It was automatically formed after the module from the initial exploration finished. The seamless repetition was made in the 15 × 15-cm² size. As seen below, the composition is seamless, dynamic, and still has the characteristics of Sumba ornaments.

4 DISCUSSION

Based on experiments, the digital approach using Escher type should begin with (1) determine the basic geometry shape, (2) develop basic geometry shape into the typical form of visual reference

Figure 3.   Results of seamless Eshcher-Repeat of Sumba woven textile.

silhouette (in this case, horse and chicken forms of Sumba ornament) considering the Escher principles become one module, then (3) seamlessly repeat the motif module, and (4) complete the step with color rendering and detail and finally the arrangement of motifs in accordance with the method in the Escher technique applied.

The innovations that emerged from these experiments are: (1) the new composition form of Sumba ornaments, from the one flat single pattern to a seamless repeat pattern by using the Escher-Repeat method. But still have traditional Sumba characteristic forms: the horse and chicken shapes; and (2) the digital techniques, and the results of this research are more complex than the last existing modern product. The complexity can be seen in the interlace pattern structure and the details inspired by the Sumba motif elements such as lines and dots.

5   CONCLUSIONS

This research aims to produce more innovative motif pattern forms by utilizing the typical East Sumba woven textile ornaments through digital techniques. The innovation of the motif pattern was made with the Escher–Repeat method, using four principles: translation, reflection, glide-reflection, and rotation. The best visual form of this research was formed by the translation and glide-reflection method. There is an aesthetic value addition on the visual of the East Sumba motif pattern—previously in the form of fabric sheets that were mainly made with a woven technique—becoming digital and seamless forms that are more dynamic and can be applied to fashion contemporary industries. This digital approach is the beginning of the textile and fashion revolution. Using the digital method to develop some traditional visual forms could lead us to further research on information technology utilization in motif pattern making for contemporary fashion design.

REFERENCES

Chun, J.H. 2011. A review of the Characteristics of Digital Art Expressed in Contemporary Fashion. *International Journal of Fashion Design, Technology and Education* 4(3):161–171.
Kartiwa, S. 2007. *Tenun Ikat : Ragam Kain Tradisional Indonesia*. Jakarta: Gramedia Pustaka Utama.
Kight, K. 2011. *A Field Guide to Fabric Desig.*, Stash Books, Lafayette.
Ningsih, Y.S. 2019. Revitalization f Sumba Woven into Fashion Product for Urban People as a Target Market. *Serat Rupa Journal of Design* 3(1):61–76.
Nizam, A. 2019. Viabilitas Ragam Hias Sulur Gelung Teratai. *Jurnal Corak: Jurnal Seni Kriya* 8(2).
Taschen. 2009. *M. C. Escher: The Graphic Work.* New York: Barnes & Noble, Inc.

Dynamics of Industrial Revolution 4.0: Digital Technology Transformation and Cultural Evolution –
Wulandari et al (eds)
© 2021 The Author(s), ISBN 978-1-032-04451-4

Issue of wayfinding concept in museum interiors

T. Sarihati, R. Firmansyah, S. Salayanti & N. Hasanah A. Rosyad
Telkom University, Bandung, Indonesia

ABSTRACT: The main purpose of museum management is to build knowledge and recreational facilities. Wayfinding has an important role in ensuring museum visitors get the most out of the purpose of visiting the museum. The presence of well-designed wayfinding encourages exploration, facilitates accessibility, and increases visitor interest in museums. This paper discusses to which extent interior wayfinding in museums is applied. The research derived from literature reviews in the form of books and journals, taken from academic research in the similar field related to the role and type of wayfinding in museums. The results achieved from this study were that museums have specific types of road search that are tailored to the information to be conveyed. The existence of wayfinding also provides another option for finding various ways.

Keywords: museum interior, wayfinding, flexibility, literature reviews

1 INTRODUCTION

Wayfinding is a means to provide information related to directions, special signs for certain locations. It is also an important factor to influence the people ability to find a way. Through experience with space, people acquire and encode environmental cues as spatial knowledge in cognitive maps that can be taken to improve road search performance (Lin et al. 2019). Road finding as a design problem outlines the logic of the design approach and illustrates that wayfinding design is fundamentally congruent with universal design (Romedi 1996). These design features include spatial planning, architectural features related to circulation, and graphic display including audible and touch (Romedi 1996).

The application of wayfinding in public spaces has been done, but only as information without a conceptual basis. Graphic marking or information systems are often presented to show space or direction and are generally in the form of written signs. The museum as a facility for obtaining information through collectibles or other objects should apply the concept of a good and clear interior wayfinding to facilitate visitors in exploring exhibitions displayed, achieving access to exit the museum, or reaching other areas easily and efficiently.

This research tried to find out the provisions about wayfinding in the museum and what the museum requires for its environmental development. It collected information about the museum, wayfinding in the museum, and how wayfinding influences the flexibility in public space especially museums.

The definition of a museum has evolved, in line with the development of society. Exhibition organizers and designers began to formulate how visitors to the exhibition could become the main characters in their experiences and see it from their perspective (Erlhoff & Marshall 2007). Understanding a successful museum in the 21st century is supporting visitors to their interests, needs, learning methods to participate in educating the public, socializing, and public meetings. Museums are no longer just institutions that preserve heritage (Crimm et al. 2009).

A museum is a place that stores history. Museum understanding of history is divided into four concepts of thinking: the concept of chronological thinking, periodization, diachronic, and synchronous. The concept of chronological thinking is the appreciation of visitors in the museum that consists of contemplation, understanding, discovery, and interaction. Visitors are invited to be more active and can be directly involved in an exhibition. One of the concepts put forward by Simon (2010) is participatory museums, a two-way interpersonal communication model that can be achieved through educational programs, participatory, living interpretations, and interactive exhibitions through various media such as audiovisual, touch screen, and multimedia.

Wayfinding is a system that provides predictable locations by various types of information and hierarchical instructions that enhance understanding and navigation in an environment. Multi-story rooms that are not connected are often faced with the complex problem of providing a readable, economical, and easy-to-treat sign at every possible decision point in the search for this road (Gibson 2009). The function of the wayfinding is to give instructions to visitors who find it difficult to interpret the floor plan, the solution is to install navigation (number, sign, code) near the exhibition or at points of interest (Roussou & Katifori 2018).

In the thesis "Effects of Design Features on Visitors' Behavior in a Museum Setting", it was stated that museums can play more than protectors of collections and accumulators of educational material, but also as providers of entertainment experience services. To offer the best possible service, wise decisions need to be made by considering how the arts and their environment interact with customers through the big picture formed by signage, the range of art exhibited, the time of the exhibition, and the placement of objects in space (Chang 2008).

Next, is the question on how the museum's interior environment, the quality of interior circulation design, and visitor satisfaction are interrelated in the context of the interior environment and museum space design. Whether the quality of interior circulation design and interior space design are direct determinants of visitor satisfaction or is there another significant relationship between the interior environment and interior elements such as lighting design, furniture, and material arrangement (Elottol & Bahauddin 2011).

2 METHOD

This study used qualitative research methods through systematic, careful data collection, using comparisons and critical thinking. This method collects, analyzes, and interprets shared data. In interpreting data, qualitative researchers theoretically create new concepts and interpretations. Qualitative research methods do not only use or test past theories but also builds new theories (Berg & Lune 2011; Groat & Wang 2013; Lune & Berg 2016; Neuman & Neuman 2006).

Literature reviews is a method of selecting documents available on topics that contain information, ideas, data, and evidence written from a particular perspective to meet certain objectives or express certain views about the nature of the topic and how the research will be investigated, and effective evaluation of documents related to the proposed research. The purpose of the literature review is to show the subject area and understand the problem; to justify research topics, designs, and methodologies (Hart 2018; Rowley & Slack 2004).

The data used in this study were obtained from other research conducted by previous researchers, taken from books and primary or original scientific reports contained in articles (printed or non-printed) regarding wayfinding and its placement in the interior, especially of a museum. Source selection was based on (1) provenance (evidence), the aspects of the author's credentials and evidence support, (2) objectivity, whether the perspective idea from the author has many uses or is it detrimental; (3) persuasiveness, whether the author is a person who can be trusted; and (4) value, whether the author's argument has contributed to other significant research.

One of the main sources was a journal written by Heru Budi (2018), titled "Wayfinding Sign in the Permanent Exhibition Room at the National Museum of Indonesia". It was chosen for several considerations: its relevance with this study and the journal's reputation for content validity. Other main sources used were journals and books from D. Gibson (2009) and Lin et al. (2019). The data was analyzed through annotated bibliography and then concluded.

3 RESULTS AND DISCUSSION

3.1 *Types of wayfinding in museums*

Table 1. Types of wayfinding.

No	Type	Example	Description
1	Orientational Sign	 Figure 1. Floor plan sign *Sentralen*. (Source: www.metricdesign.no)	Orientational sign is a panel of signs that contains clear information about the position of a person in an environment, such as maps, architectural references from a building, and the plan of the circulation of lanes in and out. Road search is characterized by knowledge of the route obtained through procedural rules.
2	Information Sign	 Figure 2. Historical timeline. Museum Gedung Sate, Bandung. (Source: https://museumgedungsate.org/galeri Museum)	Informational sign refers to the specifics and details of information, with the sign form being adjusted to the information that is to be conveyed.
3	Directional Sign	 Figure 3. Floor direction. Science Museum of Minnesota. (Source: http://www.nicolesuek.com/museum-signage)	Directional sign shows the direction or location of the destination to be directed by visitors. This sign is an explicit navigation tool. It is expected to make visitors more efficient and comfortable in an environment.
4	Identificational Sign	 Figure 4. Auditorium. The Design Museum, London. (Source: https://cobal.co.uk/projects/the-design-museum/)	Identificational sign gives the identity of an object or place according to its type and function.
5	Statutory Sign	 Figure 5. Statutory fire signage. Wollongong. (Source: https://visualenergysigns.com)	Statutory (regulatory) sign is in the form of regulations, general restrictions, or permits for a particular activity. Its main function is to maintain one's safety from danger and informs what to do and not to do.
6	Ornamental Sign	 Figure 6. Gedung Sate Museum signage. (Source: google image)	Ornamental sign serves as a decorative element that aims to beautify, enhance, or beautify an overall appearance of an environment or as a complement to the elements of a sign (Kusuma 2018).

3.2 Wayfinding function

The function of wayfinding in buildings is to provide ease of circulation. The difficulty of finding a road is more difficult for people with physical impairments, particularly for people with sensory impairments. These difficulties can become architectural barriers that are psychological in terms of reducing accessibility as much as physical barriers (Romedi 1996). Wayfinding is associated with building security as a marker for emergency evacuation routes. Wayfinding design is intended to give users an easy understanding of space and time efficiency for museum staff so that the staff does not need to provide information to visitors.

Interior signage is displayed in color, size codes, and typographic style as information on objects and circulation. With many codes affecting interior signage, visual information content used on signage instead of words, must still be effective and easy to understand (Nabila & Sarihati 2016).

There are many forms of information that can be used by designers to help build users understanding in navigating efficiently through the built space. Two types of information were assessed, the form of floor plans and signboards. They were found to interact in ways, sometimes, unexpected. The usefulness and types of signage varies greatly, although sometimes the difference is only a little in the complexity of a floor plan. Various aspects of wayfinding performances are affected differently depending on the combination of available architectural cues (O'Neill 1991).

The ease obtained in understanding space by wayfinding/signage includes aspects such as look and feel physically the use of signs in its colors or shapes, and the information to be conveyed. Wayfinding involves complex cognitive processes which include goal setting, perception, acquisition, judgment, and movement (Lin et al. 2019).

Wayfinding is an important factor to influence people's ability to find a way. The presence of signage in the form of a floor position in the room will make it easy for visitors to determine their location and provide clear instructions about circulation within. A person acquires and encodes environmental cues as spatial knowledge in cognitive maps that can be taken to improve the performance of ease of circulation and road search (Lin et al. 2019).

Figure 7. Floor position signage. The Design Museum, London. (Source: *https://cobal.co.uk/projects/the-design-museum/*).

Wayfinding or topographic orientation is the ability to determine location, find a place in building facilities. The application of wayfinding can be in the form of very detailed details to form a pattern that can direct the flow of circulation of an environment (Kusuma 2018).

Built environment features are related to deliberate human circulation and their ability to mentally place themselves in an environment (Romedi 1996). These design features include spatial planning, architectural features related to circulation, and graphic display including audible support and touch (Romedi 1996).

In conditions of high density, wayfinding arrangements can help someone to find another way when there is a crowd on a route to be headed. The wayfinding also provides options for someone to look for other destinations that could be more interesting, to carry out a different direction search strategy, and choose different initial route options. As an anticipation, while we did not find the effect of density at the strategic or tactical level, participants in conditions of high density are more likely to move along environmental boundaries to avoid crowds (Li et al. 2019).

4 CONCLUSION

The concept of wayfinding in museums is based on its function as a means of education and recreation. Museums have a type of wayfinding that is more widely used, which is the informational sign. An informational sign consists of more to the specifics and details of information. The form of this sign is adjusted to the information to be conveyed.

The influence of wayfinding on the ease of upholding is to know one's position in a room and give clear instructions about circulation within. For example, it gives people another option to look for other goals that can be achieved when faced with the situation of a crowd. It becomes a special marker for some facilities that are specific to some extent such as destined to people with disabilities that affect the additional spatial planning.

REFERENCES

Berg, B.L. and Lune, H. 2011. *Qualitative Methods for the Social Sciences*.

Chang, T.-J. 2008. *Effects of Design Features on Visitors' Behavior in a Museum Setting*. The University of Kansas.

Crimm, W.L., Morris, M., and Wharton, C.L. 2009. *Planning successful museum building projects*. Rowman Altamira.

Elottol, R. and Bahauddin, A. 2011. The Relationship Between Interior Space Design and Visitors' Satisfaction: A Case Study of Malaysian Museums (Interior Circulation Scheme). *International Journal of Organizational Innovation* 3(4).

Erlhoff, M. and Marshall, T. 2007. *Design dictionary: perspectives on design terminology*. Walter de Gruyter.

Gibson, D. 2009. *The wayfinding handbook: Information design for public places*. Princeton Architectural Press.

Groat, L. N. and Wang, D. (eds). 2013. *Architectural Research Methods 2nd Edition*. New Jersey: John Wiley & Sons.

Hart, C. 2018. *Doing a literature review: Releasing the research imagination*. Sage.

Kusuma, H.B. 2018. Wayfinding Sign pada Ruang Pameran Tetap di Museum Nasional Indonesia – Jakarta. *Mudra Jurnal Seni Budaya* 33(2):242. doi: 10.31091/mudra.v33i2.331.

Li, H. et al. 2019. The Effect of Crowdedness on Human Wayfinding and Locomotion in a Multi-Level Virtual Shopping Mall. *Journal of Environmental Psychology* 65. doi: 10.1016/j.jenvp.2019.101320.

Lin, J., Cao, L., and Li, N. 2019. Assessing the Influence of Repeated Exposures and Mental Stress on Human Wayfinding Performance in Indoor Environments Using Virtual Reality Technology. *Advanced Engineering Informatics* 39:53–61. Elsevier. doi: 10.1016/j.aei.2018.11.007.

Nabila, S. and Sarihati, T. 2016. Peran Elemen Interior Sebagai Wayfinding Sirkulasi di Showroom Galeri Selasar Sunaryo Bandung. 3(3):1138–1149.

Neuman, W.L. and Neuman, L.W. 2006. *Workbook for Neumann Social Research Methods: Qualitative and Quantitative Approaches*. Allyn & Bacon.

O'Neill, M.J. 1991. Effects of Signage and Floor Plan Configuration on Wayfinding Accuracy. *Environment and Behavior* 23(5):553–574. Thousand Oaks, CA: Sage Publications.

Romedi, P. 1996. Wayfinding Design: Logic, Application and Some Thoughts on Universality. *Design Studies* 17(3):319–331.

Roussou, M. and Katifori, A. 2018. Flow, Staging, Wayfinding, Personalization: Evaluating User Experience with Mobile Museum Narratives. *Multimodal Technologies and Interaction* 2(2):32. Multidisciplinary Digital Publishing Institute,

Rowley, J. and Slack, F. 2004. Conducting a Literature Review. *Management Research News*. Emerald Group Publishing Limited.

Wulandari, A. A. A. 2014. Dasar-Dasar Perencanaan Interior Musem. *Humaniora*, 5(1):246.

Dynamics of Industrial Revolution 4.0: Digital Technology Transformation and Cultural Evolution –
Wulandari et al (eds)
© 2021 The Author(s), ISBN 978-1-032-04451-4

The influence of digital technology on the cultural evolution of a city's monumental icons

G.A. Prahara
Telkom University, Bandung, Indonesia

M.Y. Suhairi
University Computer Indonesia, Bandung, Indonesia

ABSTRACT: Sculptures serve as a symbolic reflection of a spirit that contains philosophical, historical, and aesthetic elements. Digital technology makes it easy to replicate and reduplicate, as well as speed up, the process of working on the pre-production process and the production of three-dimensionally built objects. A society's misinterpretation turned the monumentally built objects in Bandung into a decorating tool for the city, yet visually borrowing form from cultural objects with philosophical value. The method used in this study was ethnography-descriptive observations on three-dimensional spatial objects to explore relationships between the physical form of the objects with cultural philosophical beliefs of today's society. There has been a decrease in philosophical significance because of cultural objects' replication through the use of digital technology.

Keywords: digital technology, spatial objects, cultural symbol

1   INTRODUCTION

Bandung is a historic city, the center of West Java's cultural development, where various historical events became iconic symbols. Heritage buildings have become symbols of modern cultural acculturation based on historical narratives currently used as symbols of civilization. In Bandung, there are objects built with a spatial approach such as statues, monuments, buildings, and symbols. The current municipality uses duplicated cultural objects in form of figures, typography, and cultural symbols in public areas in Bandung. Bandung's green open space was revitalized into a friendly open park with a community's physical activity and became a comfortable place to interact.

Bandung City Square was revitalized into a playground for children and families with synthetic grass flooring. Spatial typography serves as identity in an open space such as a city park or identification of a location. The Siliwangi Tiger statues, facing the four wind directions, became decorators at several crossroads in Bandung. The Kujang (traditional weapon) symbol was built as part of border signs on street gates as well as an iconic element of the philosophical character of West Java society. Kujang monuments in several places stand as a reminder of the Sundanese people's ancestors related to the Padjadjaran Kingdom. All objects are imitations or artificial replications of their original form functioning as aesthetic elements of the city.

The development of digital technology, especially three-dimensional printing presses, revolutionized the industry's design and manufacturing. The creation of a prototype in three-dimensional design takes a short time, as the capabilities of the three-dimensional print machine are advanced. Solid materials of both color and type can be cheap and easy to make into a prototype according to the design on a digital computer (White Clouds 2019).

The development of production techniques and tools based on digital technology can answer design needs including laser cutting tools for large scale objects, where shapes can be printed on metal at the desired scale. Materials are increasingly flexible so that they can be easily transformed

DOI 10.1201/9781003193241-54

into any statues or monumental objects. It gives ease of replicating objects into mimesis on spatial objects in public spaces. The artificial nature found in spatial objects in public spaces create a new interpretation by the city community. The purpose of this research is to explore the shift of symbolic significance of spatial built visualization using digital technology.

Research on public spaces and the growing monumental build-up and its challenges to public art is a comparison of the changing society in living the art of public spaces (Remesar 2005). Public pedagogy is part of the process of a learning society in public spaces through public art (Schuermans et al. 2012). Monuments function as witnesses to cultural identity (Johnson 2002). The statue as an urban monument is the basis of its regional culture (Jixin 2019).

In other research, it is stated that the current spatial build in public spaces has a relationship with the lifestyle of urban society, namely as a tool of individual and communal expression as a universal part (Nursaiman 2012). The research only discusses spatial stimulate functions that are more associated with people's emotional approaches, especially on lifestyles in public spaces. Other research on spatial builds and public spaces were also discussed in Aulia (2014) that viewed the space of the interior and some technical standards that should be considered in its design.

Another related research with a different study object is the research on monumental spacial builds in tourist areas in Yogyakarta. Many typographies are applied in public spaces as identity as well as branding but less emotive from psychosocial aspect, especially typographic approached with the value of a region (Noordyanto 2017). The study emphasizes the branding elements that can affect perception in public spaces. In other research it was also discussed that the use of public spaces as gathering places for communities at the thematic park in Bandung (Ilmiajayanti 2015).

This research discovers a spatial build development in the monumental ornaments of the city that are used as a form of decorative elements, a marker of cultural identity, which uses digital technology. It is also determined to deepen the influence of these objects on the direction of a symbolic meaning desired by the proponents on the development of an urban society.

2 METHOD

In this research, Barthes' semiological theory was applied to reveal the meaning of the artificial monumental symbolic object. Ethnographic studies were used as a benchmark for text narrative analysis contained in an object. Advanced analysis was done by linking text with a micro understanding of the community related to symbols contained in each object of inclusion (Piliang 2003). It implies that the meaning begins with an understanding of the denotative conception continued by knowing its connotative meaning.

The research was done in the qualitative descriptive method with semiological disclosure of meaning through the analysis of content on awakened objects. It found meaningful relationships based on narrative structures that have been built up through generations with current artificial replication. Textual analysis of the development of digitalization through technology relates to contemporary styles that are imitations of cultural philosophical traditions. The data was collected through an object's deep understanding and community interpretation based on the character of the traditional icons.

3 RESULT AND DISCUSSION

The city square, once a place used as a dialogue space between the city's stakeholders and citizens, now is the center of crowd and celebration. It is the trigger for changes in function and historical significance of the place. The change in the layout of the square is a sign of the development of social civilization in the city of Bandung (Figure 1).

The Bandung City Square had changed into a modern space. Digital technology plays a role in its design. Its conception today is more open and heterogeneous. Restoration was carried out by the government, functionally and structurally, by designing the square for the people (Figure 2).

Figure 1.   Journey of Bandung City Hall Square. (Source: Ichan 2015; Humas Bandung.go.id).

Figure 2.   Bandung City Hall nowadays. (Source: Tribun Jabar.com).

Figure 3.   Monument of Siliwangi Tiger. (Source: Bandung Public Art Archive 1990; TribunJabar 2018).

The current square is a playground for families and children, citizens, and tourists. The sacred value of the square faded into a playground. The text of the square that presents is a form of denotation of expression. Digital technology is very instrumental in the formation of green synthetic grass patterns that attract visitors to take selfies and become a scattering point in cyberspace.

People know the narrative about the Sundanese royal lineage Padjadjaran whose king was named Prabu Siliwangi. In addition to its pedigree, people also know about the mythical story related to the Tiger of Siliwangi. This cultural narrative remains preserved as a symbol of the spirit of patriotism. Both the tiger and king names are used as the name and symbol of the West Java military unit (Figure 3).

Maung Siliwangi (Siliwangi Tiger) figures are the result of technological advances in digital and resin printing methods, making it easy to replicate and duplicate the object. There are statues of four identical tigers pointing to four opposite directions inside a classic art deco gazebo monument. Tiger characters were duplicated. Even though they look identical, meaningfully there was a shift into an ornamental figure that serves only as an empty monument. This means that despite borrowing the symbol of the Siliwangi Tiger, it fails to foster a cultural philosophical awareness to the public (Figure 4).

Kujang is a traditional weapon typical of West Java that is a symbol of the war readiness of Padjadjaran soldiers. Kujang is also a symbol of the agrarian Sundanese community. It is currently being used as a marker pole on the entrance at some point in the city. Artificially this Kujang character is made to point upward, standing upright like a fire, with a golden color so that it looks contrasting from a distance.

Laser cutting technology that can cut metal or steel on a large scale has a role in duplication of the Kujang monument. The symbol of Kujang has become a space element as the street decorator as well as the street marker. Its meaning slowly shifting into a border sign on the entrance of the

Figure 4.   Kujang monument, Google street view 2019.

Figure 5.   Typography spacial as public park identity. (Source: Pemprov Jabar 2017).

street. Philosophical objects that changed its function obscure the meaning of the symbols. This caused society to interpretate the sign as only a passive peg or pillar.

Spatial typography is widely used as an identity marker for a location. However, there are two strong perceptions of typography: the context of the typeface and the message in which the text was formed and presented (Romano 2012). Typography is one of the relative visual elements, analogized as a dish that has different flavors according to the taste and type of food (Saltz 2013) (Figure 5).

With the conception of similar-looking letter symbols that are the result of digital technology that makes it easy in the pre-production and production process, making the same typeface and character of letters do not represent the characteristics of the location it is written for. The typeface used is an international style with sans serif type so that it looks modern to refract society from the meaning of the name and location that it shows.

A monument is "a building derived from human creation as a form of reflection of the past or something that can be remembered by future generations" (Riegl 1903, in Panico 2016). The symbol of the building generally has abstract values and meanings that are traditionally believed and used as the spirit and motivation of society. This research shows the value of a philosophical substance that shifts. It is the results of imitations of cultural symbols used as decorators or amplifiers of the city's aesthetic elements through replication using advancement of digital technology. There is a decline in the philosophical meaning of the cultural spirit today's society.

The micro-aspect of Bandung's society toward the text in the form of artificialization of monumental spatial symbols states a form of government stimulus to beautify and make an impression of the city's tingle. Aspects of the city's aesthetic reinforcement are the main factors of the denotative forces that are formed. The use of symbols in city halls, intersected with macro text narratives in the form of symbolic narratives of cultural philosophy, is revered into the middle ground as an entrance to the symbolic capital of the people. Societies, with cultural changes that occur, make connotative significance meaningless. The interpretation of existing objects become denotative in a pragmatic way. The concept comes as digital technology develops. It also facilitates and accelerates the formation of identical imitations of the same nature. The concept obscures the meaning of macro symbolic connotations into a temporary denotative structure because it is easily obsolete or damaged due to weather or time.

The micro text meaning of the Bandung people began to reduce over time in the social and cultural capital of the Sundanese people. The change of symbolic meaning relates to the change in the social, economic, political, and cultural capital of Bandung people. Although it does not change the conception of the macro narrative toward the object's ideal meaning, the construction's formation in public spaces through imitative artificial shorting results in a change in the social interpretation of the city community.

4 CONCLUSION

Built spatial monuments, that stand firmly in the middle of the city, prioritize the underlying meaning related to philosophical, ideological, historical, and aesthetic values in society. Today's advances in digital technology have transformed the work generally done through an artist's craftmanship approach into a digitally conceptualized approach through urban governance planning. Technology becomes an imitation machine that can produce symbolic objects of the city more perfectly and precisely as decorative elements, capable of replacing the emptiness of space in the city. However, without care, it can gradually erode the cultural, historical, and philosophical significance of a city symbolic spaces into just artificially plastic construction.

REFERENCES

Alfrey, S. L. 2013. Occupy Plop Art Public Sculpture as Site of Antagonism. Thesis. University of Illnois at Chicago, 26(4).

Drout, M. D. C. 2007. A Meme-Based Approach to Oral Traditional Theory. *Oral Tradition*, 21(2):269–294. https://doi.org/10.1353/ort.2007.0002

Freska Ilmiajayanti, D. I. K. D. 2015. Persepsi Pengguna Taman Tematik Kota Bandung Terhadap Aksesibilitas dan Pemanfaatannya. 1(1):21–30. https://doi.org/10.14710/ruang.1.1.21-30

Jaganath, T. 2018. The Importance of Public Spaces. medium.com. https://medium.com/@thejas009/the-importance-of-public-spaces-5bb49ba6c000. Project for Public Space.

Jhonson, N. C. 2002. Maping monuments: the shaping of public space and cultural identities. *Journal Visual Communication* 1(3):293–296. Queen University, London Thousand Oaks, CA and New Dehli: SAGE Publication.

Jixin, W. 2019. Comparative study of urban sculpture base on regional Culture. *2nd Conference Arts, Linguistics, Literature and Humanities (ICALLH 2019), Xiamen Academy of Art and Ddesign,* Fuzou University, Fujian, Xiamen. UK: Francis Academic Press.

Marsden, P. 2018. *Memetics and Social Contagion: Two Sides of the Same Coin?* Compiled By Collegiate Professor, University of Maryland University College BobF@RoboticTechnologyInc.com. March.

Noordyanto, N. 2017. Studi Tipografi Kawasan Di Yogyakarta. *DeKaVe* 9(1):65–84. https://doi.org/10.24821/dkv.v9i1.1659

Nursaiman, D. 2012. Relasi Enviromental Typography, Public Space Dan Gaya Hidup. *Visualita* 4(1):42–57. https://doi.org/10.33375/vslt.v4i1.1110

Panico, Mario. 2016. The Meanings of Monuments and Memorials: Towards a Semiotic Approach. Punctum, 2(1):28–46, 2016.

Ruki, U. A. and Nediari, A. 2014. Penerapan Tipografi dalam Sistem Signage pada Interior Ruang Publik. 5(9):822–832.

Remesar, A. (Ed). 2005. *Urban Regeneration A challenge for Public Art.* University of Barcelona, Monografies, Psico Socio Ambientals.

Schuermans, N., Loopman, M., Vandenabeele, J. 2012. Public Space, Public Arts and Public Pedagogic. *Journal Social and Cultural Geography.*

Stott, T. (2019). Operable abstraction: How toys changed the logic of modern sculpture. *Sculpture Journal* 28(2): 161–173. https://doi.org/10.3828/sj.2019.28.2.2

Velikovsky, J. T. 2018. The Holon/Parton Theory of the Unit of Culture (or the Meme, and Narreme). *Technology Adoption and Social Issues, Koestler 1967*: 1590–1627. https://doi.org/10.4018/978-1-5225-5201-7.ch075

White Clouds. 2019. https://www.whiteclouds.com/large-letters/fineartamerica2020 https://fineartamerica.com/featured/the-famous-giant-letters-of-amsterdam-georgi-djadjarov.html

Dynamics of Industrial Revolution 4.0: Digital Technology Transformation and Cultural Evolution –
Wulandari et al (eds)
© 2021 The Author(s), ISBN 978-1-032-04451-4

Visualization of princess characters in the Wayang comics of Teguh Santosa for digital graphics development

M.I.P. Koesoemadinata
Telkom University, Bandung, Indonesia

A.Z. Mansoor
Institut Teknologi Bandung, Bandung, Indonesia

ABSTRACT: Women's issues are frequently brought up within cultural studies and academic discourses in correlation with the patriarchal culture which is still embedded in traditional Javanese views. Issues that are rarely studied are women's portrayal in Indonesian comics, especially the *wayang* genre that refers to Javanese culture. *Wayang* art is significant to Javanese culture, along with its patriarchal ideology. By assumption, that ideology is also reflected in the *wayang* comics. Using descriptive qualitative analysis, preceded by aesthetical morphology, this paper discussed the way a *wayang* comic artist visualized princess characters. Teguh Santosa was chosen due to his reputation as an Indonesian comic maestro, along with his sensual visualization of women. Finally, the kind of sociocultural context with which Teguh perceived women, and the visual translation method he invented, was explored. This will complete understanding on Javanese *wayang* adaptations into comics and the possibility of it being realized in digital media.

Keywords: Teguh Santosa, *Wayang* comics, men, Javanese culture, visualization

1 INTRODUCTION

1.1 *Women issues in Javanese culture*

Most of Indonesian's cultural traditions have patriarchal tendencies, including Javanese culture. Javanese culture frequently puts women as secondary, unequal to men, although women are still regarded as having honorable values, such as fidelity, obedience, patience, and self-restraint. Those virtues are not only imposed on women of nobility, but also on peasants (Ariani 2016). A noble woman always try to bring happiness in her domestic life; there's a sort of self-identification, even a fusion, with her husband, where his happiness is also the wife's happiness. This assumption was so strong that all Javanese women try hard to make their husbands happy in many ways.

According to Franz Magnis-Suseno, Javanese women are women that follow Javanese traditions and culture in their daily lives. Their lives are much influenced by the culture that is inherent in their lives, especially the *wayang* culture with its various figures as a model. According to Javanese traditions, an ideal wife must have an attitude like the *wayang* characters of Kunti and Sinta who are devoted to their husbands, accept conditions as they are, and are willing to take part in unpleasant conditions, while reamining patient, loyal, modest, obedient, and skilled (Ariani 2016). *Wayang* art as an important part of Javanese culture certainly brings values and traits that are widely embraced and affect the lives of Javanese people, especially the lives of its women.

1.2 *Wayang comics and Teguh Santosa*

Wayang genre comics were born during the Indonesian Old Order period as an affirmation of national identity—as part of the regime's nationalist political campaign at that time, which was threatened by various Western cultural influences considered as Neo-colonialism and Neo-imperialism. In the process, *wayang* comics became characteristic of Indonesian comics and were highly promoted for their contribution in introducing traditional culture to young urban people (Gunawan 2018). The notable *wayang* comic artists were John Lo, Ardisoma, and R.A. Kosasih. R.A. Kosasih is legendary and is referred to in many *wayang* comics afterward.

After R.A. Kosasih, there was Teguh Santosa who was the second person to successfully adapt the Mahabharata story into comic form completely and also had a significant impact in introducing *wayang* stories to younger generations. Teguh was born and raised in Malang, in the family of a *ketoprak* (Javanese traditional theater) director. So, he understood very well the nuances of Javanese customs in the *wayang* that also applied in *ketoprak*. From the early 1980s until the late 1990s, he created a lot of *wayang* comics, starting with bonus series on *Ananda* children's magazines, colored comic series published by Misurind and finally several comic strips in local newspapers (Koesoemadinata 2018).

Lately, Teguh's works have been reprinted by Galang Press publisher in Yogyakarta, including the *Mahabharata* and *Bharatayudha* series compilation from *Ananda* magazine (1983–1984) in 2015, and even made into an English version. In 2015, his biography was published in the form of an anthology written by several academics and comic practitioners, entitled *Maestro of Darkness: Teguh Santosa, 1942–2000* published by Media Nusa Creative in Malang, which published its second printing in 2016. Various scholarly publications discussed his works from the perspective of humanism and pluralism, specific to the comic *Sandhora* by Aditya Nirwana and later developed into the book *Menimbang Sandhora* (Nirwana & Ginting 2017; Nirwana 2018). Others specifically discussed his *wayang* comic, comparing his visual style with the latest *wayang* comic. Some discussed how Teguh adapted the Surakarta *wayang kulit* image as a reference (Koesoemadinata & Aditya 2016; Koesoemadinata 2018). A Facebook group called *Pustaka Teguh Santosa* was created, dedicated to appreciate him and as a gathering place for his fans. All of these proved that Teguh has a significant role in the development of Indonesian comics.

Before the *wayang* genre, Teguh worked on a lot of comics. One distinctive feature of his comics, besides the dominance of his black blockings, is the graceful, sensual, and "submissive" portrayal of beautiful women. This can be seen from his legendary comic *Sandhora*, where the female protagonist was displayed in sensual poses. In general, all women in his comics were portrayed as beautiul and ideal stereotypes. The female figure was drawn with circular and pointed eyebrows, curved eyelashes, and a slightly square jaw. They are seen with closed eyelids, giving the impression of being "submissive" and sensual, referring to the female models of the 1960s or 1970s. This was not surprising because Teguh himself was said to be a fan of James Bond films that were a trend the time (Valiandra 2016).

The questions are as follows. How did Teguh Santosa describe the image of women in *wayang* genre comics? How did the portrayal of these female figures represent elements of Javanese culture? How did he translate and integrate these elements with his own distinctive visual style? What are the opportunities to be developed in digital media? The assumption is that Teguh comics certainly reflects a bit of Javanese culture, but how and to what extent?

2 METHODS

This paper is a study of art and culture, in the scope of visual arts, based on qualitative-descriptive research that contains interpretations. The object of research was visual artifacts and design works, namely *wayang* comics created by Teguh, specifically on the visual portrayals of female characters in general, which include several figures, such as Drupadi, Sumbadra, Srikandi, Banowati, and Arimbi. The discussion was not specifically on the visualization of one character by character, because the portrayal is relatively similar for all, except for the Arimbi figure. The adaptation and visual portrayal of female *wayang* characters in the Teguh puppet comic are the focus of the discussion, compared to the image of Javanese shadow puppets and the *wayang wong* costume assumed to be the main reference. The element analyzed was the visual style in the comic, which included the portrayal of anatomy and appearance, posture and gestures, hair, clothing, accessories, and others, as well as the position in the scene.

The main data samples as observed artifacts were: (1) *Mahabharata # 1–10 wayang* comic series, published by Misurind (Midas Surya Grafindo) (1986–1988); and (2) *Mahabharata* comic series bonuses *Ananda* children's weekly magazine no.17–52 & no. 06–47 (1983–1984), Kartini Magazine Publisher. Secondary data samples were graphic images of Surakarta *wayang* kulit from various printed sources such as the works of Hardjowirogo (1949) and Sudjarwo et al. (2010). The Surakarta *wayang* image was chosen as a comparison due to the information in the comic; Teguh mentioned *Sedjarah Wajang Purwa* by Hardjowirogo (1949) as the primary source together with comic works by R.A. Kosasih. Clearly, Teguh refers to the "iconography" of the *wayang* character in the book, which contains graphic images of the Surakarta *wayang* style.

The analysis method used was a modified version of Aesthetic Morphology and Art Criticism from Edmund Burke Feldman in Koesoemadinata & Aditya (2016). The stages were: visual description, formal analysis, interpretation and evaluation. The visual description stage, combined with formal analysis, will describe in detail the elements of appearance and portrayal of selected objects. Visual analysis (a combination of stages 1 and 2) of the characters was specifically carried out on: (1) biological anatomy, in part or in whole, including appearance, gesture and body language; and (2) clothing including accessories and other attributes. This stage was an analysis of the internal aspects (intra-aesthetic), the studied visual artifact object, which is considered as 'text'. Next, was the interpretation stage, where the previous stage was compared to external aspects (extra-aesthetic) such as graphic images of the same *wayang* character. It was linked to sociocultural contexts such as Javanese *wayang* traditional narratives, Javanese traditional views, women's discourses, and influences of popular culture that are contemporary with Teguh. The evaluation stage tried to comprehend the context and reasons behind the visual adaptation carried out by Teguh. Here the studied object was appreciated further.

3   THE PRINCESS CHARACTERS VISUALIZATION ANALYSIS AND DISCUSSIONS

The female characters' portrayal in *wayang* comics (also called *putri*/princess) was the same as his other comics. The female figure is drawn with circular and pointed eyebrows, curved eyelashes, and slightly square jaw, smooth arm with curling fingers, often seen lowering the head with eyelids closed, giving rise to a "submissive" and sensual impression. Almost all female characters have this similarity whether it's Drupadi, Sumbadra, or others. Without captions, it would be difficult for readers to distinguish one female character from another (Figure 1).

Figure 1.   (From left to right) Lowering head position of princess characters in Javanese *wayang* images; Teguh's typical female visualization which also the same; various images of princess characters of Surakarta *wayang* style. Beside the head and shoulder positions, also worn costumes, all share the same facial visual pattern. (Sources: Hardjowirogo 1949; Sudjarwo et al. 2010; personal documentation).

This is in accordance with the visual aspect of the *wayang* puppet which indeed always repeats the same pattern, the same types of visual elements, with the same combination. The appearance of a princess figure imaged with the aim of accommodating the beautiful impression of a beautiful person. In Javanese shadow puppet art, the face of a princess is composed of anatomical elements such as *jaitan* eyes, a sharp nose, a *salitan* mouth, which are also equally used in the *wayang* facial imagery of *satria* characters, connoted to a handsome face. In general, the female figures (princesses) are each distinguished only from the worn objects, including head jewelry (crown, etc.) and hairdos (bun rivet, unraveled), then also clothing and other accessories.

Putri figures with idealized traits such as Sumbadra, Drupadi, Kunti, and so on usually have their heads lowered. This reflects submissive, patient, calm, and refined nature, which is usually found in the *wayang* class called *putri luruh*. Some female figures are portrayed as brave, agile, even temperamental, cunning and stubborn, like Srikandi and Banowati, called *putri lanyap*. In the puppet form, their heads are depicted more raised, but still portrayed as beautiful, seen from the same eye, nose, and mouth type (Figure 2).

Figure 2. (from left to right) Graphic image of Arimbi puppet; depiction of Arimbi in Teguh's comic; a comic panel sequence which displays an interaction scene between a princess and a *satria* character. There seems to be a hierarchy between the two. (Sources: Sudjarwo et al. 2010; personal documentation).

An exception is found in the ogress princess' characters called *raseksi*, who has visual pattern different from human females. The body is slightly larger, with *peten* eyes, *bentul* nose, grinning mouth with fangs, and with the *kithingan* hand grip. *Raseksi* figures are often portrayed with such characteristics like bravery, straightforwardness, aggressive, even shameless, deceptive, and sexually proactive, is the opposition of the *Putri luruh*. Teguh visualized the *raseksi*'s anatomy as neither ideal nor sensual as human princesses. The yes are rounder with very small pupils, a round face with a larger, plumper stature in comparison to human princesses, also the fangs in her mouth. This can be seen in the portrayal of Arimbi, the ogress mother of Gatotkaca.

Another improvisation made by Teguh besides the shift from symbolic *wayang* imagery to comic visual images (that tend to be naturalistic), was his characteristic of female's sensual impressions. This sensual portrayal is certainly difficult for us to consider as a direct inspiration from the *wayang* imageries which completely deviates from the real human form, but this is very clear when looking at Teguh's track record in his comic art career. Women's sensuality was clearly inspired by trending Western popular culture at the time (1970s), like his favorite James Bond films. The portrayals of the *putri* figures are hardly distinguished from each other (except for Arimbi). Facial portrayal with eyes closed or staring down, poses and postures that are bowed and "submissive" at the same time sensual, show the patriarchal ideology, placing women as such. This is indeed relevant to the *wayang* art's narrative itself, which contains patriarchal Javanese culture.

An interesting point that can be drawn from the analysis above is how Teguh has adapted the gestures of the female characters in the *wayang* scene into modern drawing styles according to his comic visual style. This becomes a system; a method of translating the gestures of female characters from traditional visual languages, which can be applied to modern media. These gestures can be used as the main gesture to represent women's gestures on social media or virtual character designs that represent *wayang* values based on the translation method used by Teguh.

According to the methods that Teguh developed, the development of female gestures visualization as graphic digital content are as follows: (a) face tilting and body gestures, face tilting and body gestures can emphasize the dignity of visualized females, whether she's a noble or commoner status, warrior or princess attitude, seductive or submissive character, and also active and passive interaction; and (b) camera angle and visual composition, how the creator positioned the character in a relationship with others may emphasize the social relationship in the narrative (whole story) or in *moment opname* (still frame visualization).

4 CONCLUSIONS

This paper discussed the matter briefly and only on surface. It only discussed a small part of the entire study and research on the works of Teguh Santosa, especially *wayang* comics, which is still ongoing. This study has no intention to disrespect and reduce the appreciation for the late Teguh Santosa as one of the Indonesian comics maestros. It's just showing and trying to understand that he was referring to the tradition as it is, with the intention of preserving culture. The traditional Javanese patriarchal culture inherent in the *wayang* story's narrative is reflected in the princess figures' portrayal in particular, seen from their position, posture, and gesture.

The courtesy of ideal women according to Javanese culture was strongly reflected and visualized within each scene of Teguh Santosa's *wayang* comic, and more. In addition to a more realistic approach, he also gave a sensual touch to the female characters that are unlikely to be found in the original Javanese *wayang* image, as a hallmark of his comic style. This showed a comic artist who lived at that time, with the spirit of the time and the cultural background of his family. Teguh was raised in a family of traditional Javanese *ketoprak* artists in the city of Malang, who also consumed modern (Western) popular culture that was trending. As a result, these different values were mixed in his works and became a unique artistic signature. However, beyond that, Teguh gave us a 'prototype' of visual translation method or system to adopt traditional Javanese *wayang* imageries into a modern visual representation that can be implemented in the digital media, yet still conveys the values of local wisdom.

REFERENCES

Ariani, I. 2016. Feminisme dalam Pergelaran Wayang Kulit Purwa Tokoh Dewi Shinta, Dewi Kunti, Dewi Srikandi. *Jurnal Filsafat* 26(2):272–290.

Gunawan, I. 2018. Cerita-Gambar, Highlight Perkembangan CerGam di Indonesia 1925-1985. *Brosur Pameran Gudang Garam Art Award 2018: Dunia Komik "Bahasa Budaya Cerita Gambar"*, xviii–xii. Jakarta: Galeri Nasional.

Hardjowirogo 1949. *Sedjarah Wajang Purwa*. Jakarta: Penerbit Balai Pustaka.

Koesoemadinata, M.I.P. 2018. Visual Adaptation of *Wayang* Characters in the Comic Arts of Teguh Santosa. *Mudra Jurnal Seni Budaya* 33(3):401–408.

Koesoemadinata, M.I.P. and Aditya, D.K. 2016. Visualizations of *Wayang* Characters in Comics (Case Study: Bima and Arjuna Characters in the Arts of Ardisoma, Teguh Santosa and Is Yuniarto). *Proceeding The 3rd International Conference on Creative Industries, Bandung Creative Movement (BCM) 2016*:274–282.

Nirwana, A. 2018. *Menimbang Sandhora: Telaah Komik Teguh Santosa*. Malang: Ma Chung Press.

Nirwana, A. and Ginting, D. 2017. Nilai Kemanusiaan dalam Bingkai Pluralisme dan Multikulturalisme dalam Komik Sandhora (1970) Karya Teguh Santosa. *Andharupa, Jurnal Desain Komunikasi Visual & Multimedia* 03(01):92–114.

Sudjarwo, H.S., Sumari, and Wiyono, U. 2010. *Rupa & Karakter Wayang Purwa: Dewa-Ramayana-Mahabharata*. Jakarta: Kakilangit Kencana.

Valiandra, D. 2016. Mengintip Proses Kreatif Teguh Santosa. In Malik, A. and Jai, S. (eds), *Maestro of Darkness: Teguh Santosa, 1942–2000*: 3–5. Malang: Media Nusa Creative.

Digital education for creative industries

Dynamics of Industrial Revolution 4.0: Digital Technology Transformation and Cultural Evolution –
Wulandari et al (eds)

Disrupted but interactive: How online learning works in the age of a pandemic

A. Anggraeni, S. Putra & A. Nurhudatiana
Bina Nusantara University, Jakarta, Indonesia

ABSTRACT: As universities shift from face-to-face learning to distance learning, the student learning experience has dramatically changed. The classes have moved to online mode, which means that there are changes in terms of how the classes are conducted. Changes also take place in terms of how the interaction happens between the facilitators and the students as well as between the students. This study aims to investigate how different learning factors may contribute to student satisfaction. In total, there are 100 respondents that comprise both undergraduate and Master's students. The findings suggest that only interactivity and course suitability were found to have a positive influence on student satisfaction. These imply that an educational institution needs to design their online class delivery in such a way so that the interaction will be similar to the interaction in offline classes. Moreover, making sure that the courses are suitable to be delivered in an online mode is crucial as well.

Keywords: online learning, learner characteristics, learning satisfaction

1 INTRODUCTION

Since the beginning of the COVID-19 outbreak, universities around the world began shifting educational activities from physical classrooms to virtual ones. For example, the Chinese Ministry of Education launched the *"Disrupted Classes, Undisrupted Learning"* initiative, providing flexible online learning to over 270 million students from their homes (Huang et al. 2020).

The flexible learning approach provides learners with choices about where, when, and how learning occurs, by using a range of technologies to support the teaching and learning process (Lee & McLoughlin 2010). Flexible learning encompasses multi-dimensional aspects, including infrastructure, learning tools, learning resources, teaching and learning methods, services for teachers and students, and cooperation between government, enterprises, and schools (Huang et al. 2020). The unplanned and rapid move to online learning might result in a poor learning experience since students, lecturers, and university staff generally had not been prepared through simulations or practices beforehand.

To the best of the authors' knowledge, there is still very limited research on the student learning experience during the COVID-19 pandemic in Indonesia. The university students in Indonesia underwent a unique experience of having the first three to four weeks of the semester in physical classrooms and suddenly shifted to virtual classrooms for the rest of the semester. This research aims to understand the students' experience during the period and how it affected learning satisfaction. More importantly, as physical distancing measures would continue for months to come, it is very important for educational institution administrators to understand the crucial determinants that would enhance student learning satisfaction during this pandemic.

DOI 10.1201/9781003193241-56

2 LITERATURE REVIEW

2.1 Learner characteristics

Learner characteristics comprise various components, including attitudes toward computers. Attitudes toward computers include students' feelings, opinions, and perceptions toward general computer use, computer-aided instruction, computer programming and technical concepts, social issues related to computer use, and computer history (Aziz & Hasan 2012).

Aziz & Hasan (2012) emphasized the role of the user's attitudes and anxiety affect the knowledge of computers among individuals. Computer anxiety has been widely investigated in the literature. Previous studies have noted that personal characteristics of computer users (age, gender, education, etc.) can be the antecedents of computer anxiety. Somebody with computer anxiety may experience negative feelings such as fear of the unknown, frustration, embarrassment, failure, and disappointment and as a result, he or she may avoid using computers (Olatoye 2009). Therefore, it can be hypothesized that:

H1: The more positive a learner's characteristics are, the higher his or her learning satisfaction.

2.2 Instructor characteristics

Previtali & Scarozza (2019) revealed that the teaching style creates a stimulating effect on students' recognition of e-learning. In the context of online learning, there is an ever-pressing need for educators to use the tools of technology to achieve teaching goals, such as implementing the right methods, doing lesson planning and assessments, among other things (van Rensburg 2018). Instructor characteristics were also linked to class size as well as workload, as bigger class sizes and more workload could lead to less positive evaluation of the instructors (Özgüngör 2013).

Instructors in online learning can engage with the students through providing timely and useful responses or feedback to their assignments and projects (Martin et al. 2020). Therefore, it can be hypothesized that:

H2: Instructor characteristics have a positive and significant influence on online learning satisfaction.

2.3 Course suitability

Some courses may be suitable to be delivered online; however, some courses which require hands-on practices may suffer from the lack of interaction. The shift in learning mode has required all courses to be delivered in an online manner, regardless of their suitability. It was found that for online courses, subjects that are assessed by project-based assignments and involve high-level knowledge activities may increase learning effectiveness (Zheng et al. 2020).

Stier & Schneider (2009) argued that study programs do not have to choose between online and offline learning; rather, the choice should be made based on analysis of the suitability of the courses to be delivered. Courses with assignments and more theoretical components can be suitable for online learning delivery. On the other hand, courses with heavy experiential components are least suited for online delivery (Willett et al. 2019). Hence, it can be hypothesized that:

H3: Course suitability has a significant and positive influence on learning satisfaction.

2.4 Interactivity

University learning tends to be collaborative in nature, as students have the opportunity to discuss with others as opposed to pursuing their own learning goals (Koschmann et al. 1996; Yang et al. 2016 in Lin et al. 2018).

Interactivity is considered to be the key to effective learning (Blasco-Arcas et al. 2013). Interactivity can be divided into two types: interactivity with the other students and interactivity with the facilitators (Blasco-Arcas et al. 2013). The interaction with fellow students is usually in the form of group discussion, and class participation; these types of activities can improve active and high-order learning (Crouch & Mazur 2001). Active learning that involves collaboration with other students has been noted to improve students' learning experience (Blasco-Arcas et al. 2013) and possibly student satisfaction. This is due to the possibilities that interaction may enable the students to think critically and look for alternative answers, leading to deeper knowledge processing activity (Blasco-Arcas et al. 2013). Hence, it can be hypothesized that:

H4: The higher the level of interactivity during online learning, the higher the learning satisfaction.

2.5 Technological factors

Instructional support that students receive can mostly come from the course instructor and the institutions, but technology can be used to provide support to individual students and instructional contexts (Chen et al. 2010). The tools that are available online to the facilitators and learners can influence the online learning process (Deshwal et al. 2017). A previous study on the experience of online learning through massive open online courses (MOOCs) reported that internet access quality played an important factor in MOOC users' decision to continue participating in online courses. (Nurhudatiana et al. 2019). Therefore, it can be hypothesized that:

H5: Availability of the technological facilities will have a positive influence on learning satisfaction

2.6 Supporting factors

Online learning enables the learners to process learning materials based on their individual preferences at any time and from any place; they may select and examine material from a large pool of information (Artino & Stephens 2009; Narciss et al. 2007). Universities generally provide additional services such as a hotline or email address that students can contact should they encounter any problem during the online learning situation. Pieces of advice, counseling, and other facilities are also provided to improve the students' learning experience. A face-to-face consultation that complements online consultation facilities can also enable students to solve problems that may arise during online learning. Therefore, it can be hypothesized that:

H6: The availability of supporting factors has a positive and significant influence on learning satisfaction.

3 METHOD

This research utilizes the quantitative method with survey as the data collection method. The survey was distributed to undergraduate and Master's degree students who learn using an online learning method. There are seven variables investigated in this research: learner characteristics, instructor characteristics, course suitability, interactivity, technological factors, supporting factors, and learning satisfaction.

The data analysis was conducted using PLS SEM software. Construct reliability and validity as well as discriminant validity, were checked based on the Cronbach's Alpha's values, Average Variance Extracted, Composite Reliability, and Fornell-Lackner criterion. All the indicators were found to be valid and reliable.

4 RESULTS AND DISCUSSIONS

In total, 118 respondents participated in this study, with 100 usable responses which were further analyzed using PLS SEM software. Out of those 100 respondents, 31 were females (31%), 65

Table 1. Path analysis results.

Dimension	Original sample	Sample mean	Standard deviation	t-statistic	p-value
Learner characteristics	0.070	0.100	0.084	0.834	0.405
Instructor characteristics	−0.018	−0.019	0.075	0.238	0.812
Course suitability	0.412	0.408	0.068	6.072	0.000*
Interactivity	0.288	0.281	0.100	2.871	0.004*
Technological factors	0.082	0.076	0.076	1.084	0.279
Supporting factors	0.124	0.120	0.091	1.358	0.279

*significance at p-value 0.05.

males (61%), and 4 preferred not to tell their gender. A majority of them are undergraduate students with 6% being Master's degree students. The respondents come from different majors, including Business Management, Hotel Management, Computer Science, Information System, and Accounting and Finance.

The path analysis results are given in Table 1. The adjusted R square of the model is 0.575. The findings have shown that only course suitability and interactivity have a positive influence on student satisfaction. This is aligned with the studies conducted by Blasco-Arcas et al. (2013) and Chan et al. (2005). For example, interactivity may vary depending on the class dynamics as well as class size. Instructors who are livelier and better at engaging the students may foster better interaction that leads to higher student satisfaction. The nature of the courses may also vary, which means that experiential and non-experiential courses may not fare similarly. The courses with more theoretical elements can be delivered smoothly with fewer adjustments to the existing offline classes. However, courses with more experiential components may need more adjustments to improve student satisfaction during online learning.

5 CONCLUSIONS AND FUTURE WORK

The findings have shown that it is important to keep the interactivity in an online learning context as it makes the students more satisfied with their learning process. It is understandable that the respondents in this study may feel that their interactivity was reduced significantly as the institution pivoted to fully online learning mode. This implies that the facilitators would need to encourage interaction between students; either through online discussion, gamification of learning, or other activities that may foster discussion between the students.

To ensure that everyone feels comfortable to participate and contribute to the discussion, an instructor may set some rules that would encourage them to contribute to the class discussion. Interactivity also involves interaction with peers; thus, in the online setting, the students may be divided into several small groups to ease up the discussion process. In addition to that, educational institutions may need to carefully consider the courses that can be delivered online and the ones that are less likely to be delivered online. The consideration may be based on the type of the course (more practical or theoretical), the possibility of using additional means such as software, etc. This research has some room for improvement. For example, mixing both undergraduate and Master degree's students may lead to slight variance in findings, as there are differences in terms of the learning experience and maturity level of these respondents.

REFERENCES

Artino, A. R. and Stephens, J. M. 2009. Academic motivation and self-regulation: A comparative analysis of undergraduate and graduate students learning online. *The Internet and Higher Education, 12*(3–4):146–151. doi:10.1016/j.iheduc.2009.02.001

Blasco-Arcas, L., Buil, I., Hernández-Ortega, B., and Sese, F. J. 2013. Using clickers in class. The role of interactivity, active collaborative learning and engagement in learning performance. *Computers and Education*, 62:102–110. doi:10.1016/j.compedu.2012.10.019

Cao, C. and Meng, Q. 2020. Exploring personality traits as predictors of English achievement and global competence among Chinese university students: English learning motivation as the moderator. *Learning and Individual Differences*, 77:101814. doi:10.1016/j.lindif.2019.101814

Chan, Simon C. H., Wan, C. L. J., Chou, S., and Liu, C. 2005. Learning effectiveness in a Web-based virtual learning environment: A learner control perspective. *Journal of Computer Assisted Learning*, 21(1):65–76. doi:10.1111/j.1365-2729.2005.00114.x

Crouch, C. H. and Mazur, E. 2001. Peer Instruction: Ten years of experience and results. *American Journal of Physics*, 69(9):970–977. doi:10.1119/1.1374249

Deshwal, P., Trivedi, A., and Himanshi, H. 2017. Online Learning Experience Scale Validation and Its Impact on Learners' Satisfaction. *Procedia Computer Science*, 112:2455–2462. doi:10.1016/j.procs.2017.08.178

Hamid, M. R., Sami, W., and Sidek, M. H. 2017. Discriminant Validity Assessment: Use of Fornell and Larcker criterion versus HTMT Criterion. *Journal of Physics: Conference Series*, 890:012163. doi:10.1088/1742-6596/890/1/012163

Huang, R., Tlili, A., Chang, T., Zhang, X., Nascimbeni, F., and Burgos, D. 2020. Disrupted classes, undisrupted learning during COVID-19 outbreak in China: Application of open educational practices and resources. *Smart Learning Environments*, 7(1). doi:10.1186/s40561-020-00125-8

Jokisch, M. R., Schmidt, L. I., Doh, M., Marquard, M., and Wahl, H. 2020. The role of internet self-efficacy, innovativeness and technology avoidance in breadth of internet use: Comparing older technology experts and non-experts. *Computers in Human Behavior*, 111:106408. doi:10.1016/j.chb.2020.106408

Law, K. M., Geng, S., and Li, T. 2019. Student enrollment, motivation and learning performance in a blended learning environment: The mediating effects of social, teaching, and cognitive presence. *Computers and Education*, 136:1–12. doi:10.1016/j.compedu.2019.02.021

Lee, M. J. and McLoughlin, C. 2010. Emerging technologies in distance education. In G. Veletsianos (Author), *Emerging technologies in distance education* (pp. 61–87). Edmonton: AU Press.

Lin, H., Yen, W., and Wang, Y. 2018. Investigating the effect of learning method and motivation on learning performance in a business simulation system context: An experimental study. *Computers and Education*, 127:30–40. doi:10.1016/j.compedu.2018.08.008

Martin, F., Wang, C., and Sadaf, A. 2020. Facilitation Matters: Instructor Perception of Helpfulness of Facilitation Strategies in Online Courses. *Online Learning*, 24(1). doi:10.24059/olj.v24i1.1980

Narciss, S., Proske, A., and Koerndle, H. 2007. Promoting self-regulated learning in web-based learning environments. *Computers in Human Behavior*, 23(3):1126–1144. doi:10.1016/j.chb.2006.10.006

Nurhudatiana, A., Anggraeni, A., and Putra, S. 2019. An Exploratory Study of MOOC Adoption in Indonesia. *Proceedings of the 2019 5th International Conference on Education and Training Technologies - ICETT 2019*. doi:10.1145/3337682.3337690

Olatoye, R. 2009. Gender Factor in Computer Anxiety, Knowledge and Utilization among Senior Secondary School Students in Ogun State, Nigeria. *Gender and Behaviour*, 7(2). doi:10.4314/gab.v7i2.48696

Özgüngör, S. 2013. The Relationship Between Instructor and Course Characteristics and Students' Perception of Instructional quality. *Procedia - Social and Behavioral Sciences*, 93:1324–1328. doi:10.1016/j.sbspro.2013.10.037

Previtali, P. and Scarozza, D. 2019. Blended learning adoption: A case study of one of the oldest universities in Europe. *International Journal of Educational Management*, 33(5):990–998. doi:10.1108/ijem-07-2018-0197

Rensburg, E. S. 2018. Effective online teaching and learning practices for undergraduate health sciences students: An integrative review. *International Journal of Africa Nursing Sciences*, 9:73–80. doi:10.1016/j.ijans.2018.08.004

Willett, J., Brown, C., and Danzy-Bussell, L. A. 2019. An exploratory study: Faculty perceptions of online learning in undergraduate sport management programs. *Journal of Hospitality, Leisure, Sport and Tourism Education*, 25:100206. doi:10.1016/j.jhlste.2019.100206

Dynamics of Industrial Revolution 4.0: Digital Technology Transformation and Cultural Evolution –
Wulandari et al (eds)
© 2021 The Author(s), ISBN 978-1-032-04451-4

Pop-up book design of the West Sumatra endemic primates

S. Soedewi & K.K. Adha
Telkom University, Bandung, Indonesia

ABSTRACT: In 2020, the primate population in West Sumatra, Indonesia was very scarce due to a lack of knowledge and community awareness which resulted in wild forest burning, poaching, and the wildlife trade, especially in Bukittinggi, Agam Regency. Based on the author's data from the method of observation, interviews, questionnaires, and literature studies, knowledge about endemic Sumatran primates is still lacking, especially for children ages 7–12 years. The way to raise awareness for this endangered population is in the form of a pop-up book with the theme of introducing and protecting endemic primates in West Sumatra, Indonesia. The pop-up storybook's design style can attract the interest of elementary school children ages 7–12 because of its three-dimensional illustrations that can be touched and folded, creating great enthusiasm. It is hoped that this book design will provide readers with a pleasant reading experience.

Keywords: endemic primates, pop-up book, design, West Sumatra, Indonesia

1   INTRODUCTION

Rare primate populations in Bukittinggi, Agam Regency, West Sumatra, especially in the wild, are increasingly shrinking. Six endemic Sumatra primates are *Siamang Hitam*, *Simpai*, *Kukang Sumatra*, *Owa Ungko*, *Lutung Kelabu*, and *Sumatran Orangutan*. These primates are almost extinct due to a lack of knowledge and community awareness from an early age. According to West Java Profauna Coordinator (PFI), Nadya Andriani, many Indonesian people do not know the role primates play in the preservation of human life, such as playing a role in the spreading of seeds in the forest (Muhartati 2017). Many government regulations were made to protect wild animals and especially for Indonesian primates, however these regulations do not guarantee the preservation of primates. Wild animals, especially primates, are considered to be very disturbing to crop yields. When entering agricultural land, these primates will take or eat part of the cultivated plant and then leave (Wallace & Hill 2012). Due to the scarcity of primate food in nature, agricultural plants are considered more nutritious and cause primates to attack crops on agricultural land. These animals often interfere with the crop, which is why primates are called plant pests by the public (Utami 2016). According to the head of the Bukittinggi Natural Resource Conservation Center resort, the scarcity of primates in the Agam Regency is due to their habitat being disturbed by humans. This is a result of hunting wild animals, and their number of births is small because they are monogamous animals, which means they mate for life (Ciko 2020). Endemic Sumatran primates in Bukittinggi, Agam Regency, West Sumatra face extinction due to the illegal burning of forests, poaching of wild animals, and wildlife trade. This occurs because of the public's lack of awareness and knowledge about the rare species of primates that live in their environment (Aida 2020).

In Bukittinggi, Agam Regency, West Sumatra, children (boys and girls) aged 7–12 years need education about endemic Sumatran primates, which are almost extinct. Therefore, it is imperative that an awareness of these primates and their impending extinction be taught from childhood so that we can expect the next generation to protect the forest ecosystem. Therefore, the authors are interested in designing an informational medium about rare primates in West Sumatra, Indonesia, especially in Bukittinggi, Agam Regency, where they are almost extinct.

DOI 10.1201/9781003193241-57

This medium will be in the design of pop-up books that aim to provide education and awareness to children about rare primates in Bukit Tinggi, West Sumatra. The selection of books as a medium offers something concrete that children can touch. Also, books are healthier for children to use as compared to gadgets (Wulandari & Arumsari 2017). With the form of three-dimensional illustrations that can be touched and folded, children are more enthusiastic and have a pleasant reading experience. The pop-up book can arouse the interest of infants or children, increasing understanding of the story and increasing learning (Wen et al. 2015).

2 METHOD

The qualitative method was used in this study to analyze the data documentation, determine the types of respondents, display data for each variable, and test hypotheses to answer the problem formulation. The analysis is using SWOT analysis to used for this research to evaluate the strengths, weaknesses, opportunities, and threats involved in an organization, plan, project, person, or business activity (Gurel 2017).

2.1 Data collection methods

Data collection techniques were achieved through observation, interviews, and literature studies. Observations were carried out by gathering information about rare primates at the Natural Resource Conservation Center and Kinantan Buktitinggi Wildlife Park. In addition, direct observations were the best way to discover the right way to get the information about these endangered primates to the public. Interviews were conducted with experts on Bukittinggi primates, and the experts interviewed were considered part of the book design process. A literature study was completed by collecting data from various literature sources and a variety of media, such as books, articles, and the internet.

3 RESULT AND DISCUSSION

3.1 Message concept

The message in the pop-up book design is "protect primates"! It will strengthen children's understanding of rare primates whose population is diminishing and teach them the essential roles these primates play such as spreading seeds in the forest. The design contains messages and information delivered to children aged 7–12 years who are currently in elementary school. The pop-up book design expects to change children's views toward endemic Sumatran primates, which are rare, and invite them to love the forest as a place to live for endangered animals.

3.2 Creative concept

The storybook will be made in a pop-up style, using a cartoon illustration style, fonts that are simple and easy to read for children aged 7–12 years, and also use bright and natural colors. The pop-up book medium can attract children because it has a movable or three-dimensional element, thus providing a more interesting visualization of the story.

3.3 Visual concept

Visual concepts are created based on references, and the analysis results begin from sketching to the digital process.

Color
The colors used are bright, natural, and bold. Color can affect human emotions and describe a person's mood (Darmaprawira 2002). So, the use of bright colors represents the nature of cheerful

children. Natural colors use green, brown, and yellow, which represent natural colors and represent the forest where primates live in Agam District, used as a setting in for the story. Simultaneously, bold colors use red, which reflects a child's character in a pop-up book story.

Typography

The book's typeface uses Berlin Sans FB. This typeface is bold, so it gives the impression of a massive and concentrated space (Sihombing 2017). Therefore, bold letters are better suited for short words like titles. The book content uses seven Soft Sans serif typefaces. This font is easy to read for children.

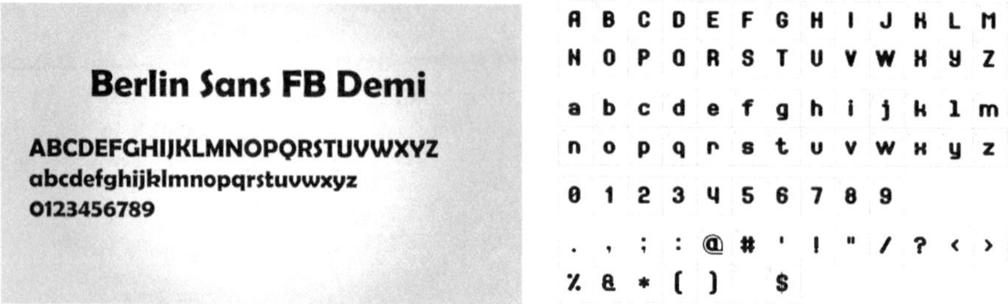

Figure 1. Berlin Sans FB Demi (left) and Soft Sans Serif 7 (right). (Source: www.fontoteka.com, www.1001freefonts.com).

Illustration style

The style of the illustrations that will be used is a cartoon style in the type of vector. Cartoon illustrations are suitable for children because cartoon characters have funny shapes that attract more attention from children. This type of vector image is used because the vector has a high resolution, so the lines and colors produced in the vector image will be sharper and can be applied to various media sizes, especially for supporting media.

Figure 2. Vector illustration. (Source: www.gumroad.com).

Character style

Character design uses references and analysis of native forms and characters from the environment in Bukit Tinggi, West Sumatra.

308

Figure 3. Main character in story (left) and endemic Sumatran primates. (Source: Kevyn Kurnia Adha 2020).

3.4 *Design result*

Character and background design

The first character in the storybook depicts a child who is active, funny, and has a caring nature about the environment wearing typical West Sumatra clothing. The second character reflects a forest ranger in Bukittinggi, Agam Regency, West Sumatra, which saves wildlife protected from genetic damage. Simultaneously, the last primates are the six species of endemic primates of West Sumatra that are protected by the government. For the background, the illustration uses the Gadang Minangkabau house, Ngarai Sianok (Sianok Canyon), and the tropical forest atmosphere in Bukittinggi, Agam Regency, West Sumatra.

Figure 4. Character and background design. (Source: Kevyn Kurnia Adha 2020).

Media design

The book is printed in hardcover with a size of 20 x 20 cm with doff laminate finishing and 230 gr art carton material for the contents page.

Figure 5. Book cover. (Source: Kevyn Kurnia Adha 2020).

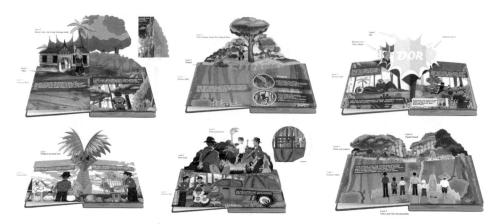

Figure 6. Pop-up book design. (Source: Kevyn Kurnia Adha 2020).

4 CONCLUSION

The primate population growth in Agam District, West Sumatra, is decreasing, causing the scarcity of these animals. Therefore, a lot of information about the rare primates in Agam Regency, West Sumatra, is needed. It is hoped that the pop-up book design regarding rare primates in West Sumatra will become one of the media that can increase public awareness of the importance of protecting rare animals so that their sustainability is maintained essentially for kids age 7–12 years. Hopefully, the information and education about the rare primates of West Sumatra can be carried out in further research through other forms of media. It is important to educate about the preservation of rare primates so that young people can be expected to preserve the natural ecosystem.

ACKNOWLEDGMENT

The authors would like to thank Mr. Vera Ciko as the head of the Bukittinggi BKSDA (Natural Resources Conservation Center) resort, and Ms. Rahmi Aida as the Curator of the Kinantan Bukittinggi Wildlife and Cultural Park. Thank you for agreeing to be interviewed so that the authors were able to get the data needed for the design process. It is our hope that this pop-up book can educate the public about the rare endemic primates of Agam Regency, Bukit Tinggi, West Sumatra, Indonesia.

REFERENCES

Aida, R. 2020. *The existence of endemic Sumatran primates in Bukittinggi, Agam Regency,* West Sumatra. Bukittinggi.

Ciko, V. 2020. *Scarcity of Primates in Agam Regency*. Bukittinggi.

Darmaprawira, S. (2002) *Warna Teori dan Kreativitas Penggunaannya*. 2nd ed. Bandung: Penerbit ITB.

Gurel, E. 2017. SWOT Analysis: A Theoretical Review, *The Journal of International Social Research*, 4(51): 9–15.

Muhartati, E. 2017. Pemencaran Tumbuhan Oleh Primata Di Daerah Lembah Harau Sumatera Barat, *Pedagogi Hayati*, 2(1).

Sihombing, D. 2017. *Tipografi dalam Desain Grafis*. 2nd ed. Jakarta: PT Gramedia Pustaka Utama.

Utami, R. 2016. Penjarahan tanaman oleh hewan Primata di Bungus dan Teluk Kabung, Padang, Sumatera Barat, 2:49–54. doi: 10.13057/psnmbi/m020110.

Wallace, G. E. and Hill, C. M. 2012. Crop Damage by Primates: Quantifying the Key Parameters of Crop-Raiding Events, *PLoS ONE*, 7(10). doi: 10.1371/journal.pone.0046636.

Wen, W. et al. 2015. Pop-up book, *Lens*.

Wulandari, C. C. and Arumsari, R. Y. 2017. Perancangan Buku Ilustrasi Tembang Dolanan Jawa Tengah, *Andharupa: Jurnal Desain Komunikasi Visual & Multimedia.*, 03(01):49–58.

Dynamics of Industrial Revolution 4.0: Digital Technology Transformation and Cultural Evolution –
Wulandari et al (eds)
© 2021 The Author(s), ISBN 978-1-032-04451-4

Digital learning innovation on concept development course. A study in visual communication design program at Universitas Ciputra

L. Indriati

Universitas Ciputra, Surabaya, Indonesia

ABSTRACT: Online learning becomes an obligation that must be undertaken by higher education during the Covid-19 pandemic. For this reason, it is necessary to adapt to technology and the learning process so that the quality of education in Indonesia can continue to improve even though delivered online. This study using a case study of online learning in the Concept Development course. This study uses a mixed-methods, by surveying a survey of 49 students of Visual Communication Design Universitas Ciputra deepened with interviews. The results of this study get recommendations for digital learning innovations that are appropriate when viewed from the TPACK framework from the aspects of technology, pedagogy, and content. Analysis of the survey results and interview resulted in several digital learning innovations that will apply in the future, including a personality assessment test, real user experience, and collaborative asynchronous learning.

Keywords: TPACK, Technology, Pedagogy, Content, Innovation, Online Learning

1 BACKGROUND

The application of information and communication technology in the development of today's education is a must, especially during the Covid-19 pandemic. Educational technology becomes very crucial as the only medium that can help the learning process at this time. All levels of education are required to adapt to technology and the learning process. Not only applying technology but also maintaining the quality of learning even though the material is delivered online.

The main problem in the world of education in the globalization era is the low level of quality, innovation, and human resources. According to Forlab Dikti data, the reality of the number of Higher Education Institutions in Indonesia is around 4,695 Universities (1,064 Academies, 278 Polytechnics, 2,534 Colleges, 217 Institutes, 583 Universities, 19 Community Colleges). A large number of tertiary institutions cause the unfocused field of science to be studied, resulting in the low quality of learning, research, and publications produced by educational institutions. To lessen the gap, digital learning innovations will be applied to Concept Development courses to prepare students for social, cultural, workplace, and technological advancements.

2 RESEARCH METHOD

The research method used in this study is a mixed-method, which combines the two approaches in research, namely, qualitative and quantitative (Creswell 2015: 5). The selected mixed method is a sequential explanatory design that is a research model characterized by collecting data and analyzing quantitative data in the first stage and followed by collecting and analyzing qualitative data in the second stage, to strengthen the results of quantitative research conducted in the first stage (Sugiyono 2011: 409).

This strategy is carried out quantitatively by survey methods. The survey was distributed to 49 respondents and analyzed descriptive statistics. According to Sugiyono (2012: 13), descriptive

DOI 10.1201/9781003193241-58

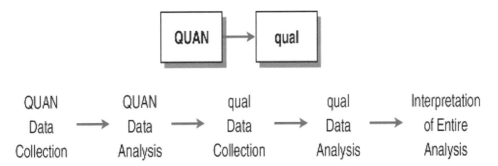

QUAN Data Collection → QUAN Data Analysis → qual Data Collection → qual Data Analysis → Interpretation of Entire Analysis

Figure 1. Sequential explanatory design.

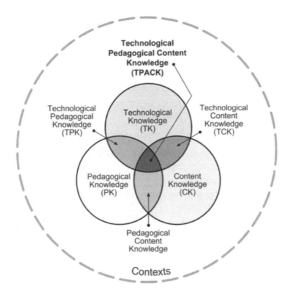

Figure 2. Framework TPACK.

research is research conducted to determine the value of an independent variable, either one variable or more (independent) without making the comparison, or connecting with other variables. In the second phase, the quantitative data obtained deepen through interviews with students associated with the study of literature about the design process and development of online courses. The framework used in this research is the TPACK (Technological Pedagogical Content Knowledge) framework, which considers three main aspects: technological, pedagogical, and content aspects (Kaplon-Schilis & Lyublinskaya 2020: 25–43).

3 DISCUSSION

Concept Development courses aim to provide an understanding of the theory and practice of the process of coordinating and directing design resources to be able to solve problems that occur. After attending this course, students are expected to be able to use design as a management tool to determine and achieve strategic goals. Based on the survey of 49 students the following is a description of the results obtained:

Table 1. Lecturer evaluation by students survey.

	N	Min	Max	Average
Course quality	49	3	5	4,2
Material quality	49	2	5	4,1
Presentation	49	2	5	4,3
Answering question	49	3	5	4,4
Express opinions	49	2	5	3,9
Assignments	49	1	5	4,2

Source: processed secondary data 2020.

From the interview with the students who took the Concept Development course, the following results obtained:

The results of the analysis in the table above produce several insights to apply in the future. The recommendations for digital learning innovation include:

Table 2. Interview.

TPACK	DESCRIPTION
Technology	• Adding translation to a presentation • More playful and interactive • Honestly online class is making this course a tough one... • Use slideshow as presentation of material cause people was too lazy to watch material from Youtube (as Youtube is for entertainment, not for study purposes, when we look at Youtube algorithm)
Pedagogy	• Tasks that directly work together to help with clients • A bigger group discussion to switch minds and opinions would be great • More personal activities • All that is gained from this learning though it feels fast to understand the steps for this semester but from here, I hope to continue to get learning related to the client so that he can understand when meeting with clients in the future
Content	• Know how to create a structural concept • Maybe invite some people to tell their experience that can be related to this class. I think that would be fun and an interesting thing to do • Conducting guidance on getting used to students doing research is good. But I feel it would be better if it was further deepened on how to do research and technical market data analysis. • Explain more about the purpose and giving tips and tricks to help understand the material • Overall I think this class is helping us to know the client's businesses or our businesses way better and improving the skill that we can use in the future! In the end, I really enjoy this class.

3.1 Personality assessment test

The user or client expects the designer to be creative, but often what the designer does not realize is that the client also expects the designer to be confident and able to manage the entrusted project well. Therefore, at the beginning of the lecturing session, students will be given a personality assessment quiz that aims to find out each strength so that they can maximize team performance. Taking the concept of team formation in the startup business, the skills needed in a team are at least three types of people: hacker (developer), hipster (designer), and hustler (communicator) (Medium.com 2018). Through this assessment, students expected to make team formations that can complement each other in impressive ways (Bakan & Bakan 2018: 119–145).

3.2 Real user experience

Students who took the Concept Development course are expected to have holistic abilities in applying design as a real-world problem-solving tool. Therefore, this course presents partners from the industry as real clients with real problems as case studies for students. The purpose of inviting clients is to foster student confidence through the opportunity to make decisions in designing and presenting the idea in front of real clients (Coleman et al. 2016). Thus, students are expected to be able to explain the design concept, why use the design approach, and how the idea can answer the client's needs. This method can also train students' soft skills in managing a design project, such as how they present design concepts and how to answer questions raised by clients. Besides, by introducing students to real clients, they are expected to be able to open opportunities and build their connections to the internship program or even get a job. The learning scheme by involving partners is as follows:

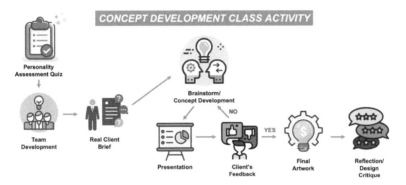

Figure 3.   Concept Development course learning activity.

3.3 Collaborative asynchronous learning

This course will apply the learning flexibility with asynchronous learning, collaboration, and multiplatform. Students can still study the subject even though the connection access barriers or conflicting schedules with courses or activities at each campus. The obstacle when carrying out collaborative learning experiences in online learning is when there are limitations to carrying out asynchronous interactions (Hafner & Ellis 2004). For example, students from other universities who take this course and have conflicting class schedules can still learn by watching the learning videos provided by the lecturer. Besides, each week will have periodic assignments that will be

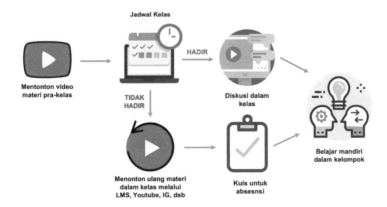

Figure 4.   Collaborative asynchronous learning method on Concept Development course.

compiled at a certain as proof of attendance. All material, modules, worksheets used in this course will be uploaded through the Learning Management System (LMS), or other media to facilitate easy access for students. Video material uploaded on YouTube or Instagram, worksheets are shared via email or group chat, presentations through Zoom Meeting media, and so on.

4 CONCLUSION

Based on the results and discussion above, the conclusion is as follows:

1. Digital learning innovations carried out mainly for creative subjects are expected to meet technological, pedagogical, and content aspects such as the TPACK framework to produce ideal online learning innovations.
2. The use of technology and social media can help students feel that courses are more accessible and flexible in using various platforms so that they can be more engaged in online learning
3. Innovations generated in this study, also can be applied to other subjects within the scope of the Visual Communication Design program whose application needs to be adjusted to the learning achievements of each course.

ACKNOWLEDGEMENT

The researcher would like to thank especially the respondents, students of Visual Communication Design Universitas Ciputra class of 2018 which were willing to fill out the survey and were interviewed for this research.

REFERENCES

Archambault, L.M. & Barnett, J.H., 2010. Revisiting technological pedagogical content knowledge: Exploring the TPACK framework. *Computers & Education*, *55*(4), pp. 1656–1662.

Bakan, U. & Bakan, U., 2018. Game-based learning studies in education journals: A systematic review of recent trends. *Actualidades Pedagógicas*, *72*(72), pp. 119–145.

Coleman, R., Clarkson, J.. & Cassim, J., 2016. *Design for inclusivity: A practical guide to accessible, innovative and user-centred design*. CRC Press.

Guetterman, T.C., Fetters, M.D. & Creswell, J.W., 2015. Integrating quantitative and qualitative results in health science mixed methods research through joint displays. *The Annals of Family Medicine*, *13*(6), pp. 554–561.

Hafner, W. & Ellis, T.J., 2004, October. Asynchronous collaborative learning using project-based assignments. In *34th Annual Frontiers in Education, 2004. FIE 2004.* (pp. F2F-6). IEEE.

Kaplon-Schilis, A., & Lyublinskaya, I. (2020). Analysis of Relationship Between Five Domains of TPACK Framework: TK, PK, CK Math, CK Science, and TPACK of Pre-service Special Education Teachers. *Technology, Knowledge and Learning*, *25*(1), 25–43.

Koehler, M. & Mishra, P. (2009). What is Technological Pedagogical Content Knowledge (TPACK)? *Contemporary Issues in Technology and Teacher Education*, *9*(1), 60–70. Waynesville, NC USA: Society for Information Technology & Teacher Education.

Yargın, G.T., Süner, S. & Günay, A., 2018. Modelling user experience: Integrating user experience research into design education.

Dynamics of Industrial Revolution 4.0: Digital Technology Transformation and Cultural Evolution –
Wulandari et al (eds)
© 2021 The Author(s), ISBN 978-1-032-04451-4

Online learning and design lectures during the COVID-19 pandemic: A student's experience

A.R. Adriyanto, I. Santosa & A. Syarief
Bandung Institute of Technology, Indonesia

ABSTRACT: The COVID-19 pandemic of 2020 caused changes in learning patterns throughout the world. Higher education was unprepared to provide online lectures to students and different learning platforms only were used sporadically for courses. Negative experiences therefore arose from this new learning process. This study uses a qualitative strategy approach to analyze a survey distributed to 193 students in April 2020. The survey aims to examine the experience of students in attending online lectures. Survey questions that are open-ended questions were analyzed by the affinity diagram technique. Four themes were found to be issues in the negative experiences of online learning, namely the reliability of information technology infrastructure, management of online learning, social presence, and student motivation. The results of these findings are expected to provide input for universities to manage future online learning in higher education.

Keywords: online learning, higher education, learning platforms, negative experiences

1 INTRODUCTION

In the face-to-face method in the physical classroom, the teacher is the center that controls the content and the learning process. Face-to-face learning is limited by space and time and the cost of learning is increasingly expensive. In online learning, students become the center of learning and demand independence, and the flexibility of location and time and unlimited access to knowledge are its strengths (Zhang et al. 2004).

The COVID-19 pandemic of 2020 caused changes in learning patterns throughout the world. Countries enforced rules that demanded that citizens stay at home, therefore teaching and learning activities that were previously carried out face-to-face in classrooms were replaced by using internet media to deliver lessons. Various types of platforms were used so that lectures could run, and these lectures were synchronously and asynchronously. However, in the process of all of this, various negative experiences emerged. A survey conducted by Adnan and Anwar (2020) in Pakistan found that most of the problems were related to limited access to the internet due to technical and financial problems. Students still prefer face-to-face meetings. The same situation occurred in West Bengal, India during the regional lockdown that occurred in the region. Students experienced problems such as depression, anxiety, poor internet connection, and uncomfortable learning environments at home (Kapasia et al. 2020). The qualitative study was carried out by Khalil et al. (2020) who analyzed synchronized online learning from the perspective of medical students. The thematic content analysis found four core themes, namely the educational impact, time management, challenges encountered, and preferences for the future. The challenges and opportunities for higher education in this pandemic were presented by Toquero (2020). This study recommends rearranging curriculum competencies and improving training for lecturers for online learning. This article aims to analyze the experience of higher education students attending online lectures during the COVID-19 pandemic in Indonesia.

DOI 10.1201/9781003193241-59

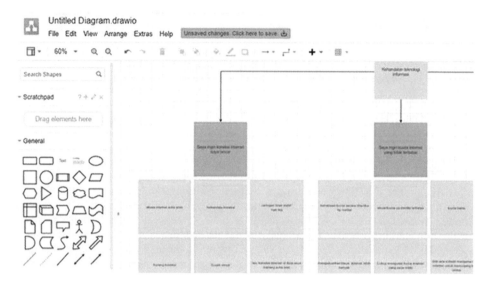

Figure 1. Diagram processing software (app.diagram.net).

2 METHODS

This study uses a qualitative strategy approach with data collections through online surveys. The online survey was conducted from April 7–17 2020 to obtain information related to student experiences with online learning. It used Google Forms by distributing the link via WhatsApp to students living in Indonesian cities such as Bandung, Jakarta, Yogyakarta, Surakarta, Pekanbaru, Makassar, and Semarang. In total, 193 students responded.

The survey consisted of 16 questions, some of which were closed, some of which were open-ended. This article focuses on respondents' answers to questions related to negative experiences in online learning during the pandemic. Online learning is focused on design courses which consist of practical and studio courses.

Open-ended questions produce a variety of answers from respondents. To analyze the diversity of answers, the affinity diagram technique was used recognize certain patterns in the answers. To process these answers, a diagram processing software (app.diagram.net) was used by entering each respondent's answer in a box (Figure 1). Boxes containing answers that are similar were grouped into one specific part. And in the end, the main themes of each group that are studied in this article were analyzed.

3 RESULTS AND DISCUSSION

The learning platform most widely used during this pandemic is Google Classroom, a learning management system from Google. Furthermore, the use of instant messaging such as on WhatsApp or LINE dominates the methods of learning through online media. Another popular platform was Zoom, a video-conferencing application that can sync face-to-face remotely. The Learning Management System (LMS) of educational institutions did not seem to be optimized to online learning during the time of the pandemic because of its non-dominant position. It is suspected that the issue of institutional readiness in preparing teaching material makes the choice of institutional LMS not the dominant usage (Figure 2).

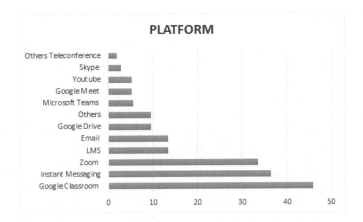

Figure 2. Learning platforms.

Figure 3. Online learning experience.

Google Classroom is asynchronous online learning when teachers and students are in different places at different times. It requires independence from students to understand the system and work-flow in learning. In contrast, the Zoom application is an application that can be used for direct or synchronous learning. Teachers and students are present at the same time but in different locations. Assuming a stable internet connection, interactivity between teachers and students can run well. Instant messaging applications were widely used because of their popularity in everyday communi-cation. The use of group features in communication allows one to communicate between people in groups that are created. Instant messaging is an application that has synchronous communication but can sometimes be delayed resulting in asynchronous communication.

On a scale of 1–10 respondents, were asked to rate the online learning they were taking. Score 6 became the most popular choice of respondents, followed by a score of 5. Looking at this data, it is suspected that there were negative experiences experienced by respondents when attending online lectures. (Figure 3).

From the analysis of respondents' negative experiences in online lectures for practical and studio courses, four themes emerged:

a. the need for information technology infrastructure reliability,
b. the need for good online learning management,
c. the need for social presence and interaction, and
d. the need for student motivation in learning.

3.1 The need for information technology infrastructure reliability

The problem that was primarily negative in online learning was that of information technology infrastructure when online lectures take place. This problem includes three groups of problems: internet network problems, internet quota limitations, and device problems used in the online lectures.

According to Bhuasiri et al. (2012), one dimension that influences the acceptance of online learning systems in developing countries is system dimension. System dimensions include infrastructure elements, and the quality of the internet infrastructure and the level of user information technology literacy is fundamental in the online learning process. To measure the level of information and communication technology development in an area, an index of information and communication technology development is used (BPS 2018). The index value is on a scale of 1–10, with the higher the index value indicating the more rapid development of information technology in a region.

Jakarta Province obtained the highest index value of 7.61, which contrasts with Papua province's index of 2.95. This shows that in a region that has a good internet network infrastructure, easier access to the internet network and the population allows for a greater ability of users to master computer technology. The lowest index besides Papua included the provinces of West Kalimantan, Lampung, Aceh, West Nusa Tenggara, North Maluku, West Sulawesi, and East Nusa Tenggara. Inequality in the development of information technology can be an obstacle to the implementation of online learning, especially if it is associated with the aim of increasing access to quality higher education.

3.2 The need for good online learning management

The next problem that contributes to the negative experience of respondents in online learning is the problem of managing online learning. This problem is covered in four groups of problems, namely lecture procedures, material understanding, assignments, and assistance processes.

Based on the negative experiences of students in managing online learning, several things can be concluded. Lecture procedures that are not clear and complicate the learning process are related to the application of rules in the online learning system used. Systems and procedures in online learning have not been optimally disseminated to teach participants. Sporadic use of various types of platforms is thought to create a large cognitive burden for teaching participants to understand each system one by one (Sweller et al. 2011).

Related to practical and studio courses contained in the design study program in general, an understanding of materials and tools is a major element in the design curriculum (Buchanan 1995). In distance learning in two different places, initial conditioning becomes a fundamental thing in practical and studio lectures. Both students and lecturers need to have the same material for the optimal learning process. The problems experienced in the survey were related to conditions that do not allow for material presence. The COVID-19 pandemic situation did not allow students and lecturers to get materials easily. In normal situations, learning materials might be presented more optimally for distance learning needs.

3.3 The need for social presence and interaction

The next problem that added to the negative experience of respondents in online learning was the absence of social presence and interaction. Although the distance between learners becomes virtually close, physical absence causes invisible nonverbal communication. Richardson and Swan (2003) discuss aspects of social presence in online learning in terms of satisfaction levels. The results of his research resulted in the discovery that there was a good level of satisfaction in students with the application of social presence aspects.

Rourke et al. (1999) focus on aspects of social presence by examining deeper aspects of the affective, interactive, and cohesive aspects of text-based material on computer media. The results of his research found that to create a social presence in computer-based media related affective, interactive, and cohesive aspects are needed. Affective aspects have indicators of emotional expression, use of humor, and self-disclosure. The interactive aspect has indicators of reconnecting the communication process, reference from other messages, explicit, reference, asking questions, expressing, and appreciating, and expressing signs of agreement. The cohesive aspect has vocative indicators aimed at a particular person, and refers to the group inclusively, making an open greeting. From these studies, it was concluded that social presence in online learning is realized through interaction with peers by including affective aspects in this digital realm.

3.4 *The need for student motivation in learning*

The negative experience of respondents in subsequent online learning is a matter of student motivation. Motivation can be divided into two parts, namely intrinsic motivation originating from within and extrinsic motivation that is triggered from outside the self. In the survey distributed to respondents, there are two groups that arise in motivational issues, namely self-motivation issues and learning environment problems.

On the environmental and personal dimensions in the online learning entities examined by Bhuasiri et al. (2012), there is intrinsic and extrinsic motivation. Intrinsic motivation is a voluntary drive from a person toward activity and aims to satisfy one's psychological needs. Motivation from within a person can be influenced by outside influences such as material use, clarity of instructions, regulations, social pressure, and competition.

According to Kawachi (2003), intrinsic motivation is stronger than extrinsic motivation and is directly related to the quality of deep learning. The formation of motivation is related to educational orientation. Educational orientation is divided into four parts, namely vocational, academic, social, and personal orientation. Vocational orientation is related to skill development while academic orientation is related to achieving intellectual interest. The formation of motivation related to vocational and academic orientation is obtained by bringing out the expressiveness in online teaching. The expression is defined as enthusiasm, friendliness, humor, dynamism, and charisma.

In online learning, students are physically separated from their peers and only meet virtually through the online class provided. The main factor in student failure in distance learning relates to students' feelings of being isolated without the support of their peers. In forming motivations related to this social orientation, online learning must facilitate the building of interaction between students in groups. Developing a sense of community can make learning effective.

4 CONCLUSION

Problems that arise in online learning vary. The government can increase investment in the development of information technology infrastructure so that various regions receive the same facilities as other regions. It is time for universities to focus on developing online learning management that takes into account social aspects and good interaction with learning content. For this reason, it is necessary to further analyze learning content that supports these aspects. Online learning user experience related to motivation deserves attention because of its independence in learning. Factors that can motivate students to learn in a fun way need to be further analyzed.

REFERENCES

Adnan, M. and Anwar, K. 2020. Online learning amid the COVID-19 pandemic: Students' perspectives. *Journal of Pedagogical Sociology and Psychology*, 2:45–51.
Bhuasiri, W., Xaymoungkhoun, O., Zo, H., Rho, J.J., and Ciganek, A.P. 2012. Critical success factors for e-learning in developing countries: A comparative analysis between ict experts and faculty, *Computer & Education*, 58:843–855.
BPS, Biro Pusat Statistik. 2018. Tingkat pengangguran terbuka, data obtained from https://www.bps.go.id/pressrelease/2018/11/05/1485/agustus-2018-tingkat-pengangguran-terbuka-tpt-sebesar-5-34-persen.html.

Buchanan, M. 1995. *Making art and critical literacy: a reciprocal relationship* in Prentice, R., ed. Teaching art and design, addressing issues and identifying direction, London: Continuum.

Kapasiaa, N., Paulb, P., Royc, A., Sahac, J., Zaveric, A., Mallickc, R., Barmanc, B., Dasc, P., and Chouhanc, P. 2020. Impact of lockdown on learning status of undergraduate and postgraduate students during COVID-19 pandemic in West Bengal, India, *Children and Youth Services Review*, 116,:1–5.

Kawachi, P. 2003. Initiating intrinsic motivation in online education: Review of the current state of the art, *Interactive Learning Environments*, 11:59–81.

Khalil, R., Mansour, A.E., Fadda, W.A., Almisnid, K., Aldamegh, M., Al-Nafeesah, A., Alkhalifah, A., and Al-Wutayd, O. 2020. The sudden transition to synchronized online learning during the COVID-19 pandemic in Saudi Arabia: a qualitative study exploring medical students' perspectives, *BMC Medical Education*, 20:1–10.

Richardson, J.C. and Swan, K. 2003. Examining social presence in online courses in relation to students' perceived learning and satisfaction, *Journal of Asynchronous Learning Networks*, 7:68-88.

Rourke, L., Anderson, T., Garrison, D.R., and Archer, W. 1999. Assessing social presence in asynchronous text-based computer conferencing, *International Journal of E Learning & Distance Education*, 14: 50–71.

Sweller, J., Ayres, P., and Kalyuga, S. 2011. *Cognitive load theory*, New York: Springer Science+Business Media.

Toquero, C.M., 2020. Challenges and Opportunities for Higher Education amid the COVID-19 Pandemic: The Philippine Context, *Pedagogical Research*, 5:1–5

Zhang, D., Zhao, J.L., Zhou, L., and Nunamaker, J.F. 2004. Can e-learning replace classroom learning?, *Communication of ACM*, 47:75–79.

Dynamics of Industrial Revolution 4.0: Digital Technology Transformation and Cultural Evolution –
Wulandari et al (eds)
© 2021 The Author(s), ISBN 978-1-032-04451-4

Meeting the needs of children in islamic boarding school with monitoring child growth

F.E. Naufalina & M. Hisyam
Telkom University, Bandung, Indonesia

A. Ahmad
Universitas Bunda Mulia, Jakarta, Indonesia

ABSTRACT: The parenting of children by their parents is very instrumental in forming the basis of children's education and development. The connection between children, parents, and the boarding school system is also very important in the process of continuing that education. Parental concerns for children have become very common, especially for children who have just graduated from elementary school. The purpose of parenting is to build bonds between children and their parents and guide children to be able to adapt well to their social environment. With everyone so connected to their gadgets to meet their daily needs these days, a digital application is necesawry solution to overcome these concerns is monitoring children with the content of an application for their parents.

Keywords: Islamic Boarding School, Children Growth, Parenting, Application, Graphic Design

1 INTRODUCTION

Education plays a critical role in helping to raise children to be quality people who are able to socialize well with their environment. The way parents educate and care for their children is a form of education. Good development and growth of a child are determined by the way parents to raise, care, pay attention, and educate them as they grow up. The boarding school environment must therefore be formed at least in the same way as the family environment so that it can contribute to developing the character of children.

The study of parenting from an Islamic or psychological perspective has been widely discussed, resulting in a variety of parenting styles that do not have targets on how to create children who can become a quality generation. Many studies on how to parent children still do not take into account the current time or religious teachings. The character of a child and his/her concept of self is a reflection on the parenting they received by their parents (Fawaid & Hasanah 2020).

Boarding schools are primarily designed with the vision and mission to educate students, help them develop good morals, and guide them to use their abilities to best serve the community. Boarding school modernization aims to perfect the Islamic boarding school educational system and also establish boarding schools as centers for community development (Hasbullah 1999). Boarding school is an option for parents who are not able to oversee their children's education at home due to lack of time or knowledge.

In previous research (Azizah 2013), many parents sometimes mistakenly interpret the role of Islamic boarding schools as a system that totally takes over the entire education of children, however, students still need the support of their parents back home. Added by Katz (1997), children who get receive and assistance from their parents are able to learn and progress better than children who do not receive it. Many studies have shown that parental support offers infinite benefits to their children.

DOI 10.1201/9781003193241-60

In psychological research (Devi & Pihasniwati 2017), the adjustment of children in Islamic boarding schools is closely related to the communication that exists between parents and children. Therefore, the better the communication between parents and children, the better the level of self-adjustment, and conversely, the worse the communication between parents and children, the lower the level of self-adjustment in the boarding school. Due to the boarding school system which requires students to live in dormitories, the number of meetings between parents and children is reduced, therefore according to Fatimah (2008) higher quality interaction between them is more important that quantity as quality communication can build a sense of closeness between parents and children.

In other psychological research, Monica (2017) reports that the closeness of parents to children also plays a significant role in a child's self-confidence while away at Islamic boarding school. The closer the parents are to the children, the higher the level of self-confidence in a child. In addition, according to Nurjanah & Heryadi (2020), parental closeness also has a significant effect on children's social intelligence. At the Modern Miftahunnajah Islamic Boarding School, the effective contribution of parent–child closeness contributed 12.1% to children's social intelligence. It can be concluded that the closeness of parents to children also has a significant effect on the development process of children in Islamic boarding schools.

The purpose of this study is to help parents monitor development and meet the needs of their children while they are away at boarding schools. Parental support usually includes moral support for psychological fulfilment which includes affection, modeling, guidance and direction, encouragement, enthusiasm, motivation, and confidence, where the attention of parents is the hope of all children in their growth and development. With the development of technology, one solution to help parents monitor their children is the creation of a digital application.

2 METHOD

The method used in this research is a qualitative approach by collecting data through literature study, interviews, observations, and questionnaires. After data collection, the next method is to analyze data using SWOT for application content design requirements.

2.1 *Method of collecting data*

Through the literature study method, data collection is done by looking for references on how parents care for children so that there is a correlation with the needs of the main subject on this research topic and the perspective and context. The interview is a conversation that aims to explore thoughts, concepts, personal experiences, convictions, and views of sources, or to obtain information from sources about events that cannot be observed directly by the researcher or about events that occurred in the past (Soewardikoen 2013). Interviews conducted are direct and indirect. In addition, this method will be carried out together with the observation method. Observations were made at the Daar El-Qolam Islamic Boarding School. The resource persons to be interviewed were the boarding school and the parents. The questionnaire is a way to obtain data in a relatively short time because at the same time many people can be asked to fill in the written answer choices provided (Soewardikoen 2013). The questionnaire was made as secondary data and distributed to the parents. The results obtained from the SWOT analysis will be designed to suit the needs of children in boarding schools and their parents.

3 RESULT AND DISCUSSION

3.1 *Segmentation, targeting, and positioning*

The customer segmentation of this application is parents aged 30–50 years, both male and female. Social status is emphasized more for middle- to medium- and upper-middle class in big cities in

Indonesia. The target users are parents who use smartphones to meet their daily needs, with a medium lifestyle that prioritizes practicality in carrying out daily activities. As a parent who wants to monitor the development and meet the needs of their children easily, efficiently, and practically, application content will be created that can be used to monitor developments and meet the needs of children in the Daar El-Qolam Islamic Boarding School.

In this application, parents receive various kinds of information about health, education, finance, and children's activities in Islamic boarding schools. However, parents can also purchase items for their children's needs through the app as well as communicate through social media features provided in the application with the school, as a means to convey messages to their children. This application is designed to be modern and dynamic, targeted at the middle- to upper-middle class.

3.2 *SWOT analysis*

From the SWOT analysis, we obtained the desire of boarding schools, as well as the government, to develop application design content for parents designed to suit the needs of their children in boarding schools.

Table 1. SWOT analysis from the interview and observation method.

	Strength	Weakness
	Accredited Education (A) Have an international program The slogan "Caring for tradition and responding to modernization"	Do not have an application that can be used by parents to monitor children's development
Opportunity The phenomenon of technological development 4.0 as well as government support for the development of Islamic boarding schools	With the development of technology 4.0 and support from the government for the development of Islamic boarding schools, Daar El-Qolam Islamic Boarding Schools better can realize their slogans	The design of this application could be one step for the Daa El-Qolam Islamic Boarding School in responding to the development of technology 4.0
Threat Some Islamic boarding schools have implemented applications for parents	Accreditation (A) and international programs can be one aspect of excellence in competing with other Islamic boarding schools that have applied applications for parents	A good application design in accordance with user needs will make this application more functional for all needs

3.3 *Message and communication concept*

Based on the data obtained through interviews, questionnaires, and observations that were made to answer the background of parents' concerns about the needs of children in Islamic boarding schools, the concept of this application was born. The concept of the message to be conveyed is the trust of parents about child parenting in Islamic boarding schools. This is one of the important factors that can influence the success of children in boarding school. With this platform, it is expected that parents can increase trust in children and Islamic boarding schools, especially Daar El-Qolam.

The concept of communication that will be made in this design is an application related to the User Interface and User Experience which is one of the fields of Graphic Design. Mobile apps are used as the output of this design because they are in accordance with the target, specifically parents who prioritize ease in their daily activities. To achieve the engagement of design functions and user needs, in this study the AISAS (Attention, Interest, Search, Action, Share) approach is used as a conceptual strategy to attract the user's attention to find out more about this application. Besides that, boarding schools will also place ad banners to advertise their boarding school environment.

Figure 1.   Strategy to attract the user's attention: (1) stand banner, (2) poster (both placed at boarding school) and (3) billboard and (4) poster (both placed in public places).

After the users see large-scale advertisements, they will be able to use this application by downloading it at which point they will see promotional media, such as social media, brochures, and x-banners, are placed there by their school. Users can download this application on the Google Playstore or Apple Store, followed by downloading and using this application as a medium to monitor their children's development so as to meet their needs.

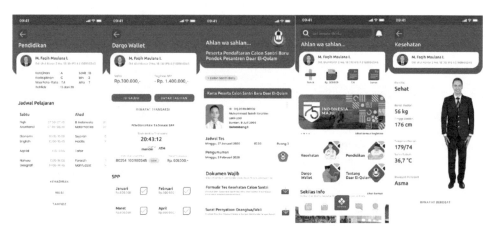

Figure 2.   Example of the mobile application, showing strategy for encouraging users to utilize the application.

Furthermore, after users use the design content contained in this application, they will share their experiences on social media sites such as Instagram, WhatsApp, Line, Facebook, and others.

4 CONCLUSIONS

Parents' concerns about wrong parenting, as well as the perception that children who attend a boarding school will be good children, can be seen as a solution to keep monitoring child development from both the point of view of the school and of parents. By utilizing UI/UX technology, it becomes possible for a parent to meet their child's needs while away from home.

The design of this application was carried out during the COVID-19 outbreak, which certainly made obtaining maximum data impossible. However, the design content that exists in the current design can be developed not only for boarding schools, but also for playgroups or daycare.

ACKNOWLEDGMENTS

The author would like to thank Mr. KH. Ody Roshihuddin, Chairman of the Islamic Boarding School Daar El-Qolam, for allowing us to conduct interviews, as well as the teachers of the school who helped the process by collecting data such as questionnaires and observations in the midst of the current pandemic. It is expected that the outcome of this research will enable parents to mee the needs of their children by monitoring their growth and development.

REFERENCES

Azizah, Nur. 2013. *Dukungan Orangtua Bagi Anak yang Belajar di Pondok Pesantren. Prosiding Seminar Nasional Parenting*. STAIN Purwokerto: 133–141.

Devi, Linggarsari, and Pihasniwati. 2017. *Hubungan antara Komunikasi antara Orang Tua-Anak dengan Penyesuaian Diri Santri di Pondok Pesantren Tradisional dan Modern*. UIN Sunan Kalijaga Yogyakarta.

Fatimah, E. 2008. *Psikologi Perkembangan: Perkembangan Peserta Didik*. Bandung. Pustaka Setia.

Fawaid, Achmad and Hasanah Uswatun. 2020. *Pesantren dan Religious Authoritative Parenting: Studi Kasus Sistem Wali Asuh di Pondok Pesantren Nurul Jadid*. Ilmu Ushuluddin 19(1):27–40.

Hasbullah, Drs. 1999. *Sejarah Pendidikan Islam di Indonesia: Lintasan Sejarah Pertumbuhan dan Perkembangan*. Jakarta: PT Raja Grafindo Persada.

Katz, Adrienne. 1997. *Membimbing Anak Belajar Membaca*. Alih Bahasa: Liliana Wijaya. Arcan: Jakarta.

Monica, Anggita Eva. 2017. *Hubungan Kelekatan Orangtua-Anak dengan Keperecayaan Diri Santri Pondok Pesantren di Surakarta*. Universitas Surakarta.

Nurjanah and Heryadi, Adi. 2020. *Jurnal Psikogenesis: Kelekatan Orang Tua dan Kecerdasan Sosial pada Remaja di Pondok Pesantren Modern*. STIPSI Yogyakarta.

Soewardikoen, D. W. 2013. *Metodologi Penelitian Visual*. Bandung: Dinamika Komunikasi.

Digital technology and cultural evolution

Dynamics of Industrial Revolution 4.0: Digital Technology Transformation and Cultural Evolution –
Wulandari et al (eds)
© 2021 The Author(s), ISBN 978-1-032-04451-4

Investigating the Zen concept in the interior setting to engage customer place attachment: An interior design for a Japanese restaurant in Bandung

D. Murdowo & S.M. Lazaref
Telkom University, Bandung, Indonesia

ABSTRACT: This study investigates how a Japanese restaurant incorporates the attributes of Japanese culture and the Zen concept in its interior setting to engage customer place attachment. The research used a qualitative method with a case study at the Shabu Kojo restaurant in Bandung. Qualitative research was performed by conducting interviews and distributing questionnaires to customers. To implement the research, the Zen concept was applied in the form of natural colors, shapes, artificial lighting, and traditional furniture with Kanji letters, as well as comfortable rooms for gathering. The research demonstrated that the principles of the Zen concept, style of Japanese culture, and Japanese philosophy can be used to produce interior design and engage customer attachment. These research findings will be a reference for to enrich further research.

Keywords: interior setting, customer place attachment, Zen concept, Japanese restaurant

1   INTRODUCTION

Most customers visiting ethnic restaurants expect to engage in place attachment and experience the authentic atmosphere of the restaurant's origin. The phenomenon of place attachment is one potentially important characteristic of satisfied and loyal customers (Rojak & Cole 2015). One aspect that supports place attachmen is its interior design. As has been stated by Andreani et al. (2013), the unique and ancient interior and exterior design of a restaurant can easily attract consumers. In fact, a restaurant's interior design is one of the essential factors that helps make a restaurant a destination (Rahma et al. 2017). Meanwhile, Levy & Weitz (2001) state that adequate interior design creates a feeling of comfort, pleasure, relaxation, and calm that creates a feeling of satisfaction from the customer. The Shabu Kojo restaurant is a typical Japanese traditional-style restaurant designed to connect it to Japanese culture via its interior design. Some traditional Japanese ambiance applications are used such as in lighting, furniture, and atmosphere.

Based on the observations conducted through customer interviews and questionnaires at the Shabu Kojo restaurant, a restaurant's interior design aspects that best represent Japanese culture and philosophy are its atmosphere, colors, natural materials, lighting and ambience, furniture, and comfortable private rooms. However, the Shabu Kojo restaurant has not applied all those representations. Therefore, there is a need to create an interior design that will engage customer place attachment. This study investigated the restaurant's visitor experience and comfort perceptions and then demonstrated how to apply the Zen concept in a Japanese restaurant.

The Zen concept as a Japanese cultural principle is well known among Indonesians. The Zen concept is a classic trend that brings a sense of peace and balance. The principle in Zen interior is to balance the arrangement of life and the rooms, life in the room and the room itself are two things that affect each other (Ashralika 2019). Wirayuda (2020) explains that the Zen concept can be applied to in the following ways: (1) color selection; (2) shapes; (3) lighting and ambience;

Figure 1.　Color application. (Source: Personal Documentation, 2020).

(4) furniture; and (5) comfortable private rooms. Therefore, there is a need to improve Sabu Kojo restaurant's aesthetics and functionality so as to be strongly identified as a Japanese restaurant.

2　RESEARCH METHODS

The research uses a qualitative method with a case study from the Sabu Kojo restaurant in Bandung. The restaurant was chosen as the research object because it is one of the local Japanese restaurants with a definite connection to Japanese culture.

The research started from data observation and data collection by interviewing 4 customers and distributing 20 questionnaires. The interviews and questionnaires explored how the existing interior represented Japanese culture, as well as questions about the overall interior and expectations of what interior could be. The next step was analyzing what concept was relevant to customer expectation. The final step was to design the interior.

3　RESULTS AND DISCUSSION

3.1　*Theme and concept design*

The Zen concept is a classic trend that can bring a sense of peace and balance. The theme design of this Japanese restaurant was "beauty is the harmony of purpose and style" and the atmosphere created by the interior was comfortable, warm, friendly, and homey.

3.2　*Color application*

Zen is the path to enlightenment and its design theory is based on light. The theory of color psychology mentions that brown is identical to something natural. These colors have the power to create relaxation and calm. The colors expressed by light are the calmest and most harmonious when the colors are natural like sunlight (Ashralika 2019). Darker colors evoke different moods and can be preferred in different dining situations, leading to different colors choices for tableware (Bao et al. 2018). When the color white is used properly, it is an effect that will not disappoint. The use of natural colors is the hallmark of the Zen concept, as seen in Figure 1.

3.3　*Architectural shape*

The application of interior shapes such as rectangles to the design theme brings in the feeling of natural resources which correlates to the principle of Japanese life that it is important to always

Figure 2.   Implementation of natural resources. (Source: www.google.com).

Figure 3.   Lighting application (Source: www.pinterest.com).

being close to nature (Widjaja 2013) and in harmony with nature (Inayah 2017). The restaurant wall is designed to resemble the shape of a traditional Japanese house to give the impression of being in a Japanese environment (Figure 2), further enhanced with aesthetic elements such as paintings, ornaments, and lanterns that adorn other dining areas. In addition to massive walls, temporary walls are used in the stretch area to maintain privacy between customers. The partition that would use shoji is a panel made of a wooden frame and transparent paper, with the addition of a curtain cloth to better maintain customer privacy.

3.4 *Lighting*

The implementation of lighting in restaurant can be divided into two categories: natural and artificial (Figure 3). Natural lighting is optimized through relatively large glass windows with Japanese patterned shading. Artificial lighting uses general lighting and accent lighting used in the form of hanging lamps, downlights, and track lamps. Hanging lamps are used in the circulation and dining areas, as general lighting and accent lighting use lanterns installed in each bulkhead between the tatami dining areas. Chandelier lights are used in the buffet area. The lighting is bright to accommodate cooking and eating activities, but the outside dining area is relatively dimmer by only using hidden lights on the floor area for direction, in addition to a hanging lamp that further lights the way.

3.5 *Furniture*

The furniture concept based on the Zen style is designed with simple characteristics and natural materials. The main furniture application concept is used in the form of a dining table and tatami made of wood and bamboo, serving as a dining area. Other supporting accessories used in restaurants are Japanese decorative accessories, such as typical Japanese paintings and Japanese patterns. According to Rucitra & Permatasari (2017), chair furniture is designed according to function, while still paying attention to elements of Japanese culture such as the shape of the Kanji letters and the application of Kanji in the form of chair furniture designs (Figure 4).

Figure 4. Kanji letters in furniture application (Source: Personal Documentation 2017).

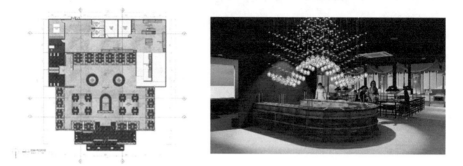

Figure 5. Buffet area visualization. (Source: Personal Documentation 2020).

3.6 *Space classification and a comfortable room*

Customer expectations of a comfortable room can be designed with two dining areas, namely a public dining area that has a four-seat tatami dining area and a six-seat tatami dining area. The classification of the space is based on the needs and activities that occur in the restaurant during the activity.

Figure 5 showcases the design of the buffet area. The center of visitor activities takes place inside the restaurant so this area is in the middle making easier to access for visitors. The application of wood on the buffet table and natural stone on the walls creates a natural atmosphere that increases the comfort of visitors.

4 CONCLUSION

This study examined the Sabu Kojo restaurant, a Japanese restaurant in Bandung. The restaurant's Japanese design style has a theme of "beauty is the harmony of purpose and style."

The application of the Zen concept is represented by calm and harmonious colors. Architectural shapes such as rectangles are designed for using natural materials such as exposed concrete flooring, tatami, and granite that are applied in paintings, ornaments, and dining area. Natural lighting is applied through large glass windows with Japanese patterned shading, meanwhile artificial lighting is used in the form of hanging lamps, downlights, and track lamps. The furniture concepts applied in the dining table and tatami are made of wood and bamboo in the shape of the Kanji letters. The comfortable room is designed as a public dining area that features a large sitting table in the middle of the room at which one can relax and be comfortable together.

The Zen concept can meet customer place attachment which can enrich the customer experience. This research can be used a reference for other ethnic restaurants.

REFERENCES

Andreani, F., Kristanti, M., and Yapola, A. 2013. Pengaruh Store Layout, Interior Display, Human Variable Terhadap Customer Shopping Orientation di Restoran Dewandaru Surabaya. *Jurnal Manajemen dan Kewirausahaan*, 15(1), 65–74.

Ashralika, P. A. 2019. Menyeimbangkan Hidup & Mendapatkan Suasana Menenangkan dengan Zen Interior Design. Retrieved from interiordesign.id: https://interiordesign.id/menyeimbangkan-hidup-zen-interior-design/.

Suomiya Bao, Yusuke Shokawa, Satoshi Suzuki, and Toshimasa Yamanaka. 2018. Exploring the Role of Color in Dining Experience: Preference and Relationship between Tableware Color and Dining Scenes in Japanese Young Females. *International Journal of Affective Engineering*, 17(1), 19–26.

Inayah, N. H. 2017. Gaya Desain Zen, Ciptakan Suasana Ruang dengan Keseimbangan dan Keselarasan yang Sempurna. Retrieved from interiordesign.id: https://interiordesign.id/gaya-desain-zen/

Levy, M. and Weitz, B. 2001. *Retailing Management*, 4th Edition. New York: McGraw Hill Irwin.

Rahma, Miranti Sari, Prabu Wardono, and Lies Neni Budiarti. 2017. Pengaruh Elemen Interior Restoran terhadap Pengalaman Nostalgia Konsumen. *Journal of Visual Art & Desain Institut Teknologi Bandung*, 9(2), 67–86.

Rojak, D. and Cole, L.B. 2015. Place Attachment and the Historic Brewpub: A Case Study in Greensboro, North Carolina. *Journal of Interior Design* 41(1), 33–50.

Rucitra, A. R. and Permatasar, R. A. L. 2017. Dekorasi Gaya Jepang dalam Desain Interior. *Jurnal Dimensi Interior*, 15(1), 56–61.

Widjaja, E. 2013. Studi Terapan Gaya Desain Interior Jepang Restoran Tomoto, Imari, Kayu, Nishiki Surabaya. *Jurnal INTRA*, 1(1), 1–10.

Wirayuda, Wisesa. (2020). *7 Alasan Mengapa Desain Gaya Zen Patut Dipilih untuk Hunian.* Retrieved from: https://narasidesign.com/7-alasan-mengapa-desain-gaya-zen-patut-dipilih-untuk-hunian/.

Dynamics of Industrial Revolution 4.0: Digital Technology Transformation and Cultural Evolution –
Wulandari et al (eds)
© 2021 The Author(s), ISBN 978-1-032-04451-4

Visualization of Indonesian culture as backgrounds in Pocari Sweat Ads "Bintang SMA"

A. Syafikarani, T.R. Deanda & G.P. Nabila
Telkom University, Bandung, Indonesia

ABSTRACT: COVID-19 made the advertising business drop forcing shifts in its media strategy toward digital media. One of them is by using animation media, such as the Pocari Sweat animation ad "Bintang SMA", where the ad also carries some cultural values. This research studies how Indonesian culture is represented in the animated background of the Pocari Sweat animation ad "Bintang SMA". The data obtained from case studies, documentation, and distributing questionnaires methods were analyzed using the theory of cultural movement and local culture. From this study, it is known that the Indonesian culture is represented in Balinese and Jakarta culture through location, architecture, and property settings. The results of this research can be used as input for those involved in the world of advertising, especially in compiling an animated media advertisement by raising cultural elements as an advertising solution in the middle of the pandemic.

Keywords: advertising, animation, Indonesian culture, Japanese visual style, COVID-19

1 INTRODUCTION

The COVID-19 pandemic has triggered a decline in activity in various fields, including in the world of advertising. As stated by the Association of Indonesian Advertising Companies (P3I), the advertising business has decreased by 35% from March to April in the last two months. This requires creative industry players to innovate in making advertising strategies and adjusting to the current situation. According to Janoe Arijanto, chairman of P3I, the advertising industry is currently trying to encourage "goodvertising", which is a form of communication that is more empathetic, relevant, and provides solutions to the complexities experienced by the public (Jawa Pos 2020).

This is because the pandemic is expanding and the work from home policy has also increased as has watching television and internet consumption. Therefore, brands are starting to shift their media strategy toward digital by using simple and efficient material without reducing their advertising goals and intentions. One of the efforts that can be made by a brand in advertising with simple and efficient media is using animation media. By switching to using animation media, it can be a substitute for shooting commercials that are done directly at several shooting locations. Therefore, this can be used as an alternative to keep health protocols running during a pandemic and remain productive to increase the creative economy. This is also supported by the results of the questionnaire that showed that 97% of respondents stated that animated ads were effective in delivering product promotions and 97.3% also stated that animated advertisements could be used as an alternative choice for an advertising solution during the COVID-19 pandemic. Therefore, in this study, researchers introduced a case study on the animated advertisement of the Pocari Sweat "Bintang SMA", where the advertisement carried several cultural values which were met with the right momentum, namely the limited production of advertisements due to the COVID-19 pandemic and taking advantage of the development of the Makoto illustration style trend, who is very popular in the world of animation. So, the creative industry movement is not just a fleeting trend, not just a lifestyle, but a continuous opportunity. This also fits perfectly with the concept of goodvertising that is being developed. In previous research conducted by the Munggaran, entitled "The Meaning

DOI 10.1201/9781003193241-62

of Cumulonimbus Clouds as Background Art in the Animated Film The Girl Who Leapt Through Time by Mamoru Hosoda", it is known that the background has an important role and it contains a representation of culture (Munggaran 2019).

This paper stated that natural objects, namely clouds in Japanese animation, contain certain meanings in Japanese culture. There it can be seen that the background has a role that is no less important than the presence of characters. However, there has been no further research that discusses the representation of Indonesian culture on an animated background, therefore this study intends to study how Indonesian culture is represented in the animated background of the Pocari Sweat advertisement "Bintang SMA". So that the results of this study can be used as input for parties involved in the world of advertising, especially in compiling an animated media advertisement by raising cultural elements as an advertising solution amid the COVID-19 pandemic.

2 RESEARCH METHOD

This research is included in the qualitative paradigm. Research was conducted by looking at specific patterns is then developed into more general patterns and aims to generate hypotheses from field research. This is supported by Judistira K. Garna's statement which states that a qualitative approach is characterized by the aim of the researcher who seeks to understand symptoms in such a way that does not require quantification, or because these symptoms are not possible to measure quickly (Afdjani 2010). The method used is a case study on advertisements that are in accordance with the research objectives, namely the animated ad Pocari Sweat "Bintang SMA". This is because the ad has succeeded in attracting the attention of the audience. On YouTube, the advertisement has been watched more than 14,714,720 times. Besides that, the Japanese anime-style illustration style wrapped with the diversity of Indonesian culture makes the advertisement have its own charm. Data collection techniques used are field studies to obtain primary data obtained through documentation and collecting animated media advertisements in image format derived from recorded advertisements on YouTube media. As well as distributing questionnaires online, to obtain data on audience perceptions of the animated Pocari Sweat "Bintang SMA" ad. From the distribution of the questionnaire obtained data of 303 respondents, with a dominant age between 15–20 years, who are in junior high and high school. In addition, a literature study was also carried out to obtain secondary data through books, journals, articles, and some literature on internet sites. The data that has been obtained is analyzed using the visual discourse analysis method, a method that has a function to find meaning and discourse in a work based on capital such as visual, verbal, and sound (Kress & Leeuwen 2006). In addition, it is supported by cultural movement theory, which is a theory that explains that a brand is not just designing a logo and developing a narrative but is much more fundamental, namely re-coding it culturally or culturally (Hendroyono 2019).

3 RESULT AND DISCUSSION

The 60-second Pocari Sweat animation ad "Bintang SMA" tells the story of two students: Ayu slive in Bali and Reza lives in Jakarta. Both want to achieve their goals by participating in Bintang SMA. This ad is directed by Shinomiya Yoshitoshi, a Japanese animator who is heavily involved in animation production, especially in the case of illustration and background design. Some of the anime that he has worked on are anime by director Makoto Shinkai, such as "Children Who Chase Lost Voices", "The Garden of Words", and "Your Name" (Kusumanto 2019). Therefore, this ad also utilizes the right momentum by carrying the nuances of the Japanese anime style to represent the origin of the Pocari Sweat drink, but still wrapped in the diversity of Indonesian culture as local wisdom where the ad is located. Based on the results of the questionnaire, obtained data showed that the background scenes that stand out in representing Indonesian culture are the statue scene at 74.4%, the Bundaran HI scene at 66.8%, the offering scene at 60.5%, the school gate scene at 58.8%, class atmosphere scenes at 48.8%, kite festival scenes at 33.9%, bus stop scenes at 19.9%, and Wisma 46 scenes at 7.6%. Therefore, this research will be divided into three parts, First, the school which consists of the school gate scene and classroom atmosphere. Second, Bali, which consists of a statue sculpture scene, a scene of offerings, and a kite festival scene. Third, Jakarta, which consists of the Bundaran HI, bus stop, and Wisma 46 scenes. After that, each of these parts will be analyzed more deeply based on the location, architecture, and supporting properties because based on the results of the questionnaire, 59.8% stated that the architecture of these animated advertisements had a majorly contributed to representing Indonesian culture.

3.1 *School*

a. Location Settings

The ad begins with a frame that shows the location setting of a school by displaying two different school gates side by side. In image (1), the background is seen in the form of buildings and gates of Bintang Pratama and Ganesha Denpasar High Schools. The gate as the "face" of a building is used as a sign of place identity (Pattymahu 2016), supported by the placement of scenes in the first frame. In one frame, there are two gate facades with two different identities. On the left side, the gate structure is commonly found in schools in Indonesia. On the right side of the frame, local identity is more focused on Balinese culture, which can be seen from the variety of decorations and archways. In picture (2), the building background is visible and there are windows, curtains, and poster frames. This shows that the background of this frame is in the form of classrooms of Bintang Pratama High School and Denpasar Ganesha High School. This frame shows that at the beginning of the ad the chosen location setting has been explained in this animated advertisement, which shows that modern urban locations are represented through the Bintang Pratama High School. From success comes growth, which is in line with urban conditions that are moving toward modernization. In addition, locations that represent regions can be seen throughout the dominant Ganesha Denpasar High School that use brown as a symbol of simplicity, classics, and tradition. Besides the frames that are displayed in parallel, it also represents that the frame intends to compare two different locations with the same time or condition.

3.2 *Bali*

a. Location Settings

The next frame shows the location setting of Bali which represents Ayu's residence. The Dvarapala statue, flower offerings, and the Balinese kite festival characterize the unique atmosphere of the island of Bali. If analyzed further, Bali Island is the choice of setting of this animated ad location because it represents the regional lifestyle in Indonesia which is still calm and beautiful. This is because Bali, despite being a tourist destination visited by tourists from abroad, can still maintain its local culture so that it becomes a special attraction for tourists. Therefore, Indonesia, besides being known as having Jakarta as its capital, is also known as Bali as a tourist area that is thick with Indonesia's local culture.

b. Architecture

The identity of Balinese culture in this advertisement animation was first shown through the first scene at the school gate. The school gate is filled with Balinese decoration. The decoration on the Balinese architectural gate has a symbolic meaning which also is used as a sign of building function and the position of the building owner (Suryada 2011), whereas the Balinese-style ornamental gates shown in this animation represent no special forms or motives that have any particular meaning behind it. It's just that from the material and shape used, it's enough to show the identity of typical Balinese architecture.

c. Properties

- Dvarapala Statue

  According to Arina (2019), the Dvarapala statue consists of a pair of large muscular statues with bulging eyes, a large fanged smiling smile, and usually carries a mace in charge of guarding the temple gate. It has a philosophical and deep meaning behind it. This statue is believed to reflect human beings who will enter the sacred area and remind them to be introspective and clear their thoughts, actions, and words.

- Bali Kite Festival

  The Bali Kite Festival is an international event that is held on an annual basis in Padang Galak, Sanur, Bali. There are various forms of kites shown in this event, such as fish (*Bebean*), birds (*Janggan*), and leaves (*Pecukan*). Usually, people fly and compete with traditional giant kites. This is wrapped by religious events with the intention of sending messages to Hindu gods so that they can bless them with abundant agricultural produce (Freidin 1989).

- Offerings

  Offerings are offerings to Hindu deities, usually in the form of flowers or food. The offerings are placed in a container (such as a leaf or tray) and placed in a certain place. The Balinese have a belief that if they make their offerings they will be kept away from bad luck and will be blessed with safety and prosperity (Tracy 2016).

3.3 *Jakarta*

a Architecture

The location shows the hustle and bustle of the city of Jakarta such as the Bundaran HI and Bung Karno bus stop. This can immediately inform the audience that these two student residences have very different atmospheres. The frame that shows Jakarta's city landscape which is a metropolitan city can be seen from skyscrapers and the dense traffic conditions that are the face of Jakarta. One of the landscapes that became the icon of the city of Jakarta in this animation is the Selamat Datang Monument which is located right in the middle of the Bundaran HI or the Bundaran Hotel Indonesia and the Bung Karno Bus Stop. Besides that, the pen-shaped blue skyscraper clearly visible in the Reza scene inside the subway is Wisma 46, which is the second tallest building in Indonesia after Gama Tower (Wahyudewi

2016). With its unique shape, Wisma 46 is one of Jakarta's most notable icons, besides the National Monument.

4 CONCLUSION

From the analysis provided here, it can be concluded that Indonesian culture is represented in the background of the Pocari Sweat advertisement "Bintang SMA" through the location, architecture, and property settings. The Indonesian culture presented in this animated advertisement is Balinese culture, which is thick with various decorations in the form of carvings both in architecture and property, such as the Dvarapala statue and events such as the kite festival and offerings. Meanwhile, the culture or lifestyle of Jakarta is conveyed through architecture such as skyscrapers like Wisma 46 and the Welcome Monument, as well as the congested traffic conditions at the HI Roundabout or the Hotel Indonesia Roundabout. The animated Pocari Sweat ad "High School Star" shows that cultural values are the main concept in their advertisements. In recent times, a brand will increasingly exist if it has strong ties to certain cultural values (Hendroyono 2019). Makoto Shinkai's beautiful visual style and detail are at the peak of his fame and are utilized in this animated advertisement which can attract buying interest from certain groups. This is also being developed in the world of advertising in this pandemic era, which is called "goodvertising". Besides, when viewed from the media selection in the form of animation, based on the results of the questionnaire, it can be concluded that animated advertisements are effective in promoting products and can be used as alternative advertising choices during the pandemic. Thus, it can be understood that making an advertisement is not only about persuasion and selling products or services, but also must pay attention to the situation and take advantage of opportunities, enabling the brand to survive through various situations.

REFERENCES

Afdjani, H. 2010. Makna Iklan Televisi (Studi Fenomenologi Pemirsa di Jakarta terhadap Iklan Televisi Minuman " Kuku Bima Energi" Versi Kolam Susu. *Jurnal Ilmu Komunikasi,* (8)1:96.
Arina, M. 2019. *Mengenal Dwarapala, Patung Penjaga Tempat Suci di Bali*, Etnis, accessed July 10, 2020, < https://etnis.id/mengenal-dwarapala-patung-penjaga-tempat-suci-di-bali/>
Freidin, S. 1989. *Return to Bali.* Kite Lines, 7(3)31–35.
Hendroyono, H. 2019. *Artisan Brand, kenapa Begitu Penting?* Jakarta: PT Gramedia.
Kress, G. and Leeuwen T. V. 2006. *Reading Images: The Grammar of Visual Design*, Taylor and Francis Group, pp. 46–214, New York.
Kusumanto, D. 2019. Yoshitoshi Shinomiya Berbagi Cerita tentang Pembuatan TVC Pocari Sweat - Bintang SMA, Kaori Nusantara, October 25, 2019, https://www.kaorinusantara.or.id/newsline/138511/yoshitoshi-shinomiya-berbagi-cerita-tentang-pembuatan-tvc-pocari-sweat-bintang-sma.
Munggaran, G.A. 2019. Representasi Awan Cumulonimbus Pada Background Art Film Animasi Jepang. *Prosiding Seminar Animasi dan Visual Media Digital.* Jakarta, September 19, 2020.
Pattymahu, D. R. 2016. Gerbang Sebagai Pembentuk Identitas Kota Studi Kasus Koridor Jalan Trans Sulawesi Di Malalayang Manado, *Daseng: Jurnal Arsitektur*, 5(2,3): 68–82.
Pilihan Promosi yang Tepat dalam Masa Pandemi Covid-19, Jawa Pos, June 26, 2020, Accessed July 25, 2020, < https://www.jawapos.com/ekonomi/26/06/2020/pilihan-promosi-yang-tepat-dalam-masa-pandemi-covid-19/>.
Pocari Sweat Bintang SMA. 2020. online video, accessed July 1, 2020, < https://www.youtube.com/watch?v=DCfk7tc_KqE>
Suryada, I.G.A.B. 2011. Varian-varian Ornament di Bagian Atas Lubang Pintu Masuk Bangunan Gerbang Berlanggam. *Jurnal Sulapa* 3(1):17–28.
Tracy, M. 2016. Menginjak Sesajen di Bali Bisa Celaka?, Pegi Pegi, accessed 1 July 2020, < https://www.pegipegi.com/travel/menginjak-sesajen-di-bali-bisa-celaka/>
Wahyudewi, P. 2016. Ini Dia 10 Gedung Pencakar Langit Tertinggi di Indonesia, *IDN Times*, accessed August 20, 2020, < https://www.idntimes.com/hype/fun-fact/putri-wahyudewi/ini-dia-10-gedung-pencakar-langit-tertinggi-di-indonesia/10>

Dynamics of Industrial Revolution 4.0: Digital Technology Transformation and Cultural Evolution –
Wulandari et al (eds)
© 2021 The Author(s), ISBN 978-1-032-04451-4

Adaptable and Instagrammable features in the interior of a University Library

A.D. Purnomo, N. Laksitarini & A.N. Jihad
Telkom University, Bandung, Indonesia

ABSTRACT: The existence of a library is very important for the sustainability of a university. However, in reality there is still the assumption that a library is just a complement to accreditation. In addition, libraries aren't being used as much by current millennial academics who are more interested in and pampered by gadgets than visiting to the library. The ease of getting information, entertainment, and socialization can be found online, therefore the university library needs to change from rows of bookshelves and tables to a more varied of layout. This paper examines the interior of modern and contemporary university libraries. Being adaptable and instagrammable becomes one of the considerations of a library's updated interior. The research methodology is implemented using the descriptive qualitative method at the Open Library at Telkom University, Bandung. The conclusion of this paper is that a university library must support "work–leisure–learning" activities.

Keywords: adaptable, instagrammable, interior, library

1 INTRODUCTION

The changing world of technology requires that every aspect of our lives to adapt, and universities are no exception. The university campuses of old must transform themselves into appearing young, energetic, and fun. Their learning atmospheres must be created with enthusiastic "work–leisure–learning" in mind so as to appeal to the current generation cof college students (Kasali 2013).

The existence of a library is at the very core of a higher education institution and can been seen as the "the heart of university" (Darwanto 2015; Mubasyaroh 2016). The library is a vital facility for the improvement and sustainability of a university. But in reality, many at the university assume that a library only acts a complement for the school and that its function is sub-optimal at best. Few in the academic community take advantage of that facility. The academic community, especially lecture and college students, are dominated by millennials who are all-too familiar with electronic gadgets. They are the modern generation born between 1980–2000, and, generally, this generation tends to place more trust in user-generated content (UGC) than unidirectional information, prefers cellphones to TVs, must have social media, do not like to read conventionally, more flexible with commitment at works, conduct cashless transaction, know more about technology, utilizing information, and communication technology, multitask, and tend to be lazy and consumptive (Hidayatullah 2018). Therefore, this generation sees the world differently than previous generations, lives in an online world, and uses social media as a tool for expression and to make a living. (Kasali 2017).

The interior of a building is a form of a built environment that embodies all human activities. The physical, physiological, and psychological needs of humans factor into the design of a room (Rengel 2016). The library is not only a place but also a space that encompasses a lot of activities, from user interactions to a room for creating a learning atmosphere. As the millennial generation has very different way of studying than their previous generations (Ertel 2019; Priyanto 2015), a modern library's interior needs to support their needs.

Andrew McDonald said there are ten factors plus one that important to note in the ideal library interior: functional, adaptable, accessible, varied, interactive, conducive, environmentally suitable, safe and secure, efficient, equipped with information technology, and the extra factor "the oomph' or 'wow' (Letimer 2007). Adaptable is important for libraries to be able to change and adapt to the changing times. While the factor 'the oomph' or with terms 'wow' means that the library not only becomes an inspirational and fun room but it also gives spirit for the academic community. In the end, the library has the function to not only as a place to lend a book and read it but can also be a place to create an atmosphere 'work-leisure-learning'. For it, interior design for the library is important to note character from the user, such as age, gender, culture, and other (Majidah 2019).

2 METHOD

This paper analyzes the interior design of the Open Library at Telkom University (Openlib Tel-U) in Bandung, West Java. The modern library is located at Telecommunications Street no.1, Sukapura, Terusan Buah Batu, Bandung, and encompasses an area of 3200 m^2 with a total collection of 150,971 books and 95,891 titles. The vision of Openlib Tel-U is to become the leader of the scientific center with world-class governance. The missions are active in knowledge acquisition, knowledge management, and knowledge sharing, active in reading and writing improvement in the community, and working together with institutions that have the same vision. The interior design has a "green futuristic" concept and international standard.

The descriptive qualitative research method was used. The primary data was obtained by field observation and interviews with the developer and respondents who are students. Secondary data was obtained from printed as well as electronic (internet) literature. Printed literature includes reference books and newspapers while electronic literature involves websites, profile videos, Instagram, blogs, social media, scientific journals, and online proceedings.

3 RESULT

3.1 Interior of Openlib Tel-U

The interior of Openlib Tel-U utilizes green futuristic and modern concepts. The interior layout is split into three areas. The left side consists of a special collection room, a reading area, library café, and discussion rooms. The right side is utilized for general book collections, a reading area, discussion rooms, a mini theater, and a sit-down reading area. The middle area consists of the circulation area and a reading area equipped with tables, chairs, and sofas, utilizing an open area without any partitions. Several corners of the area are attractively designed with sofas and bookshelves. The interior concept minimalizes the use of a partition, and only discussion rooms have a glass partition. The application of colorful and bright colors on the wall provide fresh and cheerful stimulation for the users.

3.2 Adaptable for Library interior

Being adaptable means being able to easily and quickly adjust, and be inconsistent and flexible. Adaptable concepts can also mean something that is not monotonous. The nature of adaptability in a room includes three components: expandability, convertibility, and versatility. Adaptable spaces can accommodate expansion, change in function, and provide multifunctional space (Ballast 2007). The adaptable concept in the Openlib Tel-U interior was applied with minimal implementation of a massive wall so as to maximize the use of an open space concept. The impressions of an adaptable concept and the feeling of friendliness can be experienced once entering the center area. A curved partition gives a familiar but not rigid impression. The ability to change or expand in the future as needs change was also considered. The computer area for internet browsing was restricted with

Figure 1. The reading area provides an information feeling. (Source: desinovs.blogspot.com).

Figure 2. The steps used to sit. (Source: openlibrary.telkomuniveristy.ac.id).

an iron pipe mounted vertically, as if a giant birdcage was surrounding the computer desk. The reading area with bookshelves is separated with different floor heights and does not use a closed partition.

The adaptable concept was also seen in the reading area with the procurement of furniture variations. There are several reading areas and discussions room with no seats. This situation giaves an informal and more relaxed impression. Meanwhile, near the bookshelf area there is a multifunctional stair. That stair connects the bookshelf area to the mezzanine floor which uses the reading area. The stair is used as the way to go up and down to the mezzanine floor. Some part of the stairs are utilized as seating and reading areas. Some areas are equipped with a sofa for reading with in more relaxed position. The rest of the area consists of tables and upright chairs for single users or groups.

Most furniture layout and interior elements are in the form for a cursve, following the room's shape to create an exciting and fun atmosphere. The atmosphere is informal, curved in shape, and furniture can be dragged out for interaction and to attract communication. Also, the material used in the seating facility at the lobby and book display are made of materials that give a bright and light impression. Some area even use a short table for a writing facility so the user can sit on the floor that utlizes synthetic grass. The use of colors that are not monotonous, and reading area placement makes user activity more interactive and supports a "work–leisure-learning" atmosphere.

3.3 *Instagrammable*

Instagram is one of the social media apps that is very popular with the millennial generation. Instagram is a platform whose usage is similar to their character—energic and up to date. The applicative social media is used to represent the user themself. Instagram makes it possible for a user to post a photo or video so that another follower can see and comment on it. The satisfaction

Figure 3. The midlle area as a photo spot. (Source: openlib.telkomuniveristy.ac.id).

of the user on Instagram is the effort to get the angle of shooting a photo as good as possible to appeared very excited or as it is known: "instagrammable". Millenials will always stay at a place for a long time if get they are instagrammable sites. Instagrammable pictures can be realized via an interesting interior pattern.

Based on student respondents at Telkom University, an area that is considered quite interesting and instagrammable is the middle area of Openlib Tel-U due to its stair and ramp that connect it to the mezzanine, the birdcage area, the colors used, and the corner reading area. The middle area of the Openlib Tel-U is the first area that vistor enters into. The circulation in the service room is radial, and its counter table is marked by a curve as a focal point. The stair and ramp on the left side has a stair and ramp is seen as an instagrammable spot because its radial pattern is quite interesting. The use of the green artificial grass floor covering provides a connection to a futuristic green concept.

The entrance of the book collection area also has an instagrammable design. Besides the function as an access to the reading room in the upper floor, the stair can be used as a seat. The red color on the cushions is in contrast with the reading room area. This is the focal point, so the sub-stair is used as a photo spot area.

The birdcage area is shaped as a radial area that is made similar to a birdcage by using iron pipe and finished a white color. It is an area for browsing the internet and is very memorable and always remembered by librarians because it is unique and instangrammable.

The discussion rooms are available for visitor use and and the sizes of the rooms vary. Each room uses a different color and features inspirational quotes on the wall. By using a fresh color, it makes the atmosphere of the discussion room more lively. Color plays an important role and has the extraordinary power to remove emotionality. The colorful discussion rooms are also photo spots used by the students.

4 CONCLUSION

The library at a university provides a big contribution to the provision of learning resources and information access for the academic community. A library with adaptable and instagrammable concept for the interior can create an interesting, and not monotonous, atmosphere. The use of fresh color and a curved shape concept for furniture and Openlib the Tel-U layout become important aspects of creating a fun learning atmosphere. Variation in learning areas provide college students with a way to obtain an alternative are for reading book or taking a test. Therefore, the interior of the library can support "work–leisure-learning", which is very suitable for the millennial generation. It is the hope that all of this will attract students to visit the library more often.

REFERENCES

Darwanto, Utami, Anggun Kusumah Tri, and Gusniawati, Nia. 2015. *Pedoman Penyelenggaraan Perpustakaan Perguruan Tinggi*. Jakarta: Perpustakaan Nasional Republik Indonesia.

Ertel, Monica. 2019. *Change Literacy: Digital, Collaborative, Creative*. Summary of the 2019 World Library and Information Congress Knowledge Cafe Program, August 27, 2019: Athens, Greece.

Hidayatullah, Syarif, Abdul Waris, Riezky Chris Devianti, Syafitrilliana Ratna Sari, Irawan Ardi Wibowo, and Pande Made PW. 2018. *Perilaku Generasi Milenial Dalam Menggunakan Aplikasi Go-Food*. Jurnal Manajemen dan Kewirausahaan, 6(2): 240–249.

Kasali, Rhenald. 2013. *Change!* Jakarta: PT. Gramedia Pustaka Utama.

Kasali, Rhenald. 2017. *Disruption*. Jakarta: PT. Gramedia Pustaka Utama.

Letimer, Karen and Hellen Niegaard. 2007. *IFLA Library Building Guidelines: Developments and Reflections*. Munchen: K. G. Saur Verlag.

Majidah, M., Hasfera, Dian, and Fadli, M. 2019. *Penggunaan Warna Dalam Desain Interior Perpustakaan Terhadap Psikologis Pemustakala*. Jurnal Bimbingan dan Konseling, 4(2):95–106.

Mubasyaroh. 2016. *Pengaruh Perpustakaan Bagi Peningkatan Mutu Pendidikan Perguruan Tinggi*. Jurnal Libraria, 4(1):77–104.

Priyanto, Ida F. 2015. *Perkembangan Baru Dalam Dunia Perpustakaan*. Makalah Seminar Universitas Brawijaya, Malang, September 29, 2015.

Rengel, Roberto J. 2016. *The Interior Plan – Concepts and Exercises*. New York: Bloomsbury.

Dynamics of Industrial Revolution 4.0: Digital Technology Transformation and Cultural Evolution –
Wulandari et al (eds)
© 2021 The Author(s), ISBN 978-1-032-04451-4

The influence of existing activities around public spaces on the selection of location and type of street vendors' business. Case study: Tegallega Park, Bandung, West Java

I. Sudarisman, M.B. Mustafa, M.H.B.M. Isa
Universiti Sains Malaysia, Penang, Malaysia

H.F.S. Rusyda
Telkom University, Bandung, Indonesia

ABSTRACT: The presence of street vendors who use public spaces as places of activity has caused various problems. Tegallega Park as a public space in the form of a park is also affected due to the presence of street vendors in it. This study aims to see and understand the relationship between activities around the park and the location selection and type of goods that are traded by street vendors. The research was conducted using a qualitative descriptive method. Data collection was carried out by observation and field documentation. Based on the results of the study, it was found that the level of crowd, type of activity, needs of the community, and goods traded around the park had an effect on the choice of location and goods sold by street vendors. This understanding can be used as a basis for consideration in planning public spaces.

Keywords: Tegallega Parks, existing activities, street vendors

1   INTRODUCTION

The number of migrants moving to the city driven by the need for better jobs and income cannot be matched by the growth of formal sector employment in the destination city. This condition causes migrants to find alternative employment or other sources of income to meet their daily needs through the informal economy. One form of the informal economy is street vendors. This phenomenon occurs in major cities in Indonesia, including Bandung.

Bandung as a big city that continues to grow has a great attraction for newcomers, so the growth in the number of street vendors also experiences a high increase. The number of street vendors in the city of Bandung in 2015 based on data from "Bappeda" reached 22,359 traders (Nugraha Ginanjar 2016).

McGee and Yeung (1977) mentioned that "hawkers as those people who offer goods or services for sale from public spaces, primarily streets and pavements". Siti Salamah & Luthfi Muta'ali (2019) stated that "street vendors generally grow and occupy strategic locations such as trading areas, residential areas, education areas and other public facilities that create attractiveness. These street vendors violate existing regulations because they grow in public spaces that can interfere with public activities, change the function of public spaces, and create a slum impression."

The street vendors use public spaces as a place to run their business. One of the public spaces that are favorite places is a city park.

1.1   *Tegallega Park*

Tegallega Park has a land area of 19.65 Ha (Muhammad Ramadhan & Pranggono 2018). Tegallega Park is used for various activities such as sports, playing, relaxing, ceremonies, night markets,

DOI 10.1201/9781003193241-64

music performances, and others by residents and the city government of Bandung. Tegallega Park in the center of Bandung has a strategic location, namely the main city road that connects the residential area with the city center and is surrounded by a variety of activities. This condition causes street vendors in large numbers to carry out their activities in Tegallega Park.

1.2 Street vendors and Tegallega Park problems

Street vendors occupy areas both inside and outside Tegallega Park. In carrying out their activities they tend to be in groups and can be differentiated based on the type of goods sold or the services they offer. The problem arose because Tegallega Park was not designed to facilitate their activities. Street vendors use various areas or facilities whose function is not to facilitate their activities. These problems cause a decrease in the physical condition of the park and discomfort for other park users, especially in the areas used by street vendors.

This study aims to see whether there is a relationship between existing activities outside the park with the location selection of street vendors to carry out their activities. This study also aims to look at the relationship between the types of existing activities with the types of merchandise and services offered by street vendors. Through this relationship, it is hoped that the consideration of street vendors in choosing a location and determining the types of goods or services they offer can be understood. The results of this study can be used as a basis for consideration of planning and designing public spaces such as parks in the city of Bandung. Planning a public space in the form of a park in the future is expected to consider the existence of street vendors as part of it and facilitate their needs, so that current public space problems due to the presence of street vendors can be anticipated.

2 RESEARCH METHODS

This research was conducted with a qualitative descriptive method, trying to understand a phenomenon experienced by researchers in this case is the behavior of street vendors in carrying out their activities in Tegallega Park and explaining it in words (Setyowati 2011). According to Sugiyono in Setyowati (2011), qualitative research uses a "social situation" which consists of three elements, namely: place, actors, and activities that interact synergistically.

This research was conducted by direct observation and data collection in the field of existing activities outside the park, as well as the location that was chosen by street vendors in conducting their commercial activities. Observations and data collection were also carried out on the types of goods traded and services offered by street vendors at each location in Tegallega Park. Then analysis and conclusions are drawn from the results of the field data to see the relationships that occur.

3 RESULTS AND DISCUSSION

3.1 Relationship between activities around the park and the location selection of street vendors

Tegallega Park is located in the southern part of Bandung city. The location of the park is flanked by roads connecting the southern area of the city with the city center. Tegallega Park in the east is bordered by Mohammad Toha Road, the western part is bordered by Otto Iskandardinata, and the south is bordered by the BKR road. Jalan Otto Iskandardinata is a road that connects Tegallega Park with the famous shopping center in Bandung, namely "Pasar Baru" and is a route for Bandung citizens returning to work or traveling from the city center. This road is passed by two kinds of mass public transportation, namely "angkot" (a vehicle that can accommodate 12 passengers) and city buses. On the west side of the park next to Otto Iskandardinata Street, there is a public transportation stop. Jalan Mohammad Toha is a route for city residents who will travel or work to the city center.

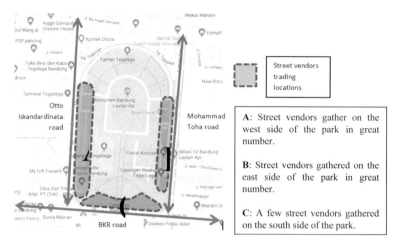

	Street vendors trading locations

A: Street vendors gather on the west side of the park in great number.

B: Street vendors gathered on the east side of the park in great number.

C: A few street vendors gathered on the south side of the park.

Figure 1. Map of Tegallega park, the road that borders the park area and the location of street vendors. (Source: Google maps & personal analysis).

Public transportation is "angkot" and buses via this road. On the eastern side of the park adjacent to Jalan Mohammad Toha there is a public transportation stop. Meanwhile, the BKR road is the main street of the city of Bandung, which serves as a gateway to the city for immigrants from outside the city of Bandung. This road is traversed by "angkot" and buses. There is also a public transportation stop in the part of the park next to this road. The three roads are very congested every day because many private vehicles, public vehicles, and pedestrians pass them so that congestion often occurs, especially during the hours of leaving for work (6–8 in the morning) and returning from work (4–6 in the afternoon).

The park area in the East and West is the area most densely occupied by street vendors because it is busy with the movement of vehicles and people, so the possibility of interaction between large traders and potential buyers occurs. In the southern area, there are not too many street vendors because this area is an area that is prohibited from being used as a place to sell by the city government. In that area, officers are stationed to keep it free from street vendors.

3.2 Relationship between activities around the park and the type of goods that are traded by street vendors

Types of street vendors who carry out business activities in Tegallega Park are grouped based on the goods sold or the services offered, namely:

- raw material traders: sell raw food ingredients for household needs such as vegetables, fruits, meat, fish, and cooking spices;
- food and beverage traders: sell ready-to-consume food and beverages;
- grocery dealer: sells household items;
- fashion traders: selling clothes, shoes, and accessories;
- electronics trader: sells a variety of electronic equipment;
- mixed trader: sells house decorations/decorations, toys, and others (family and home needs);
- sports equipment rental services: rent sports equipment;
- children's game rental services; renting out children's play services; and
- medical services: selling drugs and conducting medical therapy.

In the road section of Mohammad Toha, various activities that take place are household activities (residential areas), educational activities (school areas), and work activities (private and government office areas). In the eastern part of the park which is adjacent to Jalan Mohammad Toha, street

Figure 2.   Street vendors in the eastern part of Tegallega Park. (Source: personal).

Figure 3.   Street vendors in the western part of Tegallega Park. (Source: personal)

vendors gather and carry out their business activities around the park entrance. In addition, street vendors also gather in areas outside the park, namely along the pedestrian paths and along the roadside of motorized vehicles from Jalan Mohammad Toha. The street vendors selling in this area are dominated by raw material traders, food and beverage traders, grocery merchants, fashion traders, and mixed traders.

Based on observations and analysis, street vendors who are in the eastern area of the park choose the type of merchandise that is suitable or needed by the actors in the surrounding activities, such as providing for families, school children, and office employees.

On the road section of Otto Iskandardinata, the various activities that take place are household activities (residential areas) and commercial activities (shop and shop areas). This section of the road is known as a shopping area, and the famous shopping center in the area is "Pasar Baru". In the west part of the park which is adjacent to Otto Iskandardinata Street, street vendors gather and carry out their business activities around the park entrance. Also, street vendors gather in areas outside the park, namely along the pedestrian paths and along the roadside of motorized vehicles from Jalan Otto Iskandardinata. Street vendors selling in this area are dominated by food and beverage traders and fashion traders.

Based on observations and analysis, street vendors who are in the western part of the park choose the type of merchandise that is suitable or needed by the actors in the surrounding activities, such as providing for the needs of shoppers and shop employees in the Otto Iskandardinata area. In addition, street vendors also sell items that are similar or complementary to those sold in shops (the types of goods sold in shops are mostly fashion items) along Otto Iskandardinata Street, but at a more affordable price.

In the BKR road section, various activities that take place are household activities (residential areas), work activities (private and government office areas), and educational tourism activities (museums). In the southern part of the park which is adjacent to Jalan BKR, street vendors gather and carry out their business activities outside the park along the pedestrian path from Jalan BKR. The street vendors selling in this area are dominated by food and beverage traders.

Based on observations and analysis, street vendors who are in the southern part of the park choose the type of merchandise that is suitable or needed by the activity actors in the vicinity, such as office employees, pedestrians, and motorized vehicle users passing on the BKR road.

In the area south of the park, there are not many street vendors selling because this area has been designated by the city government as a prohibited area for street vendors to occupy. Apart from that, the municipal police officers, "Satpol PP", are assigned to guard the area so that there are few

Figure 4.   Street vendors in the southern part of Tegallega Park. (Source: personal).

street vendors, they do not sell various types of goods, and they only occupy the pedestrian lane outside the park.

4   CONCLUSION

Based on the above analysis, street vendors choose a place to run their business based on several considerations:

- There is a high movement of people or vehicles, allowing interaction with potential buyers.
- There are large associations of people who carry out various activities.
- Government regulations governing an area and the presence of officers in that place.

Meanwhile, in determining the types of goods sold or services offered by street vendors, consider the following:

- The type of activity that takes place around the area is chosen as the place to run the business.
- The needs of people who are active in the area where the business is located.
- Types of goods sold in commercial areas (shop houses and shops) adjacent to the place of business. Goods that are sold are usually more of a trap or the same but at a more affordable price.

The existence of public spaces in the city of Bandung today cannot be separated from the presence of street vendors in it. Therefore, public spaces also need to be designed to facilitate the needs of street vendors. Through understanding the considerations of street vendors in determining the location and type of business, the city government is expected to be able to make careful planning in making public spaces by considering the presence of street vendors as part of it in the future. It is hoped that this approach to public space planning can overcome problems in the public space faced in the city of Bandung today.

REFERENCES

McGee, T. G. and Yeung, Y. M. 1977. Hawkers in Southeast Asian cities: planning for the bazaar economy. Ottawa, IDRC.

Muhammad Ramadhan, E. and Pranggono, B. 2018. Transformation of Tegallega Park In Bandung City. *Prosiding Perencanaan Wilayah dan Kota* 4(2):331–341.

Nugraha Ginanjar, A. 2016. *Gaya Kepemimpinan Walikota Menertibkan Pedagang Kaki Lima di Kota Bandung.* Bandung: Program Studi Ilmu Pemerintahan Fakultas Ilmu Sosial dan Ilmu Politik Universitas Komputer Indonesia.

Salamah, S. and Muta'ali, L. Analisis Pemanfaatan Ruang Oleh Aktivitas Pedagang Kaki Lima (PKL) di Koridor Jalan Dipati Ukur Kota Bandung. *Jurnal Bumi Indonesia* 8(4).

Setyowati. 2011. *Pengelolaan Pembelajaran IPS Terpadu Berbasis Kurikulum Tingkat Satuan Pendidikan (KTSP) (Studi Situs di SMP Negeri 1 Wonogiri).* Surakarta: Program Pascasarjana Universitas Muhamadiyah Surakarta.

https://www.google.com/maps/search/taman+tegallega/@6.9349232,107.6023988,17z/data=!3m1!4b1

Dynamics of Industrial Revolution 4.0: Digital Technology Transformation and Cultural Evolution –
Wulandari et al (eds)
© 2021 The Author(s), ISBN 978-1-032-04451-4

Trend genre mobile app content on Sundanese Folklore

D. Hidayat, R.T. Afif
Telkom University, Bandung, Indonesia

A.B.M. Desa
Universiti Sains Malaysia, Penang, Malaysia

ABSTRACT: Trends in the development of car applications continue to develop along with technological developments. This study explains a trend in the development of mobile applications within the genre of Sundanese cultural folklore. Folklore is folk art that can be in the form of songs, music, legendary stories, or humorous stories that are passed on orally rather than written down. The research method used is a qualitative method of content analysis that emphasizes content analysis about the development trends of the Sundanese folklore genre. It can be concluded that Sundanese folklore is a culture that is conservative, and technology that is innovative can be integrated with it in mobile applications. The form of application can be as a game or an education app. As the current trend shows us that the majority of people have and use smartphones in their daily lives, there is an opportunity to introduce and develop Sundanese folklore into technology.

Keywords: applications, folklore, mobile, sunda

1 INTRODUCTION

Generally, people know of folklore usually only in story form. Folklore is defined as regional folklore which can provide life lessons therein. However, folklore is more than just a story but has broad meaning such as folk art. Sundanese folklore culture especially has an important position and role as an ambassador of Sundanese culture in the form of folk literature. Folklore can be interpreted as literature in the form of unwritten stories that spread around society from word of mouth. The term *folklore* can be broken down into two words: "folk" which has a collective meaning and "lore" which means a collective and cultrual tradition that is handed down (Danandjaja 2007).

Folklore is the body of expressive culture, including tales, music, dance, legends, oral history, proverbs, jokes, popular beliefs, customs, and so on within a particular culture, subculture, or group. It is also the set of practices through which those expressive genres are shared (Supendi 2008). From the description above, it can be concluded that folklore has a broad scope covering many aspects of cultural expression such as dance, music, humorous stories and legends, *lalaguan*, or *kakawihan barudak*.

The industrialization of technology is providing a lot of innovations which greatly affect all of society. There is an increasing number of smartphone users because this technology provides a lot of convenience. One product of this technological innovation is a mobile application. Mobile applications are software that run on mobile devices such as smartphones or tablets. A mobile application is also known as an application that can be downloaded and has certain functions that increase the functionality of the mobile device itself (Irsan 2020).

These mobile applications can make for an interesting educational method when the values of Sundanese folklore culture are conveyed through it in the form of games, animation, and other digital products. It can be interpreted as preserving the existence of Sundanese culture with technology intermediaries. For example, a mobile game application can be categorized as an educational game that is not only fun but a way to educate the user (Andang 2009). Mobile games are also the same as video games but are played on mobile devices. Video games can provide interesting social experiences that are both cognitive and emotional which have the potential to improve the mental health of children and adolescents. Video games can also make the user feel more prosperous (Garnic 2014). Therefore, it can be concluded that culture that carries traditional values and technology that carries a breath of innovation can be integrated to bring educational value to the community.

2 RESEARCH METHODS

This study uses a qualitative method of content analysis which is a method that examines documents in the form of a general category of meaning. Researchers can analyze a variety of documents, from personal papers (letters, psychiatric reports) to history (Richard 1967). The content analysis method is basically a systemic technique for analyzing the contents of messages and processing messages, or a tool for observing and analyzing the contents of open communication behavior from the chosen communicator (Richard 1967). Another understanding according to Berelson (1952), which was then followed by Kerlinger (1986), is that content analysis is defined as a method for studying and analyzing communication systemically, objectively, and quantitatively against messages that appear (Wimer & Dominic 2000). This study examines the Sundanese folklore culture and its integration with technological innovations in mobile applications to affect Sundanese folklore trends.

3 RESULTS AND DISCUSSIONS

3.1 *Result*

Over time, the development of the technology industry is a phenomenon that can lead its users to forget the language and culture of their own regions. People often ignore their mother tongue or their respective regions, including Sundanese culture. Only about 40% of West Javanese children know and are able to speak Sundanese (Antaranews 2020). Therefore, mobile applications in the form of games can be an effective and fun tool for introducing Sundanese cultural folklore. Games provide great educational opportunities by analyzing a group of players and individuals using rational strategies (Leyton-Brown & dan Shoham 2008).

Figure 1. Example of cultural education through a mobile application. (Source. Google Play Store, Marbel Budaya Nusantara 2020).

Sundanese folklore educational media with mobile applications are seen as very effective learning tools. Learning media with mobile applications or M-learning can also deliver Sundanese cultural values more efficiently. Mobile learning has the same meaning as e-learning, only mobile learning can only be accessed via mobile devices. M-Learning has the following advantages:

1. Portability means the device is more portable.
2. Supports learning because the younger generation is more familiar with devices such as tablets than conventional learning methods.

3. Increases the motivation of ownership of the device and can also increase the commitment to use and learn it.
4. Has a broader reach because its use reaches all levels of society.
5. Timely learning enhances learning as needed (Andy 2007).

The results are a trend where cultures that are considered conservative and technology that is considered innovated can be integrated into a learning medium that creates current trends about the concept of an introduction to Sundanese folklore and cultural values.

3.2 *Discussions*

A mobile application game is designed for fun so if education can be combined with it, there is added value. Educational games are games that are designed with the specific purpose of teaching users about something, be it developing concepts, increasing understanding, or guiding and training its users' abilities. This game must also be able to provide motivation to users to continue playing it (Hurd 2009).

Sundanese folklore expresses its identity in folk art, in which there are songs, rhymes, and legend stories which makes it an ideal genre for preservation within technology, such as mobile applications, that will trend within a community. This form of mobile application can be in the form of games or educational applications.

4   CONCLUSIONS

Although Sudanese folklore culture plays an important role as guardian of a community's identity, it tends to be conservative. Therefore, it could benefit greatly from the innovation of technology such as in the form of a mobile application game that would provide education and increase awareness to its rich culture and history.

According to Andang Ismail (2009), a mobile application game has two purposes:

1. as a pure play activity that aims to find pleasure not based on winning and losing or
2. as a fun play activity that is based on winning and losing.

Mobile applications will be an effective medium to be linked to Sudanese folklore culture because the majority of Indonesian people already have smartphones. Noted in 2015 on gs.statcounter.com, 68.75% of Indonesians were Android smartphone users (Statcounter.com 2020). This high number of users provides a great opportunity for people to use their smartphones to connect to their Sundanese folklore culture.

ACKNOWLEDGMENTS

The research team would like to say thank you to all those who helped carry out this research, especially the Visual Communication Design Study Program, Telkom University. Hopefully, this research can be useful for many people who like and study culture in relation to design and creative industries.

REFERENCES

Andy, Yonatan. 2007. *Perancangan dan Implementasi Mobile Learning untuk Pembelajaran Bahasa Jepang Berbasis Brew*. Bandung: STEI ITB.
Budd Richard, Atal, 1967. *Content Analysis of Communication*. New York: The Mac Millan Company.
Danandjaja, James. 2007. *Folklor Indonesia, Ilmu Gosip, Dongeng, dan lain-lain*. Jakarta: Grafiti.

Garnic, I., Adam Lobel, and Rutger C. M. E. Engels. 2014. *The Benefits of Playing Video Games.* Jurnal American Psycologist: 69(1):66–78, 28 Maret 2015.

Hurd, Daniel dan Jenuings, Erin. 2009. *Standardized Educational Games Ratings:Suggested Criteria.* Karya Tulis Ilmiah.

Irsan, Muhammad. 2020. *Rancang Bangun Aplikasi Mobile Notifikasi Berbasis Android Untuk Mendukung Kinerja Di Instansi Pemerintahan.* Program Studi Teknik Informatika Fakultas Teknik Universitas Tanjungpura.

Ismail Andang. 2009.*Education Games.*Yogyakarta: Pro U Media.

Leyton-Brown, K. and dan Shoham, Y. 2008. *Essentials of Games Theory.* United States of America: Morgan & Claypool.Usman Supendi. 2008. *Folklore Jawa Barat.* Artikel. Tidak Diterbitkan

Wimer, Roger, D. and Dominic, Josep R. 2000. *Mass Media Research.* Six Edition, New York: Wadsworth Publishing Company.

http://www.antaranews.com/berita/392249/bahasasunda-terus-tergerus diakses pada August 1, 2020 pukul 22.30

http://gs.statcounter.com/#mobile+tablet+consoleos-ID-yearly-2015-2015-bar diakses pada August 1, 2020 pukul 22.30

Dynamics of Industrial Revolution 4.0: Digital Technology Transformation and Cultural Evolution –
Wulandari et al (eds)
© 2021 The Author(s), ISBN 978-1-032-04451-4

Millenial Generation's Online Behavior in the humanity of the Pancasila

R. Machfiroh & M.F.A. Zahra
Telkom University, Bandung, Indonesia

ABSTRACT: The development of digital technology as a feature of globalization has shortened distance, space, time, and is inevitable. Indonesian citizens as internet users are always increasing. This study analyzed the development of digital citizenship in Indonesia and whether it can provide an alternative solution in the establishment of digital citizenship. The method used in this research was case study. The data collection techniques used questionnaires and interviews with junior high school students in Bandung, Indonesia, with a sample of 450 people. Data analysis was descriptive analytics. The results indicate that the millenial generation's online behavior, in the humanity of the Pancasila, still needs to be improved regarding digital etiquette competence, through group power in social media "who controls social media, he controls the world" to make it happen. The implications are to reconstruct rules of use and users of social media and appropriate educational models for digital citizens.

Keywords: civic education, digital era, online behaviour, millenial generation, humanity of the Pancasila

1 INTRODUCTION

Based on Van Dijk's research, presented at the Sharing Session event at Directorate of Research and Community Service of Telkom University in 2015, the number of internet users in Indonesia increases every year, reaching 19.460 million as of 2015. Indonesia experienced a sharp increase associated with the use of Information Communication Technology ICT. However, currently only part of Indonesia is on the level of the digital world used for education and employment. Other influences result from the exposure of negative access to children and adolescents with bad information flooding the internet (Setiawan 2009). Shock culture and the influence of bad information construct Indonesian citizens' low attitude of communication, tolerance, and care, while in this current digital era the value to be upheld is tolerance and care for others. Education is one of the principal pillars to the development of moral quality (Komalasari 2017).

The rapid development of technology had an impact on the behavior and character of people who lived the area. Junior high-school adolescents, the object of this research and based on theories, fall into the birth category of 2001–2010. Characteristics of generation Z are being able to describe actual conditions occurring to and serving adolescents. They also have an instant mindset, are technology dependent, tend to be popular in social media, have minimal social interaction power, and even manage to be individualistic (Renzulli, available at https://goo.gl/cTymz4, accessed on December 10, 2018). Therefore, it is foreseen that teenagers use the internet not to find learning resources, but to stream and play social media. Line/WhatsApp, Instagram, Twitter, and Facebook are favorite social media sites. However, there was an imbalance between digital knowledge and skills, and the ability to operate them fully.

2 RESEARCH METHOD

The research approach used in this case study is the descriptive analytics method. Data collection techniques used books, journal articles, research studies, and other materials are related to the impact of the development of information technology, digital citizenship, the civilization of Indonesian citizenship, including interviews with students, teachers of civics educations, headmasters, observations, and documentations. Data was analyzed after data reduction was done, followed by data presentation, data verification, and conclusion.

3 DISCUSSION

Digital citizenship in Indonesia discusses "internet usage and digital safety". Globalization demands civic education to develop civic competence involving civic knowledge, civic skills, and civic disposition, which are multidimensional (Komalasari 2009). Technology is a catalyst of change, making change to be revolutionary, very fast, and intense (Suryadi 2006). However, the positive side of the world of education and knowledge, is that revolution is happening and has double dimension that connects astonishing modern brain research with the power of information and knowledge that can be accessed quickly and easily through information and communication technology. Suryadi (2006) asserts that the joint revolution of the internet-computer-World Wide Web has formed a new generation, with new values, new social styles, new cultures, and even new economies called the digital economy.

Indonesia, with a population of 290 million people, has 51.5% of internet users, a great potential for citizen development in the digital age. Research by Machfiroh (2016) indicated that 85% of junior high-school students in Bandung City are mobile phone users. APJII research in 2016 showed that 18.4% of internet users in Java Island are aged between 10–24 years old. In the United States, the PEW research results showed that 75% of kids aged 12–17 years old have smartphones (White 2016). However, between the United States and Indonesia there are differences in security and safety. In the United States, parents supervise their children's mobile phone usage for 36% of the time, but in Indonesia this supervision is still low. Currently, parents or teachers are experiencing gadget addiction. Children who do not get enough parenting acts, due to parents who get addicted to their digital devices, grow up with negative emotions and cannot control sadness, anxiety, or even anger. Developed countries, such as Germany and Finland, have limited the use of mobile phones for children.

It is in accordance with Buckingham (2000) that many children lose their childhood due to consuming too much electronic media in the form of adult material, so that children quickly become adults. Teenagers are already able to operate the internet and can upload content, but are not accompanied by the ability to create their own content. Therefore, it is common for teenagers to just "copy–paste". Such an attitude indirectly accustoms teenagers to acts of plagiarism toward other people's work without mentioning sources. The characteristics of adolescents of junior high-school age are at the stage of showing their existence; they like to look for wise words/quotes without trying to construct their own thoughts on the things being quoted. They are also lacking the ability to cross-check data regarding information obtained on the internet. The implication is that the information shared by teenagers on social media can become a means of spreading hoaxes for free. To see the digital skills of adolescents, the following will explain the triangulation results based on three data collection techniques (Table 1).

Along with this phenomenon, speaking textually in the digital era is needed. Teenagers act not only as users but also producers (pioneers) of news useful to others, as well as making themselves exist in social media. In this connection, the skills of adolescents as the subject of knowledge construction need to be continuously built. Some of the skills that teenagers must-have in the digital era include (a) operational skills, (b) formal skills, (c) information skills, (d) communication skills, (e) strategic skills, and (f) content creation skills (Van Dijk 1999, 2012).

Table 1. Triangulation of digital skills based on data collection techniques.

Interview	Observation	Documentation
Cellphones and social media are not only a lifestyle but a necessity for adolescents. Social media is a means of actualization and self-expression for teenagers.	Teens are often caught accessing social media and lifestyle websites, rather than looking for study materials.	The results showed that children aged 11–15 years have an instant mindset, depend on technology, and seek popularity through social media channels.

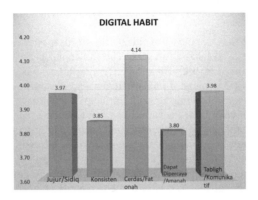

Figure 1. Youth digital habit (digital skill). (Source: compiled by Researchers 2018).

Digital skills need to be mastered by creating Z in the 21st century to dominate the competitive world (Velden 2012). This is in line with the shift in the industrial society toward an information and knowledge society, which has implications for the mastery of various skills needed in job placement and the world community (Voogt & Roblin 2010). Based on the research findings, education has a role in preparing the skills and competencies of adolescents in facing the digital era. Trilling and Fadel (2009) revealed that three 21st century competencies are often referred to as "the rainbow of 21st-century knowledge skills": life and career skills; learning and innovation; and media and information technology. The digital habits of adolescents are determined by the extent to which they can demonstrate aspects of universal and responsible positive behavior as values and characters that everyone needs to have, e.g., honesty, firm in upholding consistency (*istiqomah*), intelligence (*fathonah*), disbelieving (mandate), and a conveyor of values (*tabligh*). Diagrammatically, the habits of digital youth can be seen in Figure 1.

Based on Figure 1, the digital habits of adolescents, including honesty (*sidiq*), consistency (*istiqomah*), intelligence (*fatonah*), trustworthiness, and communicative/convey good things (*tabligh*) are in the high category. The value of honesty is 3.97, consistency 3.85, intelligence 4.24, trustworthiness 3.80, and communicative/conveying good things 3.98, while the average value is 3.95. The habit of being honest in adolescents is shown by the habit of providing correct and impartial information. Adolescents' persistence is demonstrated by five characteristics: relying on one's abilities, the courage to admit mistakes, the courage to obey school rules, studying seriously, and always upholding principles in relationships. Intelligence (*fatonah*) in using the internet/social media based on the habit of asking questions about things not understood, being able to select and sort information, and respecting differences in beliefs. Intelligence in choosing news and opinions on social media must be accompanied by the ability to present real data and facts not to cause public confusion. Trustworthiness includes being brave enough to admit mistakes and being willing to apologize, not being careless, and maintaining harmony in friendship. Conveying good things (*tabligh*) includes sharing information according to facts and politeness in giving information.

The five dimensions of truth values above must be developed as a benchmark for adolescent digital habits. Then, two previous components (digital knowledge and digital skills) must be understood completely and comprehensively to effectively develop good morals as digital habits. In another perspective, noble morality is equated with moral intelligence because it contains a person's ability to judge good things and bad things. Moral intelligence is seen as a person's ability to understand right and wrong, to have strong ethical beliefs, and act on these beliefs to be correct and honorable (Borba 2008). Moral intelligence is needed for kindness, strong character, and to become a good citizen. The results of the study showed that the most dominant is intelligence or *fatonah*. A person who has high intelligence is supported by an attitude of wanting to communicate with others coupled with an honest or *sidiq* character. By having a consistent nature and being trustworthy, these citizens have a sense of responsibility. There is an oddity in this finding, that honesty is supported by intelligence and others follow.

To face the 21st century, the competence of citizens that needs to be improved includes increasing awareness, understanding, and legal awareness. The millennial generation tends to use digital technology in various aspects of life. Therefore, forming citizens is on a legal understanding in IT to prevent cyberlaw (IT crimes). In today's digital era, the values that must be upheld are tolerance and caring for others following the second principle of Pancasila, namely fair and civilized humanity. Jeffery (2012) revealed that the value of humanity is one of the obligations as citizens of the world, that is respect for the rights of others and tolerance. Insulting and defaming other people, including deception to others in any national society, is not justified, especially in cyberspace where individuals can easily access and influence the perceptions of others.

Advances in information and communication technology must be useful for the welfare of the community. This technology is a tool to create an intelligent and advanced nation. The Internet can provide immense benefits to education, research, commerce, and other aspects of life. Citizens who are civilized in the digital era should use technological devices that can be used according to their designation as a mirror of digital society (digital citizenship) that upholds civilized values, awareness of brotherhood and humanity, supports human rights, makes themselves citizens with dignity as a human being, and there is also a balanced attitude between local interests (local awareness) such as love of family, ethnic identity, awareness of the community and self-interest, and global interests such as universal awareness of human equality and obedience to the constitution in each of its actions as manifestations in the second principle of Pancasila, which is a just and civilized humanity. Aristotle in Heater D. (2004) said that if citizens behave and follow the constitution, they can be said to be good citizens. Still, good humans do not see the state because, basically, humans are right from their conscience. This means that the behavior and attitudes of good citizens in the digital era are based on their conscience.

Indonesia has different characteristics in fostering civilized citizens in the digital era. Based on the objectives of national education, article 3 of Law No.20/2003 concerning the National Education System imperatively outlines that: national education functions to develop abilities and shape the character and civilization of a nation with dignity to educate the life of the country, aimed at developing the potential of participants educated to become human beings who believe and fear the Almighty God, have a noble character, are healthy, knowledgeable, capable, creative, independent, and become democratic and responsible citizens. Things to be developed are noble and intelligent characters in the use of social media. Efforts in forming civilized citizens in the digital era are not only able to understand but are able to show morality, intelligence, tolerance, caring, and human value development that can be done through social media.

Social media is very influential in various kinds of decision making. On the other hand, this digital era must be able to form smart citizens. Smart in choosing information and smart in providing information. Van Dijk's (2011) writing showed that citizens of countries such as Korea, China, and the United States must be cultivated or well educated in the current era of globalization, an are not easily influenced by information alone. This is reinforced by the opinion of Cogan and Derricot (1998) that global citizens must have several multidimensional national characteristics, namely: (a) the ability to understand, accept, and respect cultural differences; (b) the ability to think critically and systematically; and (c) the ability to resolve conflicts peacefully without violence. Such characters are necessary for citizens in the digital age. The development of information, communication, and technology is one of the causes of the world revolution (Waters in Sunarto 2004). That is the importance of rebuilding noble morals for young citizens in the digital era.

4 CONCLUSIONS AND IMPLICATIONS

Digital citizenship in Indonesia needs to be upgraded to digital etiquette and digital law competencies toward good and intelligent digital citizens. The strategy was undertaken to realize it through the power of groups in social media "who controls social media, he controls the world". The implications of this research are to reconstruct the rules (UU ITE) in the usage and users of social media and the appropriate education model for digital citizens. It focuses on freedom of opinion, which still has multiple interpretations.

ACKNOWLEDGMENT

Gratitude is given to the Directorate of Research and Community Service of Telkom University who provided facilities that helped in the research process. Contributions from each author—first author: research conduct and design early writing; second author: writing language and content.

REFERENCES

Bernier, A. 2008. *Making Space for Young Adults: Three Stages Toward Success*. Montreal: San Jose State University.

Buckingham, D. 2000. *The Making of Citizens: Young People, News and Politics*. London and New York: Routledge.

Budimansyah, D. 2008. *Membangun Karakter Bangsa Di Tengah Arus Globalisasi dan Gerakan Demokratisasi: Reposisi Peran Pendidikan Kewarganegaraan*. Inauguration speech of Professor of Civic Education, Social Studies, IKIP, Bandung.

Budimansyah, D. and Suryadi, K. 2008. *PKn dan Masyarakat Multikultural*. Bandung: Study Program of Civic Education, Graduate School Universitas Pendidikan Indonesia.

Chapman, J.A. and Robertson, M. 2015. *Youth Leisure, Places, Spaces and Identity*. New York.

Cloudry et al. 2013. *Digital citizenship? Narrative exchange and the changing terms of civic culture*. http://www.tandfonline.com/loi/ccst20

Cogan, J.J. 1998. *Citizenship for the 21 Century: An International Perspective on Education*. London: Cogan Page.

Djahiri, A.K. 2006. *Esensi Pendidikan Nilai Moral dan Pendidikan Kewarganegaraan di Era Globalisasi*. Bandung: Civic Education Laboratory, Faculty of Social Studies, Universitas Pendidikan Indonesia.

Komalasari, K. 2009. *The Effect of Contextual Learning in Civic Education on Students' Civic Competence*. Journal of Social Sciences 5(4):261–270.

Komalasari, K. (2017). *Value-Based Interactive Multimedia Development through Integrated Practice for the Formation of Students' Character*. The Turkish Online Journal of Educational Technology 16(4).

Machfiroh, R. 2016. *Digital Citizenship*. Research final report: Telkom University.

Machfiroh, R. et al. 2017. The 2nd International Conference on Sociology Education. DOI: 10.5220/0007107408730877

Saripudin, D. and Komalasari K. 2015. *Living Values Education in School's Habituation Program and Its Effect on Student's Character Development*. The New Educational Review 39:51–62.

Van Dijk. 2015. Presentation on Sharing Session at Directorate of Research and Community Service, Telkom University, August 13, 2015.

Dynamics of Industrial Revolution 4.0: Digital Technology Transformation and Cultural Evolution –
Wulandari et al (eds)
© 2021 The Author(s), ISBN 978-1-032-04451-4

Ergonomics aspect review: Effectiveness of information-based technology display at the Mpu Purwa Museum in Malang

T.I.W. Primadani, I.A. Agustina & I.B.A. Wijaya
Bina Nusantara University, Malang, Indonesia

ABSTRACT: In Indonesia, to support their exhibition, some museums have been already been applying multimedia and interactive technologies in their presentations, including the Mpu Purwa Museum in Malang. The purpose of this study is to find the ease of the ergonomic aspect so that the stored information can be easily obtained by visitors and to determine the effectiveness of the QR code label at the Mpu Purwa Museum in terms of ergonomics. The problem is the application of the QR code as part of a display object in a museum exhibition in Indonesia is still relatively new, so its effectiveness needs to be reviewed. The method used in this research is qualitative, with data collection in field studies, visitor interviews, and literature studies. The results of this study conclude that the ergonomics of anthropometry, display location, lighting, and circulation areas must adapt to each other with the type of technology-based media used in the museum.

Keywords: ergonomic, QR code, display, technology, museum

1 INTRODUCTION

One thing that supports a visitor's multidimension experience in museum exhibitions is the concept of audience participation. In participatory-concept museums, the two-way interpersonal communication can be achieved by interactive exhibits through various media such as audiovisual, touchscreen, and multimedia (Wulandari 2014). The format of delivering information in a different packaged museum will be easier for visitors to remember than passive writing without meaningful interaction, such as typographic presentations on walls or information that can explore through gadgets (Palmyre Pierroux 2019).

Technology developments, especially smartphones, affect emerging behavior (Weilenmann et al. 2013). With the increasing use of smartphones and sensory system technology developments, public spaces such as libraries or museums now have the opportunity to enhance their visitor experience and further achieve their institutional goals (Mar Perez-Sanagustín 2016). The strategy of using technology, such as mobile applications, touchscreens, and websites, is considered one of the most effective design systems for presentation methods in museums and learning environments (Al-Hajji 2017). Technology in the museum also uses existing historical collection objects, for example, to explain and describe the collection's background story. By utilizing technology, the museum's display collections are expected to provide a new experience in interacting with objects that are in the museum display.

A QR code consists of a black box module, which is a code that can be read by a scanner or a gadget camera that has been facilitated by this QR code reader application, and that code links with the digital information storage of the related object on the internet. By that explanation, it can be seen that QR code technology allows visitors to interact with collections in the museum by utilizing their smartphone. According to previous research, a QR code is an option for cost-effectiveness in museums and has been applied by several museums to guide visitors and contains information that supports exhibitions or libraries (Schultz 2013).

DOI 10.1201/9781003193241-67

1.1 *Ergonomic display in museum*

Ergonomics is a scientific discipline that is concerned with understanding the interactions between humans and other elements of a system, providing theoretical principles, data, and methods for designing how to optimize human well-being and overall system performance (Erminia Attaianese 2012). The goal of the ergonomic design of the museum environment is to create prevailing ambient conditions that are comfortable and acceptable accommodations of activity performance or visitor health (Stanton 2005). The aspects of the physical environment in the museum that can affect the effectiveness of information presented are noise, lighting, ergonomics of the eye line (anthropometry), the connectedness of the content and objects on display, visual elements, and their location to the visitor's circulation flow (Screven 1992; Wulandari et al. 2017). Effective layout and display designs are designed to engage visitors for self-education on a subject and to inspire the visitors to learn more (Wolfgang Leister 2016). If there is any display design's fault and improper arrangement both visually or physically, that means the collection will potentially be overlooked by visitors.

Labels on collection displays also play an important role in providing information to visitors. Information labels are important to provide a deep understanding of a display object in a museum (Wulandari et al. 2017). Labels refer to all types of media—print, audio, graphics, and presentation formats—used to help visitors interpret and connecting with exhibition content, have an emotional impact, or to motivate visitors to get to know more (Screven 1992). The presentation aspect of label format includes all type of media used such as interactive, sound, image, and video.

In order to be easily read by visitors, object information labels need to be designed in accordance with human ergonomic standards by paying attention to attractive visualizations and placing them according to the normal human eye line (Wulandari et al. 2017). Several techniques have been used in previous research to display effective information designs in the form of graphics, sculptures, boards, or other information products in museums by following UX design principles (Al-Hajji 2017). Principles of UX Design are easy to use, to find the function, and to understand; users do not have to get help to do the task; visual focus, direction are clear; and users can perform their task efficiently and correctly, works for the user (Rosenzweig 2015).

Another supporting factor for the ergonomics of the interior environment is lighting. Lighting has an important role in the exhibition space, both for the conservation of collections and visitors (Hunt 2009). With an appropriate light, exhibition organizers are present with an influential tool that enables the definition of the atmosphere for viewing art, establishes a sense of drama to support its reception, and generally contributes to the success of the exhibition (Schielke 2019). The lighting intensity is very important for visitors to be able to easily observe the collection and read the label information clearly (Wulandari et al. 2017).

1.2 *Objectives*

In this study, we will discuss the effectiveness of a QR code as a label for statues collection at the Mpu Purwa Museum in terms of the ergonomics placement. A QR code label contains descriptions and explanations of the statue collection in Bahasa and English in the Mpu Purwa Museum. The Mpu Purwa Museum is a public museum located on Kota Malang, East Java. Most of the Mpu Purwa Museum collections are statues and inscriptions from the Mpu Sindok period to the Majapahit Kingdom (year 929–947 AC).

Ergonomic problems in placing QR codes as information labels for collections in museums that will be discussed in this paper are lighting and anthropometry related to the placement of QR codes. Based on visitor interviews and field observations, the problem found in implementing QR codes as collection information is that not all of them can be seen by visitors and require more effort to aim the smartphone camera at the QR code. Other problems are the material selection, QR code image placement, and lights position that cause a very bright reflection on a QR code.

2 METHODOLOGY

The research method used in this research is the qualitative method by conducting literature studies, field studies, and interviews. Studies conducted to search for reference data and analyzing the

Figure 1. QR code placement case A.

Figure 2. QR code placement case B.

Table 1. QR Code label location identification.

Case Study	QR Code Location	Circulation Dimension	Standart Dimension (Panero and Zelnik 2003)		Effort
			Line-of-sight place-ment	Minimum circulation area	
A - Figure 1	10 cm from the floor	200 cm	107–170 cm from the floor	167.6 cm (accommodate two people viewed the display and cir-culation for one person.)	Visitors must bow their heads or their bodies to read labels or scan QR codes with their smartphones.
B - Figure 2	50 cm from the floor	140 cm			Visitors must squat down to read labels or scan QR codes with their smartphones.

interior aspects that affect the display of museum collections, lighting, sirculation and ergonomics anthropometric display design technology based on museum collections. Meanwhile, field studies were conducted to determine the ergonomic aspects of anthropometric display arrangement equipped with QR codes and the size of the circulation area. Interviews were conducted with managers and visitors about the purpose QR code application and comfort when reading QR code in the museum.

3   RESULT AND DISCUSSION

Based on field studies in the statues collection area, there is a QR code label on each collectable. QR code labels are placed near the object and located on the front of the display case. Placement of the labels next to the object makes it easier for visitors to see the object and read the label at the same time (Bitgood 2002). However, in case study A (Figure 1), the label was placed at a height of 10 cm from the floor. In case B (Figure 2), the label was placed on the front of the display case at a height of 50 cm from the floor.

The black QR code is printed on a white paper measuring 10 x 15 cm and laminated by plastic. Label not only contains a QR code but contains collection name and description in Bahasa and

English in terms of visibility, the label applies a ground-figure contrast. Not only is it easier to attract attention with a ground-figure contrast, but it is easier to read text when the letters and background have high contrast (Bitgood 2002). Labels that are located in line of sight will be easily detected and legible, however, the QR code label on the study object (Figures 1 and ;) is located far from the eye line area in a normal standing position and using small font size results, cause information on the label is not easy for visitors to read. Labels that are not in the eye line area will affect the effectiveness because it will tend to be overlooked and unreadable by visitors. Visitors have to spend extra effort by squatting or bending in the attempt to read the QR code label. The extra effort is one of the distractions that affect motivation and focus the attention of visitors (Bitgood 2002).

Based on field studies, represented by cases A (Figure 1) and B (Figure 2), the circulation width inside the museum is quite narrow to accommodate the activities of a squatting visitor while aiming smartphone cameras at the QR code and tend to disturb other visitor circulation areas. The circulation width area in the museum does not yet meet the minimum required standard for circulation width according to anthropometric ergonomics (explanation in Table 1).

Placement of objects and the space provided in the museum should pay attention to the comfort of visitor's activity. Object and space can become the focus of attention, facilitate or encourage the movement of visitors, provide a rhythm or balance, and can improve visual and physical abilities to enjoy the collection in the museum (Swathi Matta Reddy 2012). If there is one that doesn't meet the standard, the activity comfortability will be disturbed. Squatting and bowing while aiming the cellphone camera at the QR code will take up a wider space, so it can interfere others circulation area, especially if the museum has a lot of visitors. Circulation disturbances can also cause crowds, thus disturb visitors' comfort while observing collections in museums or reading the existing information. This disturbance can cause the object around it to be less notified by visitors.

In arranging and placing technology to support historical collections, several things need to be considered in order to be effective, one of which is the interior environmental conditions. Physical aspects of the environment such as visibility generated from lighting effects, visual barriers, and glare will affect the appearance of the display so that it also affects the attention of visitors (Schielke 2019). Based on the existing, the lighting used at the Mpu Purwa Museum is 25% natural lighting and 75% artificial lighting. Artificial lighting is used as a general light and decorative light to expose the collection. There is no special lighting that exposes QR code labels, so the lighting takes advantage of general light or spotlight that leads to the display object.

QR code labels must be well lit. Based on research on the mobile phone audiovisual guide tour at Ueno Zoological Gardens and the National Science Museum in Tokyo, visitors find it difficult to scan QR codes in a dark gallery area (Sakamoto & Sakamoto 2007). However, lighting that is too bright must also be considered, because it can cause a glare effect both in camera phone and visitor's eye. If there is glare or too much reflective light, guests may experience discomfort while interacting in the museum, and their experience will be greatly altered (Hunt 2009). Based on a case study at the Mpu Purwa Museum, there are several QR codes that reflect light from a spotlight that illuminates the collection object, so visitors must find the right position so that the scanned QR code does not have a white spot reflected by the light.

The problem with the appearance of a white spot is that the QR code label has a shiny plastic material facing the spotlight so that a bright light reflection occurs. This condition can be overcome by moving it to a part that is not directly facing the direction of the light, moving the location of the spotlight or replacing the QR code label material with a non-reflective material. From this condition, it can be concluded that physical environmental aspects such as lighting also play an important role in influencing the effectiveness of the information on labels, even though the presentation and type of labels displayed are based on the latest technology. Determination of the placement and type of lamp used has a correlation with other elements in an interior space (Swathi Matta Reddy 2012). The placement of lights, QR code labels, and materials used must be considered so that the information presented can be easily accessed by museum visitors.

4 CONCLUSION

The advantage of using a label that uses a QR code at the Mpu Purwa Museum provides a new experience for visitors to use a smartphone to get information about the object collections in the museum. Tshe drawback is the location QR code label placement that does not comply with ergonomic standards anthropometry, so the label of QR code placement on at the Mpu Purwa Museum is still not effective. To maximize the benefit by QR code label, the label should be moved to a place that meets the anthropometric-ergonomic standards of human activity and aligns it with the lighting placement in the interior of the Mpu Purwa Museum. Based on the ergonomic analysis of the QR code label at the Mpu Purwa Museum which was described above, it can be concluded that the physical condition of the environment must be reconsidered and redesigned in order to maximize the benefits of using digital technology to increase visitor engagement with museum collection objects. Physical environmental factors such as ergonomics of object's placement, lighting, and area of circulation must be adapted to the type of technology-based information media used in the museum. If visitors can take full advantage of it, it is hoped that the information conveyed by utilizing digital-based technology can be well received by visitors.

ACKNOWLEDGMENTS

This paper is part of the results of a beginner lecturer research (PDP) scheme, a research grant from Ministry of Research and Technology Indonesia (RISTEKDIKTI).

REFERENCES

Al-Hajji, Z. 2017. *Applying user experience (UX) design in interior space for art, science museums, and learning environments.* [Online] Available at: https://commons.emich.edu/theses/791/ [Accessed October 5, 2020].

Bitgood, S. C. 2002. Environmental Psychology in Museums, Zoos, and Other Exhibition Centers. In: *Handbook of Environmental Psychology.* New York: John Wiley & Sons, Inc, pp. 461–480.

Erminia Attaianese, G. D. 2012. Human factors and ergonomic principles in building design for life and work activities: an applied methodology. *Theoretical Issues in Ergonomics Science*, 13(2):187–202.

Hunt, E. G. 2009. *Study of Museum Lighting and Design.* [Online] Available at: https://digital.library.txstate.edu/handle/10877/3203 [Accessed October 5, 2020].

Julius Panero, M. Z. 2003. *Dimensi Manusia dan Ruang Interior.* 1st ed. Jakarta: Erlangga.

Mar Perez-Sanagustín, D. P. R. V. G. G.-G. 2016. Using QR codes to increase user engagement in museum-like spaces. *Computers in Human Behavior*, 60:73.

Palmyre Pierroux, A. Q. 2019. *Wall texts in collection exhibitions: Bastions of enlightenment and interfaces interfaces for experience. Nordisk Museology*, 1:39–50. [Online] Available at: https://www.duo.uio.no/handle/10852/75254 [Accessed October 2020].

Panero, J. and Zelnik, M. 2003. *Dimensi Manusia dan Ruang Interior.* 1st ed. Jakarta: Erlangga.

Rosenzweig, E. 2015. *Successful User Experience: Strategies and Roadmaps.* MA-USA: Morgan Kaufmann-Elsevier.

Safavi, S. 2013. *Eastern Mediterranean University Institutional Repository: Effects of Design Principles on Visitors' Perception in Museum Spaces.* [Online] Available at: http://hdl.handle.net/11129/3495 [Accessed October 10, 2020].

Sakamoto, H. and Sakamoto, K. 2007. Using a Mobile Phone Tour to Visit the Ueno Zoological Gardens and the National Science Museum in Tokyo, Japan. *Journal of Museum Education*, 32(1):35–45.

Salim, P. 2018. Persepsi Kualitas Ruang Pamer Museum Seni: Sebuah Studi Observasi. *NARADA, Jurnal Desain & Seni, FDSK - UMB* 5(2):23–32.

Schielke, T. 2019. Interpreting Art with Light: Museum Lighting between Objectivity and Hyperrealism. *LEUKOS : The Journal of the Illuminating Engineering Society.*

Schultz, M. K. 2013. A case study on the appropriateness of using quick response (QR) codes in libraries and museums. *Library & Information Science Research*, http://dx.doi.org/10.1016/j.lisr.2013.03.002.

Screven, C. G. 1992. Motivating Visitors to Read Labels. *ILVS*, 2(2).

Stanton, N. A. 2005. Human Factors and Ergonomics Methods. In: N. A. Stanton, ed. *Handbook of Human Factors and Ergonomics Methods.* Neville: CRC Press, pp. 1-1–1-9.

Swathi Matta Reddy, D. C. S. K. 2012. *Emotion and interior space design: an ergonomic perspective.* s.l., IOS Press.

Weilenmann, A., Hillman, T,. and Jungselius, B. 2013. *Instagram at the Museum: Communicating the Museum Experience through Social Photo Sharing.* Paris, ACM Press.

Wolfgang Leister, I. T. T. S. G. J. A. L. M. d. B., 2016. Assessing Visitor Engagement in Science Centres and Museums. *International Journal on Advances in Life Sciences*, 8(1 & 2):50–64.

Wulandari, A. A. 2014. Dasar-dasar Perencanaan Interior Museum. *Humaniora* 5(1):246–257.

Wulandari, A. A. A., Fajarwati, A. A. S., and Latif, F. 2017. The Relationship of Exhibition Space Design and The Success of Delivering Messages To Museum Visitors In Jakarta. *Humaniora* 8(3):219.

Author index